CITIZENSHIP AND ADVOCACY IN TECHNICAL COMMUNICATION

In *Citizenship and Advocacy in Technical Communication*, teachers, researchers, and practitioners will find a variety of theoretical frameworks, empirical studies, and teaching approaches to advocacy and citizenship. Specifically, the collection is organized around three main themes or sections: considerations for understanding and defining advocacy and citizenship locally and globally, engaging with the local and global community, and introducing advocacy in a classroom.

The collection covers an expansive breadth of issues and topics that speak to the complexities of undertaking advocacy work in Technical and Professional Communication (TPC), including local grant writing activities, cosmopolitanism and global transnational rhetoric, digital citizenship and social media use, strategic and tactical communication, and diversity and social justice. The contributors themselves, representing fifteen academic institutions and occupying various academic ranks, offer nuanced definitions, frameworks, examples, and strategies for students, scholars, practitioners, and educators who want to or are already engaged in a variegated range of advocacy work. More so, they reinforce the inherent humanistic values of our field and discuss effective rhetorical and current technological tools at our disposal. Finally, they show us how, through pedagogical approaches and everyday mundane activities and practices, we (can) advocate either actively or passively.

Godwin Y. Agboka is an associate professor of technical and professional communication and director of the Master of Science in Technical Communication program at University of Houston-Downtown, where he teaches graduate and undergraduate courses, including intercultural communication, medical writing, and science writing. Agboka's research interests include intercultural technical communication, social justice and human rights perspectives, research methodologies, and the rhetoric of science and medicine. He is the author of several journal articles and book chapters.

Natalia Matveeva is an associate professor of technical and professional communication and the co-director of the Institute for Plain English Research and Study (IPERS) at University of Houston-Downtown. Matveeva teaches undergraduate and graduate courses in intercultural technical communication, grant writing, web writing, research methods, and plain language. She has published a number of articles and book chapters in technical and business communication journals and edited collections.

ATTW Book Series in Technical and Professional Communication
Tharon Howard, Series Editor

Communicating Project Management
Benjamin Lauren

Lean Technical Communication: Toward Sustainable Program Innovation
Meredith A. Johnson, W. Michele Simmons, and Patricia A. Sullivan

Scientific and Medical Communications: A Guide for Effective Practice
Scott A. Mogull

Plain Language and Ethical Action: A Dialogic Approach to Technical Content in the 21st Century
Russell Willerton

Rhetoric in the Flesh: Trained Vision, Technical Expertise, and the Gross Anatomy Lab
T. Kenny Fountain

Social Media in Disaster Response: How Experience Can Build for Participation
Liza Potts

For additional information on this series please visit www.routledge.com/ATTW-Series-in-Technical-and-Professional-Communication/book-series/ATTW, and for information on other Routledge titles visit www.routledge.com.

CITIZENSHIP AND ADVOCACY IN TECHNICAL COMMUNICATION

Scholarly and Pedagogical Perspectives

Edited by Godwin Y. Agboka and Natalia Matveeva

Routledge
Taylor & Francis Group

NEW YORK AND LONDON

First published 2018
by Routledge
711 Third Avenue, New York, NY 10017

and by Routledge
2 Park Square, Milton Park, Abingdon, Oxon OX14 4RN

Routledge is an imprint of the Taylor & Francis Group, an informa business

© 2018 Taylor & Francis

Library of Congress Cataloging in Publication Data
Names: Agboka, Godwin, 1979- editor. | Matveeva, Natalia, 1978- editor.
Title: Citizenship and advocacy in technical communication :
scholarly and pedagogical perspectives / edited by Godwin Agboka and
Natalia Matveeva.
Description: New York : Routledge, 2018. | Series: ATTW book series in
technical and professional communication
Identifiers: LCCN 2017058042| ISBN 9781138560796 (hardback) |
ISBN 9781138560802 (pbk.) | ISBN 9780203711422 (ebk.)
Subjects: LCSH: Communication of technical information—Study and
teaching. | Citizenship. | Social advocacy.
Classification: LCC T10.5 .C47 2018 | DDC 607.1/1—dc23
LC record available at https://lccn.loc.gov/2017058042

ISBN: 978-1-138-56079-6 (hbk)
ISBN: 978-1-138-56080-2 (pbk)
ISBN: 978-0-203-71142-2 (ebk)

Typeset in Minion
by Keystroke, Neville Lodge, Tettenhall, Wolverhampton

We dedicate this book to our families and parents who have supported us all these years, to our teachers who inspired us to strive for the best, and to our past, current, and future students who make our lives meaningful each and every day.

CONTENTS

PART ONE: DEFINING CORE COMPETENCIES FOR LOCAL AND GLOBAL ADVOCACY AND CITIZENSHIP   1

FIGURES AND TABLES

Figures

Tables

AUTHOR BIOGRAPHIES

Peter Cannon is a PhD student in Rhetoric and Composition at the University of South Florida. His research interests are rhetoric of health and medicine, library science, and technical communication. Recent publications examine bibliotherapy and addiction treatment.

Lucía Durá is a program director and an assistant professor of Rhetoric and Writing Studies in the English Department at The University of Texas at El Paso (UTEP). Her work on positive deviance, intercultural communication, and participatory methodologies focuses on understanding and leveraging the assets of vulnerable populations to solve complex problems. To do this work, she collaborates with local and global organizations including the Housing Authority of the City of El Paso, Creative Kids, the YWCA, Project Vida, Save the Children, and Minga Perú. Dr. Durá was a UTEP nominee for the UT System Regent's Outstanding Teaching Award in 2016 and is the author of numerous publications.

Jessica Edwards is an assistant professor of English at the University of Delaware (UD) in Newark, DE. Dr. Edwards has developed and taught courses in professional writing, critical race studies, diversity studies, composition studies, and African American literature. Her scholarship considers ways to engage critical race theory, the intersections of race, racism, and power, in writing classrooms. Dr. Edwards was a Faculty Scholar with the Center for Teaching, Learning, and Assessment at UD and her scholarship has appeared in *Computers and Composition Online* as well as the edited collection, *Key Theoretical Frameworks for Teaching Technical Communication in the 21st Century*.

Laura A. Ewing currently serves as the Station Chair at the American Red Cross Kadena Station, Service to the Armed Forces Far East Division in Okinawa, Japan. She has been living and working in Japan since 2012. She received her PhD from the University of South Florida in Rhetoric and Composition Theory with a focus in intercultural technical communication. Her research interests include intercultural communication, digital communication, and military rhetoric.

Ann Marie Francis is an assistant professor in Composition and Technical Writing for the University of North Georgia. She earned her PhD in rhetoric and composition, her MA in English, and her BA in technical writing. Her primary research interests include technical writing, multimodal composition, community-based writing, and composition pedagogy. In addition to her teaching and research duties, she serves as the Coordinator of the English Department for the Cumming Campus.

John R. Gallagher is an assistant professor at the University of Illinois at Urbana Champaign. He studies interfaces, digital rhetoric, and technical communication on the World Wide Web. He has been published in *Computers and Composition*, *enculturation*, and *Written Communication*. He thanks his participants for donating their time to the project that appears in this edited collection.

Elisabeth Kramer-Simpson directs the Bachelor of Science in Technical Communication Program at New Mexico Tech and teaches classes on grant writing and technical writing. She researches feedback and mentoring in technical communication internships and writing for non-profits, and her work can be found in *IEEE Transactions on Professional Communication* and *The Journal of Technical Writing and Communication*.

Diane Martinez is an assistant professor of English and director of the Professional Writing Program at Western Carolina University (WCU). Prior to teaching at WCU, she worked as a technical writer in engineering and an online writing instructor. Her research interests include social justice in technical and professional communication, intercultural communication, the Bologna Process, globalization and technical communication, and online writing instruction.

Megan M. McIntyre is the Assistant Director of Dartmouth's Institute for Writing and Rhetoric. Her research focuses on how technologies alter conceptions of rhetoric, pedagogy, and writing program administration. She has published work in *Composition Forum*, *Peitho*, and *Kairos*.

Zsuzsanna Palmer is an assistant professor in the Department of Writing at Grand Valley State University. She teaches business and technical communication and document design. Her interests include intercultural online collaboration projects, visual rhetoric, and website accessibility. Her research has appeared in the *Journal of Technical Writing and Communication* and *The International Journal of the Image.*

Emily January Petersen holds a PhD from Utah State University and is an assistant professor of technical and professional writing at Weber State University in the Department of English Language and Literature. Her research focuses on professional identities from a feminist perspective, examining how women act as technical communicators in the workplace, online, and historically. Her work has appeared in various peer-reviewed journals, including the *Journal of Technical Writing and Communication, Communication Design Quarterly,* and *Technical Communication.*

Joshua M. Rea is a PhD student in Rhetoric and Composition at the University of South Florida. His research interests include digital rhetoric, ethics, and composition theory. His current projects examine the mediation and rhetoric of scientific and political discourses in digital spaces, especially Reddit.

Derek G. Ross is an associate professor in the Master of Technical and Professional Communication Program at Auburn University, where he specializes in document design, ethics, and environmental rhetoric. His work has appeared in such journals as *Technical Communication Quarterly, Technical Communication, Written Communication, IEEE Transactions on Professional Communication,* and the *Journal of Technical Writing and Communication,* among others. He is the editor of *Topic-Driven Environmental Rhetoric,* from Routledge, and editor of the journal *Communication Design Quarterly.*

Robert M. Rowan is a writer, teacher, and database designer currently living in Cleveland, Ohio. He holds a doctorate in English Studies (Technical Communication) from Illinois State University and teaches technical and professional writing at Case Western Reserve University. His interests include open-source projects, humor and its uses, creative writing, video games, science fact and fiction, computer programming, neuroscience and adult education, technical communication pedagogy, and contemporary politics and culture. He specializes in teaching technical and professional communication to STEM majors.

Alysia Sawchyn is an MFA candidate in non-fiction at the University of South Florida. She holds an MA in Rhetoric and Composition, and her writing has appeared/is forthcoming in a number of literary journals including *Indiana Review* and *The Southeast Review.* She is the most recent winner of *Cutbank*'s 2016 Flash Prose contest. Her research interests include service-learning, transgressive pedagogies, and mental health narratives.

Steve Simpson is Chair of the Department of Communication, Liberal Arts, and Social Sciences at New Mexico Tech, and teaches courses in science communication and technical editing. He has published widely on communication support for graduate students in STEM disciplines and is a founding board member of the Consortium on Graduate Communication. His co-edited book, *Supporting Graduate Student Writers: Research, Curriculum, and Program Design,* was published through the University of Michigan Press (2016).

Katie L. Walkup is a PhD student in Rhetoric and Composition at the University of South Florida. Her research focuses on rhetoric of health and medicine, advocacy, and new media. Recent publications examine health and identity from a networked perspective.

Xiaobo Wang is the Writing Center Director of Oxford College, Emory University, where she teaches Writing Center Practicum and Critical Reading and Writing. Her research interests are transnational rhetoric and communication, technical communication, cultural rhetoric, and literary studies. She earned her PhD in Rhetoric and Composition from Georgia State University, where she was a 2CI (Second Century Initiative) doctoral fellow, teaching assistant, and writing tutor. She had been an intern of Business Communication Strategy at the Goizueta Business School, Emory University. Her works appeared in *Communication Design Quarterly Review* and *International Research and Review,* among others.

Sarah Warren-Riley is a PhD student at Illinois State University specializing in Rhetoric, Composition and Technical Communication. Her research and pedagogical interests include the intersections of digital rhetorics, public rhetorics, technical communication, and critical digital literacies with an ultimate focus on enacting social justice.

SERIES EDITOR FOREWORD

Tharon Howard

It has been my pleasure to include Godwin Agboka's and Natalia Matveeva's edited collection *Citizenship and Advocacy in Technical Communication* in the ATTW Series in Technical and Professional Communication. The use of service learning projects in technical communication has been steadily increasing in popularity over the past two decades, making the subject of this book extremely timely. I know that back in 1992, I wanted my students to become more than simple wordsmiths and to embrace the idea that they could be what we once called "user advocates." To that end, I started incorporating real usability testing clients into my classes. If only I had had a collection like Agboka and Matveeva to guide my practice; I shudder to think of the number of pedagogical disasters my classes suffered which could have been avoided.

Today, our Technical and Professional Communication (TPC) classrooms are uniquely positioned in the academy to prepare our students to become productive citizens and valued advocates for social, economic, and environmental issues in the workplace. The chapters in this collection are all intended to move our courses beyond merely training students to "translate" scientific and technical content into a language which laypersons can understand; the authors help us see ways to make our courses pathways to citizenship in both local and global contexts. Yet, beyond the usefulness of this collection for TPC classroom pedagogy, there is a decided lack of empirically driven scholarship on service learning, and particularly on service learning involving civic engagement and social advocacy, so readers will be pleased to see chapters in this collection which addressed this need in the field. Agboka and Matveeva have solicited some of the best and brightest scholars in the field as contributors to this volume. As a result, this book provides an important contribution to our field's understanding of the theoretical frameworks and empirical research methodologies which are being used to approach advocacy and civic engagement in TPC classrooms.

Again, I'm thrilled that this collection is part of the ATTW Series in Technical and Professional Communication. The topic is totally consistent with and wholly appropriate for the ATTW Series and provides exactly the blend of solid scholarship and pedagogical application that we're seeking in the Series.

FOREWORD

Of Access, Advocacy, and Citizenship: A Perspective for Technical Communicators

Kirk St.Amant

The Components of Access and Advocacy

At its core, advocacy is about effective *access* to information. After all, information is central to understanding the nature of the problems we seek to rectify. It is also crucial to identifying the options available to address a problem and undertaking the processes related to solving it. In these ways, knowledge becomes power, for it provides us with the tools needed to effect change in the world around us. These connections between information and action are what allows advocacy to move from the conceptual to the actual as individuals build upon their knowledge to identify, coordinate, and enact actions that can foster change.

In terms of information, the concept of access involves two interlocking parts. The first is *availability* – that is, the sources of information are available for us to consult as needed. If I wish to challenge a particular policy, for example, I need access to that policy (and the related items noting its application and interpretation) to understand how it works and to plan for how to respond to it. The second concept is *comprehensibility* – or information presented in a way we can easily understand and act on. It is one thing to have formal policy documents available for review; it is another to understand what the policy is based on and how it is written and designed. Effective advocacy requires both, and it is in relation to this idea of access that technical communicators can make important contributions to advocacy.

Connecting Advocacy to Technical Communication

As individuals trained in the study of audience and audience expectations, technical communicators are well aware of the mechanics of access that can hinder or facilitate the *availability* of information. We are, for example, experts at examining how different audiences use media to access information. Conversely, we are also aware of how a failure to address such factors can affect how available – and thus accessible – information can be.

Through our knowledge of rhetoric, design, and usability, we can determine the most effective mechanisms for sharing information with different audiences to make it readily available to them. Thus, we can facilitate advocacy by taking a more involved role in providing information via the media that different groups use to engage in the advocacy of certain causes. This same skill set can help us identify where disconnects in expectations of availability and design can hinder advocacy efforts. In such cases, we – as technical communicators – are often well positioned to suggest improvements that allow for information to be available and related advocacy activities to succeed.

We, as technical communicators, are also experts in addressing comprehensibility – particularly related to conveying technical or specialized information from one group to another. As such, we are the ideal individual to design materials so the information they contain can be understood by the intended audience to engage in the advocacy of a cause or idea. Moreover, the fact we specialize in working with highly technical scientific and/or technical data makes us well suited to conveying that data effectively to a range of audiences. In these ways, we – as technical communicators – are professionals who can foster effective advocacy by addressing availability and understandability in the information age. Such connections also mean technical communicators are well poised to play a central role in fostering engaged citizenship within a society.

Technical Communication and Engaged Citizenship

Advocacy is often connected to the idea of citizenship: that is, for citizens to take an active role in their society – be it local, regional, or global – they need access to information that is easily available and readily understandable. The empowerment that can come through access to available and understandable information can empower citizens by making them aware of the forces affecting their lives. Such knowledge can also form a foundation on which citizens can advocate for a course of action that reflects the dynamics of their daily lives, as well as their current needs and future aspirations. This raised awareness fosters engagement as individuals seek to interact with others in their society (or with society itself) to advocate effectively for a course of action.

Such engagement connects to fundamental technical communication activities of media selection and the formatting and sharing of information. It also connects to rendering ideas in a way that makes them readily understood (and thus able for others to engage with) by a given group. At this citizen level, however, the contributions technical communicators can make to advocacy changes. Rather than focusing on the informational nature of materials (i.e., providing content for others to process and act upon), the focus of the citizenship level moves to instructional: that is, the key becomes teaching others – i.e., citizens – how to create messages and share information that allows others to access it and to thus engage in greater interactions around a topic. At this level, technical communicators can greatly contribute by making available and understandable information that teaches others 'how to do' in relation to addressing availability and comprehensibility. In so doing, technical communicators become engaged citizens, for they need to work with various citizen groups to understand and address expectations when crafting instructional materials.

Addressing Advocacy and Citizenship across Technical Communication

As with many fields, technical communication exists across a range of individuals working in different domains. These audiences include academic researchers, industry practitioners, professional educators, and students in the discipline. Each group can play an important role in addressing access via availability and comprehensibility. What such contributions can entail, however, can often seem daunting due to the complex and nuanced nature of access, availability, and citizenship. Such understanding, however, is paramount for technical communicators to address both issues of advocacy and of citizenship in what they do. As such, individuals across the field can benefit from resources that guide how to apply one's knowledge and skills effectively to the areas of informed advocacy and engaged citizenship. This text represents such a resource.

By examining advocacy and citizenship across segments of the field, the collected work of the contributing authors offers an effective framework for understanding availability and understandability at different levels within society. Technical communicators can use such approaches to address such factors. The collection's contributors present different approaches to applying their own special knowledge and skills within technical communication to advocacy practices and the actions of engaged citizens. In so doing, they provide us – as members of a common field – with a new perspective of what constitutes value in the modern global age: value based on one's ability to interact with and contribute to society on a range of levels. In short, the authors make the concepts of advocacy and citizenship available to and comprehensible to members of the field in ways that allow them to become engaged citizens and participate in effective advocacy for different causes.

The editors of this collection have also done a masterful job of compiling individuals who can address a range of topics relating to advocacy and citizenship across a variety of settings – from the university classroom to the global stage. By organizing these entries into three thematic sections, the editors make central ideas available in ways that allow the reader to build on prior concepts as she or he moves through the text. In so doing, the structure created by the editors allows a degree of engagement with ideas and approaches that can empower by revealing what technical communicators can do to facilitate effective advocacy and engaged citizenship in modern society. As such, they establish their status – as well as that of their contributors – as advocates and citizens whose model can be followed by others across the field.

Advocacy is often a matter of investment. If you feel invested in a topic, you are more likely to advocate on its behalf. In so doing, you are more likely to engage others in society to foster more coordinated and more effective advocacy for that topic, thus making all of you engaged citizens. This text represents a similar approach. By investing in reading it and learning from it, technical communicators can more effectively become advocates of various ideas and become more engaged citizens working with others for a common cause.

PREFACE

Advocating for the Good of Humanity: Technical Communication as a Tool for Change

Godwin Y. Agboka and Natalia Matveeva

The thematic strands of advocacy, citizenship, and civic engagement are not new to technical and professional communication (TPC), although historically the field has been slow to embrace them. Around the late 1980s and the 1990s, TPC faced mounting criticism, from scholars within and outside the field, for its overemphasis on vocationalism, or what Engell & Dangerfield (1998) called the "market model." The market model, with its capitalist undertones, sought to teach marketable and innovative skills with the goal of "producing" skilled labor for the corporate sector. This model was (and still is) an important component of higher education.

However, critics, concerned about the "corporatization" of education, decried the field's attachment to the apron strings of these functionalist, skill-based approaches to the neglect of democratic, humanistic, and social justice approaches that were more responsive to social, economic, cultural, and environmental issues in the community (Ansley & Gaventa, 1997; Bushnell, 1999; Dubinsky, 2002; Grabill, 2001; Herndl, 1993; Miller, 1979, 1989). Miller (1979) had initiated discussions about the place and value of technical writing within English departments, highlighting the problematic positivist view of the discipline and its pedagogical practices. While rejecting such misconceptions, Miller suggested that when introducing students to mechanical rules and writing strategies, teachers should also help students gain "a broader understanding of why and how to adjust or violate the rules, of the social implications of the roles a writer casts for himself or herself and for the reader, and of the ethical repercussions of one's words" (p. 617). In a later rebuke, Bushnell (1999) argued that technical communication had "become training departments for corporate 'clients' who provide us with internships and fellowships for our students, and ever-increasing numbers of good-paying jobs for our graduates" (p. 175–176). Thus, it was important for TPC pedagogical approaches to prepare more rounded "public intellectuals" (Cushman, 1999) who would be knowledgeable in their subject matter areas, but also be willing and able to interrogate ways in which their activities would impact their communities of practice.

As a consequence of these growing criticisms, Sapp & Crabtree (2002) recount the increasing pressure on ". . . faculty and administrators to find ways to empower students in communities of living and learning, to provide education that is concerned with more than merely training students to be effective engineers, system analysts, or technical writers" (p. 412). Fortunately, TPC rose to the challenge and embraced notions of "education for the public good" by encouraging pedagogical and research approaches that have sought to train and prepare civic minded students who advocate a critical perspective that engages the political, economic, social, and cultural issues that impact communities (Breuch, 2002).

Thus, for the past 20 years, TPC has looked to areas such as service-learning (Bourelle, 2014; Cook, 2014; Dubinsky, 2002; Henson & Sutliff, 1998; Huckin, 1997; Judge, 2006; Matthews & Zimmerman 1999; McEachern, 2001; Sapp & Crabtree, 2002; Turnley, 2007; Walton, 2013;) and radical pedagogical and research approaches (Bowden & Scott, 2002; Clark, 2004; Cushman, 1999; Dubinsky, 2002; Herndl, 1993; Walton, 2013) to infuse the discipline with civic engagement and advocacy perspectives. New approaches in research methodologies and practices, such as participatory design (Crabtree, 1998; Spinuzzi, 2005), decolonial methodologies (Agboka, 2014; Beeman-Cadwallader et al., 2012; Haas, 2012; Mutua & Swadener, 2004; Smith, 1999); and user-centered design (Johnson, 1998) are leading the way in involving actual users and various stakeholders in product development and devising solutions that work within given contexts rather than the one-solution-fits-all approach.

As knowledge mediators and users' advocates, technical writers, communication specialists, grant writers, public relations managers, web designers/content developers, and social media managers employ "practical rhetoric" as "a matter of arguing in a prudent way toward the good of the community rather than of constructing texts" (Miller, 1989, p. 23). Technical and professional communicators play various roles in shaping democratic discourses locally and globally. Not only do teachers, researchers, and practitioners produce artifacts that contribute to advocacy and global citizenship, but they also conduct important research and work in governmental and civil society organizations that all shape these practices. (See Agboka, 2013a/b, 2014; Walton, 2013; Walton & DeRenzi, 2009; Walton & Jones, 2013; Walton et al., 2015).

Tools for Advocacy and Active Citizenship in Technical Communication: Service Learning and Community Engagement in the Digital Age

In the 2012 report produced by the National Task Force on Civic Learning and Democratic Engagement formed by the Association of American Colleges and

Universities (AAC&U), the group calls for the greater civic participation of colleges and universities in the communities they are located and recommends "strengthening students' civic learning and democratic engagement as a core component of college study" (p. vii). AAC&U has sounded the alarm that without increased civic participation by students and faculty "the United States risks becoming a second-rate democracy and an increasingly fragmented society" (Woods et al., 2013, p. 67). In the follow-up report (2016), the AAC&U claims that many institutions of higher education have answered the call and have introduced initiatives (grant development, scholarships, collaborative projects, curricular changes, and pedagogical approaches) to advance the vision of "civic learning" that "should prepare students with knowledge and for action in our communities and at their workplaces" (AAC&U, 2016, p. 1).

The field of technical and professional communication has a long-standing commitment to connecting to and improving lives of people in the local communities. In fact, the very skills and knowledge we teach are effective advocacy tools and can empower students to be informed and effective participants in civic discourse. Students' solid understanding of advocacy genres, such as proposals and grants, effective research and writing skills, and the knowledge of available tools can bring needed funding for programs and projects that aid people in need. The use of appropriate workplace genres and document design can inform and persuade employees in a workplace context and empower them to take action if a problem arises. Good rhetorical skills can also help future practitioners analyze and refute flawed arguments, while the knowledge of new communication technologies and delivery modes may allow for a wider reach of potential audiences. However, teaching the right skills and knowledge is not enough for building strong ties between the academy and the outside world.

At the turn of the last century, Thomas Huckin (1997) published a seminal article which formally introduced service-learning into the TPC literature. Huckin's work spurred a great many publications, case studies, and teaching cases on service-learning. Elsewhere, two other important publications followed, which cemented the value of advocacy work in TPC. In 2000, Carolyn Rude edited a special issue of *Technical Communication Quarterly* on "The Discourse of Public Policy," which argued that technical communication is inextricably linked to public policy issues of relevance to communities. Then, when Dubinsky & Carpenter (2004) introduced their special issue on "Civic Engagement" in the same journal, they insisted that education should prepare students for critical citizenship so that they can, more thoughtfully, analyze the sociopolitical implications of their communication decisions. However, this movement also invited its fair share of resistance. Among them, critics were concerned that civic engagement would be a convenient platform to indoctrinate, "radicalize," and "propagandize" students for political gains (Sapp & Crabtree, 2002).

The suspicions notwithstanding, the recognition that professional and technical communication occurs in and impacts local and global communities motivated a significant paradigm shift in pedagogy and research. Often called the "change" paradigm (Kathne & Westheimer, 1996), the shift towards engaged citizenship enabled students, faculty, and administrators to become more civic minded and to think more critically about their role in society as they develop a reciprocal relationship with their organizations (p. 595). Evidently, more and more technical communication teachers are merging classroom learning and community engagement to enable students to apply their academic skills to projects within the community. Through internships, innovative writing assignments, and direct requests from community partners, students are able to come face-to-face with expectations of the workplace, enact social justice by helping vulnerable populations address a problem, negotiate socio-political issues, and develop practical skills that a traditional classroom assignment would not provide.

As our commentary has shown, advocacy and citizenship occur on several platforms, the most popular of which is service-learning—which is not surprising because of its connections with social justice (Mitchell, 2008). On the one hand, service-learning provides opportunities for students to learn and offers community service, which itself teaches students about action, social responsibility, and citizenship. Our field's literature is replete with scholarship about the merits and forms of service-learning (Dubinsky, 2002; Huckin, 1997; Sapp & Crabtree, 2002), the role of technology in enacting service-learning (Turnley, 2007), the challenges of integrating service-learning in online classes (Bourelle, 2014), and the problems associated with implementing service-learning (Matthews & Zimmerman, 1999; McEachern, 2001; Scott, 2004)—just to highlight a few. With its emphasis on experiential learning in which students apply academic skills to the needs of a local nonprofit (Huckin, 1997), service learning can have many benefits for students, community partners, and the university. First, it "offers students opportunities to develop, reflect about, and enact civic responsibility" (Scott, 2004, p. 289); it ". . .prepares students to be responsible community members," and provides ". . .education in engaged citizenship" (Sapp & Crabtree, 2002, p. 412); it produces "critical citizens who produce effective and ethical discourse and work to create more inclusive forms of power" (p. 304); it exposes students to real-world problems (Matthews & Zimmerman, 1999); and, it also offers a real-world context in which students can more effectively develop as writers" (Ashworth & Bourelle, 2014, p. 65).

As scholars and pedagogues who write and teach about these issues, we are excited about the promising scholarly work in the field and the tremendous opportunities for further work. But we also share in the concerns of several scholars that a lot more work needs to be done (Dubinsky, 2002; Eyler et al., 1996; Simmons & Grabill, 1998). Recent challenges to racial, class, gender, disability, and economic issues raise significant concerns and provide excellent opportunities for our field to engage, forge relationships, and build new relationships with communities. Scholars very often question the commitment of civic engagement assignments to social justice (Herzberg, 1994), decry the quality of deliverables to community members (Brizee, 2015), raise concerns about the theoretical grounding motivating service learning projects (Matthews & Zimmerman, 1999), wonder about the value of community engagement to students (McEachern, 2001), and worry about the asymmetrical posture of student-community member relationships. Indeed, when we titled the 2016 ATTW conference "Citizenship and Advocacy in Technical Communication," it was in recognition that the field needed to reconsider advocacy and civic engagement in the many ways they manifest themselves in our discipline.

This edited collection attempts to answer these questions in our field. It's an attempt to re-engage and re-interrogate our practices. As scholars and teachers of social justice, we see advocacy work as important in not only connecting us to communities, but also in imbuing in our students a sense of social responsibility, engaged citizenship, and social justice towards their communities of practice when they join the workforce, whether locally or internationally. Already, technical communicators play various roles in shaping democratic discourses locally and globally. Ultimately, we see advocacy as the process of using a combination of academic and practical skills and knowledge systems to enact social justice with the goal to improving the quality of life for communities. In essence, we argue that our pedagogies and scholarly practices must create the opportunities, through political and non-political means, to positively impact communities.

Certainly, we acknowledge the important work of scholars before us; thus, in many ways, this collection builds on their legacy—but this project also offers new perspectives on teaching, undertaking, and writing about advocacy work in our field. Although our collection is not the first to raise and address questions about advocacy, it represents the first book-length attempt, since the early 2000s, to provide a comprehensive look at advocacy and active local and global citizenship as core topics in technical communication.

Goals of This Collection

The chapters assembled in this collection cover an expansive breadth of issues and topics that speak to the complexities of undertaking advocacy work in technical and professional communication, including local grant writing activities, cosmopolitanism and global transnational rhetoric, digital citizenship and social media use, strategic and tactical communication, and diversity and social justice. The contributors themselves, representing 15 academic institutions and occupying various academic ranks, offer nuanced definitions, frameworks, examples, and strategies for students, scholars, practitioners, and educators who want to or are already engaged in a variegated range of advocacy work. More so, they reinforce the inherent humanistic values of our field and discuss effective rhetorical and current technological tools at our disposal. Finally, they show us how, through pedagogical approaches and everyday mundane activities and practices, we (can) advocate either actively or passively.

The collection consists of three parts and 14 chapters that are grouped based on their general focus and purpose. The chapters in Part One define major competencies and provide important definitions for discussing advocacy and local and global citizenship. Part Two delves into various approaches and heuristics for engaging with local and global communities. Finally, Part Three offers specific pedagogical tools and considerations for various teaching or training situations.

PART ONE: Defining Core Competencies for Local and Global Advocacy and Citizenship

In Part One, readers will familiarize themselves with the concepts of advocacy and local and global citizenship. It offers important definitions and frameworks and discusses the role of advocacy and citizenship in the field of technical communication and beyond.

In Chapter 1, "Female Practitioners' Advocacy and Activism: Using Technical Communication for Social Justice Goals," Emily January Petersen claims that advocacy and activism are at the core of what technical communicators do and defines the meaning of these concepts in our field. To support her argument, she introduces two case studies of female practitioners, one working in a religious organization and another an employee of a nonprofit providing social services, who served as advocates for others officially/strategically and extra institutionally/tactically. By analyzing the women's approaches to dealing with various challenges, Petersen concludes that each woman has employed effective strategies as a technical communication practitioner, including employing careful audience analysis, preparing effective documents, and collaborating, that allowed them to advocate successfully for themselves and others.

In Chapter 2, "Expanding Inventional and Solution Spaces: How Asset-Based Inquiry Can Support Advocacy in Technical Communication," Lucía Durá proposes a framework for working with local communities and integrating community representatives into technical communication research and practice, which she calls "asset-based thinking," a derivative of asset-based community development and community-based participatory research. The author introduces two case studies, one describing an afterschool program on the US-Mexican border and the other focusing on a program in a public hospital in Texas. With each of the cases, the author describes two techniques—Appreciative Interviews, and Discovery and Action Dialogues—that were used to collect vital information from community representatives. Durá suggests that by employing "asset-based thinking," researchers can advocate for the needs of the community to ensure that all voices are heard and effective solutions are implemented.

In Chapter 3, "Enabling Global Citizenship in Intercultural Collaboration: Cosmopolitan Potential in Online Identity Representation," Zsuzsanna Palmer expands on the ideas of cosmopolitanism and proposes developing in future practitioners the "cosmopolitan outlook" that can serve as a basis for active global citizenship. Working around the themes of interconnectedness, cosmopolitanism, and common ground, the chapter analyzes the cosmopolitan potential represented on online blogs by students involved in an intercultural pedagogical project in two universities: Pazmany Peter University in Hungary and Davenport University in Michigan. Ultimately, the author concludes that when instructors teach the principles of cosmopolitanism to students, the students become more aware of the cosmopolitan elements of their identities and can use this awareness as the basis for finding common ground with their international counterparts and ultimately explore their cultural differences.

Similar to the previous chapter, Chapter 4, "Building the Babel of Transnational Literacies: Preparing Education for World Citizens," by Xiaobo Wang, explores effective frameworks for responsible global citizenship. Wang supports Palmer's position and uses cosmopolitanism as a foundation for developing her model of transnational and transcultural rhetoric and communication. The new theoretical model serves as an analytical tool for reviewing different types of variables in the contents of technical communication textbooks. Wang then categorizes these variables in current textbooks to determine the scope of relevant content on transnational and transcultural rhetoric. The author makes important conclusions about deficiencies in the chosen textbooks and re-emphasizes the importance of introducing the concepts of cosmopolitanism and transnationalism in techni-cal and professional communication. These approaches can help people find common ground and promote ethical and responsible global citizenship.

PART TWO: Choosing the Right Approaches to Advocacy and Community Engagement: Working with a Real Client

Part Two contains case studies that report a variety of techniques and approaches to advocacy and civic engagement. Practical examples and strategies found in the chapters will help those who plan to start advocacy projects in their commu-nities, locally or globally. It also discusses available tools for effective advocacy campaigns.

Part Two starts with Chapter 5, "Technical Communication Client Projects and Nonprofit Partnerships: The Challenges and Opportunities of Community Engagement," by Elisabeth Kramer-Simpson and Steve Simpson who present the results of their successful community engagement project between faculty and students at New Mexico Institute of Mining and Technology and Puerto Seguro (PSI), a homeless day shelter in Socorro, NM. The authors have built a strong partnership. Working with the homeless shelter over the years, the authors and their students in various classes had an opportunity to help those in need, prac-tice their skills, and build important relations with the local organization. This collaboration has resulted in acquiring much needed funding for the organization and establishing productive relations with the local community. After collecting feedback from various stakeholders in this long-term project, the authors discuss numerous benefits of such collaborations and offer solutions to some potential challenges.

In Chapter 6, "An Intercultural Analysis of Social Media Advocacy in Disaster Response," by Laura A. Ewing and Megan M. McIntyre, the use of social media advocacy in disaster response comes into focus. The authors examine potential cultural similarities and differences in the way social media is employed by governmental and non-governmental organizations in the U.S. (FEMA and United Way of Southeast Louisiana) and Japan (Kumamoto Prefecture and the Nippon Foundation) for the purpose of disseminating information to and advocating for their constituents. By conducting content analysis of social media messages produced by the organizations after the historic August 2016 floods in Louisiana in the U.S., and the 2016 Kumamoto earthquake in Japan, the researchers have concluded that the use of social media in managing the disaster response was less prominent or even non-existent in the communications by the two Japanese organizations, potentially due to cultural differences as they exhibit themselves in organizational structures and the use of social media and other technologies. Technical communicators must be aware of such peculiarities when using social media platforms across cultures and national borders.

Continuing the focus on electronic communication from the previous chapter, John R. Gallagher, in Chapter 7, "Monitoring and Managing Online Comments in Science Journalism," explores the intricacies of responding to and building rapport with the readership of online scientific publications. The author reports the results of five interviews with professional online journalists whose task is to respond to readers' comments. Through his analysis, Gallagher identifies common strategies that these journalists use "to advocate for civic engagement: (1) ignoring (2) establishing forums, (3) correcting/updating, and (4) textual listening." Such strategies help build online communities and maintain inter-actions between the publications and the readers to ensure that credible and truthful information is disseminated, which also leads to advocacy on the part of scientific community.

In Chapter 8, "Journaling and Bibliotherapy Participatory Design as a Heuristic for Program Development," Joshua M. Rea, Peter Cannon, Alysia Sawchyn, and Katie L. Walkup discuss journaling as an advocacy tool in seeking social justice for vulnerable populations. They interrogate issues of mental health literacy, usability for vulnerable populations, and effective service-learning techniques through a case study of bringing journal writing out of the classroom and into a community learning space. While pointing out some of the challenges that occur when advocating for and working with vulnerable populations, their work suggests how the needs of vulnerable populations shape design, and that when designing for unenfranchised audiences, technical communicators must be responsible and reflexive.

In Chapter 9, "Résumé Design and Career Advocacy in a Goodwill Career Center," Derek G. Ross, working around similar themes, demonstrates ways in which résumé writing might be used as a conduit to advocate for those seeking help in a job search. He has worked as a writing coach at a Goodwill Career Centre and has had an opportunity to build connections with and survey those who came seeking help with résumé design. Ross concludes that volunteerism, through offering help with résumé writing, could be an important locus for discussing ways for "technical and professional communicators to become more involved with their local communities, and to discuss ways that our expertise might better serve our communities."

PART THREE: Introducing Advocacy Techniques in a Classroom

This final part offers teaching strategies for those interested in introducing advocacy, social justice, and diversity issues in a classroom and suggests methods of engaging with the local and global communities.

In Chapter 10, "Inclusive Practices in the Technical Communication Classroom," Jessica Edwards reports the results of a study on strategies to promote more diverse curricula in technical communication and better prepare students for working in diverse contexts. After conducting focus groups with faculty and students, she provides a list of effective assignments and strategies for introducing the discussions of diversity and social justice in a technical communication classroom. Edwards suggests that there must be more effective efforts and strategies, both institutionally and in the classroom, that go beyond paying lip service to diversity and diverse practices, to more intentional and engaged approaches.

In Chapter 11, "Community-Engaged Learning in Online Technical Communication Classes: A Tool for Student Success," Ann Marie Francis discusses service-learning activities in online technical writing courses, or service eLearning, which is a relatively new phenomenon. She examines some of the problems associated with organizing and motivating students in an online setting and concludes that working with a community partner, although at times a challenging task, provides an invaluable experience to the students as it allows for building important community relations and better prepares students for future careers.

Chapter 12, "Teaching Proposal Writing: Advocacy and Autonomy in the Technical Communication Classroom," by Diane Martinez, discusses how proposal writing courses in technical communication can be a good site for teaching about advocacy. Specifically, she demonstrates how a graduate-level proposal writing course that includes theoretical foundations in social justice and cultural studies in TPC can be used to teach students about advocacy for others. In the sample assignment she shares, students analyzed requests for proposals (RFPs), explored the rhetorical nature of proposals, and learned about the complexity of the proposal writer's role. Martinez argues that because the proposal writing process allows students to gain a sense of autonomy as they have to develop their own position on issues that are important to and affect them, the course is a good platform for teaching undergraduate and graduate students how to effectively advocate through inquiry, critical thinking, problem-solving, and professional writing.

Robert M. Rowan's Chapter 13, "Open-Source Technical Communication in the Classroom: Digital Citizenship, Communities of Play, and Online Collaboration," provides a rationale and methods for encouraging and guiding student participation in online communities of interest. The chapter makes a case for using our technical communication skills to participate in the world—particularly, for this chapter, the digital world—and using the technical communication classroom as a platform for developing and focusing those skills. It concludes by providing discussion questions, exercises, and assessment methods—options for integrating the approaches as a course module.

Finally, the last chapter of the book, Chapter 14, "Social Media and Advocacy in the TPC Classroom: A Social Justice Pedagogical Approach," by Sarah Warren-Riley, focuses on teaching advocacy and social engagement as "a mindset." Specifically, the author suggests that by asking students to interrogate everyday social media text, the students will gain new perspectives on the power and effect of writing in advocacy. The chapter offers sample activities and assignments that include textual analysis of social media posts and discussion questions targeting advocacy tools in social media spaces. The goal of the activities is to help students "develop technical and critical literacy which can be further translated into a more socially just approach to creating all texts."

Implications for Research, Teaching, and Practice

The value of this book is in its systematic approach to building bridges with the outside world that can benefit both the students and the community. However, building long-term community relations is not easy and can rarely be done effectively by just one faculty member in just one semester; it requires a broader institutional commitment and resources. In recent years, many institutions have made such a commitment and have promoted community engagement, i.e. a broader involvement of an institution in the life of the community in which it is situated through building long-term relations and conducting collaborative projects to benefit the community.

This book takes a step further and examines how the work we do in the communities locally and globally manifests itself as advocacy and active citizenship. The chapters of this book discuss what it means to advocate, how technical and professional communicators advocate, and how advocacy and citizenship manifest themselves in either the workplace or local communities. The collection skillfully meshes perspectives on pedagogy, theory, and practice with the goal of helping technical and professional communicators engage in advocacy and civic engagement in their various contexts. Finally, the collection addresses the needs of multiple audiences. It is a useful guide for people who are new to work in civic engagement and advocacy because it provides definitions, approaches, and best practices. However, even for those who are already familiar with work in this area, the collection suggests news ways of implementing practices in the classroom and the field.

References

All website URLs accessed February 2018.

Agboka, G. (2013a). Participatory localization: A social justice approach to navigating unenfranchised/disenfranchised cultural sites. *Technical Communication Quarterly, 22*(1), 28–49.

Agboka, G. (2013b). Thinking about social justice: Interrogating the international in international technical communication discourse. *Connexions. International Professional Communication Journal, 1*(1), 29–38.

Agboka, G. (2014). Decolonial methodologies: Social justice perspectives in intercultural communication research. *Journal of Technical Writing and Communication, 44*, 297–327.

Ansley, F., & Gaventa, J. (1997). Researching for democracy & democratizing research. *Change,* 46–53.

Ashworth, E., & Bourelle, T. (2014). Utilizing critical service-learning pedagogy in the online classroom: Promoting social justice and effecting change? *Currents in Teaching and Learning, 7,* 64–79.

Association of American Colleges and Universities. (2012). A crucible moment: College learning & democracy's future. Retrieved from www.aacu.org/civic_learning/crucible/documents/ crucible_508F.pdf

Association of American Colleges and Universities. (2016). A Crucible Moment: College Learning and Democracy's Future How the National Report Has Spurred Action 2012–2016. Retrieved from http://aacu.org/sites/default/files/files/crucible/CrucibleUpdate 2016.pdf

Beeman-Cadwallader, N., Quigley, C., & Yazzie-Mintz, T. (2012). Enacting decolonized methodologies: The doing of research in educational communities. *Qualitative Inquiry, 18*(1), 3–15.

Bourelle, T. (2014). Adapting service-learning into the online technical communication classroom: A framework and model. *Technical Communication Quarterly, 23,* 247–264.

Bowden, M., & Scott, J. B. (2002). *Service-Learning in technical and professional communication.* New York: Longman.

Breuch, L. A. K. (2002). Thinking critically about technological literacy: Developing a framework to guide computer pedagogy in technical communication. *Technical Communication Quarterly, 11,* 267–288.

Brizee, A. (2015). Using Isocrates to teach technical communication and civic engagement. *Journal of Technical Writing and Communication, 45*(2), 134–165.

Bushnell, J. (1999). A contrary view of the technical writing classroom. Notes toward future discussions. *Technical Communication Quarterly, 8,* 175–188.

Clark, D. (2004). Is professional writing relevant? A model for action research. *Technical Communication Quarterly, 13,* 307–324.

Cook, K. C. (2014). Service learning and undergraduate research in technical communication programs. *Programmatic Perspective, 6*(1), 27–51.

Crabtree, R. D. (1998). Mutual empowerment in cross-cultural participatory development and service learning: Lessons in communication and social justice from projects in El Salvador and Nicaragua. *Journal of Applied Communication Research, 26,* 182–209.

Cushman, E. (1999). The public intellectual, service learning, and activist research. *College English, 61*(3), 328–336.

Dubinsky, J. (2002). Service-learning as a path to virtue: The ideal orator in professional communication. *Michigan Journal of Community Service Learning. 8,* 61–74.

Dubinsky, J.M., & Carpenter, J. H. (Eds.) (2004). Civic engagement and technical communication. *Technical Communication Quarterly, 13,* 13.

Engell, J., & Dangerfield, A. (1998). The market-driven university, humanities in the age of money. *Harvard Magazine,* (48–55), 111.

Grabill, J. (2001). *Community literacy programs and the politics of change.* Albany, NY: SUNY Press.

Grabill, J. T., & Simmons, W. M. (1998). Toward a critical rhetoric of risk communication: Producing citizens and the role of technical communicators. *Technical Communication Quarterly, 7*(4), 415–441.

Haas, A. (2012). Race, rhetoric, and technology: A case study of decolonial technical communication theory, methodology, and pedagogy. *Journal of Business and Technical Communication, 26,* 277–310.

Henson, L., & Sutliff, K. (1998). A service learning approach to business and technical writing instruction. *Journal of Technical Writing and Communication, 28,* 189–205.

Herndl, C. G. (1993), Teaching discourse and reproducing culture: A critique of research and pedagogy in professional and non-academic writing. *College Composition and Communication, 44,* 349–363.

Herzberg, B. (1994). Community service and critical teaching. *College Composition and Communication 45,* 307–319.

Huckin, T. (1997). Technical writing and community service. *Journal of Business and Technical Communication, 11,* 46–59.

Johnson, R. (1998). *User-centered technology: A rhetorical theory for computers and other mundane artifacts.* Albany, NY: SUNY Press.

Judge, T. M. (2006). Service-learning on campus. *Business Communication Quarterly, 69,* 189–192.

Kathne, J., & Westheimer, J. (1996). In service of what? The politics of service learning. *Phi Delta Kappan, 77,* 593–600.

Matthews, C., & Zimmerman, B. B. (1999). Integrating service learning and technical communication: Benefits and challenges. *Technical Communication Quarterly,* (4), 383–404.

McEachern, R. W. (2001). Problems in service learning and technical/professional writing: Incorporating the perspective of the nonprofit management. *Technical Communication Quarterly, 10*(2), 211–224.

Miller, C. (1979). A humanistic rationale for technical writing. *College English, 40*(6), 610–617.

Miller, C. (1989). What's practical about technical writing? In B. E. Fearing & W. K. Sparrow (Eds.), *Technical writing: Theory and practice* (pp. 14–24). New York, NY: Modern Language Association.

Mitchell, B. (2008). Traditional vs. critical service-learning: Engaging the literature to differentiate two models. *Michigan Journal of Service-Learning, 14*(2), 50–65.

Mutua, K., & Swadener, B. B. (2004). *Decolonizing research in cross-cultural contexts: Critical personal narratives.* Albany, NY: State University of New York Press.

Rude, C. (Ed.) (2000). The discourse of public policy. *Technical Communication Quarterly, 9.*

Sapp, D. A., & Crabtree, R. D. (2002). A laboratory in citizenship: Service learning in the technical communication classroom. *Technical Communication Quarterly, 11*(4), 411–431.

Scott, J. B. (2004). Rearticulating civic engagement through cultural studies and service-learning. *Technical Communication Quarterly, 13*(3), 389–306.

Smith, L. T. (1999). *Decolonizing methodologies: Research and indigenous peoples.* New York, NY: Zed Books Ltd.

Spinuzzi, C. (2005). The methodology of participatory design. *Technical Communication, 52*(2), 163–174.

Turnley, M. (2007). Integrating critical approaches to technology and service-leaning projects. *Technical Communication Quarterly, 16*(1), 103–123.

Walton, R., & DeRenzi, B. (2009). Value-sensitive design and health care in Africa. *IEEE Transactions on Professional Communication, 53*(4), 346–358.

Walton, R. (2013). Civic engagement, information technology, & global contexts. *Connexions. International Professional Communication Journal, 1*(1), 147–154.

Walton, R., & Jones, N. N. (2013). Navigating increasingly cross-cultural, cross-disciplinary, and cross-organizational contexts to support social justice. *Communication Design Quarterly, 1*(4), 31–35.

Walton, R., Zraly, M., & Mugengana, J. P. (2015). Values and validity: Navigating messiness in a community-based research project in Rwanda. *Technical Communication Quarterly, 24*(1), 45–69.

Woods L., Willis J., Wright D. C., & Knapp, T. (2013). Building community engagement in higher education: Public sociology at Missouri State University. *Journal of Public Scholarship in Higher Education, 3,* 67–90.

Defining Core Competencies for Local and Global Advocacy and Citizenship

PART ONE

1

FEMALE PRACTITIONERS' ADVOCACY AND ACTIVISM

Using Technical Communication for Social Justice Goals

Emily January Petersen

Introduction

Women must navigate power structures in workplaces (Dragga, 1993; Bergman & Hallberg, 2002; Guy & Newman, 2004; Hamel, 2009; Favero & Heath, 2012; Budig, 2014), and they may react in various ways, including by claiming authority and agency in their interactions with those hierarchies (Schneider, 2007). As this chapter will show, a few women take authority a step further by becoming advocates. These women have experienced traumatic or disappointing events, and they use this understanding to advocate for others. They do not wish only to work within or around systems; they work to change them and use personal experiences to speak up and act on behalf of others through technical and professional communication (TPC).

My workplace experiences (and my inability to fully advocate for myself and others) inform this research on female technical communicators in workplaces. I worked in a department that was composed of some 300 men and six women. I was the only technical communicator and the only woman in a non-secretarial position. In upper-level staff meetings for the research and analysis division, I often heard inappropriate jokes from male colleagues. In fact, when interviewing for the position, the director of the division asked me when I planned to start a family and expressed anxiety over the possibility of me becoming pregnant. I am sure he did not extend these same questions to his male employees. I saw power dynamics and hierarchy in action. I learned that women were often objects for sexual jokes, and that my biology made me a liability to my company, no matter how good my work ethic, training, and abilities were. I did figure out ways to claim authority for myself through my supervisory role over an assistant writer, by being friendly with SMEs, and asking for leadership roles. However, I never advocated for anybody else. I did not use my experiences to change the system. It did not occur to me to use documentation to highlight inequalities or to persuade decision-makers.

The 39 women I interviewed had similar experiences. While almost all of them were content with their jobs and mostly felt valued, they had experienced feeling undervalued and shuffled aside for male employees. Very few of the women I talked with made hierarchical or organizational decisions. While some of them acted as managers for their teams, not many of them enjoyed this role, and those who did conceded that they did not have the power to fire, hire, or make decisions for their employees. I wondered: What power do female TPC practitioners have in the workplace? How do they find ways to overcome difficulties and, more importantly, to change the systems? This chapter will examine what two of the interviewees revealed about advocacy and activism through the use of TPC. It is important to understand how workers innovate and advocate in difficult situations through documentation, in order to prepare students and inform practitioners of what tools are available to them in tricky workplace situations. The information in this chapter suggests how such work in TPC can be accomplished. By conducting two case studies, I focused on answering two major research questions: How do women enact change on the workplace via genres, practices, tools, and texts? In what ways do practitioners engage in problem-solving?

The practitioners in this chapter's case studies used both tactical (unofficial) and strategic (official) communication to achieve advocacy goals for marginalized groups within their contexts. They employed TPC expertise to advocate for others, and they engaged in forms of communication to counter the oppressive messages received from powerful hierarchies. The final section will elucidate the advocacy practices that emerge. These include (1) recognizing the relationship TPC has to advocacy; (2) appealing to powerful and political audiences and organizations; (3) using documentation to make advocacy official; and (4) engaging in coalition-building.

Advocacy and Activism in TPC

Advocacy is inherent to a technical communicator's experiences because the field is concerned with users (Johnson, 1998), and essentially practitioners are constantly engaging in user advocacy. One of my interviewees stated, "I feel like I am the advocate for the users. . . . I speak up . . . because I've gotten to know these systems so well that I can speak up for the users." She took responsibility for being accountable to her audience and future users of her documentation. While TPC practitioners do this routinely, as professionals who apprise users of technology and its intricacies, a few of the 39 women I interviewed saw themselves as formal advocates.

This sort of user advocacy in TPC has flourished into social justice, beyond civic engagement (Rude, 2008; Jones, et al., 2014). Social justice provides context for focusing on "the multiple voices of the marginalized, the discriminated, the colonized, and the oppressed" (Muñoz, 2014, p. 11). According to Walton and Jones (2013), "Centrally relevant to social justice is work that examines the importance of the role of technical communication for activist groups and other stakeholders involved in affecting change for disenfranchised and marginalized populations" (p. 31). So practitioners who keep the experiences of users in mind and advocate for better documentation as a result are working to equalize inequities. To take this a step further, the case studies in this chapter address specific ways to change conversations about inequities in the workplace and in nonprofit work. Many of the women I interviewed engaged in some form of advocacy or activism. They promoted 508 Compliance for users with disabilities, edited an app that provides the day's history from a queer perspective, expressed interest in being a straight ally, advocated for same gender health benefits, and taught diversity training.

Women's Experiences as Knowledge

The advocacy of these women highlights the importance of valuing mundane and everyday experiences as a source of knowledge. Experience as knowledge is central to feminist standpoint theory, the idea "that knowledge is situated and perspectival and that there are multiple standpoints from which knowledge is produced" (Hekman, 2004, p. 226). In other words, knowledge is built and shared. Those who are not in official positions of power may see breaks in the power structure and act to make concerns known. Therefore, those with experiential knowledge must act because not all women (or men) are willing to advocate for themselves or others. In addition, those being oppressed and those engaging in advocacy must value their own knowledge. As Collins (2004) stated, "First, defining and valuing one's consciousness of one's own self-defined standpoint in the face of images that foster a self-definition as the objectified 'other' is an important way of resisting the dehumanization essential to systems of domination" (p. 108). Becoming aware of one's ability to act in the face of oppression is a form of knowledge built from experience.

Tactical and Strategic Communication

Once aware, being able to act requires tactical and strategic communication, central to understanding organizations. Those in power employ strategic communication to contain tension and keep disruptive forces at bay while reifying the power structure. Strategic communication includes the culture of the organization, specific policies, and the ways in which employees are promoted or ignored. Hallahan, et al. (2007) defined strategic communication "as the purposeful use of communication by an organization to fulfill its mission" (p. 3). They suggest that this type of communication "implies that people will be engaged in deliberate communication practice on behalf of organizations" (p. 4).

However, I argue that strategic communication messages are also subtle, such as men making up most of the management structure, or suits and ties being part of the dress code. Support for this more nuanced understanding of strategic communication comes from Reicher & Levine (1994) who stated: "Those with power . . . take advantage of favourable [sic] power relations in order to give full expression to their social identities" (p. 512). They argued that strategic communication affects and is linked to social identity, and that "behaviour [sic] is an act of communication deployed to strategic ends. . . . [Groups] serve a crucial communicative role which is essential in achieving self-definitions" (p. 515). Those who maintain forms of strategic communication may not realize they are participating; however, such communication excludes particular workers and reinforces organizational strategies. Those enacting reified strategies have social privilege, or "entitlement, sanction, power, immunity, and advantage or right granted or conferred by the dominant group" (Black & Stone, 2005, p. 245). Such privilege blinds them to the oppression of others, and they may not realize that not all members of the group are granted the same status.

Privileged groups or individuals then participate in strategies, which are "systems, plans of action, narratives, and designs created by institutions to influence, guide, and at worst manipulate human society" (Kimball, 2006, p. 71). De Certeau (1984) defined *strategy* as "the calculation (or manipulations) of power relationships that becomes possible as soon as a subject with will and power . . . can be isolated. . . . As in management, every 'strategic' rationalization seeks . . . the place of its own power and will" (pp. 35–36). Similarly, Feenberg (2002) described *operational autonomy* or "the power to make strategic choices among alternative rationalizations without regard for externalities, customary practice, workers' preferences, or the impact of decisions on their households" (pp. 75–76). Those who are interested in keeping organizational norms intact engage in this strategic choice-making and rationalization.

Those who disrupt norms respond through tactics. Tactical TPC is "the capability of the user to produce his or her own products from the detritus of the strategic, industrial world" (Kimball, 2006, p. 79). Furthermore, "users become producers of documents and artifacts that subtly resist authority" (p. 82). Kimball identified tactical communication as extra institutional in nature. While strategic communication occurs within organizations, tactical communication can be "influential in creating and shaping cultures," and tactical communication occurs when a person might feel helpless in a dominant culture (p. 67). Feenberg (2002) described this as "reactive autonomy" or the "margin of maneuver," which "may be reincorporated into strategies, sometimes in ways that restructure domination at a higher level, sometimes in ways that weaken its control" (pp. 84–85).

Tactics are kairotic, and workers who do not fit the dominant power structure of an organization might engage in such maneuvering. To do so, they must attune themselves to moments for tactical action in order to reterritorialize the system of the workplace. For technical and professional communicators, texts "produce a stable representation of shifting reality, [and] are among the tools used both to create common objects and to coordinate activity over time" (Winsor, 2007, p. 4). In other words, practitioners can use the tools available to them, such as documentation, to shift the narratives they encounter. Such tools will be detailed in the case studies presented in this chapter.

Case Study Methodology

In order to explore women's experiences in the TPC workplace and answer how women enact change and engage in problem-solving, I used qualitative interviews and observations. I used these methods because they are suited to the idea that women's experiences are best understood through their own voices, according to feminist theories. In TPC, feminist theory has been defined as including women's experiences as legitimate subjects of study because female experience "reveals what is missing within other discourses and theories" (Lay, 2004, p. 431). Therefore, interviews and observations were my most effective tools in gaining a sense of how women view and experience the workplace.

After interviewing 39 female practitioners of TPC and using content analysis to analyze the data, I saw the theme of advocacy and activism emerge, most clearly in the two interviews presented here as case studies. Their specific workplace experiences give perspective to the ways practitioners engage in advocacy and activism within specific contexts. As Sullivan & Spilka (2011) explained, "Case studies gather descriptive information about a phenomenon of interest" (p. 21). I focused on the patterns of advocacy and activism that the two individuals shared, leading to an in-depth exploration of processes and activities bounded by time and activity (Creswell, 2009, p. 13). Furthermore, because case studies can be misunderstood, I did as Willerton (2011) suggested and studied about and became sensitive to the context in which the women's advocacy work was happening (p. 218), considered both interview and observation data, and used documents and work products to additionally illuminate what the women had reported about their advocacy practices.

Interviews began with a brief written questionnaire about demographics, including age, education level, job title, location, marital status, household income, and subfield of TPC. To recruit participants, I shared a call for participants on Twitter, Wordpress, Facebook, and on TPC listservs (the Association of Teachers of Technical Writing, the Council for Programs in Technical and Scientific Communication, and TechWhirl). As a result, I solicited interviewees in various U.S. locations, including: Washington state; Washington, D.C.; California; Texas; Utah; Florida; Virginia; Maryland; Arizona; Massachusetts; Illinois; Idaho; and Colorado. The project was approved by my university's Institutional Review Board, and all names used in this chapter are pseudonyms.

Two of the 39 interviewees focused on practicing advocacy and activism through TPC. These two women's experiences are the case studies presented in this chapter. One of the participants allowed me to observe her work. I spent one day with her, observing her interactions with others, taking notes on genres and asking clarification questions. I also followed her to different locations throughout the day to see her advocacy on the ground. At the end of the observation, I conducted an informal open-ended interview about what I had seen and heard. She clarified statements, documents, actions, and policies. The other participant was not able to spend a day with me as an observer, so I rely on her interview data to present her advocacy work in this chapter.

The data I collected was analyzed through critical theories of strategic and tactical communication, taking social justice literature from TPC into account. I transcribed all interviews and observations, developing research notes and memoing. I pulled data about advocacy and activism into a new document, which I re-read and memoed again, tightening themes and identifying useful approaches for TPC. I then analyzed the tension between organizational strategies and extra institutional tactics present in these women's experiences.

Results of Case Study 1: "I Just Won't Let Anybody Go Alone"

The first case study looked at Virginia, who worked for a large nonprofit organization that was also a religious institution. Because of the patriarchal structure in that organization, Virginia faced situations that many women in the workplace no longer face to the same degree. Virginia was under 30 years old and had some eight years of experience as an editor for a specific department within the organization. Her stories of sexism and harassment were some of the most egregious I encountered during participant interviews.

Strategically, Virginia's organization slighted women through policies and workplace culture. Virginia had heard managers say they wanted to hire somebody "who didn't have an expiration date," meaning they were uninterested in hiring married and/or pregnant women. When Virginia became engaged to be married, an important project was taken from her; however, she stood her ground, claimed authority over the project, and had the work reinstated. In general, women are seen as a threat to the patriarchal and hierarchical structure of this organization as their presence may disrupt the way it has always done business. The strategic communication of the organizational culture elucidates which kinds of employees are acceptable and useful.

As a result of her experiences, Virginia decided to engage in regular tactical communication to modify and transform this organization. Virginia acted as a self-appointed advocate for women by going to human resources (HR) with them or stepping in when she noticed unfair situations. Through observations, or her tactical surveillance of those in power, Virginia noticed, "men are promoted on potential and women are promoted on past performance." Favero & Heath (2012) noted that "structures (norms and policies) of the gendered workplace still prioritize work over family; men's work and careers still take precedence over women's work and careers. . . . These workplace practices traditionally privilege men and work and subordinate life and family" (pp. 334–335). Because Virginia knew that managers were uninterested in hiring those who might also play a principal role in family life, she understood that women were often viewed as having no future at work.

Virginia had experienced the double standard that women must work harder than men to receive the same compensation. In a performance review, Virginia was told to be more vulnerable. She took a few days to think about why that feedback bothered her and then returned to her manager to discuss. She said to her manager, the feedback was "troubling to me because I know the men are never asked to be more vulnerable, and I don't feel like it's very fair for me to be asked to look dumber than I am in order to make other people comfortable." She also noted the power differentials present in her division, which employed older male colleagues with advanced degrees, and she felt she had to be able to prove her competence in order to be treated professionally: "I can't do my work if people don't take me seriously." While she was troubled by her manager's feedback, a form of strategic communication meant to promote submissiveness, she used it as an opportunity to tactically educate him about her perspective. She made him aware of her standpoint and highlighted the problem with power differentials.

These personal experiences were foundational to the tactical advocacy she had engaged in for others. Virginia used her TPC expertise to write a report detailing the problems for women in the organization. Virginia inserted herself tactically into the project when she heard that "Sherry" was gathering stories from women about what it was like to work for the organization. Sherry had a meeting scheduled with a senior executive, who had publicly made comments about family-friendly workplace policies and commitment to supporting women and families. Sherry wanted to make him aware of the many crises occurring within his own organization, as his strategic comments did not represent women's realities.

Virginia knew that such tactical communication required caution. Given the hostile nature of her workplace, subordination was often viewed suspiciously and could result in formal discipline. Virginia emailed Sherry and said, "Are you for real? Are you legit? Are you being careful? And if you are, do you need help?" Virginia knew that stakes were high for any woman who dared to challenge the organization so officially. She also knew that her expertise in TPC would benefit the project because of her understanding of rhetoric and audience and her ability to research and document. She understood, as Rude (2008) claimed, "the field's knowledge gives it the potential to contribute to social justice" (p. 267).

Sherry and Virginia moved forward, soliciting stories through private social media groups and networks, tactically seeking out the antenarrative (Boje, 2007), or prestory and fragmented voices that needed to be heard. Virginia "recommended that we put together some materials that [Sherry] could leave with him, so that she has her conversation but then he has in his hands something that he can refer back to and remember." Virginia used the stories they collected to create a dossier on a number of topics, including maternity leave, sexual harassment, intimidation, and sexism.

Virginia spent some 150 hours composing this document over two weeks. She described her work:

> I designed it all and got stock photography, and so each section laid out what the problem is and gave some stories from women who had experienced it to illustrate the problem. And then [it] talked about what possibilities are out there that [are] being done by other companies or countries to mitigate the problem and what specifically we could do . . . to make it better. And then I had infographics and the whole nine yards.

While acting tactically, Virginia included forms of strategic communication to offer solutions to these problems and to allow the senior executive ways of seeing and engaging with the organizational cracks that would benefit both groups: the disenfranchised women and the powerful men, who were unaware of the occurring crises. The senior executive's strategic communication would be challenged by presenting him with the antenarrative women's voices of the crisis of his workplace.

In soliciting the women's stories, Sherry and Virginia promised not to use the women's names, which gave them the freedom to explain their experiences any way they wanted to without fear of reprisal. It also prevented Virginia from allowing me to analyze a copy of the report because she felt uncomfortable sharing information with me that she had promised to keep proprietary. However, the report, as she explained it, represented what Kimball (2006) described as sharing challenges and problems within a system and posing ideal narratives that illustrated how processes should work, could work, or did work (p. 73). She employed the strengths and purposes of TPC to narrate the culture of her workplace through the experiences and perceptions of female employees.

This documentation represented formal advocacy. Her communication was meant to address larger concerns for thousands of women who worked at this organization. Virginia reflected:

> I learned a lot doing it, but I was also just appalled by the things that I read from women who work here: intimidation of women in the workplace, terrible handling of sexual harassment, and putting . . . a very junior woman alone in the room with her very senior male harasser and [HR] tell[ing] them to work it out. I was shaking in fury for most of the two weeks. It was really a lot to take in.

While engaging in this advocacy, she became more aware of the institutionalization and pervasiveness of the problem for nearly every woman who had worked there.

While the results of this advocacy are ongoing, Virginia noted that the senior executive turned the dossier over to the manager of another department. That manager put together a focus group to discuss how the organization's culture could be improved. However, Virginia was discouraged by the outcome, as "That group put together a document . . . [that] accepted the premise that no woman would work if she had another option." Nevertheless, the organization is talking about the need for more family-friendly policies, and a task force has been assigned to work with HR on policy recommendations. Virginia reported that "paid family leave [i]s on the way as a result of all of this." Other policies are under review, but unfortunately, as Sherry and another manager who got involved no longer work for the organization, progress may be stalled as a consequence.

When I asked Virginia if she considers herself to be an "activist," she reframed herself as an "advocate." She believed activism was more public, and while her work had certainly had public implications, she tended to work in the background. She regularly speaks with "other women, both under my purview and not, about how to navigate different situations. And I talk regularly with my immediate supervisor and the managers about problems that I see, especially gender-based problems. I try to educate them about power differentials in the workplace." She is dedicated to acting tactically, as she is fully aware of the organization's hierarchical problems. This tactical advocacy includes engaging in conversations at opportune moments. This sort of work is invisible, as Virginia explained:

> I feel like I'm rarely a visible face, whether it's because I want a man to make the point, I'm going to feed him his lines or whether it's because somebody else has this in, and I'm going to give them all their information to go and talk to somebody in power, but I tend to be behind the scenes.

Her tactical advocacy reflects the profession of TPC, as the work is often invisible, translated, and meant to inform users through the expertise of others (Neeley, 1992). Virginia does the research and the translation necessary for those in power to ensure that pertinent information is not forgotten or unknown. In other words, she communicates to make problems visible and to increase the agency of those who are affected. She is a technical and professional communicator of workplace culture, in addition to her formal work, identifying sites of conflict and disseminating information to decision-makers.

Her work is important, even if behind the scenes, because "if you come to [HR] and you clearly don't know what you're entitled to, it's much more likely to be brushed under the rug." This is exactly why she has taken on the role of advocate. While she has taken steps to connect with people in power, she has also "told all the women who work here [to] never go by themselves to HR, and I'll go with them. They can take somebody else with them, but they ought never to go by themselves. . . . I just won't let anybody go alone."

Results of Case Study 2: "Be Patient, Bearing with One Another in Love"

While the woman in Case Study 2 had experienced harassment and gender bias, her TPC advocacy work is focused on benefitting various marginalized populations within her larger community rather than her workplace.

This second study looks at Edith, a policy analyst for a nonprofit organization focused on providing services to low-income families and individuals. Edith was responsible for writing a report on state poverty each year. She had an up-to-date [State] Poverty Facts for the year taped to her computer screen. She explained:

> [W]hen I'm working with legislators, I can talk about poverty rates, food stamp usage, families on welfare, et cetera. . . . We actually do some lobbying, [but] very little of my job is actual lobbying. But there is a lot of educating and a lot of advocacy based on the information that we get from that poverty report.

She additionally held events to raise awareness. Therefore, her TPC work was the impetus for her advocacy and activism and was official and strategic within her nonprofit organization.

A motivating factor for advocates is experience; an individual engaged with social justice concerns has most likely experienced the problem, or a form of it, herself. Edith explained:

> I grew up rather poor, but the kind of poverty that I experienced was more situational, so that it was a crisis that led us into poverty. My father was quite sick and my mom decided that rather than put him in a nursing home, she was going to take care of him at home. So that meant that we had a limited income from social security benefits. While we were poor financially, I still had two very middle class parents, so we were eating government cheese, but my grammar was still being corrected at the dinner table.

Edith, while having experienced the poverty that prompted her to act, also experienced privilege through education and class. She opted to use her privilege to improve the situation for those who did not have the same advantages.

Her poverty report, while a strategic document mandated by her non-profit organization, was composed tactically through her engagement with it. When Edith came to the job, she had a copy of the previous year's "official" report that she described as "graph salad." It lacked a consistent voice because of many contributing agencies. She updated the report to be consistent, engaging as the only author, fixing inconsistencies, and making graphs and tables. Yet, as she described this report and its effects, she referred to the efforts as collaborative and networked by using the pronoun "we." Her work resisted traditional notions of what it meant to engage in strategic communication through systems of power.

She recognized that politics played a major role in the type of advocacy she engaged in and that she would not always be able to make a difference from her ideological standpoint; however, her work represented the idea that the personal is political, as politics is "an ongoing process of negotiating power relations" (Coole & Frost, 2010, p. 18). Therefore, if technical and professional communicators create documents that affect people personally, their work is inherently political. Blyler (1998/2004) noted that researchers "must in a self-conscious way attempt to understand and to articulate the values and interests they as researchers bring to their tasks" (p. 272). Their research should "address questions that, first and foremost, their participants want to have answered" (p. 277). Similarly, the work practitioners do for users, especially work that is connected to advocacy, social justice, or politics, must take into account the contexts and needs of users. As Albers (2008) defined, "Information is not a commodity to be transferred from person to person. It is inherently value laden and the social and political framing of the source strongly influences the overall presentation" (p. 119).

One communication tactic is to put a human face on the statistics. Edith emphasized, "The legislature sometimes gets really hung up on costs of things, but we were continually trying to make sure that there was a human face on this." This fact highlighted the importance of an ethic of care, as those in power must be reminded that actual people were affected by their decision-making. Advocacy then becomes about putting humans first and ensuring that those in positions of power can see situations clearly and view the standpoints of others.

One way of humanizing poverty is through social media campaigns. Edith understood that a video, available online, would reach more people and was easily transportable. She recently created a video "on issues around earned income tax credit." Her nonprofit organization had a tax specialist on staff, and they, along with a representative from another nonprofit organization, interviewed families who used the Volunteer Income Tax Assistance program, which provided free tax services, and posted it to YouTube. The video used pathos, identifying families by names and places. These families put a human face on the program by simply talking about their situations. All different ages, ethnicities, and socioeconomic statuses were highlighted in an effort to reach diverse audiences.

Written materials supplemented videos. Edith created a full-color booklet with stories from specific families about how Medicaid or the Children's Health Insurance Program (CHIP) helped them. She was discerning with these stories, choosing those that best fit her organization's strategic narrative. She wanted stories that pulled at heartstrings and featured employed parents, racial and ethnic diversity, and people across the state. She traveled to meet all of the families and left certain details out because "to use it for lawmakers, you can't reinforce the stereotypes they might have." Her booklet focused on the success of the program. She avoided using numbers and statistics and said, "Advocacy is about putting a face to the story, so people can identify and see themselves in those images." She saw the effectiveness of this approach when a lawmaker identified with one of the stories and retold it at every rally. To Edith, this was the first step to success. She knew her audience and appealed to them in a way that would bolster her nonprofit organization's social justice work.

Edith's audience awareness stemmed from her interactions with those who opposed advocacy. In fact, Edith was puzzled by some of the religious people she had met over the years who opposed "entitlement" programs, as her religious beliefs had led her to the opposite conclusion. In fact, she has a tattoo of the scripture Ephesians 4:2 on her arm that reads, "Be completely humble and gentle; be patient, bearing with one another in love" from the New International Version of *The Holy Bible.* She expounded, "It is such a strange political dichotomy to me . . . I feel like my religious beliefs influence me toward more social justice issues." She was aware of some of the misconceptions of the poor; that they might be lazy or cheating the system. But she suggested, "There are jerks at every level. There are jerks in the upper class, there are jerks in the middle class, and there are certainly jerks in the lower class, but it is probably about the same distribution in every single population." She explained that people liked to demonize the poor and reward the rich, noting that people tended to ignore other people who cheat on their taxes. She knew the people for whom she advocated, and she realized what she was up against in terms of cultural norms, expectations, and ideologies about class. This audience awareness, at all levels, helped her to enact social justice through TPC.

Edith recognized her audience in other ways as well. She knew from her report that 38.1 percent of women who were single parents with children under five years old were in poverty (Annual Report on Poverty in [State], 2014, p. 20). She recognized that it was a problem, but she suggested:

> You have to think about women because they are, by and large, the ones utilizing those programs, but you can't assume that everybody who's going to be using those programs are going to be single moms. You have to make room for single dads. You have to make room for relatives who have taken on those kids and who need help with the programs also. So one-size-fits-all programs are not a good idea for those reasons.

She was aware of typical situations but also mindful of other possible audiences and users. She wrote inclusively, and she was sensitive to gender, class, sexuality, and other categorizations: "There are so many misconceptions about poverty and who's there and why, so you have to be really careful . . . The words that you choose are so incredibly powerful." Edith understood, as Rude (2008) reasoned, that "[l]anguage is a means of policy negotiation and of social transformation" (p. 267). Knowing which language to use in specific situations, especially when social services are on the line, is a skill that TPC practitioners possess. The words used to represent marginalized people are vital in their effect on decisions about people's lives.

Another audience for Edith was lawmakers, as she distributed her reports to them. When she identified a problem—such as lack of education, lack of outreach, or onerous applications—she distributed information to lawmakers to encourage their outreach. However, she realized that the problem was often budgetary, and she called the results of her campaign to distribute the materials "squishy." It was "a really hard road to haul because of money. No measurable results. But working on these unpopular issues, you have to say, 'This may not go anywhere but the conversation is worth having.' We need to keep reminding people that we are doing a poor job of insuring kids."

Edith also got a sense of her legislative audience based on social media conversations that occurred tactically outside of regular legislative sessions. When I observed her work for a day, we spent time at the state capitol attending an interim legislative session, where she noted that Twitter was particularly important. She monitored a hashtag related to her state's politics, and it exposed the tactical conversations occurring during sessions. Some of the state representatives tweeted all day, and by monitoring these social media avenues, Edith got a sense of her audience's opinions, who had aligned with them, or what communication was happening besides the motions on the legislative floor. Furthermore, tweeting functioned as a way for the gallery to join the conversation, "especially when controversial. The gallery tweets instead of bursting out, because you have to be quiet." Edith used this approach to enhance her understanding of audience and the issues facing lawmakers.

In this advocacy work, Edith noticed different approaches to social justice and a move from traditional activism to those who had gone through graduate school and tended to engage in more talking and community building: "There are ones who are like we should go up and have a demonstration, and others are like me. I'm kind of like, 'We look like crazy people when we do that!'" She suggested taking into consideration how actions related to advocacy would be viewed. To her, the long game was important: "I'm not crazy about having to do it [the long game], but I'm getting there." She understood that dialogue, tactical communication, patience, and community building would effect change, even if it felt like she was moving backwards or making backroom deals. Part of this process was being physically present at the state capitol. She did it "to be seen." Anybody could watch the legislative sessions streaming online, but Edith felt it was important to be physically present to make personal connections.

Coalitions are vital to making an impact politically. Edith participated in and chaired meetings of nonprofit advocates who shared information with each other and strategized about how to approach social justice issues. While Edith focused on poverty, her colleagues focused on housing, education, disabilities, and homelessness. An important feature of communication among nonprofits is a coalition of advocates, and this coalition's communication is often tactical, as it must approach those in power to move forward. Edith said, "It won't just ever be one advocate or one group pushing it. It has to be a big strong coalition of people, but it takes people being invested in that to make that happen, so that's probably where . . . I see the most impact."

I observed one gathering of the meeting that Edith chaired. The conversation was a give and take of tidbits that would allow the nonprofit communicators to act tactically when the time was right. They were informing each other of situations, opportunities, and kairotic moments to act. Sharing such information was a way of researching their intended audience. Those in attendance shared the official ways in which their nonprofit partner organizations could strategically participate and bolster varied efforts. The meeting itself was strategic, but tactically, the group shared how to make their efforts visible at the upper levels of the legislature and state government. They did not have official access to policy-making, but they could inform each other of the tactics that made it possible to influence. All of the nonprofit representatives in the coalition meeting were willing to work together in order to fight social injustices. Some of the attendees asked each other to share flyers for particular events. While Edith spent time in her cubicle gathering stories and statistics to write reports and pamphlets, she also engaged in networking to be apprised of her audience and various social issues. This part of her work had a community atmosphere, necessary to accomplishing social justice work. She had to tie her documentation into public networks. Ultimately, her practices illuminate the way TPC practitioners can engage in advocacy within their own contexts.

Implications of the Case Studies: Intersections of Advocacy and Activism with TPC

What can be learned from how these women enacted change and solved problems via genres, practices, tools, and texts? The case studies contain rich information and exemplary stories about how advocacy and social justice intersect with TPC. From Virginia's and Edith's experiences, the skills and actions necessary for engaged and effective advocacy emerge. They teach us about what it means to be a civically engaged technical communicator, including (1) recognizing the obvious intersection between TPC and advocacy; (2) appealing to audiences, especially those in powerful positions; (3) using documentation to make concerns official and recognizable; and (4) forming a coalition. A detailed account of these core competencies follows.

First, advocacy is a "natural" part of TPC work, as practitioners are engaged in the work of mediating, accommodating, and translating for users. Both Virginia and Edith used expertise in TPC to engage in documentation that addressed problems they were passionate about solving. Practitioners have the ability to mediate between and among levels of power, meaning that TPC should be engaged in advocacy work at more visible and political levels. There is room for practitioners and scholars to argue that our genres and knowledge of audiences and contexts and the significance of human-information interaction (Albers, 2008) are essential to advocacy and activist work. TPC must be recognized as political communication, and therefore extends into fields that are inherently political or activist. TPC can and should "assist" beyond the fields in which practitioners and scholars traditionally engage.

Second, because of practitioners' knowledge of language and rhetoric, they can appeal to an audience effectively when political concerns are at stake. Both Virginia and Edith used careful, tactical communication. They highlighted the importance of using language and rhetoric that appealed and the essentiality of knowing an audience. When advocating, those in power are usually those who must be persuaded to view the situation differently. Because of their training in rhetoric, technical communicators are particularly suited to advocacy that requires this expertise.

Third, practitioners must use documentation to make advocacy and activism official. While scholars have established that speaking up is important (Schneider, 2007; Hamel, 2009), the impact of communication is in its documentation. Virginia tactically documented the problems for women in her workplace by strategically making them visible to the hierarchy. Edith created reports, social media posts, and videos that would make an impact. Because practitioners are documentation experts, they can document the voices of those who are disenfranchised. Those in power must have tangible documentation in order to remember the issues being advocated for and to cite such information.

In general, practitioners must use documentation to make advocacy visible. It might take the form of social media, as many technical communicators participate in communities on Twitter and Facebook. It might be networking with communicators across the organization to form groups that support each other through difficult or proprietary work situations. Podcasts might also be a method of advocacy, as seen with the communicative work that Haven and Harper do in the knitting community (Petersen, 2016). Speaking up through documentation is an effective way to claim agency. Documentation can be easily shared and can become widespread in a way that word-of-mouth communication cannot. However, such "official" documentation creates questions about what *should* be documented. Further research might address the nuanced and complex negotiation involved with social justice work that becomes "official" and therefore possibly as bureaucratic and oppressive as the structures it attempts to expose.

In addition, official documentation can affect larger numbers of people. Speaking up on a case-by-case basis is important, but it does not enact large-scale change. Both Virginia and Edith noted that their documentation allowed them to reach larger audiences and to influence on a broad scale. Making public the problems faced in a particular situation is a way of "forcing" those in power to engage with the issue, for they may lose support if they ignore a large enough public effort. While such advocacy can backfire, as embarrassing those in power can lead to the closing of communication lines, it can also raise awareness and lead to larger numbers of people becoming engaged and exerting pressure where it is needed.

Furthermore, documentation of silent or distressing issues might not get official recognition. Maneuverable documentation—like Virginia's extra institutional dossier of problems in the workplace—might be more appropriate in particular situations. Such documentation can be developed in teaching social justice techniques to students; students should be identifying their own advocacy concerns and documenting them in unique ways. Instructors can facilitate student practice and disseminate their advocacy by requiring a practical task that allows for creativity and passion in its execution.

Such ideas include: live tweeting (or using another social media platform) of a student-led protest on campus; writing a blog post or editorial for a newspaper; collecting and writing a report on social media activism that is delivered to the head of a department or organization; creating an online magazine (Stephens, 2016), podcast, or zine; or publishing concerns in a research article. For example, my undergraduate research methods students investigated the fairness of YouTube copyright claims for narrators and examined volunteer recognition in nonprofit organizations. Both projects are publishable and will impact a larger consortium of digital activists and nonprofit organizations. Digital media platforms and awareness of social issues make for endless possibilities in teaching, collaborating, and disseminating information.

Lastly, forming a coalition of advocates is key to performing advocacy and social justice work, as noted by Edith. While technical communicators are often characterized as "lone" workers, this stipulation does not reflect reality. Practitioners have the ability to interact with and interview subject matter experts, meaning that coalition-building, especially when it comes to documenting social or political issues, is not foreign to their work. Practitioners are always networked and situated, and such positioning and the skills of TPC lend themselves to advocacy. Bowdon (2004) summed up the exigence for such work: "The complicated world in which we live and write and teach demands nothing less of technical communication educators and practitioners than our willingness to be civically engaged ... [to] contribute to public understandings of complex issues" (p. 325). The field of TPC is positioned to influence social matters and policies, but not all of us have been talking about it and engaging in it, as Virginia and Edith have. Social justice advocacy and activism is not reserved for those marching in protests. Students, practitioners, and scholars can engage in activism and advocacy through the norms, genres, positionalities, and spirit of TPC.

Conclusion

The case studies of Virginia and Edith illuminate some of the best practices for engaging in advocacy through TPC. Scholars and practitioners must recognize that discourse and documentation are political; therefore, TPC's knowledge can and must extend into fields that are inherently political or poised to be activist, such as women and gender studies, political science, environmental studies, humanities, education, and sociology. There is room for TPC to "assist" beyond the fields in which it traditionally engages, especially because genres have power in tactical use. Unofficial, unarticulated, and unrecognized forms of communication are essential to advocacy work. Those who wish to disrupt, reterritorialize, and maneuver within/around organizations must engage in unofficial forms of communication that can change and inform the situations of users. Core competencies in advocacy emerge from the work of Virginia and Edith, and from them, the field can hypothesize and innovate further ways of engaging in activism and advocacy.

Discussion Questions

1) What role does empathy play in advocacy and activism? In what ways do ideas about empathy intersect with advocacy practices and goals in technical communication?
2) Virginia's advocacy focused on solving problems surrounding the discrimination of women in the workplace. What other sorts of discrimination can affect workers and how could technical communication play a role in reducing those problems?
3) Motherhood is an identity that is often depicted as in conflict with the workplace. Using some of the sources in the "Further Reading" section and doing your own research, create a list of the ways in which motherhood could be beneficial to organizational environments. How can we reframe conversations about working mothers based on what you found?
4) What genres of technical communication may be best suited for advocacy work? How could you promote the use of those genres for advocacy purposes at your university, workplace, or community organization?
5) What social issues are of concern to you? Based on what you learned from Virginia and Edith, how can you engage in documentation that joins those conversations and makes a difference in your community?
6) Have you ever spoken up in a difficult situation? What happened? How could you have documented that experience, and would documentation have changed the outcome? In what ways?

Further Reading

All website URLs accessed February 2018.

Gomstyn, A. (2015). Demoting employees on maternity leave is not just bad for women. *Babble.com*. Retrieved from www.babble.com/parenting/demoting-employees-on-maternity-leave-is-not-just-bad-for-women

Herndl, C. G., & Licona, A. C. (2007). Shifting agency: Agency, kairos, and the possibilities of social action. In M. Zachry & C. Thralls (Eds.), *Communicative Practices in Workplaces and the Professions: Cultural Perspectives on the Regulation of Discourse and Organizations* (pp. 133–154). Amityville, NY: Baywood.

Lewis, K. R. (2015, March 31). How to make your company less sexist and racist. *The Atlantic*. Retrieved from www.theatlantic.com/business/archive/2015/03/how-to-make-your-company-less-sexist-and-racist/388931

Miller, C. C. (2017, April 10). It's not just Fox: Why women don't report sexual harassment. *The New York Times*. Retrieved from www.nytimes.com/2017/04/10/upshot/its-not-just-fox-why-women-dont-report-sexual-harassment.html

Petersen, E. J. (2017). Empathetic user design: understanding and living the reality of an audience. *Communication Design Quarterly Review*, 4(2), 23–36.

Porath, C. (2017, September 15). The silent killer of workplace happiness, productivity, and health is a lack of basic civility. *Quartz*. Retrieved from https://qz.com/1079344/the-silent-killer-of-workplace-happiness-productivity-and-health-is-a-lack-of-basic-civility

Rivera, L. A. (2015, May 30). Guess who doesn't fit in at work. *NYTimes.com*. Retrieved from www.nytimes.com/2015/05/31/opinion/sunday/guess-who-doesnt-fit-in-at-work.html?_r=0nytimes.com

Sandberg, S., & Grant, A. (2015, January 12). Speaking while female: Sheryl Sandberg and Adam Grant on why women stay quiet at work. *NYTimes.com*. Retrieved from www.nytimes.com/2015/01/11/opinion/sunday/speaking-while-female.html

Slaughter, A. (2012, July–August). Why women still can't have it all. *The Atlantic*, 85–102.

References

All website URLs accessed February 2018.

Albers, M. J. (2008, September). Human-information interaction. In *Proceedings of the 26th Annual Association for Computing Machinery International Conference on Design of Communication* (pp. 117–124). Association for Computing Machinery.

Annual Report on Poverty in [State]. (2014). Community Action Partnership of [State].

Bergman, B., & Hallberg, L. R. M. (2002). Women in a male-dominated industry: Factor analysis of a women workplace culture questionnaire based on a grounded theory model. *Sex Roles*, 46(9–10), 311–322.

Black, L. L., & Stone, D. (2005). Expanding the definition of privilege: The concept of social privilege. *Journal of Multicultural Counseling and Development*, 33(4), 243.

Blyler, N. (2004). Taking a political turn: The critical perspective and research in professional communication. In J. Johnson-Eilola & S. A. Selber (Eds.), *Central works in technical communication* (pp. 268–280). New York, NY: Oxford University Press. (Original work published 1998.)

Boje, D. M. (2007). The antenarrative cultural turn in narrative studies. In M. Zachry & C. Thralls (Eds.), *Communicative practices in workplaces and the professions: Cultural perspectives on the regulation of discourse and organizations.* (pp. 219–238). Amityville, NY: Baywood.

Bowdon, M. (2004). Technical communication and the role of the public intellectual: A community HIV-prevention case study. *Technical Communication Quarterly, 13*(3), 325–340.

Budig, M. J. (2014). *The fatherhood bonus and the motherhood penalty: Parenthood and the gender gap in pay.* Washington, DC: Third Way.

Collins, P. H. (2004). Learning from the outsider within: The sociological significance of Black feminist thought. In S. Harding (Ed.), *The feminist standpoint theory reader: Intellectual and political controversies* (pp. 103–126). New York, NY: Routledge.

Coole, D., & Frost, S. (2010). Introducing the new materialisms. In D. Coole & S. Frost (Eds.), *New materialisms: Ontology, agency, and politics* (pp. 1–43). Durham, NC: Duke University Press.

Creswell, J. W. (2009). Research design: Qualitative, quantitative, and mixed methods approaches. Thousand Oaks, CA: SAGE Publications, Inc.

De Certeau, M. (1984). *The practice of everyday life.* Berkeley and Los Angeles, CA: University of California Press.

Dragga, S. (1993). Women and the profession of technical writing: Social and economic influences and implications. *Journal of Business and Technical Communication, 7*(3), 312–321.

Favero, L. W., & Heath, R. G. (2012). Generational perspectives in the workplace: Interpreting the discourses that constitute women's struggle to balance work and life. *Journal of Business Communication, 49*(4), 332–356.

Feenberg, A. (2002). *Transforming technology: A critical theory revisited.* New York, NY: Oxford University Press.

Guy, M. E., & Newman, M. A. (2004). Women's jobs, men's jobs: Sex segregation and emotional labor. *Public Administration Review, 64*(3), 289–298.

Hallahan, K., Holtzhausen, D., Van Ruler, B., Verčič, D., & Sriramesh, K. (2007). Defining strategic communication. *International Journal of Strategic Communication, 1*(1), 3–35.

Hamel, S. A. (2009). Exit, voice, and sensemaking following psychological contract violations: Women's responses to career advancement barriers. *Journal of Business Communication, 46*(2), 234–261.

Hekman, S. (2004). Truth and method: Feminist standpoint theory revisited. In S. Harding (Ed.), *The feminist standpoint theory reader: Intellectual and political controversies* (pp. 225–242). New York, NY: Routledge.

Johnson, R. R. (1998). *User-centered technology: A rhetorical theory for computers and other mundane artifacts.* Albany, NY: State University of New York Press.

Jones, N., Savage, G., & Yu, H. (2014). Tracking our progress: Diversity in technical and professional communication programs. *Programmatic Perspectives, 6*(1), 132–152.

Kimball, M. A. (2006). Cars, culture, and tactical technical communication. *Technical Communication Quarterly, 15*(1), 67.

Lay, M. M. (2004). Feminist theory and the redefinition of technical communication. In J. Dubinsky (Ed.), *Teaching technical communication: Critical issues for the class-room* (pp. 428–445). Boston, MA: Bedford/St. Martin's. (Original work published October 1991.)

Muñoz, C. (2014). *Transformative pedagogy for social justice education: Teaching technical communication students to bridge with Anzaldúan theories of social change.* Master's Thesis. Cheney, WA: Eastern Washington University.

Neeley, K. A. (1992). Woman as mediatrix: Women as writers on science and technology in the eighteenth and nineteenth centuries. *Professional Communication, IEEE Transactions on, 35*(4), 208–216.

Petersen, E. J. (2016, October). Reterritorializing workspaces: Entrepreneurial podcasting as situated networking, connected mediation, and contextualized professionalism. In *Professional Communication Conference (IPCC), 2016 IEEE International* (pp. 1–8). IEEE.

Reicher, S., & Levine, M. (1994). On the consequences of deindividuation manipulations for the strategic communication of self: Identifiability and the presentation of social identity. *European Journal of Social Psychology, 24*(4), 511–524.

Rude, C. D. (2008). Introduction to the special issue on business and technical communication in the public sphere: Learning to have impact. *Journal of Business and Technical Communication, 22*(3), 267–271.

Schneider, B. (2007). Power as interactional accomplishment: An ethnomethodological perspective on the regulation of communicative practice in organizations. In M. Zachry & C. Thralls (Eds.), *Communicative practices in workplaces and the professions: Cultural perspectives on the regulation of discourse and organizations* (pp. 181–199). Amityville, NY: Baywood.

Stephens, E. J., (2016, April 6). Advocating for the inexperienced: Teaching social justice and citizenship with limited time, resources, and experience. Presentation. Association of Teachers of Technical Writing.

Sullivan, P., & Spilka, R. (2011). Qualitative research in technical communication: Issues of value, identity, and use. In J. Conklin & G. F. Hayhoe (Eds.), *Qualitative research in technical communication* (pp. 1–24). New York, NY: Routledge.

Walton, R., & Jones, N. N. (2013). Navigating increasingly cross-cultural, cross-disciplinary, and cross-organizational contexts to support social justice. *Communication Design Quarterly 1*(4), 31–35.

Willerton, R. (2011). Proceeding with caution: A case study of engineering professionals reading white papers. In J. Conklin & G. F. Hayhoe (Eds.), *Qualitative research in technical communication* (pp. 212–234). New York, NY: Routledge.

Winsor, D. (2007). Using texts to manage continuity and change in an activity system. In M. Zachry & C. Thralls (Eds.), *Communicative practices in workplaces and the professions: Cultural perspectives on the regulation of discourse and organizations* (pp. 3–19). Amityville, NY: Baywood.

2

EXPANDING INVENTIONAL AND SOLUTION SPACES

How Asset-Based Inquiry Can Support Advocacy in Technical Communication

Lucía Durá

The "How" of Everyday Advocacy Is in the Questions We Ask

At the 2015 Association of Teachers of Technical Writing (ATTW) conference in Orlando, Florida, a group of technical communication scholars came together around the value and influence of social justice work and the different contexts that are ignored, such as the Global South as argued by Godwin Agboka, or subsumed under the auspices of effective communication and dominant transactional or for-profit ideologies, as argued by Kristen Moore, Rebecca Walton, and Natasha Jones (Moore, 2015). The roundtable undoubtedly demonstrated a commitment to social justice by panelists and participants; it also raised an important question: "How do we incorporate social justice into existing frameworks, institutional contexts, and disciplinary contexts?" How we answer this question depends on how we define social justice and our economic, social, and political realities and ways of understanding the world. It also depends on how our commitments and ideologies interact with systems, institutions, methodologies, norms, and values. We have all been there—that place where our idealism is confronted with a brick wall of exigency. The place where doing the right thing, like advocating for the voiceless, seems to be at odds with getting the job or the funding. We tend to think of social justice as involving big decisions, but we forget that our everyday work comprises micro-decision points, and that these micro-decision points can be leveraged as advocacy moments. Let me offer a brief example.

Recently, I was invited to work with faculty from the chemistry program at my institution seeking to "improve the reading and writing skills of students in first-year chemistry courses through a team-based peer leader program" (e-mail communication). The head of the program was writing a grant proposal and was excited about the prospect of students "writing their way to better thinking" (e-mail communication). I found the invitation an exciting challenge on one level, but on another, I experienced a dissonance. The dissonance I experienced was from the assumption that together, we would fix things—together we, the experts, would fix this deficit in student knowledge and capacity. In my feedback on the pre-proposal draft, I asked the team via e-mail if we could consider the following questions in the project: "What's working?" I clarified, "Are there any students who read and write *well*, and how can we engage them to see what they are doing and if they have suggestions?" As I typed, my research biases crystalized into an explanation that I felt compelled to articulate in my e-mail response: "I always ask the question about what's working, particularly when it shouldn't be working, because this aspect of problem-solving is often overlooked. When we want to fix something, we look at what's broken—not what's going right in the midst of it all." I reasoned with myself after sending the e-mail: "I'm not here to change this team's focus; I am not the principal investigator or team leader. But I can put the 'assets' question up for consideration without losing political face as an untenured faculty and new collaborator."

This anecdote speaks to our everyday realities as technical communicators; in collaborative opportunities, we face micro-decision points about the ways we present ourselves and our work. Sometimes our levels of agency in terms of social justice and advocacy (or in terms of project design) are very much in our hands, as may be the case when we are project leads or when we are invited to collaborate based on our experience with advocacy or community engagement. But other times, we work within institutional and group constraints, and these are predominantly embedded within Western business models. We are invited as collaborators for our technical expertise. In this capacity, we enter into fairly traditional projects within hospitals, businesses, non-profits, and government offices. Or, as my story illustrates, we work to solve problems within our own institutions of higher education, which despite progressive thinking, still operate in very traditional modes that seek to "fix" or "solve" problems, e.g., the needs assessment as a way to understand audience, task, context, and genre (Society for Technical Communication (STC), 2014). In the case above, I wanted to advocate for problem-solving based on cultural capital. While students at my institution are in large part the first in their families to attend college and they often struggle to balance work, family, and school responsibilities, they also bring strengths. I think it is critical to advocate for those strengths in problem-solving because the already existing solutions of successful students might surprise us. Advocacy at the inquiry level, therefore, in the way we ask questions, is very much within our purview—even for those of us in junior or contingent positions working to advance our careers.

In this chapter, I respond to the 2015 ATTW roundtable's call for the "hows" of advocacy. Drawing from my experiences as an action researcher, I propose asset-based thinking as a core competency for advocacy in technical communication. Asset-based thinking, I argue, can be used at a macro level, i.e., in methodology design, and it can be used at a micro level to make a difference through micro-decision points and inquiry framing. I define *asset-based thinking* as a disposition derived from asset-based community development (ABCD) and community-based participatory research (CBPR), and in this chapter I describe how we can tease out these tested approaches' inventional heuristics for advocacy purposes in a variety of settings, including industry and healthcare as much as the non-profit sector. I propose that while ABCD and CBPR are in and of themselves advocacy methodologies, their inquiry structures are accessible during the "smaller" or everyday moments that make up our working lives. Using a brief review of literature and two case examples as a basis, I discuss the ways asset-based inquiry frameworks: (1) expand the solution space in technical communication, by asking questions that complement deficit-based thinking; (2) legitimize local ways of knowing and enable community-naming and community-building that does justice to a community's strengths and agentic potential; and (3) can be implemented immediately into the inquiry processes of technical communicators.

From ABCD Models to Asset-Based Inquiry Frameworks

Asset-based community development (ABCD) models arose in the early 1990s from the critique of needs- or deficit-based orientations, and they tend to be applied as interventions. ABCD models:

- Focus on the discovery, mapping, and mobilization of a community's strengths rather than on its deficits;
- Take on problem-solving at a local level; and
- Rely heavily on relationships among individuals, associations, and institutions (Kretzmann & McKnight, 1993; Grabill, 2001; Mathie & Cunningham, 2003; Blythe, et al., 2008).

Some examples of ABCD approaches are Appreciative Inquiry, Participatory Rural Appraisal, and Positive Deviance. I call them approaches and not methods or tools because they are presented to the world as interventional methodologies; that is, in manuals and handbooks, which are accessible online and in print and describe ABCD implementation from start to finish, usually in terms of months— from the perspective of community-based, practitioner-led projects. In this sense, ABCD approaches comprise multiple methods and tools. Take Positive Deviance, for example, the approach with which I have the most experience (see Durá, 2015). Practitioners in nutrition settings developed a CBPR "Hearth model" for Positive Deviance. It combines participatory asset-mapping with rapid ethnography, qualitative interviews, and hands-on workshops. In other settings, Positive Deviance has been adapted to include Discovery and Action Dialogues, an inquiry framework I describe in one of the case examples for this chapter. Additionally, in other spaces, practitioners use theatrical improv and participatory sketching to facilitate the Positive Deviance inquiry process. So ABCD models are not static. They are continually adapted by their users and often combined. Notwithstanding, some of the tools and frameworks used in ABCD have been refined, tested, and proven effective. The argument for the inclusion of these approaches in our methodological toolboxes is not new. Grabill (2001), Simmons (2007), Blythe, et al. (2008), and Diehl, et al. (2010) have argued that they can be useful complements to our methodological repertoires. Asset-mapping is perhaps the most prevalent example of a tool technical communicators have adapted for advocacy.

In a 2010 *Technical Communication Quarterly* article, Diehl, Grabill, & Hart-Davidson described *Grassroots*, an asset-mapping tool combining cutting edge technology and the ABCD concept of localizing and mobilizing assets. Asset-mapping in the field can be as simple as drawing on dirt with a stick or with pen and paper, or as complicated as using Google maps and more complex GIS software (Durá, 2015). No matter the tool, the benefits of mapping come from its potential as a rhetorical act. Diehl, et al. (2010) noted that mapping allows "the map's writer to socially construct a viewpoint: a way of looking at a space selectively" (p. 417). Further, they proposed, maps are primarily arguments, representing different visions. Mapping then becomes important as a process of selection and interpretation. Map writing is very often invisible work, and maps as products are presented and taken as facts. After all, maps are created from data. What Diehl, et al. (2010) pointed out, however, is that each map tells a story of a community based on data available, and "for certain communities, the story is almost always a negative one because the data collected focuses on deficits" (p. 422). When community members hear stories identifying them as deficient, they begin to see themselves and to identify as clients in need of help from outsiders (Kretzmann & McKnight, 1993). Indeed, communities may need help and outside expertise to affront certain issues; Diehl, et al. did not aim through their work to do away with needs-based maps or outlooks. Instead, they proposed mapping processes and software that harness collective intelligence and allow experts and community members to co-construct and co-name realities. Aside from the contribution of mapping as a tool or of *Grassroots* itself, in this proposal are two different and important contributions: (1) foregrounding assets as much as deficits; and (2) participatory involvement.

In the context of inquiry or research, focusing on assets has the power to shrink the distance between the researcher as the expert and the participant as the client. At minimum, asset-based inquiry offers a different and complementary perspective for problem-solving. But at its best it positions the participant as expert (Cushman, 1998), fostering what Foss & Griffin (1995) termed the condition of value in their proposal for invitational rhetoric:

The condition of value is the acknowledgment that audience members have intrinsic or immanent worth. This value is what Benhabib (1992) calls *"the principle of universal moral respect"*—"the right of all beings capable of speech and action to be participants" in the conversation (p. 29). Barrett (1991) describes this condition as "respectfully, affirming others" while at the same time "one affirms oneself."

(p. 148)

When participants are seen as co-contributors, they are respected at a different level. They are not just clients but whole persons with agentic value. While a project does not have to be participatory to ask an asset-based question—it all depends on the degree of commitment the project has to social justice (Blythe, et al., 2008)—the more participatory a project, the richer and wider the scope of the data. This is not new to technical communication scholars, many of whom have made the shift from usability to user-centered design and are increasingly working in global and complex settings where stakeholders have varying degrees of language fluency, literacy practices, and cultural expectations (see for example Simmons, 2007; Walton & DeRenzi, 2009; Evia & Patriarca, 2011; and Yu & Savage, 2013). Positioning the participant as expert has effects at the meta-level. The addition of a strength-based reality has an epistemological and behavioral impact on culture (Grabill, 2001; Arduser, et al., 2015; Durá, 2015). It challenges "stabilized representations" of culture and knowledge (Bazerman, 1999). While a community or organized group can exist without naming its strengths, "stabilizing" it as asset-based enables the type of community-naming and community building that supports community-owned change (Cushman, 1998; Grabill, 2001; Grabill, 2007; Simmons, 2007).

Asset-based inquiry frameworks then, such as *Grassroots*, i.e., mapping tools and other inventional heuristics that are practicable, can be inserted into larger or more traditional projects without need to commit to the entire ABCD or CBPR process from which they are derived. They are as simple as asking a different question, a question about assets instead of deficits, and as complicated as mapping and telling a different story. In essence, while scholars in technical communication have advocated for asset-based orientations, I argue inquiry frameworks take one aspect of asset-based thinking and make it operational for other uses—for our purposes in technical communication, for research and problem-solving. In the next section I present two case examples, and I elaborate with a discussion of asset-based thinking as a core competency for advocacy in our field.

Asset-Based Inquiry Frameworks in-Use: Two Case Examples in Technical Communication

The case examples presented here intend to show how asset-based inquiry frameworks can function within technical communication projects. To construct these case examples, I draw from two published studies in which I participated as a co-principal investigator and as a research consultant, respectively (Durá, et al., 2015; Sreeramoju, et al., 2015). My rationale for selecting these two examples is based on two factors:

1. I am well-versed with the larger interventional Asset-Based Community Development (ABCD) models undergirding both inquiry frameworks: Appreciative Inquiry and Discovery and Action Dialogues.
2. Both case examples deal with topics relevant for technical communicators. One case is situated in a community-based setting and the other in a healthcare setting, which shows the versatility of asset-based thinking.

While these case examples focus on the practicality of inquiry frameworks, they also include background information on the larger case studies and a synthesis of the principles and broad steps of Appreciative Interviews and Discovery and Action Dialogues, the ABCD models from which they are derived. This contextual information sheds light on the theoretical roots of the two inquiry frameworks, which I argue is useful in keeping the big picture purposes of their heuristic questions in mind. The two case examples are presented separately, with the purpose of offering a snapshot of the asset-based inquiry frameworks in-use. They are followed by a synthesis of key insights and implications.

Appreciative Interviews: Recipes, Nostalgia, and Cultural Wealth at the "Escuelita"

Case Example 1 depicts the use of Appreciative Interviews (AI/AIs) in an after-school program in public housing for children and their parents on the U.S.-Mexico border. The program has been running for four consecutive years and brings together partners from the city's public housing organization, the local university, and local school districts. It is informally known as the "Escuelita" project. Due to the high levels of bilingualism and translingualism in the area, what counts as literacy or as legitimate knowledge is contentious (Scenters-Zapico, 2009). Its purpose was to facilitate a space where parents and children could use food to bridge home and school knowledge with the ultimate aim of increasing traditional literacy practices by boosting confidence about cultural wealth. The team piloted a curriculum that integrated food pedagogy with traditional school subjects like reading, writing, math, science, and geography. The study as it is written up in Durá, et al. (2015) was funded by a small grant from our college of education. One of the ways we fostered family involvement was through the use of AIs with participating families early in the academic year.

AIs are a heuristic framework inspired by Appreciative Inquiry, a prominent ABCD model. Appreciative Inquiry has is generally described as being about:

"the coevolutionary search for the best in people, their organizations, and the relevant world around them. . . . It involves systematic discovery of what gives 'life' to a living system when it is most alive, most effective, and most constructively capable in economic, ecological, and human terms."

(Cooperrider, et al., 2008, p. 101)

Appreciative Inquiry is grounded in principles of social construction, simultaneity of inquiry and change, poetics (stories as data), and asset-based thinking. These principles are enacted through a process involving four broad steps:

1. Discovery. Mobilizing a whole system inquiry into the positive change core.
2. Dream. Creating a clear results-oriented vision in relation to questions of higher purpose.
3. Design. Creating possibility propositions for the ideal organization.
4. Destiny. Strengthening the affirmative capability of the whole system, enabling it to build hope and momentum around a deep purpose and creating processes for learning, adjustment, and improvisation like a jazz group over time.

(Cooperrider, et al., 2008)

Because of its emphasis on system change, Appreciative Inquiry is most prevalent in organizational settings.

AIs are compressed or simplified version of Appreciative Inquiry, allowing for a speedier process. In essence, AIs as an inquiry framework ask a "positive question" aimed at revealing hidden success stories (see McCandless & Lipmanowicz, 2014). The positive question is generally phrased in the form of a prompt, e.g., "think of a time when you were successful working with a group of people from different programs and are proud of what you accomplished—tell that story." The prompt takes a well-known assumption, i.e., group work is challenging, especially across difference, and asks participants to think of the opposite scenario. "Have you had positive experiences, and what made them so?" This shift is significant for those of us who gravitate towards identifying problems and their causes. Of further significance is that the prompt asks for a story. A story increases the likelihood of rich and vivid descriptions by positioning the narrator as a participant, i.e., it makes the scenario more personal. Table 2.1 shows the heuristic questions offered on www.liberatingstructures.com and our adaptations for the Escuelita program.

AIs arose as a possibility in the Escuelita when we decided to engage parents and family members in co-designing the curriculum. While we knew that we would be bringing sanctioned, expert knowledge into Escuelita sessions, e.g., the Michelle Obama "my plate" depicting food variety and portion size, we wanted equally to respect and feature local funds of knowledge (Moll & Greenberg, 1992), or the cultural wealth (Yosso, 2005) of community participants. AIs

TABLE 2.1 Appreciative interviews inquiry framework and adaptations

Appreciative interviews heuristic questions	Adaptations for Escuelita Program in a community-based setting
1. Tell a story about a time when you worked on a particular challenge and are proud of what you accomplished. 2. Engage in sense-making about patterns for success and what made the success possible.	1. In pairs, tell your partner (preferably someone you don't know or whom you know the least) a story about your favorite food or recipe growing up. Who cooked it? When did you eat it? What made it special? 2. In fours, tell your partner's story to the group. 3. Once everyone has told their story, talk about the patterns and the differences amongst yourselves. 4. At the end of this session, the research "harvests" top patterns and insights from each group.

Source: www.liberatingstructures.com

allowed us to collect data on assets from the entire group at one time: we collected stories from 20 participants in one hour, as opposed to conducting individual focus groups or interviews. We foregrounded the notion of "story," in keeping with AI principles and processes, to encourage the use of vivid details, concrete examples, and self-authoring of a strengths-based landscape.

At the end of one hour, participants had each told one story, heard three, and engaged in collective sense-making and data coding for 15 more stories. The process of arranging conversations in pairs and in fours (in a "think, pair, share" fashion) allowed for everyone to participate at the same time and for participants themselves to vet data and learn from each other's experiences. That is, we went around the room and asked groups to report on the patterns, insights, and differences they found. We recorded these in a collective Cultural Memory Bank (see Nazarea, 2001; Handa & Tippins, 2012), which became an ongoing repository and organizational tool for what we learned together throughout the school year. The Cultural Memory Bank served as an ethnographic tool that combined cultural practices and academic knowledge (Durá, et al., 2015). Within the overall purpose of the project, which aimed to bridge home and school literacies, the information we collected on assets became our baseline. The data on cultural wealth and home knowledge helped to counter the other baselines: readily available regional data depicting low literacy levels and educational attainment (Scenters-Zapico, 2009). For example, we learned that whether in rural or urban households, the parents grew up with knowledge of how to cook outside and that they had collectively lived in five Mexican states. We used this information to probe further for home science and cultural heritage throughout the course of the project. The asset-based tone of this program continues as the program goes into its sixth year. Families return year after year claiming greater confidence in their own and their children's abilities; some families bring before and after report cards to show this change.

Discovery and Action Dialogues: Practices that "Stop a Bug, Save a Life"

Case Example 2 draws on the experience of implementing Discovery and Action Dialogues (DAD/DADs) as part of a Positive Deviance interventional study "Stop a Bug, Save a Life" to decrease healthcare-associated infections in a public Texas hospital. The study was funded by the National Institutes of Health. The Centers for Disease Control and Prevention (CDC) reported 722,000 healthcare-associated infections (HAIs) and 75,000 deaths in the U.S. in 2011 (CDC, 2016). This particular hospital faced re-accreditation issues and was trying different approaches to HAI prevention during the intervention period: April 2011 to March 2013.

The purpose of the intervention study was to see if Positive Deviance, which I define below, was effective in reducing HAI. This study was the first of its kind. The intervention was structured as a clustered randomized controlled trial in which three inpatient hospital wards received the Positive Deviance intervention and three inpatient wards received standard practices for infection control. The research team was led by an infectious disease specialist-medical doctor and comprised an interdisciplinary team including other medical doctors, an epidemiologist, an economist, and me, a technical communicator. My role as technical communicator was to contribute to the participatory design process and to visit the hospital once a month and help facilitate inquiry and brainstorming sessions.

Positive Deviance is premised on the idea that in every community facing an intractable issue there are individuals and groups whose uncommon practices enable them to find better solutions than their peers. As an ABCD and CBPR model, Positive Deviance provides a systematic framework "to identify assets, indigenous knowledge, and home-grown solutions, and to amplify them for wider adoption" (Singhal & Durá, 2017). Although it is best known in non-profit and community-based settings, Positive Deviance has been applied to problems in areas from pharmaceutical sales to prison recidivism and in sectors as varied as business, education, and healthcare/public health. Positive Deviance as a process is divided into two parts: inquiry and action. These two larger parts are broken down further into steps known as the "6 Ds":

1. Define the problem.
2. Determine the existence of positive deviants.
3. Discover positive deviant practices and behaviors.
4. Design the positive deviance intervention.
5. Discern effectiveness.
6. Disseminate results, expand, scale.

Steps 1–3 make up the inquiry portion, and steps 4–6 make up the action portion. Because Positive Deviance can be executed any number of ways, the methods used to carry out the 6 Ds vary by community and local context—in rural Uganda, for example, a community engaged in asset-mapping by hand to locate returned abductees during civil conflict (Durá, 2015). In a study to assess successful teen pregnancy prevention, a survey was combined with semi-structured interviews (Diaz, 2010). In hospital settings, DADs have become a common way to facilitate Positive Deviance.

DADs are similar to AIs in that they too ask a "positive question," but there are some differences. First, the DAD setup begins by asking about a common problem, which is how it fulfills the first step in a Positive Deviance Inquiry. Second, DADs are aimed at coming up with outliers and their concrete behaviors. Third, DADs follow up with questions about generating new ideas and an action plan for implementation. So, DADs intend to generate new ideas in addition to "discovering" existing ones. In this sense, DADs and AIs are mini-versions of their parent approaches, Positive Deviance and Appreciative Inquiry. Table 2.2 provides a side-by-side comparison of the DAD heuristic questions and adaptations in practice for "Stop a Bug, Save a Life."

As the technical communicator on the team, during the initial phase of the project I worked with the medical doctor-epidemiologist and the epidemiologist to design the kick-off meeting for the project and adapt the Discovery and Action Dialogue (DAD) process for this setting. Together we thought of the best wording possible for the context, not just for the DAD itself but for the invitations to

TABLE 2.2 Discovery and action dialogues inquiry framework and adaptation

Discovery and action dialogues heuristic questions	Adaptation for "Stop a Bug, Save a Life" program in a hospital setting
1. How do you know when X problem is present?	1. How do you know or recognize when healthcare associated infection is present?
2. How do you contribute effectively to solving problem X?	2. How do YOU protect yourself, patients, and others from transmission of any microorganisms?
3. What prevents you from doing this or taking these actions all of the time?	3. What prevents you from taking these actions all the time?
4. Do you know anybody who is able to frequently solve problem X and overcome barriers? What behaviors or practices made their success possible?	4. Is there any group or anyone you know who is able to overcome the barriers frequently and effortlessly? How?
5. Do you have any (other) ideas?	5. Do you have any ideas?
6. What needs to be done to make it happen? Any volunteers? Who else needs to be involved?	6. What initial steps need to be pursued to make it happen? Any volunteers?
	7. Who else needs to be involved?

Source: www.liberatingstructures.com

ward managers. I conducted the first DAD rounds with the team and visited the site once a month as a research consultant and DAD co-facilitator. The team conducted 54 DADs over six months with frontline medical staff (sometimes one-on-one and sometimes in small groups) including doctors, nurses, patient transporters, cleaning staff, and patient family members (Sreeramoju, et al., 2015). The DADs all followed the heuristic structure presented in Table 2.2. Interviews took place in ward break rooms, included one to four participants, and lasted between five and 30 minutes.

Through the DADs, participants generated 210 ideas for infection prevention (a combination of "hidden" current practices and new ideas). The research team worked with participants to vet the epidemiological effectiveness of the ideas and to prioritize the ones they could put into action right away. The "Stop a Bug, Save a Life" program, as it came to be known after a naming contest in the intervention wards, worked to operationalize the top three ideas:

1. Using flash cards to teach patients how to participate in their own care. The flash cards contained visuals of important infection prevention steps, from handwashing to hub scrubbing. Caregivers wanted patients to understand these processes and talk with them about it—even to remind them if they skipped a step.
2. Engaging patients to teach visitors about the handwashing process. The rationale behind this was that while staff can't keep track of all visitors, patients generally can. Further, patients can make the most compelling case for handwashing by making it a personal issue for friends and family.
3. Adopting a patient care technician's checklist for hygiene competency. A patient care technician had developed a list of 64 items that he used for onboarding new patient care technicians. This list was adapted and used with roughly 50 staff members from each intervention ward (Sreeramoju, et al., 2015).

In the final assessment by the medical doctor-epidemiologist and her research associate, the intervention wards showed a gradual exponential decline in HAI over the nine-month intervention period, compared to a one-time drop only in the control wards (Sreeramoju, et al., 2015). The gradual exponential decline was sufficiently significant to show that the intervention had made a difference.

Key Insights: Expanding Inventional and Solution Spaces

What key insights can technical communicators glean from these two case examples illustrating asset-based inquiry frameworks in use? The first key insight is asset-based inquiry frameworks' inventional value. As can be seen in the tables from Case Examples 1 and 2, the form and content of the heuristic questions can be easily adapted. Questions can be dropped and added, and the heuristics can be used in many formats, from one-on-one interviews to focus group discussions (as seen in Case Example 2), to simultaneous group discussions (as seen in Case Example 1) and beyond. The inquiry frameworks can be combined as they were in the case examples with other methods, from highly participatory improvisational theater sessions to the highly scientific clustered randomized control trial process. Also compelling, is the relative efficiency of using tested and tried inquiry heuristics. Practitioners who use AIs and DADs have adapted the question structure over thousands of iterations, and the result is quite dependable. In Case Example 1, hearing stories, systematically analyzing them, and vetting their patterns and insights resulted in rapid data gathering. In Case Example 2, the rapid interview sessions allowed for participants to confirm and expand their responses over time, yielding breadth and depth of data.

From an advocacy perspective, perhaps the most compelling insight of using asset-based inquiry frameworks is the value of adding a previously overlooked perspective to the solution space. Similar to Diehl, et al.'s proposition about asset-mapping as a complement to deficit-mapping, asset-based inquiry frameworks can enrich technical communication projects. Case Example 2 illustrates through the use of the DAD inquiry framework that it is possible that solutions to problems may come from the bottom-up, e.g., utilization of checklist developed by a patient care technician, as opposed to best practices imported by hospital administration. In Case Example 1, the extraction of home knowledge relative to science, culture, and geography brought forth funds of knowledge available to participants that were beyond the research team's experience and expertise, e.g., a connection to the earth and seasonal cooking through ranch life, and the use of traditional tools to grind and prepare corn for tortillas and for all of its uses. Further, the ideas garnered from both cases were put on equal terms as the ideas were generated through academic or "official" sources.

There is also a transformational aspect to legitimizing local ways of knowing. In Case Example 1, hearing stories and seeing data from these stories recorded in the Cultural Memory Bank engendered an instant and collective sense of pride, according to participant responses after an informal feedback session. Similarly, the emphasis on inside resources vs outside resources in Case Example 2 generated lateral and bottom-up leadership within a very hierarchical system. In both cases, the effectiveness of asset-based inquiry frameworks can only be judged against the alternative. The alternative in HAI prevention in the U.S. has followed a top-down infection control paradigm where interventions and protocols are designed by experts and imported as "best practices." In Case Example 1 we can assume that schools and teachers utilize best practices with their students. Best practices are good for a reason—they have been vetted as effective across contexts.

Typically, healthcare organizations establish a reward or recognition system for appropriate follow-through. But best practices require "buy-in," which assumes that the users must "buy" what the experts are "selling." The process of DADs within the Positive Deviance interventional study described in this case example changes that paradigm by saying, "yes, best practices are out there, and they are evidence-based, *and* there are adaptations and innovations at a local level, i.e., practice-based evidence that can make us more effective at infection prevention." Asset-based inquiry prompts us to see ownership as an alternative to buy-in. In Case Example 1, ownership is such that the program continues without funding. In Case Example 2, ownership of the problem was as great a milestone as the solutions; because of the accreditation issues the hospital faced, employee turnover was high, and staff hesitated to compromise their job security.

In essence, while a community can exist without naming its strengths—that is, without going the asset-based route—"stabilizing" it as asset-based enables the type of community-naming and community-building that supports community-owned and sustainable social change (Cushman, 1998; Grabill, 2001; Grabill, 2007; Simmons, 2007). So, although technical communicators, with established expertise in research and language, have much to contribute in the realm of user-centered and participatory design, asset-based inquiry is not where we go by default. Asset-based inquiry as a competency for technical communicators adds value to the work we do in problem-solving and research. In the section that follows, I summarize the core skills necessary to develop this competency.

Asset-Based Inquiry: Core Skills

On its website, the Society for Technical Communication (STC) lists core competencies for technical communicators and specific competencies relative to ethical and multicultural communication, demonstration of professionalism, communication publication/production processes, communication technologies, communication design and development, and balance of communication theory and practice. Within these lists the following competencies are most relevant to the work of this chapter:

- design with users in mind (core competency as explained by Hayhoe, 2002);
- work collaboratively with subject-matter experts and co-workers (core competency derived from Rainey, et al. in 2005);
- analyze communication problems (competency for communication design and development); and
- conduct needs assessment to understand audience, task, context, and genre (competency for communication design and development).

While the lists posted on the STC website are not exhaustive, they point to our assumptions and to prevalent ways of working. Asset-based inquiry as a competency meshes well with other competencies, and it provides an important avenue for advocacy by amplifying local knowledge, cultural wealth, and strengths. Developing this competency entails three core skills: asking the positive question, becoming attuned to deficit-based discursive cues, and practice.

Skill 1: Ask the Positive Question

Asset-based inquiry is developed as a competency by sharpening our inquiry design skills to include "the positive question." This can mean drawing from asset-based inquiry frameworks like AI or DAD, which entails building these into a research design. But it can also mean something even simpler, which is being mindful of micro-decision points that fall into the deficit trap.

Skill 2: Be Attuned to Deficit-Based Discursive Cues

When we hear the words "best practices," that is a cue that local solutions might be ignored. This is a micro-decision point for asset-based advocacy. Similarly, when we hear the words "buy in," someone is discursively constructing a reality whereby another must be persuaded. Persuasion is not innately negative. However, it does signal, much like in the best practices reality, that ownership lies in outside expertise. This is a discursive cue about ownership and another opportunity for asset-based advocacy. When we hear these phrases, we can ask ourselves, "Whose best practices are being imported? Who is buying in, and is this justified?"

Skill 3: Look for Opportunities and Practice

Designers use the concept of rapid prototyping to create and test a model. Such testing can include one or many failed attempts. Becoming good at asset-based inquiry, at knowing when to ask a positive question and how to phrase it, takes practice—a phronesis of sorts. The upside is that opportunities to practice abound because we are always attempting to solve problems big and small, at school, at home, and at work. All it requires is asking oneself, "Can changing the discourse/question alter the outcomes?" Despite the magnitude, complexity, or messiness of a problem, has the positive question been asked? If it hasn't then there might be a glimmer of hope that has gone unnoticed.

Concluding Thoughts

The work in this chapter opens up a couple of avenues for further exploration. First, technical communicators, from students to established scholars and practitioners, are in a prime position to not just adopt and adapt asset-based thinking as a new competency, but to test and create inquiry frameworks as simple and elegant as those presented here. These frameworks can be used within classrooms and group discussions in the field to facilitate conversations. Second, asset-based inquiry frameworks can be combined with deficit-based method-ologies for advocacy in research. The frameworks for asset-based inquiry proposed in this chapter are not meant to replace traditional inquiry frameworks or even deficit-based frameworks. Pointing out and understanding deficits helps us problem-solve and find root causes of systemic issues. But by dismissing local knowledge and purely favoring traditional expertise, we fail to tap into existing resources and we overlook the capable, apt, and rich aspects of participants' identities. Even more profound, by dismissing local knowledge, we engage in an act of disrespect. In today's political climate, more than ever, innovative inquiry and dialogue may yield surprising and refreshing results.

Discussion Questions

1) Let's debrief using a *What? So What? Now What?* structure. Work in pairs and then in fours to answer the following:

   a. What facts or observations stand out about this chapter?
   b. What is significant about them? How has what you read influenced you or provoked further thought?
   c. What will you do next, or how does what you've learned change the way you do things?

2) Observe and keep track of the number of deficit-based frames, labels, or descriptions used in a given time period—it can be a conversation, a class period, a lecture, a reading, or a day. Record your observations. How many of these would benefit from asset-based language? What does this tell you?

3) Use an internet browser to navigate to a mainstream news site and choose a current event or topic to research. How many articles or write-ups use a deficit-based lens vs an asset-based lens to tell a story? What kind of language is used to indicate assets? How is that language different from labels or descriptors that indicate deficits?

4) Think more deeply about the relationship between using an asset-based framework and advocacy. What are some current social issues or situations that might benefit from this lens?

5) Work with a partner to develop an asset-based research question around a problem that you care about. If possible, share this question with another pair of students and help each other refine your questions. What did you learn about the process of formulating questions around assets?

Further Reading

Brown, T. (2009). *Change by design: How design thinking transforms organizations and inspires innovation.* New York, NY: HarperCollins.

Durá, L. (2018). Leveraging assets through Appreciative Interviews in classrooms and communities. In *High Impact Practices in Community Settings.* (Eds.) A. Gonzalez & G. Nunez-Mchiri. Dubuque, IA: Kendall Hunt Publishing.

Durá, L. (2015). What's ~~wrong~~ right here? Introducing the positive deviance approach to community-based work. *Connexions, International Professional Communication Journal,* 4(1), 57–89.

Kretzmann, J. P., & McKnight, J. L. (1993). *Building communities from the inside out: Asset-based community development.* Chicago, IL: ACTA Publications.

Mathie, A., & Cunningham, G. (2003). From clients to citizens: Asset-based community development as a strategy for community-driven development. *Development in Practice, 13*(5), 474–486.

McCandless, K., & Lipmanowicz, H. (2014). *The surprising power of Liberating Structures: Simple rules to unleash a culture of innovation.* Seattle, WA: Liberating Structures Press.

Singhal, A., & Durá, L. (2017). Positive Deviance: A non-normative approach to health and risk messaging. In *The Oxford encyclopedia of health and risk message design and processing.* (Ed.) R. Parrott. New York, NY: Oxford University Press.

Acknowledgments

This work is the product of extensive work, conversations, and prototyping. I am grateful to Laura Gonzales for reading several drafts of this chapter and to Jason Rosenfeld for his early inputs. I especially thank Pranavi Sreeramoju and the Escuelita participants for inviting me to work and learn with them. And I thank Arvind Singhal, Henri Lipmanowicz, and Keith McCandless for their ongoing mentorship.

References

All website URLs accessed February 2018.

Arduser, L., Durá, L., & Malkowski, J. (2015). Rhetorical agency in the face of uncertainty. *POROI, 11*(1), 1–8.

Bazerman, C. (1999). *The languages of Edison's light.* Cambridge, MA: MIT Press.

Blythe, S., Grabill, J., & Riley, K. (2008). Action research and wicked environmental problems: Exploring appropriate roles for researchers in professional communication. *Journal of Business and Technical Communication, 22*(3), 272–298.

Centers for Disease Control and Prevention/CDC (2016). HAI data and statistics. Healthcare associated infections. Retrieved from www.cdc.gov/hai/surveillance

Cooperrider, D., Whitney, D., & Stavros, J. (2008). *Appreciative Inquiry handbook,* 2nd Ed. Brunswick, OH: Crown Custom Publishing, Inc.

Cushman, E. (1998). *The struggle and the tools: Oral and literate strategies in an inner city community.* Albany, NY: SUNY Press.

Diaz, A. (2010). *A positive deviance inquiry of communicative behaviors that influence the prevention of Hispanic teenage pregnancy* (Master's thesis). Retrieved from ProQuest Dissertations and Theses database. (UMI No. 2280752981)

Diehl, A., Grabill, J., & Hart-Davidson, W. (2010). Grassroots: Supporting the knowledge work of everyday life. *Technical Communication Quarterly, 17*(4), 413–434.

Durá, L. (2015). What's wrong right here? Introducing the positive deviance approach to community-based work. *Connexions, International Professional Communication Journal, 4*(1), 57–89.

Durá, L., Salas, C., Medina-Jerez, W., & Hill, V. (2015). *De aquí y de allá:* Changing perceptions of literacy through food pedagogy, asset-based narratives, and hybrid spaces. *Community Literacy Journal, 10*(1), 21–39.

Evia, C., & Patriarca, A. (2011). Beyond compliance: Participatory translation of safety communication for Latino construction workers. *Journal of Business and Technical Communication, 26*(3), 1–28.

Foss, S., & Griffin, (1995). Beyond persuasion: A proposal for an invitational rhetoric. *Communication Monographs, 62*(1), 2–18.

Grabill, J. (2001). *Community literacy projects and the politics of change.* Albany, NY: State University of New York Press.

——. (2007). Sustaining community-based work: Community-based research and community building. In *Labor, Writing Technologies, and the Shaping of Composition in the Academy.* (Eds.) P. Takayoshi and P. Sullivan. Cresskill, NJ: Hampton Press, pp. 325–339.

Handa, V., & Tippins, D. (2012). Cultural memory banking in preservice science teacher education. *Research Science Education, 42*(6), 1201–1217.

Hayhoe, G. (Nov. 2002). Core competencies: The essence of technical communication. *Technical Communication 49*(4), 397–398.

Kretzmann, J. P., & McKnight, J. L. (1993). *Building communities from the inside out: Asset-based community development.* Chicago, IL: ACTA Publications.

Mathie, A., & Cunningham, G. (2003). From clients to citizens: Asset-based community development as a strategy for community-driven development. *Development in Practice, 13*(5), 474–486.

McCandless, K., & Lipmanowicz, H. (2014). *The surprising power of Liberating Structures: Simple rules to unleash a culture of innovation.* Seattle, WA: Liberating Structures Press.

Moll, L., & Greenberg, J. B. (1992). Creating zones of possibilities: Combining social contexts for instruction. *Vygotsky and education: Instructional implication and applications of sociohistorical psychology,* (Ed.) Luis Moll. London: Cambridge University Press, pp. 319–348.

Moore, K. (2015). The value of technical communication in enacting social justice. Open Grounds. Retrieved from: www.depts.ttu.edu/english/grad_degrees/Open_Grounds/Spring_2015/moore_tcr_socialjustice.php

Nazarea, V. (2001). *Cultural memory and biodiversity.* Tucson: University of Arizona Press.

Rainey, K. T., Turner, R. K., & Dayton, D. (Aug, 2005). Do curricula correspond to managerial expectations? Core competencies for technical communicators. *Technical Communication 52*(3), 323–352.

Scenters-Zapico, J. (2009). *Generaciones' narratives.* Logan: Utah State University Press.

Simmons, W.M. (2007). *Participation and power: Civic discourse in environmental policy decisions.* New York, NY: SUNY Press.

Singhal, A., & Durá, L. (2017). Positive Deviance: A non-normative approach to health and risk messaging. In *The Oxford encyclopedia of health and risk message design and processing,* (Ed.) Roxanne Parrott. New York, NY: Oxford University Press.

Society for Technical Communication. (2014). Core competencies. Retrieved from www.stc.org/bodyofknowledge/wiki/categories/core-competencies

Sreeramoju, P., Durá, L., Fernandez-Rojas, M., Minhajuddin, A., Simacek, K., Fomby, T., & Doebbeling, B. (2015). Positive deviance intervention to reduce healthcare-associated infections in medical wards: A pilot cluster randomized controlled trial. *American Journal of Medical Quality, 30*(2S) 43S–47S.

Walton, R., & DeRenzi, B. (2009). Value-sensitive design and healthcare in Africa. *IEEE, 52*(4), 346–358.

Yosso, T. (2005). Whose culture has capital? A critical race theory discussion of community cultural wealth. *Race, Ethnicity and Education, 8*(1), 69–91.

Yu, H., & Savage, G. (2013). (Eds.) *Negotiating cultural encounters: Narrating intercultural engineering and technical communication.* Hoboken, NJ: Wiley & Sons, IEEE Press.

3

ENABLING GLOBAL CITIZENSHIP IN INTERCULTURAL COLLABORATION

Cosmopolitan Potential in Online Identity Representation

Zsuzsanna Palmer

Introduction

Most technical communication instructors agree that in order to teach inter-cultural communication successfully, students should be given the opportunity to have meaningful intercultural encounters (St.Amant, 2011). For this reason, a number of intercultural collaboration projects have been organized that focus on training students in how to collaborate on international technical writing projects (i.e. Maylath et al., 2008; Starke-Meyerring, 2010). Although this utilitarian approach equips students with useful skills in the globally networked workplace, it does not acknowledge the importance of educating students for global citizenship.

Global citizenship, the rights and responsibilities inherent in being part of humanity, has often been posited as a utopian concept due to the lack of unity in the world community (Carter, 2006). Openness towards linguistic and cultural difference and identification with the issues affecting others and humanity as a whole are hallmarks of global citizenship. Global citizens are not only aware of concerns that arise at the local and national levels, but they are also equally interested in the issues and problems that emerge in other parts of the world and seek to find how their own background and know-how can contribute to solving some of these problems (Beck 2006). For technical communicators, this trans-lates to an awareness of communication practices—often with their built-in inequalities—around the world, and a willingness to use their own expertise for engaging with the people who have the means to improve these communication practices. This direct engagement requires that technical communicators embody cosmopolitan ideals as they approach specific communication issues around the world.

Cosmopolitan ideals have been around since the time of the Ancient Greeks and have been connected to a stance—a certain disposition that enables individuals to align themselves with entities beyond their national culture and allows them to act as citizens of the world. In a previous publication (Palmer, 2013), I explained the relevance of cosmopolitan theory to technical communication as a field and, more specifically, I described the communication skills resulting from a cosmopolitan outlook that can be effectively used when participating in or teaching intercultural communication. This chapter also argues that when cosmopolitan tendencies are observable and are highlighted at the onset of intercultural collaboration projects within the technical writing classroom, instructors will be able to create an environment where global citizenship becomes a possibility.

In order to foster students' development as global citizens in the technical writing classroom, I designed, on the basis of cosmopolitan theory (Beck, 2006; Appiah, 2006), an intercultural online pedagogical project between two groups of university students in Hungary and in the U.S. The goal of the project was to increase students' awareness of cosmopolitan principles that support viewing individuals from different cultures first as members of humanity (universality), while exploring cultural differences with an open attitude. These cosmopolitan principles then will enable the competencies: an open attitude towards people with different backgrounds, and an understanding of diversity as universality plus difference that are the building blocks of global citizenship. According to Appiah (2006), concentrating on the universality as opposed to focusing on the difference enables higher levels of empathy and allows for more fruitful cooperation.

In this online collaboration project, a group of my Professional Writing students at Davenport University in Michigan were connected to a group of Business English students at Pazmany Peter University in Hungary. The project consisted of two phases and lasted for six weeks. First, all students were introduced to the basic tenets of cosmopolitanism and developed an understanding of the varied identities that each individual brings to cross-cultural encounters. Then participants in both countries were asked to create blogs about their varied identities and languages. In the second phase of the project, students commented on the blogs written by students overseas who have described similar identity types on their blogs. After the project was finished, I analyzed all the student blogs to answer the following research questions:

1. What kind of identities did students create for the purposes of the intercultural blog exchange project?
2. To what extent can these identities and their multimodal representations be associated with traditional cultural categories and hybrid, cosmopolitan identities?

The purpose of this was to determine whether students displayed a potential for developing cosmopolitan outlook.

To answer my research questions, in this chapter I will first outline the connections between identity, cosmopolitanism, and global citizenship. This will be followed by a discussion of the results of my multimodal analysis of the most commonly chosen identity categories represented on the class project blogs by 52 participants. The categories of student identity, sports identity, and national identity will be examined in detail based on the high cosmopolitan potential observed in connection with these identities. The results of the analysis suggest that while the identities chosen by students on the blog sites include traditional notions of national identities, the presence of hybrid, cosmopolitan identities that are often represented through multimodal means creates a space for students in which they can establish connections across borders and further develop their cosmopolitan outlook: a prerequisite of global citizenship.

Approaches to Intercultural Communication and Cosmopolitanism

Widespread globalization and the accelerated cultural exchange enabled by the Internet have resulted in a revision of traditional concepts of culture, and in calls for pedagogical methods in teaching intercultural technical communication that emphasize universal skills which are much more applicable in the global communication environment (Cardon, 2008; Hunsinger, 2006; Agboka, 2012; Starke-Meyerring, 2005; Kankaanranta & Louhiala-Salminen, 2011). In this more complex global environment, there is a need for a better understanding of the complex identities that are involved in intercultural communication interactions. Jameson (2007), for example, calls for the necessity to better understand not only others' but also one's own cultural identity. She defines the concept of cultural identity as "an individual's sense of self, derived from formal or informal membership in groups that transmit and inculcate knowledge, beliefs, values, attitudes, traditions, and ways of life" (p. 199). Further, she argues that using cultural identity with this definition will help intercultural communication research overcome the traditionally overwhelming concentration on national identity and cultural categories and dimensions alone, and will help in developing an understanding of how other layers of identity play a role in intercultural communication.

The traditional line of research about intercultural aspects of professional and technical writing has been based on the assumption that cultures are something tangible, static, and monolithic; a view that was common in the social sciences of the last century. According to the contemporary philosopher Seyla Benhabib (2002), this widespread view originates in the social anthropology work of Malinowski, Mead, and Levi-Strauss and can be described as holding the assumptions that "each human group 'has' some kind of 'culture' and that the boundaries between these groups and the contours of their cultures are specifiable and relatively easy to depict" (p. 4). However, as Benhabib explains, this assumption is based on faulty epistemic premises including that cultures are homogeneous, clearly identifiable entities, that they correspond to groups of people, and that their description can be done without any controversy. Benhabib calls such an approach the "reductionist sociology of culture" (p. 4) and claims that viewing culture this way denies the historical complexity of human interaction and the resulting hybridity in culture. Sociologist and cultural studies hybridity expert Jan Pieterse (2001), describes hybridity as "multiple identity, cross-over, pick-'n'-mix, boundary-crossing experiences and styles, matching a world of growing migration and diaspora lives, intensive intercultural communication, everyday multiculturalism and erosion of boundaries" (p. 3). It is this type of hybridity frequently observed in today's global society that cannot be described by using theories that originate in the reductionists sociology of culture.

However, the reductionist sociology of culture originally served as a framework for professional communication research, especially through the work of two scholars—Edward Hall and Geert Hofstede—whose work on cultural categories and dimensions has greatly influenced the field. As several professional and technical communication scholars (Hunsinger, 2006; Cardon, 2008; Wang, 2010) who have questioned the relevance of Hall's work in this field now recognize, the drawbacks of categorizing individuals according to national cultures only, a more systematic understanding of what kind of identities people bring to communication encounters becomes necessary. Thus far in technical communication, the description of these identities has mostly been based on rigidly defined ethnic or racial identities (Medina, 2014; Kelly, 2014). The research presented in this chapter aims to find a different approach that acknowledges additional identities and recovers these identities' cosmopolitan potential and possible connection to global citizenship.

The pedagogical project that serves as the basis of this investigation was designed in the theoretical framework of cosmopolitanism (Appiah, 2006; Beck, 2006; Canagarajah, 2010). Cosmopolitan theory not only provides an overarching theoretical framework that promotes an open attitude towards hybridity and diversity, but it can also serve as a basis for developing pedagogical projects aimed at teaching students successful communication practices in actual transcultural encounters (Palmer, 2013). Diogenes of Sinope, the first cosmopolitan ("citizen of the world"), was a founder of Cynicism in Ancient Greece and rejected declaring local loyalties by defining himself in universal terms as a member of humanity. In more recent approaches to cosmopolitanism, Hannerz (1990) defines a cosmopolitan as someone who has "a stance toward diversity itself, toward the coexistence of cultures in the individual experience (. . .) an orientation, a willingness to engage with the Other" (p. 239). Vertovec & Cohen (2002) also suggest that cosmopolitans have a "capacity to engage cultural multiplicity" (p. 1) and indicate this open attitude or disposition towards cultural difference (also called "cosmopolitan outlook") as the major characteristic of the cosmopolitan identity.

According to Delanty (2012), in the presence of a cosmopolitan outlook a relativization of identity happens when a "reinterpretation of culture occurs as a result of the encounter of one culture with another" (p. 340). Through the reinterpretation of culture, people see themselves and the identities they develop differently. Beck (2006) describes this process of identity-relativization in terms of territorial allegiance by explaining that under the current social changes caused by globalization, being associated with a single country in all aspects of one's life is hardly possible. Thus it is necessary to go beyond the "territorial prison theory of identity" (p. 7) in order to understand transnational loyalties and forms of life. As Beck argues, cosmopolitan identity is not the only identity a person has but is rather ascribable to someone whose loyalties reach beyond national borders. It necessarily involves the willingness to engage with the Other, and this engagement often results in developing a mixture of different national and cultural identities such as hybrid and transnational identities. Based on this argument, then, I propose a definition of cosmopolitan identity as one of an individual's varied identities which is developed through loyalties, group memberships, or significant interests that reach beyond national borders and stems from a cosmopolitan outlook or genuine willingness to engage with the Other, physically or virtually.

Through educating students about cosmopolitan outlook and allowing them to acknowledge and act on their cosmopolitan identities, technical communication instructors can open a pathway to education for global citizenship. The contemporary philosopher, Appiah (2008), argues for the urgency in educating for global citizenship in a world where each individual and their actions can have direct positive and negative impacts on all other individuals. He grounds his discussion of global citizenship education in the ideals of cosmopolitanism, and he reasons that a true cosmopolitan approach to teaching students about global responsibilities has to start by listening to and learning from individuals of different backgrounds with an open mind. Understanding cosmopolitanism as "universality plus difference" (Appiah, 2008, p. 92), will widen the scope of teaching intercultural communication that has been very much focused on cultural difference, often ignoring commonalities: the universal part of the cosmopolitan equation. A deeper understanding of cosmopolitan identities and the inclusion of cosmopolitan principles in intercultural communication pedagogy then has the potential to support the argument for global civic engagement in technical communication (Walton, 2013), as it can provide students with the inner motivation to engage in such projects, and with the competencies they need to collaborate with people of different linguistic and cultural backgrounds.

Multimodal Analysis and Interviews

To better understand the cosmopolitan potential in the identity descriptions of the two groups of students on their blogs, I have conducted a study of the identities represented on all of the blog sites created for the "My Identities and

Languages" online collaboration project. I established the project together with Rita Kóris, professor of Business English from Hungary and her students at Pazmany Peter University. While Rita was involved in the pedagogical phase of the project, she did not participate in the research phase. During the project, students in a Professional Writing class in the U.S. at Davenport University, where I was the instructor, were connected through blog sites to students in Rita Kóris' advanced Business English class in Hungary. Most students at Davenport University, 18 out of 22, were English monolinguals, while the remaining four students were immigrants or international multilingual students. All 30 students at Pazmany Peter University were multilingual as their International Relations major required them to pass advanced proficiency foreign language exams in two languages before graduation. All but one Pazmany student spoke Hungarian as their native language.

In this study, I analyzed some modalities that students used to represent their different identities. In order to examine the blogs' multimodal components, I applied Wysocki's (2013) rhetorical approach to analyzing multimodal data. Wysocki (2013) describes her method of looking at multimodal texts as "a rhetorical approach with a strong cultural inflection" (p. 2). Her analysis rests on the tenet that multimodal text producers are motivated; they want their texts to "do some sort of work in the world" (p. 2). However, the choices composers of multimodal material make to do this work are not only influenced by the affordances of the media and tools they use, but also by the cultural conventions that surround the use of a certain media and mode in the composers' specific context. In addition, composers create their text for a specific audience to which they attribute either the same or a different set of cultural conventions and attitudes when it comes to interpreting different media and modes. These conventions and attitudes can be revealed when they are examined relative to cultural context.

Thus, when analyzing multimodal data, Wysocki suggests to start out by determining what kind of strategies producers of multimodal texts used and then connecting these strategies with assumptions about the audience, context, and purpose. As in the case with language use, multimodal composers' choices are affected by their organized knowledge based on prior experiences (what is called "structures of expectations") and these expectations can be reconstructed based on how different modes are used in multimodal texts. Further, this approach can help identify whether the reconstructed structures of expectations are based on a single culture or on a combination of cultures in the case of identities with cosmopolitan potential. If the data shows that the structures of expectations are based on a combination of cultures, then a connection between the multimodal representations of identities and cosmopolitan practice can be accomplished.

In addition, since it is the choices an individual makes from the available resources that will determine how a multimodal communication product will take shape, inquiring about this process can reveal much about the role of agency in the pedagogical project. Understanding the motivation of individuals during the decision-making/composition/design process provides researchers with further information about multimodal identity representation and its connection to cosmopolitan identity. As several studies in writing research in the digital space exemplify (Wei, 2010; Yi & Hirvela, 2010; Leon & Pigg, 2011), an effective research method to inquire about individuals' composing process is interviewing them about what motivated them while writing, and how they decided between different design choices in multimodal composition. Thus, after the end of the semester I sent out an email looking for volunteers to be interviewed about the project. Overall, nine students volunteered, and eight of them followed through to the end of the process (four from Pazmany Peter University, Hungary, and four from Davenport University, U.S.). Of the four interviewees from Davenport University, one was a bilingual student who immigrated to this country as a child, the others were monolingual English speakers. The four interviewees from Pazmany Peter University included one student whose first language was not Hungarian, one student who was part of a Hungarian minority growing up outside of the country borders, and two who were born and raised in Hungary. These interviews allowed greater insight into the data by contextualizing students' composing practices for this intercultural blog project.

Identity Representation on the Student Blog Sites

Before an analysis of students' identities represented during this project could be undertaken, I had to categorize, based on content, the different types of identities students represented most frequently on the blogs. The overwhelming majority of students (49 out of 52) introduced their different identities by describing them in different sections and including a section heading or label that stands for the identity category they discussed. In most cases, the identity labels were very explicit in referring to a specific identity category; examples for these included student, brother, soccer player, or computer technician. Building on Burke and Stets' (2009) definition of identity, and participants' characterization of identity on the blog pages as "different roles assumed" (Blog #35) or "different hats worn" (Blog #39), identity was defined for the purposes of this research project as "a set of meanings that define who one is, based on a personally or situationally significant societal role, group membership, frequent activity, or personal characteristics."

The following excerpt from Blog #1 illustrates how a specific identity described here is associated with a frequent, personally significant activity: sports.

Sportman: Posted on <u>November 12</u>

Identity: For me doing sports are meaning more than doing some hobbies. I have been doing sports actively since I was 7. At first I started to play basketball but after a year I'd decided to try judo. I did it for 6 years. In addition in elementary school I swam for 8 years. After that I started Duathlon (cycling and running) and I did it for 2 years. Then I began playing football in a professional team (in all my life I've played football). Now I play football about 4 or 5 times a week (at weekends I usually play 2 matches). 2 years ago I've started to play squash (similar to tennis) and I'm really enjoy it. Every year I do some hiking (I walk about 50–100 kilometers/each one) and in the winters I go skiing. In addition I'm a tennis fan and I love to watch tennis in live. This year I was so lucky that I could watch Roger Federer in live.

(Blog #1)

This instance of identity description by a Pazmany Peter University student then was counted as an instance for the category of identities based on a frequent activity/sports and is also listed to have cosmopolitan potential due to its cross-border reference to an international tennis player (see row G in Table 3.1).

All blog sections describing different identities were assigned to specific categories listed in Table 3.1, and each of these descriptive sections were further examined as to whether they contained any type of cosmopolitan potential. To

TABLE 3.1 Identity categories and cosmopolitan identity potential

Identity categories	Frequency in the database		Frequency of cosmopolitan potential	
	Pazmany U.	Davenport U.	Pazmany U.	Davenport U.
Identities based on societal roles or group memberships				
A. Personal relationships (family member, friend)	14	5	3	0
B. Pet owner	4	0	1	0
C. National identity	7	6	6	6
D. Region based identity	5	1	2	0
Identities based on activities				
Main activity				
E. Student	26	11	25	2
F. Employee	3	13	1	0
Free-time activity				
G. Sports	15	7	10	5
H. Hobby	3	4	0	0
I. TV	1	1	1	0
J. Music	4	1	4	1
K. Gaming	2	2	2	2

determine which of the identity categories had the highest potential to represent cosmopolitan identity, I looked for indications in students' descriptions of their specific identities that pointed to loyalties, group memberships, or significant interests reaching beyond national borders. Every instance of identity description that contained some reference to groups, people, practices, or languages that came from outside the national borders of the blog writer was counted as one potential for the representation of cosmopolitan identity. The last two columns in Table 3.1 list the number of blog sections that contained references reaching beyond national borders in each identity category type. After developing the categories and calculating the number of instances in each category, I identified the most frequently represented identity category types containing references that reach beyond national borders are: student identity (27), sports-related identity (15), national identity (12). In the following section, I undertake a detailed analysis of these three identity categories.

Student Identity: Cosmopolitan Elements

The textual references to transnational content under student identity in the blogs allow the categorization of student identity in the database as one identity that can have cosmopolitan potential. Sentences like the following exemplify interests and allegiances beyond borders:

> "I love learning foreign languages (now English and French), and I'm really interested in getting touch with other cultures." (Blog #1)
> "I love watching men's tennis in particular. Roger Federer from Switzerland is in my opinion the best player to ever step foot on a tennis court." (Blog #41)

Of the 27 student identity sections containing transnational elements, 24 were written by Pazmany University students and three were written by Davenport University students. This discrepancy in numbers between the two student groups is most likely connected to the fact that the Pazmany students were all majoring in International Relations, thus as they described their major and its language requirements they inevitably incorporated transnational elements.

Two of the Pazmany University students' blogs contain multimodal data that will constitute a more complex picture of how cosmopolitanism features into representing student identity, so this analysis will focus on these two blogs. Blog #2 and Blog #14 refer to a video on YouTube (golytabortv, 2011) with highly hybrid content. The writer of Blog #4 has embedded this video into his blog site under student identity, while the writer of Blog #14 directs her audience to the video with the link: "We always have fun at the campus and sometimes [sic] we do silly things Check it!" The video is titled *PPKE-BTK Everyday I'm Shufflin* (golytabortv, 2011) and is a remix of the music video popular in 2011 entitled *Party Rock Anthem* by an American electronic dance music band called LMFAO (LMFAOVEVO, 2011). The original video by LMFAO shows many dancers using a shuffling move while the two singers of LMFAO sing and dance along with the group on the streets. The video became viral in 2011; its YouTube page shows more than 620 million views at the end of 2013.

The remix that two Pazmany University students posted on their blog pages (golytabortv, 2011) was created by students of their university the same year at freshman camp. The remix starts out with a young man walking down a sidewalk between university buildings dressed in jeans and also wearing a jeans jacket and a baseball cap put on backwards. He has a boombox in his hand, walks to a set of stairs in the middle of a square, and turns on the music. As soon as the music is on, five dancers appear at the top of the stairs right next to a statue held up by a column and start dancing using the shuffling move. More and more bystanders also become aware of the music and either join the party or form their own little dancing groups around the square. The video ends on the main square with the original group. After the finale, a still image appears that is a modified version of the logo visible on an LMFAO t-shirts (Party Rock Clothing, 2013). This still image contains the major elements of the LMFAO logo with a slightly modified color layout and with an embedded picture of the Pazmany campus' main build-ing. Both the remix video and the final still image are true examples of hybridity because they showcase an American song and dance move in a traditional setting in Hungary and combine visual elements of both contexts to create new meaning. Cosmopolitanism as a social process is often realized in hybrid outcomes in many different domains such as music and visual representations.

While delving into the setting of the remix music video further, an element of hybridity can be uncovered in historical and symbolic connections that gain new meaning with the production of this remix video. For example, the Pazmany university campus square that students chose as the scene for the filming of the video incorporates a row of three statues along a line that cuts across campus from the East to the West. The Kozterkep (2010) website that hosts a digital catalog of sculptures around Hungary explains that these three statues symbolize the country's location and connections between East and West as well as reflect on the country's historical and Christian roots. Filming the remix video at this square thus reinforces that cultural mixture and reinterpretation of texts is something that is natural and has happened in the past as well. What is different in the present is the frequency with which such mixture happens and the widespread availability of technology that allows many people to participate in this process.

Situating the remix video in the contemporary media environment, which Henry Jenkins (2006) calls convergence culture, the relevance of this remix video becomes clear for the transcultural blog exchange project. Jenkins (2006) describes convergence culture as "the flow of content across multiple media platforms, the cooperation between multiple media industries, and the migratory behavior of media audiences" (p. 2) and emphasizes the increased participation of the traditionally passive audience as another key factor in this media culture. In a participatory culture, as Jenkins explains, the consumers of cultural products are actively involved in the creation and distribution of new media content. Active participation is enabled by distribution platforms, such as YouTube, that allow users to create new content and post it on the site. But participation does not stop there. YouTube users can select videos and utilize different digital channels to distribute them. In fact, Jenkins (2006) characterizes participatory culture specifically on YouTube as a three-stage process of "production, selection and distribution" (p. 275).

Thus, while from the blog contents, it cannot be ascertained that the students involved in the remix video production were also students enrolled in the classrooms participating in the blog project, still, the two students who posted a link to the remix of the *Everyday I'm Shufflin* song on their blogs contributed to the selection and distribution (the second and third) stage of sharing a media product with viewers. Taking part in this stage of participatory media culture provides these students with a sense of agency as they spread this remix video with highly hybrid visual content to audiences that otherwise would have been very unlikely to stumble upon this video. Adding a link to the remix video onto the blogs emphasizes what is shared between many students involved in the project who participate in practices of this musical genre's subculture regardless of their country of residence which certainly meets Appiah's (2008) description of cosmopolitanism as "universality plus difference" (p. 92).

The two Davenport University students that listed a student identity with cosmopolitan potential had direct connections with other countries as students. One of the study participants studied international business and gained this interest in international subjects through her family's frequent hosting of exchange students. Her blog section describes how she is intrigued by different countries and cultures and how this propels her to study in a field that might lead to international employment. The other Davenport student whose student identity describes allegiances across borders is an international student from Iceland. Her described experience as a student in a different country embodies the hybridity people often encounter in different cultural settings, which she expresses through the title of her blog "svartahvitu" (meaning: black and white, in Icelandic language) that introduces the three different identities she discusses on her blog. The international student identity described by this student directly connects to the languages she uses as the following quote exemplifies: "I have an Icelandic roommate so I speak Icelandic at home, but at school I only speak and write in English" (Blog #49). Maintaining her first language with her roommate and in the blog title shows that although she embraces the language and context of her new environment she also upholds connections to her origins.

All of the above examples of cosmopolitan potential connected to student identity illustrate that being a student opens up possibilities along which international connections can be forged. This is especially visible in the high level of cosmopolitan potential among the Pazmany Peter students, whose International Relations major, by its definition, directs students' attention outside of the national borders and enables them to build allegiances through foreign languages and international exchange programs. Thus, students who take advantage of the more globally-oriented higher education system that is made available to them with increasing frequency have a higher likelihood of embracing identities that reach across borders.

Sports Identity: Cosmopolitan Elements

The second most common identity category represented on the student blogs that also has a high frequency of cosmopolitan identity potential is connected to sports. As for specific numbers on sports identity, 22 students (15 Pazmany University and seven Davenport University) decided to describe this identity category. To better understand this category, it is important to consider the role sports play in the globalized world. In addition to the countless popular books on different sports and athletes with a global reach and appeal, many academically oriented books on the subject attest to the importance sports have in people's lives around the world (i.e. Maguire, 1999; Bairner, 2001; Chappelet, 2008; Marjoribanks and Farquharson, 2011). In the analysis of blog sections describing a sport related identity, this special role of global sports needs to be taken into consideration.

In order to determine to what extent sports identities have the potential to represent cosmopolitan identity in the blog database, I identified transnational elements in the text and multimodal components in the blog sections describing sports identity. I found that 15 of the 22 blog categories describing this identity contained such elements. Most cross-border references in the blog texts were connected to famous teams (i.e. L.A Lakers, Manchester United), famous players (i.e. Roger Federer, Kobe Bryant), sports organizations (i.e. National Basketball Association (NBA), National Football League (NFL)), other countries and their winter sport locations (Austria, Slovakia) and international competitions (World Cup and Olympic Games). However, in the case of sports identity, the process of determining what counts as a transnational element based on the criterion that it has connections beyond one's national borders can be difficult, and this process resulted in categorizing the same sport reference (i.e. NFL, or an NBA team) as reaching beyond national borders when it was used by Pazmany University students but not when it was used by Davenport University students. Because certain sports with international reach are located in the U.S., these sports listed in the blogs of students living in this country did not count as transnational reference.

According to sociologist Richard Giulianotti (2004), sports have a cross-cultural appeal that is similar to the universal appeal of art and truth. In addition, since sports are based on a set of rules, they are easily transferrable across cultures. As this universal appeal, explains Giulianotti, is strengthened by the coverage provided by global media, new often virtual spaces of sport spectatorship and fandom are created presenting new opportunities for identification. These new forms of identifications are based on choice and are increasingly more deterritorialized as fans of globally popular teams are dispersed across many nations as they share the language of their favorite sport's terminology. Particularly, a small number of sports such as basketball, soccer, and football referred to as "hegemonic sports" by Markovits and Rensmann (2010), have captured the imagination of audiences across the globe and have produced communities that shape identities from the local to the transnational levels.

Often the role of hegemonic sports is depicted as a one-way transfer of cultural commodity from the United States to other parts of the world (see for example Guttman, 1996). Certainly, in my data sample four different students referenced American teams and players at Pazmany University, but players and teams of other countries such as the U.K., Germany, Switzerland, and Japan were also mentioned by these same students and six other Pazmany students. Further, there were five transnational sports references in the blogs of Davenport University students, specifically to Swiss and Serbian sport stars. Regardless of the country of origin of different sports teams, my data shows that the following summary about the cosmopolitan aspects of sports by Markovits and Rensmann holds true: "The cosmopolitanism of sports not only facilitates the universal admirations of the very best – thus generating an everyday sense of global commonality and communality of sports connoisseurs – but it also transforms persistently relevant collective identities" (2010, p. 31).

One multimodal example that shows cross-border allegiances comes from a Pazmany University student that indicated his editorial role of the Hungarian Manchester United Fan Site as an important element of his sports identity in Blog #16. This student's example illustrates the wide array of possible engagements with distant sports teams. In addition, it attests to the newly emerging cosmopolitan aspect of sports as such fan sites provide an arena for a mixing and hybridization of cultural practices and languages. On the fan site, team members and symbols of the British team are displayed together with a mixture of English and Hungarian words. The website not only contains team news for the fan club members but also connects them with each other through discussion forums and social networking sites. All these platforms are sites for fan interaction where the newest line-ups and latest games are discussed with English soccer terminology mixed into the Hungarian commentary.

Another example from a Davenport University student describes her love of tennis. Her post on this sport includes the following statement: "I love watching men's tennis in particular. Roger Federer from Switzerland is in my opinion the best player to ever step foot on a tennis court" (Blog #41). This example shows that it is not necessary just the hegemonic sports (mostly U.S.-based) that have fans in different countries, but that players of other countries also inspire people in the U.S. Thus, allegiances across borders can be formed focused on sports and their top performing players around the world often regardless of the national origin of these players.

Such transcultural involvement in sports is just one way in which participants of the pedagogical project demonstrated how global sports transform identities and create a potential for developing cosmopolitan outlook. These identities that reach beyond one's national borders are difficult to describe within the national paradigm as they reveal multiple allegiances while changing traditional ideas about communities.

The question then becomes whether there is evidence in the database for more traditional communities, such as nations, still maintaining their strong appeal for individuals for the purposes of identification. If students did choose to list this identity as one of their important identities, what kind of necessary elements did they ascribe to this identity as evidenced by the expectations of content and its impact on the verbalization of this identity? To answer these questions, the following section will include a detailed analysis of the blog sections describing national identity.

National Identity: Cosmopolitan Elements

National identity, a sense of belonging to a community called nation, was the third type of identity in the blog database that had a high number of elements indicating cosmopolitan potential. Twelve of the 13 students who decided to represent national identity as one of their significant identities revealed allegiances reaching beyond the borders of their country of residency. Out of the 13 blog sections that described national identity, six were written by students who had resided in the U.S. and seven were written by students who had resided in Hungary at the time of the assignment. The careful language here (using *residency* as a descriptor rather than *nationality*) is associated with the complexity of this category that is illustrated by several blog entries where the national identity described by some students is not the same as their country of residency at the time of the project. Of the six Davenport University students who chose to represent this identity on their blogs, one was an international student from Brazil, two had moved here in their childhood from Europe, one connected to a Polish identity through his grandparents, and two described an American identity. In the group of seven students that attended class in Hungary and described national identity, two students came from ethnic Hungarian minority groups living in the Ukraine and Rumania, one student described herself as having a double Hungarian and Iraqi national identity, another student characterized his identity as simultaneously Hungarian and European, and the remaining three students labeled their identity as Hungarian.

Some of these cross-border references are associated with physical movement of the participants or their ancestors across countries, and some have developed as a direct result of historical events' influence on personal lives. One of the interviewees who gave the title "Best of Both Worlds" to the section where she describes her double national identity explains the reasons behind her title selection as follows: "I'm really into a music and there was a song that was titled 'Best of Both Worlds' and I think it really defined that I'm from two homes, I have two home. I think it . . . I don't know exactly to say it. I think I gained that from my Iraqi side and from my Hungarian side as well. If it makes sense" (Interview #8). Being connected to two worlds/countries was the experience of not only this participant, but also others who described their national identities on the blogs. This shows that lived experience often contributes to encountering hybridity when it comes to one's national identity, as through these experiences it can become difficult for people to pledge allegiance to a singular country.

Indeed, defining one's national identity can be problematic. A common practice for showing connectedness to two nations has been hyphenating the name, such as in Dutch-American. Denoting hybrid national identity this way, however, implies that the person has Dutch ancestry but is primarily American. Further, this type of description does not address whether the person herself has lived in the Netherlands earlier in her life or whether it was just one or both of her parents or perhaps grandparents who moved to the United States. In addition, hyphenating an identity is a nationality imposed on someone based on current residency or citizenship and does not take into account whether that person acknowledges this ascribed identity as his/her own. One example of such a case is from Blog #48 whose writer incorporated his Bosnian-Serb identity into his blog, without referencing his status as American citizen. By claiming a Bosnian-Serb identity without referencing place of current residence (Bosnian-American) this student prioritized his national allegiances.

Other students also illustrated in their blogs the kind of agency one can achieve through naming hybrid national identities. Two Pazmany University students (the writers of Blog #19, and #20) belong to Hungarian minorities that ended up on the other side of the newly defined national borders of Hungary after World War I. Neither of these students describe their identities as hyphenated identities, such as of Ukrainian-Hungarian or Rumanian-Hungarian, because that would mean that at some point in their lives they have been Ukrainian or Rumanian or have acknowledged such an identity. However, both of these students describe a primarily Hungarian identity in their blogs, and through the discussion of official language versus home language on their blog pages it becomes clear that they are forced to live in a different country because of the outcome of historical events.

In order to illustrate how national identity is not only a product of geopolitical contexts but is also a fluid concept recognized as such by the participants, I will provide a more detailed discussion of one student's representation of his dual Hungarian and European identity on the blog. The writer of Blog #22 introduces his blog as follows: "On this blog I would like to show how complex identities can be in Europe. For that purpose, I use my own situation as an example." He then proceeds to introduce his identities by starting out with the Hungarian identity: "First of all, I am Hungarian, that means I use our national language, I think of our history to be mine, too, and I feel that the interests of the nation are my interests, too." This unsolicited definition of national identity as determined by a shared language, history, and interest points to the need displayed by this participant to interpret identity for his individual use. Further, this definition shows that a shared language and history are as prominent elements of the national identity described by the writer of Blog #22 as a shared interest is. To this point, the way this participant represents his identity fits very much into the national framework. But what follows shows a more complex connection picture: "But in the same time I am European. That not only means that I am a citizen of the European Union, but it does mean a strong identity that roots in Europe as cultural and geographical unit" (Blog #22).

Here, the writer of Blog #22 describes a supranational identity, one that emerges as a result of the creation of a unit larger than a nation: the European Union. The writer of Blog #22 can be an example of cosmopolitan identity as he describes a double Hungarian/European identity and thus shows allegiance to a more encompassing group than just a single nation. While on the one hand this double identity is a great example of multiple allegiances reaching across national borders, these two identities, Hungarian citizen and European Union citizen, appear as two different versions of the same "old-fashioned" national identity. In fact, the writer seems to transfer the meaning of national identity to a larger unit, a union of nations even as it is acknowledged by the writer that this transfer does not work to its full extent (it excludes a shared language). A questioning of the strength of a European identity also emerged in the interview conducted with the writer of Blog #22 several months after the end of the blog project. In the interview it was obvious that he understood the problematic nature of proposing a European identity as a supranational category that is based on a national framework, but it was also evident that through this deliberation he became aware of the contextual nature of identities. The process this student encountered exemplifies the complexities that one faces when declaring multiple national allegiances and shows the insights that can be gained from such experiences. Further, this kind of process fosters active engagement with national and cultural similarities and differences and can promote the open-minded curiosity necessary for a cosmopolitan stance.

All of the above examples attest to the difficulty of describing and determining national identity in the contemporary social and geopolitical context. The difficulty comes from the fact that identity description is often attempted within the national framework, when in reality people have many allegiances in many different areas of their lives that reach beyond national borders. In the database, even those students who described their national identity had to refer to countries outside of their place of residency because of physical dislocation or as a result of larger historical events. Thus, the data shows that describing identity within the national framework, in an age when transnational movement in physical and virtual space of people is so prevalent, is becoming rather limiting, and a cosmopolitan framework needs to be adopted to better reflect reality. As can be seen in several identity categories listed by students, many project participants had allegiances reaching beyond borders associated with them. Using the cosmopolitan framework, which allows the coexistence of varied identities that are not connected to the rigid borders of countries offered more possibilities within this specific project for students to express their identities.

Conclusion

While the findings of this study are limited to the specific participants of this online blog collaboration project, these findings can serve as a starting point for discussions that illuminate the limitations of the reductionist sociology of culture (Benhabib, 2002) and of theories that are based upon rigid identity categories and borders. The cosmopolitan framework that was explicitly explained to students at the start of this project enabled participants to see their varied identities as different expressions of their allegiances and allowed them to create a better understanding of the complex interaction of global forces and individual lives as these manifested in their descriptions of identities. Seeing that many of the identity categories students chose to represent and the topics discussed within these categories overlapped regardless of what country participants lived in made it possible for participants to realize what they share with each other and then explore with openness the differences that were present on blog sites.

Thus, the above review of the cosmopolitan potential of three identity types (student identity, sports identity, and national identity) has shown that conceptualizing identity within the cosmopolitan framework has much to offer for a more nuanced understanding of identities involved in transcultural communication over digital networks. This more nuanced understanding has far-reaching implications for research. Specifically, when data analysis starts out by dividing the data into national categories -as is the case in many intercultural rhetoric studies - these categories serve as the basis for reporting results. In other words, the reporting of research results will concentrate on supporting the argument that national differences exist in writing patterns and will neglect the role of individual influences and identities. For this reason, findings from research that pre-categorizes data into national groups will often not include similarities and overlaps that result from the continuous crosspollination of ideas and practices in our global era. The description of similarities resulting from cosmopolitan social change can only be discussed by avoiding nationality as a preexisting category, since the very essence of nations lies in "denying difference internally, while affirming, producing and stabilizing it externally" (Beck, 2006, p. 56).

As cosmopolitanism entails a deemphasizing of territorial-based connections (as indicated by a person's birth place) in many domains, examining phenomena in the cosmopolitan framework necessitates an analytical approach that does not start out by dividing data sets into national categories. This analytical approach is exemplified in this research study by the absence of categories such as "Hungarian students" and "American students" and a lack of generalizations that can be made based on these two categories.

In addition to influencing research methods in technical communication, cosmopolitan principles can also inform teaching practices in the field. The ability to encounter difference with curiosity, and as part of the "universality plus difference" (Appiah, 2008) equation is a quality that global citizens need to have. If technical communication instructors can incorporate into their curriculum the understanding that transcultural and global allegiances are just as important as local connections are, they can successfully implant the values of global citizenship into their students. This can be done through explicit instruction about cosmopolitanism and its principles, and through creating opportunities for students to engage in transcultural collaboration that allows them to directly apply these principles. Based on the fundamental cosmopolitan principle of privileging humanity above local allegiances, students will be able and willing to apply their expertise in communication to the analysis and improvement of global communication processes that exacerbate inequality around the world and neglect to make visible shared interests existing beyond borders.

Due to their cosmopolitan outlook acquired in technical communication classes, students when they enter the workforce will be much better equipped to handle exchanges with their international counterparts as experiences that both parties can equally benefit from. Thus, cosmopolitan theory, or more specifically, cosmopolitan outlook as a competency or capacity to engage diversity with openness should definitely be one of the theories we introduce our students to as it has great potential for immediate application in transcultural interactions that students can transfer to their prospective workplaces.

Discussion Questions

1) When discussing intercultural communication in different contexts, what typically gets foregrounded: challenges and misunderstandings or advantages and collaboration?
2) In what way can shared identities foster dialog about difference?
3) What kind of workplace situations in technical communication lend themselves to a direct application of cosmopolitan principles?
4) What kind of advocacy work can result when someone adopts cosmopolitan principles?
5) What approach would a global citizen take to solve some of the most pressing global issues?

Further Reading

Checkel, J. (2001). Why comply? Social learning and European identity change. *International Organization, 55*(3), 553–588.

Corbett, J. (1996). From dialogue to praxis: Crossing cultural borders in the business and technical communication classroom, *Technical Communication Quarterly, 5*(4), 179–200.

de Andreotti, V. O. (2014). Soft versus critical global citizenship education. In S. McCloskey (Ed.), *Development education in policy and practice* (pp. 21–31). London: Palgrave Macmillan.

Miles, L. (1997). Globalizing Professional Writing Curricula: Positioning Students and Repositioning Textbooks, *Technical Communication Quarterly, 6*, pp. 179–200.

Matveeva. N. (2007). The intercultural component in textbooks for teaching a technical writing service course. *Journal of Technical Writing and Communication, 37*(2), 151–166.

Matveeva. N. (2008). Teaching intercultural communication in a basic technical writing course: A survey of our current practices and methods. *Journal of Technical Writing and Communication, 38*(4), 387–410.

Weiss, T (1992). "Ourselves among others": A new metaphor for business and technical writing, *Technical Communication Quarterly, 1*(3), 23–26.

Weiss, T. (1997). "The Gods must be crazy": The challenge of the intercultural. *Journal of Business and Technical Communication, 7*(2), 196–217.

Yuan, R. (1997). Yin/Yang principle and the relevance of externalism and paralogic rhetoric to intercultural communication, *Journal of Business and Technical Communication, 11*(3), 297–320.

References

All website URLs accessed February 2018.

Agboka, G. (2012). Liberating intercultural technical communication from "large culture" ideologies: Constructing culture discursively. *Journal of Technical Writing and Communication, 42*, 159–181.

Appiah, K. A. (2006). *Cosmopolitanism: Ethics in a world of strangers.* New York, NY: W. W. Norton & Co.

Appiah, K. A. (2008). Education for global citizenship. In D. Coulter, J. Wiens, & G. Fenstermacher (Eds.), *Why do we educate? Renewing the conversation* (pp. 83–99). National Society for the Study of Education.

Bairner, A. (2001). *Sport, nationalism and globalization.* Albany, NY: State University of New York Press.

Beck, U. (2006). *Cosmopolitan vision.* Malden, MA: Polity Press.

Benhabib, S. (2002). *The claims of culture: Equality and diversity in the global era.* Princeton, NJ: Princeton University Press.

Burke, P., & Stets, J. (2009). *Identity theory.* New York, NY: Oxford University Press.

Canagarajah, S. A. (2010, June). *From intercultural rhetoric to cosmopolitan practice.* Plenary speech given at the 6th Annual Conference on Intercultural Rhetoric and Discourse. Atlanta, GA.

Cardon, P. (2008). A critique of Hall's contexting model: A meta-analysis of literature on intercultural business and technical communication. *Journal of Business and Technical Communication, 22*(4), 399–428.

Carter, A. (2006). *The political theory of global citizenship.* New York, NY: Routledge.

Chappelet, J. (2008). *The International Olympic Committee and the Olympic system: The governance of world sport.* New York, NY: Routledge.

Delanty, G. (2012). A cosmopolitan approach to the explanation of social change: Social mechanisms, processes, modernity. *The Sociological Review, 60*(2), 333–354.

Golytabortv. (2011, August 25). *PPKE-BTK Everyday I'm Shufflin* [Video file]. Retrieved from http://www.youtube.com/watch?v=J6XuRf7UrLM.

Giulianotti, R. (2004). *Sport: A critical sociology.* Malden, MA: Polity Press.

Guttmann, A. (1996). Games and empires: Modern sports and cultural imperialism. New York, NY: Columbia University Press.

Hannerz, U. (1990). Cosmopolitans and locals in world culture. *Theory, Culture & Society, 7*, 237–251.

Hunsinger, R. P. (2006) Culture and cultural identity in intercultural technical communication. *Technical Communication Quarterly,15*(1), 31–48.

Jameson, D. (2007). Reconceptualizing cultural identity and its role in intercultural business communication. *Journal of Business Communication, 44*(3), 199–235.

Jenkins, H. (2006). *Convergence culture.* New York, NY: New York University Press.

Kankaanranta, A., & Louhiala-Salminen, L. (2011). Professional communication in a global business context: The notion of global communicative competence. *IEEE Transactions on Professional Communication, 54*(3), 244–262.

Kelly, K. (2014). American's changing perceptions of Indian cultural identity: An analysis of Indian call centers. In M. Williams & O. Pimentel (Eds.), *Communicating Race, Ethnicity and Identity in Technical Communication* (pp. 135–152). Amityville, NY: Baywood.

Kozterkep (2010) Szent Istvan szobor. Retrieved from: www.kozterkep.hu/~/11129/Szent_Istvan_szobor_Piliscsaba_2000.html#

Leon, K., & Pigg, S. (2011). Graduate students professionalizing in digital time/space: A view from down below. *Computers and Composition, 28*, 3–13.

LMFAOVEVO. (2011, March 8). LMFAO – Party Rock Anthem ft. Lauren Bennett, GoonRock [Video file] www.youtube.com/watch?v=KQ6rz6kCPj8

Maguire, J. (1999). *Global sport: Identities, societies and civilizations.* Cambridge: Polity Press.

Marjoribanks, T., & Farquharson, K. (2011). *Sport and society in the global age.* London: Palgrave Macmillan.

Markovits, A., & Rensmann, L. (2010). *Gaming the world.* Princeton, NJ: Princeton University Press.

Maylath, B., Vandepitte, S., & Mousten, B. (2008). Growing grassroots partnerships: Trans-Atlantic collaboration between American instructors and students of technical writing and European instructors and students of translation. In D. Starke-Meyerring & M. Wilson (Eds.), *Designing Globally Networked Learning Environments: Visionary partnerships, policies, and pedagogies* (pp. 52–66). Rotterdam: Sense

Medina, C. (2014). Tweeting collaborative identity: Race, ICTs, and performing Latinidad. In M. Williams & O. Pimentel (Eds.), *Communicating race, ethnicity and identity in technical communication* (pp. 63–86). Amityville, NY: Baywood.

MUSC Hungary (2014). Manchester United Soccer Club Hungary. Retrieved June 21, 2014 from www.manutd.hu

Palmer, Z. (2013). Cosmopolitanism: Extending our theoretical framework for transcultural technical communication research and teaching. *Journal of Technical Writing and Communication, 43*(4), 381–401.

Party Rock Clothing (2013). Unisex *Everyday I'm Shufflin* tee. Retrieved January 1, 2014 from https://partyrockclothing.com

Pieterse, J. (2001). Hybridity, so what? *Theory, Culture, and Society, 18*(2–3), 1–27.

Starke-Meyerring, D. (2005). Meeting the challenges of globalization: A framework for global literacies in professional communication programs. *Journal of Business and Technical Communication, 19*(4), 468–499

Starke-Meyerring, D. (2010). Globally networked learning environments in professional communication: Challenging normalized ways of learning, teaching and knowing. *Journal of Business and Technical Communication, 24*(3), 59–266.

St.Amant, K. (2011). Thinking globally, teaching locally: Understanding the changing nature of technical communication in the age of globalization. In B. Thatcher & K. St.Amant (Eds.), *Teaching intercultural rhetoric and technical communication: Theories, curriculum, pedagogies and practices* (pp. 1–11). Amityville, NY: Baywood

Vertovec, S., & Cohen, R. (2002). Introduction: conceiving cosmopolitanism. In S. Vertovec & R. Cohen (Eds.), *Conceiving cosmopolitanism: Theory, context, and practice* (pp. 1–22). Oxford: Oxford University Press.

Walton, R. (2013). Civic engagement, information technology, & global contexts. *Connexions. An International Professional Communication Journal, 1*(1), 147–154.

Wang, J. (2010). Convergence in the rhetorical pattern of directness in Chinese and U.S. business letters. *Journal of Business and Technical Communication, 24*(1), 91–120.

Wei, Z. (2010). Blogging for doing English digital: Student evaluations. *Computers and Composition, 27*, 266–283.

Wysocki, A. (2013, March). *Analyzing multimodal data.* A handout at the ATTW Research Methods workshop in Las Vegas, NV.

Yi, Y., & Hirvela, A. (2010). Technology and self-sponsored writing: A case-study of a Korean American Adolescent. *Computers and Composition, 27*, 94–111.

4

BUILDING THE BABEL OF TRANSNATIONAL LITERACIES

Preparing Education for World Citizens

Xiaobo Wang

Introduction

Our obligation as professional communication scholars to pursue public good in a global context, and students' participation in information technology for development are vital to contemporary advocacy in public spheres (Walton 2013: pp. 149 & 151). Ding and Savage (2013) suggest that teacher training, curriculum design, textbooks, and teaching materials should emphasize the importance of intercultural communication skills; the role and impact of mass media, new media, and the Internet in intercultural and multicultural communication should be also stressed. Matsuda and Matsuda (2011) propose to "reimagine students in the classroom as citizens of the world" (p. 189), which resonates with Thrush and Thevenot's (2011) claim of the dual task of teaching "students native to the United States the complexities of international and multicultural communication," and developing English skills of "nonnative speakers of English" (p. 65).

In addition to the intercultural and global concerns of technical communication, Eble and Gaillet (2004) call for humanistic concerns in our teaching (pp. 341–342) and state that the classical ideas of rhetoric, moral philosophy, and civic engagement are inseparable in educating "community intellectuals" (p. 353). Similarly, Ornatowski and Bekins (2004) highlight the significance of "moral imagination" in contemporary capitalist globalization in terms of how technical communication professionals impact communities of various scales (p. 267). In this regard, deliberative rhetoric with conscience and humanistic spirit of conflict solving could be the answer to pedagogies and practices of technical communication as a civic discourse (Ornatowski and Bekins, 2004: p. 251), which relates to the very idea of citizenship and advocacy. Increasingly cross-cultural, cross-disciplinary, and cross-organizational contexts require us to cultivate students' advocacy of the marginalized and the under-resourced communities with methodologies from diverse perspectives and epistemologies to understand and promote social justice (Walton and Jones 2013: pp. 31–33). In this chapter, my goal is to cultivate cosmopolitan citizens with the awareness, tolerance, literacy, and competence of addressing the complexities, conflicts, and violence in the contemporary transnational world. Recent cases such as the UK's "Brexit" from the EU has proven that many citizens do not have the kind of literacy that is needed in the information era, notably, the case of British citizens searching on Google to find out what EU means (Selyukh, 2016).

With the transnational context in mind, I respond to the complaint that textbooks have insufficient examples of intercultural technical communication and writing (Matveeva, 2008). For this purpose, I encourage students and professionals of technical communication and the general public to become better citizens of not only their own country, but also of the world in this post-modern, late capitalist, and digital era. My preliminary empirical study (that is not presented here) has revealed expectations, reflections, challenges, and current practices among administrators, instructors, and students of technical communication, which lays a basis for the transnational rhetoric and communication model and textbook analysis in this chapter. I have coded my model to examine and analyze theoretical frameworks and pedagogical practices reflected in the most popular technical communication textbooks. Finally, I discuss and envision future curriculum, textbook, and pedagogical designs to cultivate students' transnational literacy and morality of world citizenship.

Textbook analysis literature is scarce compared to current theories, models, and pedagogies in the field of intercultural rhetoric and communication. The goal of this chapter is to build a new theoretical model through the sampling and rhetorical analysis of twelve textbooks, five of which are presented due to space limit. I have collected a range of technical and professional communication and writing textbooks by reading the discussions about textbooks from the Association of Teachers of Technical Writing (ATTW) and the Conference of the Council for Programs in Technical and Scientific Communication (CPTSC) mailing lists, by searching online and in-library databases, and by visiting publishers' websites and booth exhibitions at the Conference on College Composition and Communication (CCCC), ATTW, Rhetoric Society of America (RSA) and other conferences. Because the in-depth rhetorical analysis of major and popular textbooks demonstrated gaps in teaching and research of transnational rhetoric and communication, I offer suggestions on potential theoretical and pedagogical revisions.

The chapter addresses the following research questions:

- How are transnational rhetoric and communication framed and presented in introductory technical communication/writing textbooks published in the United States?

- To what extent do they present transnational and international issues, if at all?
- Do the textbooks help students to become transnational literate technical communicators?

Cosmopolitanism and World Citizenship: Then and Now

The concept of "cosmopolitanism" can be traced to Plato's *Protagoras*, in which the Sophist Hippias addresses both Athenians and foreigners at Callias' house:

> "Gentlemen present . . . I regard you all as kinsmen, familiars, and fellow-citizens—by nature and not by convention; for like is by nature akin to like, while convention, which is a tyrant over human beings, forces many things contrary to nature."
>
> (337c7–d3)

Hippias' speech on the awareness and brotherhood of his own fellow-citizens and foreign citizens, therefore, is the first argumentation on the cosmopolitan ideal, which is significant to the contemporary world of plurality, fragmentation, conflicts, clashes, and many challenging issues of globalization.

Contemporarily, Fine (2007) states that cosmopolitanism poses challenges to the postmodern exclusion of the "Other" (pp. 133–135). The critical issue, according to Fine, is how to make the postmodern natural law an ethical and critical space where the rights of all human beings will be fulfilled (p. 141). Kemp (2011) also proposes cosmopolitanism as an answer to globalization, and he unfolds that cosmopolitanism continues to be the political, social, and educational ideal despite the anti-global capitalism movements that are actually anti-economic globalization, rather than against cultural and human globalization (pp. 41–45). Therefore, cosmopolitanism is vital in connecting nations as cultural entities and offers a sustainable dimension that will help not only our own generation, but also our successors in terms of social, scientific, economic, legal, ethical, unification, responsibility, and related issues (Kemp 2011: pp. 49–97).

Cosmopolitan Pedagogy: Moral Education and "Bildung" Formation in Writing Classrooms

Cosmopolitanism is, first and foremost, an educational mission. It is related to the moral education of citizens: their "Bildung," coming-of-age, or formation. The formation of contemporary world citizens requires us to help students and the public to become genuine world citizens, an ideal educational state (Kemp 2011: p. 147). Philosophically, cultivation, transformation, and Bildung are all equals and interrelated in terms of the responsibility for oneself and others in the globalized world (Kemp 2011: pp. 152–168). Further, education, or "moral training" (Kemp 2011: p. 165), is of vital importance in contemporary cosmopolitan practice and cosmopolitanism should not be confined to narrow patriotism if the latter means blind obedience to local loyalties rather than global responsibilities (Hooft, 2009: p. 54). Sobré-Denton and Bardhan (2013) propose to cultivate cosmopolitanism for intercultural communication, arguing that the cosmopolitan pedagogy helps human beings to understand themselves through the lens of others (p. 149).

Introducing the Transnational Rhetoric and Communication Model

The transnational rhetoric and communication model will be useful in transnational contexts based on Association of Teachers of Technical Writing (ATTW), National Committee of Teachers of English (NCTE), and Institute of Electrical and Electronics Engineers (IEEE) code of ethics, mission statements, goals, and vision statements. Moreover, this model is also based on the similarities and differences between and among the "intercultural," "comparative," and "transnational" in several overlapping disciplines.

Intercultural rhetoric was proposed by Ulla Connor (Connor, 2004: p. 312) to replace "contrastive rhetoric," and Connor thinks "intercultural rhetoric" studies can include both cross-cultural and intercultural studies. Contrastive rhetoric belongs to research on English as a second language (ESL) and English as a foreign language (EFL) in that it focuses on how a human being's first language and culture interfere with his or her writing in a second or foreign language. The term "contrastive rhetoric" was first coined in 1966 by Robert Kaplan, applied linguist, and widely expanded from 1996 to today by Connor, among others. Contrastive rhetoric brings attention to cultural and linguistic differences in the writing of English L2 students. Coincidentally, Connor adopts the postmodern mapping framework in order to conceptualize contrastive and intercultural rhetoric (2004: p. 305). Further, Connor stresses Gidden's structural theory in that it helps understand the ever-changing genres, models, and social practices (p. 306).

In June 2013, comparative rhetoric was defined in "A Manifesto: The What and How of Comparative Rhetoric" at the Rhetoric Society of America (RSA) Summer Institute Workshop:

> Comparative rhetoric examines communicative practices across time and space by attending to historicity, specificity, self-reflexivity, processual predisposition, and imagination. Situated in and in response to globalization, comparative rhetoricians enact perspectives/performances that intervene in and transform dominant rhetorical traditions, perspectives, and practices. As an interdisciplinary practice, comparative rhetoric

intersects with cognate studies and theories to challenge the prevailing patterns of power imbalance and knowledge production.

Regarding methodology, according to the Manifesto, comparative rhetoric practices the art of recontextualization characterized by a navigation among and beyond an outright rejection of assumed parity, equivalence, difference, or similarity and a readiness for interdependence and heterogeneous resonance without eliding power imbalance, and so on (Mao et al. 2015: pp. 273–274).

Transnational rhetorical studies started with transnational feminist rhetoric (Dingo, 2012) with networking arguments that investigate how women's lives are shaped by policy arguments. The "trans" before "national" indicates a state of being and a process that exists and happens between and among nation states. However, transnational phenomena can happen within one nation state when people migrate because national belonging, nationality(ies), and places of dwelling can intertwine together. For instance, a Latina's literacy can be studied as transnational and translingual literacy when it involves the nations where the languages originated from and the places/nation-states where the speaker lived (Farr, 1994: pp. 65–66). Schiller, et al. (1992) argue that the experience and consciousness of the migrant population can be called "transnationalism"[1]. They define transnationalism as a process during which immigrants build social fields that link their country of origin and their country of settlement together. The migrant population was referred to as "transmigrants."

Transnationalism can also be understood as a product of world capitalism (Block, 1987: p. 136; Nash and Fernandez, 1983; Wakeman, 1988), the result of cultural flow (Appadurai and Breckenridge, 1988; Hannerz, 1989) and as social relations (Portes and Walton, 1981: p. 60; Rouse, 1988, 1989). Dingo considers "transnational" as "networks of global institutions, supranational organizations, and nation-states" (p. 144). Owing to transnational references to address issues in fields such as international relations, global epidemics, economic stability, environmental protection, and so on, transnational rhetoric and communication tends to shed a more political and activist light on global issues, e.g., the wide spread of global communication technology and the growing economic and political interdependency, non-governmental organizations (NGOs) (Dingo 2012), etc.

I use a transnational framework to address and cope with the challenges brought forth by global capitalism, information flow and contra flow, and technological innovations, which are the result of informal and nonofficial networks, movements and exchanges among national populations (Wakeman, 1988: p. 87). Further, these issues are all embedded with postcolonial, racial, and/or rhetorical contexts. For instance, I am concerned about how postmodern identities and subjectivities are shaped, and troubled by increasing collisions of ideologies due to postcolonial influences, and world order established after World War II. I apply the comparative rhetorical framework to look at transnational texts and contexts as a way to intervene in postcolonial power dynamics and investigate the possibilities of a cosmopolitan agency in a world with overwhelming technologies and media. I explore the possible ethics, spirituality, and creativity that can be used in the teaching of technical communication to address contemporary schizophrenic rhetorical situations that are frequently associated with the growingly unavoidable but narrow-minded nationalism.

Based on, but different from, Thatcher's onion model of rhetoric and communication that excludes the postmodern subject, this model should first have a compartmental subject, which is caused by postmodern clashes of civilizations, fragmentation of the context and text, as well as the technologies (mass media, new media, artificial intelligence, and so on) in the postmodern and posthuman era; secondly, this subject, whereas being a transnational site of communication both vertically and horizontally, negotiates meanings with other subjects who are either solo cultural beings or multicultural beings; thirdly, the subjects of transnational rhetoric and communication model negotiate inside or outside themselves within different contexts.

I follow Jameson (1980) and McGee's (1991 & 1992) postmodern fragmentation frameworks that focus on how to interpret fragmented rhetorical texts and contexts. I argue that it is not only possible for postmodern and posthuman subjects to carry out intercultural and cross-cultural communication, but also promising for them to integrate the fragmented subjectivities, texts, and contexts, providing the literacy and competence in transnational rhetoric and communication. I built this model to inform the challenges that we are facing as a result of emerging technologies. For the purpose of this investigation, I have to relate to other transnational rhetoric and communication variables or codes that I include here in this model, especially how identities, media, as well as technology, are similar and different on both national and international levels. Because adapting digital communication across national borders evolves cultural differences regarding purpose, audience, information needs, organizational strategies, style preferences, and when associated with different national and international digital media, cosmopolitan approach offers a universal frame for approaching technical communication with humanistic ethics. It takes compassion, love, care, and responsibility for each other as world citizens in order to apply the transnational rhetoric and communication model in that a global vision is at the top of all sustainable and ethical communication.

Dingo (2013) regards postmodern subjects as agencies dealing with complex information in transnational literacies. Using space and time, two essential concepts in postmodern texts and contexts, I elaborate the integration tasks postmodern subjects will have to cope with providing the collapse of both in a fragmented reality. I assert that the collapse of time and space is a subjective victory of the stream-of-consciousness trend and the defeat of the overwhelming knowledge and information throughout our history.

As discussed above, transnational rhetoric is political because the word "nation" is politically charged. Secondly, it enables us to look at global rhetoric from the deliberative aspect of rhetoric, digging into the deeper structures of cultures, nations, and peoples. Thirdly, transnational rhetoric and communication is inherently cosmopolitan owing to the essential cosmopolitan values of "trans," such as awareness of others, compassion, love, care, and service beyond national borders. I am using the term "self" instead of "subject" because what I am trying to achieve is the competency of transnational literacies within the identity of world citizen. See Figure 4.1.

Therefore, awareness from the self, i.e., self-awareness, is the first and foremost issue involved in the transnational rhetoric and communication model. I am not repeating the traditional cultural variables used in inter- and cross-cultural rhetoric and communication because what I am highlighting is the national/international binary, which is crucial to identity formation, and the coming-of-age of world citizens in general. However, it will be more challenging for the postmodern and posthuman subject to become a genuine world citizen due to the increasing emergence of technologies, media, and the fast speed of information exchange. Therefore, it will be helpful to look at how these subjects interact between and among themselves (Figure 4.2).

For the purpose of this study, I relate to key transnational rhetoric and communication variables such as identities, media, as well as technology. In Figure 4.2, the interaction among postmodern and posthuman subjects requires transnational literacies on one's and others' national and international identities, national and international media, and national and international technology.

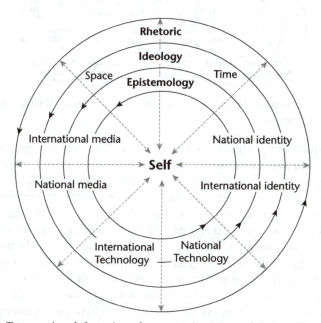

FIGURE 4.1 Transnational rhetoric and communication model: the self

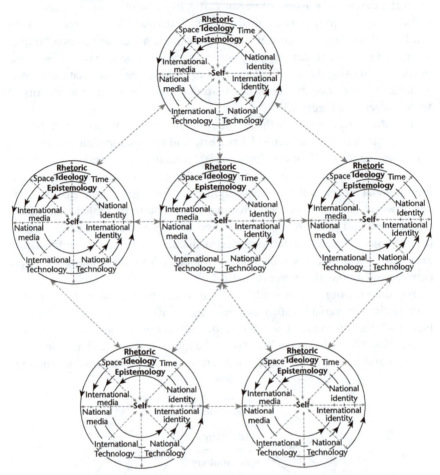

FIGURE 4.2 Transnational rhetoric and communication model: interaction among postmodern subjects

It also requires the subjects to know very well the others' epistemologies, ideologies, and how these two are reflected with rhetorical patterns that are not necessarily the same with the subjects' own ways of communication.

Also, the postmodern and posthuman subjects have to horizontally and vertically learn and examine the historical and contemporary rhetorical patterns, epistemologies, and ideologies carried with the national and international media, technologies, and identities. Therefore, in the interaction among the postmodern subjects, if any party lacks the transnational literacy needed in the above-mentioned areas, the communication will not be smooth, and misunderstandings and even conflicts and violence may happen. Because adapting digital communication across national borders involves cultural differences regarding purpose, audience, information needs, organizational strategies, style preferences, and when associated with different national and international digital media, the cosmopolitan approach offers a universal frame for approaching technical communication with humanistic ethics.

In Figure 4.2, I use dashed lines with arrows in this model to illustrate open ended possibilities among the subjects and their interior growth, thinking patterns, and the open dynamics among their identities, transnational media, technology, time, and space. I use solid lines to signify the layered relationships among epistemology, ideology, and rhetoric. The arrows illustrate directions of communication and flow of information, thinking patterns, technology, identities, and transnational time and space. I draw the six subjects and then connect them together, illustrating their interactions and communication. I have used this model to generate abstract and operational codes/variables for data analysis, which other instructors, administrators, and students can apply in their teaching, administration, and learning process. I borrowed from Thatcher's onion model the layers of self, epistemology, ideology, and rhetoric because I agree with the relationship among epistemology, ideology, and rhetoric and how they together shape a person's way of knowing, communication, and behaviors in general. My transnational model is different from Thatcher's model in that it visually presents how the self/subject resides and reacts towards national and international media and technology, and how the self/subject's identity is shaped by postmodern collapse of space and time transnationally. In this new model, the subject interacts with others' using his/her own national epistemology, ideology, and rhetoric. The transnational interaction and learning process then gradually shapes the subjects into world citizens with transnational literacy on each other's epistemology, ideology, and rhetoric from learning from each other's identities, media, and technology.

In order to evaluate and analyze the textbooks I have chosen, I have drawn code sets from the theoretical frames I adopt. I have also developed the more general and abstract codes in my transnational rhetoric and communication model into operational variables that can be used to conduct textbook analysis. In addition, I have cross-tracked indexes, references, page numbers, and most importantly, theoretical frameworks and pedagogical practices in the content of each textbook I conduct rhetorical analysis with.

Rhetorical Analysis of Textbooks

The research methodology of this chapter is informed by theory and rhetorical analysis based on both qualitative and quantitative data collected in the preliminary, institutional empirical study (empirical data is not presented in this chapter). The rhetorical analysis of five among the altogether twelve textbooks is based on the transnational rhetoric and communication model I have built above, using variables generated from the model. In the next section, before I offer my rhetorical analysis of the textbooks chosen, I present the method and process I used when selecting the textbooks.

Choosing Textbooks for Analysis

To choose the textbooks for my analysis, I collected a range of technical and professional communication and writing textbooks by reading the discussions about textbooks from Association of Teachers of Technical Writing (ATTW) and Conference of the Council for Programs in Technical and Scientific Communication (CPTSC) mailing lists, by searching online and in library databases, and by visiting publishers' websites and booth exhibitions at the Conference on College Composition and Communication (CCCC), the ATTW conference, the Biennial Conference of Rhetoric Society of America (RSA), and other conferences. I have also conducted survey questionnaires and interviews with students who are taking and/or have taken technical communication and writing classes; instructors who are teaching and/or have taught technical communication and writing courses; and administrators from different departments, who have experience in designing curriculum and assigning textbooks in technical communication and writing at a southeastern university.

I will first unfold abstract/overriding (more abstract and general) codes, operational codes (concrete codes used to operate the analysis), as well as specific codes (words, examples that represent the operational codes) for the textbook analysis. Due to space limit, this chapter will only include five of the twelve major textbooks under concern (the most republished or the most adopted textbooks in the southern, PhD granting university):

- *Technical Communication Today* (Johnson-Sheehan, R., 4th edition, 2011, Pearson)
- *Technical Communication* (Markel, M., 11th edition, 2012, Bedford/ St. Martin's)
- *Technical Communication* (Lannon, J. M., & Gurak, L. J., 14th edition, 2016, Pearson)
- *Technical Communication: A Reader-Centered Approach* (Anderson, P., 6th edition, 2007, Wadsworth Publishing)
- *Writing That Works* (Oliu, W. E., Brusaw, C. T., & Alfred, G. J., 12th edition, 2016, Bedford/St. Martin's)

Whereas some of the editions will already be dated by the publication of this chapter, instructors and students might still be using older editions due to various reasons, such as the prices of such textbooks.

Developing Codes for Textbook Analysis

In order to evaluate and analyze the chosen textbooks, I developed code sets according to the theoretical frames I designed so that the rhetorical analysis of the textbooks can be easier to understand. Specifically, I developed the more general and abstract codes in my transnational rhetoric and communication model into operational codes that could be used to conduct textbook analysis. Then I cross-tracked indexes, references, page numbers, and most importantly, theoretical frameworks and pedagogical practices in the content of each textbook I analyzed.

Abstract/Overriding Codes

I identified eight abstract/overriding codes in the transnational rhetoric and communication model, which I used to describe the current status quo of global/international/transnational rhetoric and communication on a more abstract, theoretical level. They are as follows: Space, Time, Identity, Epistemology, Ideology, Rhetoric, Technology, and Media. However. These codes could be further classified into operational codes that would be illustrated by the exact terms as the codes themselves, or specific codes that can be directly applied in textbooks analysis.

Operational Codes and Definitions

"Space" in the transnational sense will be defined/split into international, global, transnational, national, interpersonal, mapping and other kinds of spatial definitions and terminologies that define the distance and space between and among countries and people. "Time" to a transnational extent will be defined/split into different definitions of time such as historical perspectives, time zones, and values toward time, etc. "Identity" refers to both international and national identities, and most importantly transnational identity when a subject is looked at from different, transnational, and ideological perspectives: for instance, double national identities such as dual citizenship, multicultural identity, world citizenship, global citizenship, etc. "Epistemology" as the justification of knowledge can mean very different things in different cultures, nations, and within different identities. "Ideology" can be categorized into national and international ideologies, ideologies from different parties and social systems (democratic, republican, communist, socialist, capitalist, etc.). "Rhetoric" as the exterior expression of epistemology and ideology, can therefore use different appeals such as pathos, ethos, logos, as well as persuasive patterns. "Technology" means a myriad of platforms, tools, methods, and issues that surround surveillance, access, and even human rights. For instance, smartphones, i-Pads, apps, privacy settings, VPN, etc., can mean different rhetoric and ways of communication in different cultures. "Media" in the contemporary world is multidimensional and multifocal, with many issues that the designers, journalists, reporters, and other stakeholders impose on the audience. This means the audience will have to keep a critical distance from the kinds of information that media provides. National/international media represents the cultures, ideologies, and epistemologies that frame them; therefore, information flow can be an overwhelming obstacle for the audience to discern the truth. In this way, the rapid flow of information, the multifaceted nature of media and the tremendous amount of information on the Internet impose on the "self/subject" an unprecedented task. He or she will have to consider time and space, national boundaries, cultural factors, and other complex systems, even before understanding the information he or she receives on a daily basis.

Based on the values and concepts in my model, as well as the position statements and policies from the National Council of Teachers of English (NCTE), ATTW, UN, and other major transnational organizations, as well as the data gathered from the preliminary empirical study, I have summarized these codes into Table 4.1 to better serve the textbook analysis from both theoretical and practical perspectives. Only the following variables were used in the textbook analysis, whereas variables/codes in Table 4.2 were used in the empirical study. There are four major categories or dimensions of the transnational rhetoric and communication variables, or codes I used to analyze the textbooks: world citizenship, literacy, media, and traditional cultural dimensions.

TABLE 4.1 Codes of transnational rhetoric and communication model

Overriding codes	Operational codes		Specific codes	Examples
Rhetoric	Media	International Media	Global broadcasting companies, news agencies, etc.	CNN, BBC, VOA, etc.
		National Media	Local broadcasting companies	CCTV (Chinese version), Georgia Public Broadcasting, etc.
	Technology	International Technology	Social media, telecommunications, the Internet, etc.	Facebook, Twitter, WhatsApp, etc.
		National Technology		"Baidu," "CNKI," "China mobile," etc.
	Identity	International Identity	Nationality, cross border identity, etc.	"American," "German," "Japanese," "international student"
		National Identity	African American, native American, American Chinese, etc.	People of color, ethnicity, transgender, etc.

TABLE 4.2 Transnational rhetoric and communication variables

Category	Overriding variables	Operational variables
World Citizenship Dimension	international travel	visa application, passport politics, international flights, etc.
	borders	passing customs, borders, border checks, etc.
	citizenships	nationalities, dual citizenship, etc.
	tolerance and compassion	awareness, willingness, care, love, understanding, be an active listener, etc.
	humanistic dimensions	refugee, asylum, immigration, etc.
	virtual travel	doing search and research on the Internet, communicate globally online, engage in online events and activities, etc.
Literacy Dimension	ethnicity	Asian (Korean American, Japanese American, etc.), African American, etc.
	race	European (German, Irish, etc.), African, Asian, Hispanic, etc.
	class	middle class, working class, etc.
	gender	male, female, transgender
	history	world history, national history, local (city, town, etc.) history, racial history, etc.
	politics	world politics, national politics, regional politics, family politics, gender politics, etc.
	ethics	global ethics, national ethics, racial ethics, cultural ethics, etc.
Media Dimension	national and international media	various media platforms: BBC, CNN, NYT, WSJ, China Daily, etc.
	speed	information flow, Internet, WiFi, mobile data plan, etc.
	simulations	signs and symbols that represent truth/fallacy: words, phrases, ideographs, collage, pastiche, mimes, etc.
	ideological stances of media	left, right, Christian, liberal, LGBTQ, capitalist, socialist, etc.
	surveillance	firewall, virtual private network (vpn), etc.
	fragmentation	division of labor, overwhelming information, segmented identities, digital borders, etc.
	intersubjectivity	middle ground of subjects, shared identities, ideas, practices

(continued)

TABLE 4.2 Transnational rhetoric and communication variables *(continued)*

Category	Overriding variables	Operational variables
	intertextuality	translation, mistranslation, comparative rhetorical and communication studies, etc.
Traditional Cultural Dimension	political systems	American political system, European political system, communist/socialist political system
	communication pattern	direct, indirect
	power distance	institutional hierarchy, family hierarchy, gender hierarchy, etc.
	individualism vs. collectivism	behavioral patterns (individual, collective) of cultural groups
	masculinity vs. femininity	gender relations, gender issues, gender equality, etc.
	uncertainty avoidance	communication patterns, comfortable level of rejection, directness, etc.
	values on time	long-term orientation vs. short-term orientation
	cultural negotiations of English language	World Englishes (Singaporean English, Chinese English), plain English, etc.

Classifying and categorizing textbook contents

In order to analyze textbook data as well as survey data (not presented here), and interview data (not presented here), so that the analysis would answer my research questions on whether current practices help students to become genuine world citizens with transnational awareness and responsibilities, and whether current pedagogies cultivate students' transnational literacy, skills, and competence, I looked at the following:

1) Are there transnational theoretical and pedagogical frameworks in the chosen textbooks?
2) Do these textbooks mention World Englishes, multilingualism, as well as transnational cultural contexts and transnational literacy practices?
3) What cultural and national variables do these textbooks use to guide transnational communication?
4) Whether, or to what extent do the textbooks relate transnational literacy through multimedia and new media literacy?

Therefore, the analysis focused both on the process and the product with in-depth rhetorical inquiries regarding world citizenship, transnational literacy, and critical thinking of media from a world citizenship perspective. Additionally, classical models and variables were also weighed to evaluate theoretical perspectives and the pedagogical applications in these textbooks—especially when they were intertwined with new variables from the new model.

In addition, I applied active and positive connections between the textbook content and the new variables in the transnational rhetoric and communication model to avoid potential misinterpretation of the textbooks' design and potential. For instance, if the textbooks mentioned active listening, listening, comparing cultures, and/or interview, I categorized them into the "tolerance and compassion" variable in "world citizenship dimension," for such approaches would naturally stimulate dialogues and, therefore, lead the instructors and students to go beyond national and cultural borders. If the textbooks encouraged students to search and/or research on the Internet under global/international context, I categorized them into "virtual travel" in the "world citizen dimension." However, if there was zero mentioning of the key operational variables—for example, when textbooks only mention online meeting and/or collaboration online, but did not specifically talk about culture and/or national differences—then I considered the content of "virtual travel" as negative. Similarly, if textbooks had content on any possibility of students learning about different cultures, peoples, histories—such as interview and/or comparative study projects—I categorized them into the "tolerance and compassion" variable in "world citizenship dimension," and/or "race," ethnicity," "class" in "Literacy Dimension." Nevertheless, such categorization might end up romanticizing classroom instructions and learning processes, when in reality this variable depended on what instructions were given to students and what their learning processes might be. My pedagogical evaluation approach was mainly a rhetorical analysis based on the kind of assignments and projects that the textbooks designed and what kind of teaching goals they would achieve. Finally, the evaluation of transnational rhetoric and communication variables focused on whether or not such goals would be able to cultivate world citizens with transnational awareness, literacy, and competence, as well as cosmopolitan traits and responsibilities.

Results and Analysis

Tolerance, Care, Compassion, and Active Listening

Technical Communication Today (2011) considers listening and learning as the key to intercultural and cross-cultural communication. It offers four strategies to listen to and learn intercultural and cross-cultural communication:

- listen carefully,
- be polite,
- research the target culture, and
- talk to your colleagues (p. 36).

Overall, it suggests students observe and listen to what others do and say in different cultures, encourages them to do research into the expectations in other cultures, and learn from mistakes. It also assigns website analysis from different cultures, traditional intercultural communication variables (indirectness vs. directness, collectivism vs. individualism, etc.), and writing a white paper on the persuasive strategies in different cultures (pp. 61 & 138–141). Therefore, this textbook's pedagogical approach is close to the kind of tolerance and compassion in cosmopolitan pedagogy.

Mike Markel's *Technical Communication* offers political, economic, social, religious, educational, technological, and linguistic variables when providing traditional intercultural variables such as individualism vs. collectivism (p. 92). However, this textbook uses a U.S.-centered approach when teaching intercultural rhetoric and communication in that it offers the U.S. way of listening and speaking habits, such as eye contact, without addressing the needs of audiences from other rhetorical traditions (pp. 710–712). It also suggests native speakers use short, easy, and concise words, phrases, and sentences for a multilingual audience (pp. 98–99 & 710–712), which has an implied precondition that multilingual communicators are somehow incompetent in English communication.

John Lannon and Laura Gurak's *Technical Communication* follows IEEE code of global ethics and states in its communication guideline "think globally" at the end of each chapter, which gestures towards awareness, literacy, tolerance, and compassion. *Technical Communication: A Reader-Centered Approach* requires students to think about the audience's cultural background (p. 6), encourages students to think about human consequences of communication (pp. 222–223), teaches the use of inclusive language (pp. 276–277), and addresses the importance of cultural diversity by looking at the readers' backgrounds and expectations, as well as high and low context (pp. 76–82, 109–110, & 432–433). *Writing That Works* offers an evaluation form on collaborative projects and requires students to carry out interviews with collaborators from different cultures.

In general, the existing efforts in these textbooks indicate some characteristics that promote and encourage tolerance, awareness, understanding, and willingness, whereas such efforts are far from enough to cultivate essential cosmopolitan competence of love and care that would enable students to be able to actually work for and serve citizens in different cultures.

Computer Mediated Communication, Virtual Travel, and Cultural Literacy

Regarding computer mediated communication, virtual travel, and cultural literacy, *Technical Communication Today* talks about using Skype for collaboration (pp. 642–643), but the assignment on creating a Facebook page for a local university is not transnational (p. 645). In addition, this textbook, when teaching electronic resources, does not consider transnational virtual learning. For example, it does not mention information access on transnational level because it only gives examples of Google, Yahoo, etc., which are U.S.-based search engines (p. 394). Further, this textbook requires students to compare websites designed from different cultures (pp. 618–619), which cannot be sufficient when virtual traveling alone, but it can help students to be aware of culturally sensitive web design.

Mike Markel's *Technical Communication* requires students to classify their skills into hardware skills, software skills, language skills, and operating system skills (p. 15) in teaching resume and job application skills. However, no transnational component was found in the actual text. Therefore, unless the instructor designs an international job application assignment, students will have to learn about transnational literacy by themselves. Additionally, this textbook discusses online databases, social media, websites, and catalogs in contrast to traditional research tools (p. 121), with which we cannot see any transnational pedagogical possibilities unless the instructors design the assignments themselves.

Lanon and Gurak's *Technical Communication* requires students to study websites of international organizations and search the Internet for information about cultural variables and differences among cultures. *Technical Communication: A Reader-Centered Approach* mentions audio and video conferencing using computers and talks about collaboration in this regard (pp. 451–452) but does not mention specific transnational resolutions and learning processes, except for giving general guidelines at the end of the chapter (pp. 453–456). Nevertheless, when teaching details of collaborative meetings, this textbook encourages discussion, debate, and diversity of ideas (pp. 448–450). Whereas this shows a positive possibility on virtual traveling, the textbook promotes "real time" collaboration tools without discussing the specific things to consider when scheduling transnational meetings (p. 451).

Writing That Works encourages students to use collaborative writing tools such as Google Drive. The fact that there are textbooks that do not address virtual travel needs to be marked, and the ones that teach cultures and encourage students to collaborate may want to think one step further about new projects that could be designed in new editions. This would provide students more opportunities to be immersed in a transnational working environment.

Physical Travel Techniques: Passport, Visa, and Border Crossing

No textbook among the five mentions anything relevant to the technical aspects of physical travel issues such as visa application, passport and visa policies, or border passing. The authors may have to omit these aspects given the nuances of different practices from nation states, but giving students an idea about how easy or difficult international travel can be would be beneficial to the competence of world citizenship, in that it teaches students to understand each other's national identities, different restrictions on traveling, and the unequal power dynamics even regarding transnational travel. This would be conducive to cultivating their compassion and understanding toward each other, especially between the colonial national identity and the colonized national identities. For instance, teaching empathy using documentaries on developing countries such as Jamaica and China: "Life and Debt" and "Mardi Gras: Made in China." Additionally, no textbook addresses dual citizenships and nationalities, refugee, asylum, and immigration that are closely related to students' global identities, literacies, and competence to understand and communicate such problems.

Ideological Considerations: Religion

Ideological perspectives such as religion are an important variable in the transnational rhetoric and communication model. *Technical Communication: A Reader-Centered Approach* and Lannon and Gurak's *Technical Communication* do not mention the reflectivity of religious and other ideological references in global communication. The other textbooks touch upon religion to different extents. For example, *Technical Communication Today* suggests avoiding religious symbols and references (pp. 544 & 607) because the mentioning of a religious figure or saying prayers can be potentially insulting and even sacrilegious in another culture. Markel's *Technical Communication* observes that religious differences can affect diet, attitudes toward individual colors, style of dress, holidays and hours of business (p. 96). *Writing That Works* advises not to use religious symbols because they might mean entirely different things in another culture (pp. 255–256).

Historical and Ethical Aspects of Culture

Regarding the historical and ethical aspects of culture (ethnicity, race, and gender), *Writing That Works* is the only textbook that includes all these areas. It claims that identifying human beings by their racial, ethnic, or religious backgrounds is not relevant in professional writing (pp. 112 & 650). It also requires students to interview people whose work involves international travel, which might inspire them to communicate about a nation or nations' histories. Gender is mentioned in all of the textbooks, and they recommend using non-sexist language (*Technical Communication Today*, pp. 120 & 123; Markel's *Technical Communication*, pp. 240–241; *Technical Communication: A Reader-Centered Approach*, pp. 276–277; Lannon and Gurak's *Technical Communication*, pp. 86–87 & 127; *Writing That Works*, pp. 111 & 619–620), but they almost always talk about gender differences according to research findings from previous studies that oppress those who have different ways of communication and behavior patterns. For instance, Markel's *Technical Communication* reports that women value consensus and relationships more than men, that they show more empathy and demonstrate superior listening skills, and that women talk more about topics unrelated to the task, which maintains team coherence; whereas men appear to be more competitive than women and more likely to assume leadership roles. Although *Technical Communication: A Reader-Centered Approach* suggests that all professionals should be treated equally in the workplace (p. 77), this textbook presents that many American men express assertions as facts, whereas women do not (pp. 455–456). Lannon and Gurak's *Technical Communication* also reports previous studies on behavioral differences between men and women but claims the impossibility of generating gender differences (pp. 86–87). We can see that some of the comments about women and men in the workplace are fairly stereotypical, which should be noted for future research and teaching of transnational rhetoric and communication when examining the transnational gender dynamics.

Language as Cultural Variable

In terms of language as a cultural variable, only one textbook, out of the five, meets this criterion. Also, none of the five textbooks included World Englishes as a cultural dimension in their content, nor mentioned ESL at all. Nevertheless, many of them encourage the use of plain language. For example, Lannon and Gurak's *Technical Communication*, like the other textbooks, suggests the basic guideline that simple and coherent vocabulary should be used when communicating with non-native speakers, but it states that respect for the audience's fluency level is also important, which implies that the audiences' educational, working, travel, and even living experience might be different. Whereas there is no inherent connection between and among plain English, English as an international language (Lingua Franca), ESL, and World Englishes, plain English—which is supposed to use easy to read syntax, simple vocabulary, and short sentences—can be easier for ESL speakers to understand. Similarly, looking at English as an international language seems to encourage practices with simple and concise use of the English language. However, World Englishes may or may not be understood easily. For example, "people mountain people sea," a direct, literal translation from the Chinese four-character idiom 人山人海 may or may not be understood by native English speakers depending on their cultural literacy of the Chinese rhetorical context. In addition, some grammatically wrong translations cannot be considered as Chinese English, a variety of World Englishes. For instance, 人山人海 is considered as Chinglish, a non-idiomatic translation from the original language to the target language. Textbooks show concerns of native speakers not being understood by less literate (speakers of English) non-native speakers; not vice versa. This is one issue to address in the teaching of transnational and translingual technical communication. However, multilingual speakers and/or people who hold dual citizenships are mentioned in none of these textbooks.

Further, these textbooks show a lack of tolerance and understanding between and among differences, as well as the teaching on positive attitude and the courage toward dialogues between and among cultures. For the transnational rhetoric and communication variables—information dissemination and sur-veillance and fragmentation, intersubjectivity, and intertextuality—not a single textbook among the five textbooks analyzed showed any concern about the speed of information dissemination, media's ideological stances, surveillance, fragmentation, intersubjectivity, and intertextuality. This gap suggests that future textbook revision should consider the issues due to the increased speed of techno-logical development and transnational information dissemination on situated and converged information flow.

Regarding issues surrounding translation, negotiations on vocabulary, and discourse communities, all five textbooks refer to a third culture, but stop at asking students to avoid using culturally inappropriate and/or sensitive vocab-ulary and/or idioms, without mentioning the deeper causes of such avoidance, or giving any resources and/or examples. Therefore, this gap will have to be filled with more resources and examples to cultivate students' transnational literacies and competence.

Discussions

The evaluation has shown that the textbooks under consideration will need new theoretical frameworks and assignments regarding transnational and global rhetoric and communication. In addition, they still rely largely on the traditional/classical definitions of cultural awareness, literacy, and competence on broader, national borders, instead of fast-changing and ubiquitous transnational cultural exchanges, communications, and rhetorical convergences. For instance, some of the textbooks' content gives stereotypical examples based on classical cultural variables/binaries such as indirectness/directness, low- and high-context cultures, power distance, and uncertainty avoidance. However, there are some excep-tions. For instance, Lannon and Gurak's *Technical Communication* stands out in terms of stereotypical definitions of group behaviors from cultures because it tells students to respect individual characteristics of human behaviors. This textbook also follows the IEEE gender equality code (p. 77) and asks students to pay attention to social cues on gender differences, whereas others largely ignored gender issues in technical communication. *Technical Communication Today* makes an argument that women in North America are more direct (p. 35) than women from other cultures, which falls into the category of an old stereotypical cultural variable.

The literacy, skills, and competence that textbooks could teach in order for future practices to be effective while communicating across national boundaries include, but are not limited to, the following skills:

- students' self-awareness (citizenships, ethnicity, race, gender, passports and visas),
- transnational team building and relationship building,

- transnational technological literacy,
- transnational media literacy (ideological stances of media from different nations caused by previous human but not national history, and ability to recognize fake news using reliable sources),
- ability to tolerate, recognize, and comprehend cultural negotiations of the English language.

In conclusion, when we think of the achievements and failures of globalization, both economically and ideologically, it is time to shift our pedagogical focus from the small-minded national boundaries to transnational middle grounds, dialogues, and smaller institutional cultures that are already global and transnational, and historically irreversible. What world citizens should strive for is how to solve concrete problems for individuals beyond national and/or institutional authorities and boundaries. Cosmopolitanism and transnationalism is the ideal and irreplaceable strategy for each human being to go beyond ideological, geographical, and national limitations; however, this strategy is not easy to realize without the collaborative effort of world citizens.

The implications of my findings illustrate that textbooks are trying to avoid using traditional models in so-called intercultural communication, but insufficient examples were provided. The insufficient materials may be supplemented by providing more cases in transnational rhetoric and communication such as: transnational mobile apps; teaching historical and contemporary texts with readings, videos, and documentaries; simulating transnational rhetorical situations so students will have an idea of what contemporary transnational workplaces are like; using transnational websites that have different language versions to discuss implications of different design, communication, and so on.

Note

1. Develop and maintain multiple relations on familial, economic, social, organizational, religious, and political levels that go beyond national borders. Transmigrants take actions, make decisions, feel concern, and develop identities within their social networks.

Discussion Questions

1) How are your ways of communication similar and different from others from different cultures? Why? How can we communicate as equals if we are from different cultures? Give examples of miscommunications and discuss how you would handle a workplace miscommunication situation.
2) How can you contribute to your intercultural and transnational communication classrooms, the workplace, and beyond?
3) How does technical design, such as app design and web design, change from culture to culture? Give examples.

4) What are some of the better ways to communicate in a transnational context? What are the worst ways? Why?
5) Analyze a text, a visual, or a multimodal composition of your choice that reflects transnational communication context. State the positive and negative aspects from the piece and revise it into one that would facilitate the awareness, responsibility, and ability of world citizens.

Further Reading

All website URLs accessed February 2018.

Agboka, G. (2012). Liberating intercultural technical communication from 'Large Culture' ideologies: Constructing culture discursively. *Journal of Writing and Communication*, *42*(2), 159–181.

Agboka, G. (2013). Participatory localization: A social justice approach to navigating unenfranchised/disenfranchised sites. *Technical Communication Quarterly, 22*, 28–49.

Alfred, G. J. (2006). Bridging cultures: The academy and the workplace. *Journal of Business Communication, 43*(2), 79–88.

Barker, T. & Matveeva, N. (2006). Teaching intercultural communication in a technical writing service course: Real instructors' practices and suggestions for textbook selection. *Technical Communication Quarterly, 15*(2), 191–214.

Bokor, M. K. (2011). Moving international technical communication forward: A world Englishes Approach. *Journal of Technical Writing and Communication, 41*(2), 113–138.

Bray, Daniel. (2011). *Pragmatic cosmopolitanism: Representation and leadership in transnational democracy*. New York: Palgrave Macmillan.

Canagarajah, S. (2006). The place of world Englishes in composition: Pluralization continued, *College Composition and Communication, 57*(4), 586–619.

——. (2007). The ecology of global English. *International Multilingual Research Journal, 1*(2), 89–100.

——. (2013a). *Translingual practices: Global Englishes and cosmopolitan relations*. New York: Routledge.

Cárdenas, L. D. (2012). Challenges and rewards of teaching intercultural communication in a technical writing course: A case study, *Journal of Technical Writing and Communication 42*, 143–58.

Flower, L. (2003). Talking across difference: Intercultural rhetoric and the search for situated knowledge author(s), *College Composition and Communication, 55*(1) 38–68.

Foss, S. K., Foss, K. A., & Trapp, R. (1985). *Contemporary perspectives on rhetoric*. Prospect Heights: Waveland Press.

Hofstede, G. (2011). Dimensionalizing cultures: The Hofstede Model in context. Online readings in psychology and culture, *2*(1). Retrieved from http://dx.doi.org/10.9707/2307-0919.1014

Horner, B., & Lu, Min-Zhan. (2007). Resisting monolingualism in English: Reading and writing the politics of language. In V. Ellis, C. Fox, & B. Street (Eds.), *Rethinking English in the classroom*, pp. 141–157. London: Continuum.

Horner, B., Lu, M.-Z., & Matsuda, P. K. (Eds.) (2006). Cross-language relations in composition college English special issue, *College English, 68*.

Horner, B., Lu, M.-Z., Royster, J., & Trimbur, J. (2011). Language difference in writing: Toward a translingual approach, *College English, 73*(3), 303–321.

Hunsinger, R. P. (2006). Culture and cultural identity in intercultural technical Communication, *Technical Communication Quarterly 15*(1) 31–48.

Kant, I. (2006). *Toward perpetual peace and other writings on politics, peace, and history,* with essays by J. Waldron, M. W. Doyle, A. Wood, P. Kleingeld (Eds.), D.L. Colclasure (trans.) New Haven: Yale University Press.

Kristiva, J. (1977). Word, dialogue, and novel. Desire. In L. S. Roudiez, (Ed.), Thomas Gora et al., (Trans.) *Languages: A Semiotic Approach to Literature and Art,* pp. 64–91. New York: Columbia U. P.

Lyon, A. (2004). Confucian Silence and Remonstration: A Basis for Deliberation? In C. S. Lipson & R. A. Binkley (Eds.), *Rhetoric Before and Beyond the Greeks,* pp. 131–145. Albany: SUNY Press.

Mao, L. (2013). Beyond bias, binary, and border: Mapping out the future of comparative rhetoric. *Rhetoric Society Quarterly, 43*(3) 209–225.

Mao, L. (2013). Writing the other into histories of rhetoric: Theorizing the art of recontextualization. In M. Ballif (Ed.), *Re/Theorizing Writing Histories of Rhetoric,* pp. 41–57. Carbondale: Southern Illinois UP.

Mao, L. et al. (2015). Manifesting a Future for Comparative Rhetoric. *Rhetoric Review 34*(2), 239–274.

Matveeva, N. (2011) Review of *Culture, Communication and Cyberspace: Rethinking Technical Communication for International Online Environments.* In K. St.Amant & F. Sapienza (Eds.), *IEEE Transactions on Professional Communication 54*(4) pp. 406–407.

——. (2007). The intercultural component in textbooks for teaching a technical writing service course, *Journal of Technical Writing and Communication, 37*(2), 151–166.

Matveeva, N., & T. Barker, (2006). Teaching intercultural communication in a technical writing service course: Real instructors' practices and suggestions for textbook selection, *Technical Communication Quarterly, 15*(1).

Matveeva, N. (July 2005). Paralogic hermeneutics: An alternative approach to teaching intercultural communication in a technical writing course, Proceedings of the IEEE international professional communication conference, University of Limerick, Ireland.

McCarty, S. (2007). Theorizing and realizing the global classroom. In A. Edmunson (Ed.), *Globalized E-learning cultural challenge,* pp. 90–115. Hershey: IGI Global.

——. (2006). Studies and development of comparative rhetoric in the U.S.A.: Chinese and Western rhetoric in focus, *China Media Research, 2*(2), 112–116.

Miles, L. (1997). Globalizing professional writing curricula: Positioning students and repositioning textbooks, *Technical Communication Quarterly 6*(2), 179–200.

Plato, & Zeyl, D. J. (1987). *Gorgias.* Indianapolis: Hackett Pub. Co., c1987.

Plato, & Helm, J. J. (1981). *Apology.* Chicago: Bolchazy-Carducci, c1981.

Pogge, T. W. (1992). Cosmopolitanism and Sovereignty, *Ethics, 103,* 48–75.

——. (Ed.), (2001). *Global Justice.* Oxford: Blackwell.

Said, E. (1977). *Orientalism.* London: Penguin.

Thatcher, B. & St.Amant, K. (2011). *Teaching intercultural rhetoric and technical communication: theories, curriculum, pedagogies and practices.* New York: Baywood.

——. (2004). Rhetorics and communication media across cultures, *Journal of English for Academic Purposes, 3,* 305–320.

——. (2012). *Intercultural rhetoric and professional communication: Technological advances and organizational behavior.* Hershey: Information Science Reference.

——. (2010). Understanding digital literacy across cultures. In R. Spilka (Ed.), *Anthology of Digital Literacy for Technical Communication: 21st Century Theory and Practice*. New York: Routledge.

——. (2010). Reading and writing new media across cultures: Issues of fit, reciprocity, and cultural change. In C. E. Ball, J. Kalmbach (Eds.), *Raw (Reading and Writing) New Media*. New York: Hampton Press.

Wan, A. J. (2014). *Producing good citizens: Literacy training in anxious times*. Pittsburgh, PA: University of Pittsburgh Press.

You, X. Y. (2016). *Cosmopolitan English and transliteracy*. Carbondale: Southern Illinois University Press.

Yu, H. (2012). Intercultural competence in technical communication: A working definition and review of assessment methods. *Technical Communication Quarterly, 21*,168–186.

References

All website URLs accessed February 2018.

Agboka, G. (2013). Participatory localization: A social justice approach to navigating unenfranchised/disenfranchised sites. *Technical Communication Quarterly, 22*, 28–49.

Agboka, G. (2014). Decolonial methodologies: Social justice perspectives in intercultural communication research. *Journal of Technical Writing and Communication, 44*, 297–327.

Appadurai, A., & Breckenridge, C. (1988). Why public culture, *Public Culture, 1*(1), 5–9.

Block, F. (1987). *Revising state theory: Essays in politics and postindustrialization*. Philadelphia: Temple University Press.

Charles, B. (2004). Intertextuality: How texts rely on other texts. In C. Bazerman, P. Prior (Eds.), *What writing does and how it does it: An introduction to analyzing texts and textual practices*, pp. 83–97. Mahwah, New Jersey: Lawrence Erlbaum Associates.

Connor, U. (2004). Intercultural Rhetoric Research: Beyond Texts. *Journal of English for Academic Purposes 3*, 291–304.

Ding, H., & Savage, G. (2013). Guest editors' introduction: New directions in intercultural professional communication. *Technical Communication Quarterly 22*, 1–9.

Dingo, R. A. (2012). *Networking arguments: Rhetoric, transnational feminism, and public policy writing*. Pittsburgh, PA: University of Pittsburgh Press.

——. (2013). Networking the macro and micro: Towards transnational literacy practices. *JAC: A Journal of Rhetoric, Cultural, & Politics, 33*(3–4), 529–552.

Eble, M., & Gaillet, L. (2004). Educating "community intellectuals": Rhetoric, moral philosophy, and civic engagement, *Technical Communication Quarterly, 13*, 341–354.

Farr, M. (1994.) En los dos idiomas: Literacy practices among Mexicano families in Chicago. In B. Moss (Ed.), *Literacy across communities*. Cresskill, NJ: Hampton Press.

Fine, R. (2007). *Cosmopolitanism*. New York: Routledge Taylor & Francis Group.

Hannerz, U. (1989). Scenarios for peripheral cultures. Paper presented at the symposium on Culture, Globalization and the World System. Sweden: University of Stockholm.

Hooft, S. v. (2009). *Cosmopolitanism: A philosophy for global ethics*. Montreal, Ithaca: McGill-Queen's University Press.

Jameson, F. (1991). *Postmodernism, or, the cultural logic of late capitalism, post contemporary interventions*. Durham: Duke University Press.

Jameson, F. (1992). Postmodernism and consumer society. In P. Brooker (Ed.) *Modernism/Postmodernism*. New York: Longman.

Kaplan, R. B. (1966). Cultural thought patterns in inter-cultural education, *Language Learning, 16*(1–2), 1–20.

Kemp, P. (2011). *Citizen of the world: The cosmopolitan ideal for the twenty-first century*. Amherst, NY: Humanity Books.

Mao, L., & Lyon, A. (Eds.) (2013). Comparative rhetoric. *Special issue of Rhetoric Society Quarterly 43*(3), 209–309.

Matsuda, A., & Matsuda, P. K. (2011). Globalizing writing studies: The case of US technical communication textbooks. *Written Communication 28*(2) 172–192.

Matveeva, N. (2008). Teaching intercultural communication in a basic technical writing course: A survey of our current practices and methods, *Journal of Technical Writing and Communication 38*(4), 387–410.

McGee, M. C. (1980). The ideograph: A link between rhetoric and ideology, *Quarterly Journal of Speech, 66*, 1–17.

——. (1990). Text, context, and the fragmentation of contemporary culture, *Western Journal of Speech Communication, 54*, 274–289.

Nash, J., & Fernandez, M. P. (1983). *Women, men and the international division of labor*. Albany: State University of New York Press.

Ornatowski, C. M., & Bekins, L. K. (2004). What's civic about technical communication? Technical communication and the rhetoric of community, *Technical Communication Quarterly, 13*, 251–269.

Portes, A., & Walton, J. (1981). *Labor, class, and the international system*. New York: Academic Press.

Rouse, R. (1988). *Mexican migration and the social space of postmodernism*. San Diego: Center for US. Mexican Studies, University of California.

——. (1989). Mexican migration to the United States; Family relations in the development of a transnational migrant circuit, Ph.D. dissertation. California: Stanford University.

Schiller, N. G., Basch, L., & Blanc-Szanton, C. (1992). Towards a Transnational Perspective on Migration: Race, Class, Ethnicity, and Nationalism Reconsidered, *Annals of the New York Academy of Sciences, 645*, 1–24

Selyukh, Alina. (2016). After Brexit vote, Britain asks Google: 'What Is The EU'. Retrieved from www.npr.org/sections/alltechconsidered/2016/06/24/480949383/britains-google-searches-for-what-is-the-eu-spike-after-brexit-vote

Sobré-Denton, M., & Bardhan, N. (2013). *Cultivating cosmopolitanism for intercultural communication: Communicating as global citizens*. New York: Routledge.

Thrush, E., & Thevenot, A. (2011). Globalizing the technical communication classroom: Killing two birds with one stone. In B. Thatcher & K. St.Amant, *Teaching intercultural rhetoric and technical communication: Theories, curriculum, pedagogies and practices*, pp. 65–86. New York: Baywood.

Wakeman, F. J. (1988). Transnational and comparative research, *Items, 42*(4) 85–88.

Walton, R. (2013). Civic engagement, information technology, & global contexts, *Connexions. An International Professional Communication Journal, 1*, 147–154.

Walton, R., & Jones, N. N. (2013). Navigating increasingly cross-cultural, cross-disciplinary, and cross-organizational contexts to support social justice, *Communication Design Quarterly, 1*, 31–35.

Choosing the Right Approaches to Advocacy and Community Engagement: Working with a Real Client

5

TECHNICAL COMMUNICATION CLIENT PROJECTS AND NONPROFIT PARTNERSHIPS

The Challenges and Opportunities of Community Engagement

Elisabeth Kramer-Simpson and Steve Simpson

Introduction

In spring 2013, our technical communication program began a grant-writing partnership with a small homeless day shelter in our surrounding, rural New Mexico community that has resulted at the time of writing this chapter in nearly $43,000 in grant funding. In many ways, the partnership has been extremely successful. Writing grants for a nonprofit organization has provided technical communication majors with real-world writing opportunities that has assisted with their transition to non-classroom settings, which is the stated goal of many client projects and service-learning pedagogies (Huckin, 1997; Kramer-Simpson, et al., 2015; Matthews & Zimmerman, 1999; Weber & Spartz, 2014). Further, the grant money has not only helped with shelter upkeep and operations but, in the early stages of this partnership, kept the shelter from being shut down completely by the U.S. Food & Drug Administration (FDA).

Beyond these pragmatic points, our program strives for deeper goals. We aim, first of all, to instill in students a sense of civic responsibility and to expose them to career opportunities in the nonprofit sector. More importantly, we aim for this project to have long-term benefits for the organization and to build a sustainable infrastructure for future organizational growth. These objectives raise numerous challenges and ethical concerns in our ongoing community work. For example, we must ask to what degree students understand the civic impact of their work? Do they see value in this community collaboration, or is it just another line to add to their résumés? To what degree are we considering the needs of varying community stakeholders such as shelter clients or staff? Are we truly helping the organization grow, or are we just providing temporary financial relief? In building this long-term partnership with one community organization, are we overlooking other needs in the community?

In this chapter, we explore these questions using data drawn from interviews with ten students who have participated in this project over the past three years, a focus group session with the shelter's staff and board members, and observations from class interactions with students. Our immediate goal in this paper is to provide technical communication programs and instructors with strategies for developing more effective, sustainable, and community-focused service-learning partnerships. However, a broader goal is to challenge programs to take a leading role in their institutions in connecting with key stakeholders in town and on campus.

Service-Learning in Technical Communication

Service-learning pedagogies[1] have a long history not just in technical communication but also in the sister field of composition and rhetoric, and more broadly in higher education research (Bowden & Scott, 2002; Cushman 2002; Deans, 2000; Dubinsky, 2002; Kimme Hea & Shah, 2016; Jacoby and Associates, 1996; Mathieu, 2005; Stoecker, 2016). While service-learning plays a laudable goal of providing students with real-world applications for community work, we would echo Sapp & Crabtree's (2002) argument that these pedagogies are particularly important for showing technical communication majors that fulfilling employment can be found in the nonprofit sector and not just in for-profit industry. Further, such pedagogies, in theory, can provide students with a deeper sense of the civic responsibilities that accompany professional work (Cushman, 1999; Eble & Gaillet 2004).

Our own community work is situated within two ongoing discussions in the service-learning literature. The first discussion involves the structure of the service-learning relationship, namely the distinction that Cushman (2002) draws between long-term partnerships and "hit-it-and-quit-it relation[s] with communities" (p. 41). The "hit-it-and-quit-it" model might be all too familiar to technical communication practitioners; students are sent into their communities to "find a client" and perform some sort of service, whether it be creating publicity materials, documenting workplace practices, or so on. Generally, students complete this work in a semester's time and release this work to the "client" before heading off for winter or summer break.

This model certainly has its place in the curriculum in that it provides students with a better sense of audience than a strictly classroom-based project would. However, this model has been critiqued extensively. Cushman (2002) has expressed concerns with the sustainability of a model that relies on students to "create their own liaisons" with community partners with very little faculty involvement, as over time bad service-learning experiences can hurt the program's credibility. In our own case, living in a very small town, we could very quickly run through our list of community partners if we were to develop a reputation for substandard or unreliable student work. More importantly, however, many scholars have rightly indicated that this approach places too much emphasis on what the *student* receives from the experience, rather than what the *organization* receives. As Mathieu (2005) aptly argues, nonprofit organizations' needs extend beyond the confines of the semester and often require more follow-up than students can provide. Further, she recounts numerous anecdotes of nonprofits either not receiving the promised deliverables, receiving deliverables that were not useful, or taking more time than they have to give mentoring student workers. More recently, Kimme Hea & Shah (2016) noted the complexity of community partners' motivations for participating in service-learning assignments and emphasized the importance community partners placed on having a clear plan or agenda for a service-learning assignment, which can be difficult without adequate teacher involvement. Thus, while it is important to consider the educational benefits for students, reciprocity is critical to a successful service-learning partnership; the activity needs to benefit the organization and must account for the nonprofit's needs, constraints, and timetables.

As Stoecker (2016) has aptly pointed out, even the long-term partnership model has pitfalls to consider. Presumably, this approach builds better relationships between higher education and a nonprofit organization. However, he writes, "as agency staff come and go and students come and go, the bureaucratic long-term partnership is not between individuals but between organizations, neither of which may actually be controlled by the people most affected by it" (p. 71). Thus, we would stress that the concept of a "long-term partnership" does not imply an indefinite relationship. That is, the partnership needs to have sustainability in mind so that if the project runs its course for any number of reasons, the organization has the infrastructure in place to continue whatever service had been rendered by students. Further, Stoecker raises the ethical concern of whether a higher education institution or program, by entering a long-term relationship with one organization, might be taking opportunities away from other nonprofits, or might be giving this one organization an advantage over other nonprofits. We would agree that educators need to have a holistic understanding of community needs. Later in this chapter, we will discuss how we have used this one partnership as a way to bridge to other community opportunities.

The second essential discussion pertinent to our work is the definition of "community" itself, and the way students learn via the client project to position themselves in relation to it. Most important to this question, of course, is *which* community one decides to focus on. The university community is certainly the safest and easiest community to engage but arguably not the community with the greatest need. Cushman (1999) argues for academia to think beyond these comfortable communities "to address social issues important to community members in under-served neighborhoods." Cushman goes on to describe these often overlooked local communities: "You know these neighborhoods: They're the ones often located close by universities, just beyond the walls and gates, or down the hill, or over the bridge, or past the tracks. The public in these communities isn't usually the one scholars have in mind when they try to define the roles of "public" intellectuals" (p. 329).

We agree with this charge, though we would like to overlay a concern raised by both Stoecker (2016) and Ornatowski & Bekins (2004) concerning the murkiness of our assumptions about "community." Stoecker (2016) cautions us that, as members of the university, we often place ourselves in the position of identifying what this "community" needs or lacks. Further, Ornatowski & Bekins (2004) have argued that many of our uses of community in educational contexts communicate an implicit duality between "inside" and "outside" the university. That is, in the very act of sending students *out* into the community, we are defining community as "something 'outside' of whatever it is that is designated as not the community" (p. 256). In other words, while ostensibly trying to better "university-community" relations, we are reinforcing a separation between the two. Further, Ornatowski & Bekins (2004) draw attention to our assumptions that sending students into the community for "real life" experience automatically "translates into civic and, perhaps more importantly, rhetorical awareness" (p. 255).

We have wrestled with these questions with our program's community partnerships. In our situation, since very few of our students are from the small New Mexico town in which our university is situated, this divide between 'university' and 'community' can be very pronounced, and it may be very difficult for students to identify themselves as members of the surrounding community (though we do, of course, welcome when students are able to do so). In our case, we hope that through this pedagogy students are reflective of what a civic stance might mean and to differentiate it from the hyperpragmatic approach that Scott (2004) identifies. One obstacle to teaching civic engagement in the class is that students' lens for viewing learning is very often shaped by the industry-university relationship. Technical communication students express their learning in utilitarian terms, often in terms of what can be added to a résumé or TC portfolio. The struggle is helping students adjust their discourse and expand their frame of learning to account for lessons they can learn from a community-based project and possibly to expand their understanding of future career trajectories to include consideration of nonprofit sector jobs. From a programmatic perspective, *our* goal is to think more critically of how our relationship with a nonprofit is benefitting the *organization* and how the bridges that we build with the community partners enables students and community members to work together on solving community problems.

Project Description and Methodology

Client Background

Puerto Seguro (PSI) is a homeless day shelter in Socorro, a small city of about 9,000 residents in south-central New Mexico situated 70 miles south of Albuquerque and close to 150 miles from Las Cruces. It is seemingly a town in the middle of nowhere, and many New Mexicans have trouble placing it on their mental maps of the state; Albuquerque residents tend to place it much closer to Las Cruces, and Las Cruces residents place it up closer to Albuquerque. The Spanish word *socorro* comes from the same root as the English word *succor* and means "help in distress."

Socorro, NM, was slammed by the last economic downturn, and many businesses—often renting space from out-of-town landlords—recently shuttered their windows, causing many residents to lose their jobs. Many of the evaporating towns in the vicinity have been drying up for years, and these residents also rely on Socorro for services. The health of our community has become very important to our university and has been recently written into our school's strategic plan. In addition to encouraging faculty and administration to live and shop in Socorro rather than Albuquerque, our school has looked for ways to engage the community and help build better infrastructure for education and economic growth. Our technical communication program has found opportunities to lead this charge through proposal-writing initiatives such as the one we have developed with PSI.

PSI, while a small facility, serves all of Socorro, Catron, and Valencia Counties, an area roughly the size of Maryland, and also draws many clients from the nearby Navajo reservation. The day shelter offers meals, shower and laundry facilities, and emergency shelter and support paying utilities, gas and/or rent. PSI is also committed to helping clients find employment and provides clients with a mailing address when searching for jobs. The shelter operates with just two paid employees and a large volunteer base; many volunteers are previous or current shelter clients.

The uniqueness of this shelter makes it difficult to anonymize completely. We have worked with our Institutional Review Board (IRB) administrator and the shelter staff and executive board on methods of protecting participants' identities. Further, we have made sure to keep participants apprised of our progress on this study. By and large, our community partners are excited about our opportunity to share the story of our partnership.

Client Project Description

We started our project with PSI with a grant-writing unit in a required senior-level class in our Bachelor of Science in Technical Communication program in spring 2013 (TC 421: Professional Writing Workshop). Elisabeth taught this first iteration. After a successful pilot, we decided to continue the grant-writing partnership, though the project was moved to our senior-level Persuasive Communication class, which Steve taught in spring 2014. We continued from that point working on these grants in Persuasive Communication, taught by Elisabeth again in fall 2015, in addition to working smaller grant-writing and publicity tasks for PSI into other classes in the major (e.g., our 1-credit introduction to the major, TC 101). Thus, many students who partook in the third iteration of the class had already been introduced to the organization.

Service-learning client projects always involve some amount of chaos; simply bringing in stakeholders outside of the university complicates the audiences with whom students are communicating and for whom they are writing. However, it is this complexity that can lead to rich learning opportunities for students. Elisabeth had initially decided to forge a relationship with a nonprofit in the interest of streamlining the process of collecting organizational data and creating a deeper and more meaningful grant-writing experience. In preparation for the spring 2013 class, Elisabeth contacted an acquaintance at the local Episcopal church who chaired the board of the local shelter. Elisabeth had not been to the homeless shelter at that time nor did she know what services it provided. However, she believed in supporting the community and had positive experiences working with homeless shelters in other communities, and so she thought that PSI may be a good candidate for the focus of grant-writing efforts.

Initially, Elisabeth planned to work with the shelter for only part of a semester. After working with the director and board for three months, she found the work engaging, became a member of the board, and planned to engage more classes and students in writing grants for the shelter. The willingness of the board and paid staff to work with the students was a key factor in building this relationship. The staff successfully fielded many emails from students during the spring 2013 class. The accessibility and flexibility of the staff helped mitigate other complications with the partnership such as ideas posed by staff that seemed impractical or not fundable, or discrepancies with record keeping and shelter statistics. The other most central force driving this partnership was the mutual need: our students needed grant-writing experience, and the homeless shelter had a seemingly endless list of needs for funding projects. Students wrote grants for a variety of projects at the shelter in spring 2013—from winter clothes to a kitchen upgrade. We submitted three grants from the groups the semester after the class ended (for food, kitchen upgrade and utilities support) and were awarded two of the grants in spring 2014 (kitchen upgrade and utilities support).

Involvement on the shelter board gave Elisabeth access to the organization's financial records and more details about client success stories. In the second iteration of the class (which Steve taught in spring 2014), Elisabeth, as a member of the board, served as the main point of contact for Steve's students. We had very pragmatic reasons at the time for reducing students' contact with shelter staff; the board was undergoing some personnel changes, and there was tension between the staff and the board. We thought that we had the best interests of students in mind by sheltering them from this disorganization, but in retrospect, we feel that this was the wrong decision. The communication was quick and timely, but as a professor, Elisabeth missed some of the authentic stories and experiences of working at the shelter day-to-day. Students also never visited the shelter and were distanced from the experience. However, the partnership continued to be useful to the students as they found and wrote grants. Students were able to use the extensive database of information gathered over the course of the past year and a half. Also, it was very beneficial to the organization, as the second part of the grant for kitchen upgrades started in spring 2013 had to be written by students in the spring 2014 class. This grant alone secured $10,000 and allowed PSI to upgrade its kitchen with commercial-grade equipment as required by a recent FDA inspection.

Our third iteration of this class was held in fall 2015 (taught by Elisabeth), and in order to engage students better, we scheduled a field trip to visit the shelter and talk with staff. Students became more interested in the shelter (some donated food or clothes), and Elisabeth by this time had a well-established database of information about the shelter, spanning three years. Elisabeth used samples of previous grants to help students write for the shelter. Also, a student from the spring 2013 class, who had graduated and had accepted a position as a professional grant-writer for a large nonprofit, shared samples of her own grant-writing with the class. Despite this preparation, Elisabeth still phoned the staff regularly to ask student questions and clarify stories of success at the shelter. Five grants from this class were submitted between fall 2015 and summer 2016, and four were funded (for plumbing, shelving, chairs/tables, and gas for clients). The class was also featured in news articles in the local paper and on the school website.

Since piloting the grant-writing partnership, we have worked shelter work into multiple courses in the TC program. More recently, we have also run an Advanced Grant Writing course that works more in depth with the shelter (including more work on follow-up grant reporting and grant administration) and pursues a number of grant opportunities benefitting other organizations and small businesses in town. This course has been popular among community members, as well. We are constantly looking for ways to grow the impact of this partnership and other partnerships in the community and so we collected data from the stakeholders, both students and community members, to evaluate the effectiveness of the partnership with Puerto Seguro and systematically observe ways this partnership could be extended.

Data Collection

We identify strongly with Grabill's (2012) description of Community-Based Research (CBR) as "the practice of working with people to answer questions and solve problems—as opposed to researching 'on' people and their problems" (p. 212). That is, much like action research, CBR is participatory in that the researchers work directly with members of the community on tasks being studied. This research approach necessarily means that we are not as clinically removed from our subject of study as other qualitative researchers might be, and we are, in fact, directly impacting study results. However, through this approach, we have gained a much greater level of insider access to the community, and we believe that this approach allows for greater reciprocity and benefits to the community. The other side of this reciprocity is that we discuss our research with members of the community organization and account for their insight in our findings. This community participation is particularly critical in our case, since the remoteness and uniqueness of the organization with which we are working make it nearly impossible to disguise the organization's identity, though steps were taken to protect identities of the shelter's staff and volunteers.

We employ a purely qualitative approach to the study. This IRB-approved study draws from interviews with student participants, and staff and board members from the shelter, in addition to our own observations of class and shelter interactions. Students were recruited by email and participated in 30-minute, semi-structured follow-up interviews on their experiences writing for the shelter. We were careful to ensure that we had representation from all three iterations of our pilot work with our project. Because the first iteration occurred in a different class than the one that became the primary home for this project, some students participated in both the first and second iterations. Overall, ten students were interviewed. In Table 5.1, we have included their pseudonyms and an indication of which versions of the project they participated in.

In the interest of protecting the identities of shelter staff, volunteers, and board members, we conducted a one-hour focus group interview with seven participants who fill a variety of roles at the shelter. Participant responses from the focus group will be referred to only as "focus group responses"; the roles of responders will not be indicated.

Interviews were transcribed and coded for emerging themes separately by each researcher. After initial coding, the researchers shared emergent themes with each other, identified overlapping themes, and discussed passages that they coded similarly and differently and abstracted these themes to categories. We followed Hughes & Hayhoe's (2008) advice to follow the data in our qualitative examination of the transcripts, and also sought to increase reliability through collecting multiple perspectives in interviews and multiple forms of data (observation, interview and text). We triangulated these in establishing our categories.

TABLE 5.1 Community grant-writing partnership student participants

Student pseudonym	Class (Iteration / Semester)
Andrea	First Iteration / Spring 2013
Alice	First and Second Iteration / Spring 2013 and Spring 2014
Anthony	Second Iteration / Spring 2014
Jared	Second Iteration / Spring 2014
Alex	Third Iteration / Fall 2015
Alicia	Third Iteration / Fall 2015
Arabella	Third Iteration / Fall 2015
Maddie	Third Iteration / Fall 2015
Michael	Third Iteration / Fall 2015
Timothy	Third Iteration / Fall 2015

Project Outcomes

Students' Perceived Personal Benefits

In a student interview, Michael, who participated in the third iteration of the class, summarized nicely the top motivations students had for participating in this project and what students saw as the benefits of writing grants for the day shelter: "There's the one voice in the back of my head, it's like, 'This is a good thing to do.' Then there's the other one, 'This is going to look really good on your LinkedIn profile.'" Students saw both benefits to their professional development and benefits to the shelter, though the variation in how the students saw the grant-writing benefitting the shelter indicates that some students were motivated by the civic elements of writing these grants more than others.

Many students mentioned in interviews that the professional experience and the résumé line were two of the most important personal benefits that they received from this project. Jared reported that other students in the class were excited to be able to add grant-writing to their résumés, and he also mentioned that it was one benefit of working for a real organization. Anthony said, "I got a great line on my résumé that says, 'Contributed to . . .'" when discussing the grant. Alicia mentioned that it increased her "marketability," and Arabella reported that it was a skill that could help all sorts of students when entering the workforce, not just Technical Communication students. Though not mentioning the résumé in particular, Alex discussed how writing grants for the shelter was "a great opportunity to add to my repertoire of writing skills," and Alice reported that grant-writing is a possible TC career trajectory. Most students acknowledged that developing grant-writing skills would potentially benefit them as they entered the workplace. Two of the students interviewed actively sought careers in grant-writing. Andrea, a student in the first iteration of the class who became a professional grant-writer for a large nonprofit, stated that for this career:

> "[Y]ou just kind of have to start like we did, hope that somebody will give you a chance and the numbers that you need to be a grant-writer so you can build up some success so you can actually call yourself a grant-writer and then you kick off a career in grant-writing."

That is, many nonprofit grant-writing jobs require applicants to have prior grant-writing experience. Thus, even though most jobs required several years of experience, this grant-writing assignment did make Andrea marketable. For her, not only was grant-writing a résumé line but real experience for her future career. Arabella also mentioned how it was helpful to start her training for this career in the class, as it confirmed that she wanted to follow this career path in grant-writing for nonprofits.

Students' Perceptions of Civic Benefits

In addition to seeing the benefits to their professional technical communication work, many students reported in their interviews that they liked the opportunity to help people and saw their grant-writing as an opportunity to improve lives. Alex reported that "the most unique part of this class was that we got to actually engage with the community and write things that mattered." He later clarified this statement:

> "I don't like spending hours on a paper that I know somebody's going to read for five minutes and then throw out and neither of us will ever think about again. It's nice when you actually do something that makes a lasting impact."

Alex felt that the grant-writing would make a difference in people's lives as opposed to a class assignment, which might be quickly forgotten. Alicia was more specific about how this impact fit within her goals, as she said, "helping people is important to me, so I was very, very invested" in writing grants for the shelter. Arabella went a step further and described how all of the writing classes she took were helpful in preparing her to help others. In her interview, Arabella seemed to empathize with the shelter clients more than other students interviewed:

> "I don't believe it's always the person's fault as to why they can't afford things, why they're out on the streets. Situations happen and things happen and you can't really control everything. I think the more we can do to help people the better."

She approaches all of her life with this civic mindset and reported in her interview that she sees all of her TC program classes equipping her with skills to help people. Michael, on the other hand, described how grant-writing for the shelter gave him a feel-good experience that he could share with his family:

> "For this, in particular, there was some satisfaction to it. There was the nice perk of going home for Thanksgiving and talking with my nice, Christian grandmother and telling her that, 'Yes, I'm doing well. I'm writing for a homeless shelter and we're doing a lot of good for the community, and my writing is directly contributing to that.' That's a good feeling."

He appreciated the opportunity to share with his family how what he was learning would benefit the community.

Two students, Michael and Maddie, mentioned that it was nice to see the university reach out to the community. Often, the students referred to the university as its own world, and they felt good about moving out of the "ivory tower" to join in efforts to support the larger community. This stated desire to bridge the campus and community was, in our minds, a step beyond simply acknowledging the "feel-good" benefits of helping other people, and it fell in line with the university's strategic priority to "broaden the circle of community" with community initiatives (New Mexico Tech Strategic Plan).

Challenges to Community Engagement

Not all students interviewed identified with the civic goals of the assignment. Two students (Anthony and Jared) from the second class reported feeling disconnected from the organization. Anthony candidly stated that, "Even though I was persuading, I didn't necessarily feel motivated by Puerto Seguro's plight, I suppose." He further explained that he didn't go to the shelter or have contact with those he was writing for. Though Jared found that "it's always a good thing to help out people that are just helping out for the sake of it, for the sake of better living conditions and life," he also felt disconnect with the shelter and said, "to me, the organization now is still just a name." As students in the second class, neither Anthony nor Jared had direct contact with shelter staff.

Two students reported that the field trip in the third iteration of the class increased their motivation. Alex found the face-to-face field trip crucial to his investment:

> "We took a look at the facilities they were currently using and we looked at their kitchen, and we looked through their meeting areas, their shower, which was . . . I think the first grant we wrote was for the shower and their showers were definitely in need of repair and so I did like how we got to see all of that."

Alex liked seeing the issues at the shelter firsthand. Michael, also in the third iteration, remembered the visit to the shelter, and commented, "You still have that understanding of what the organization does, what kind of atmosphere it has, and what they are concerned with from the mouths of the representatives that gave us the tour." Hearing from the staff and volunteers directly was an essential part of the experience that we plan to continue in future iterations of this grant-writing client project.

Students Reported Benefits to the Client

Some students interview comments did focus more on benefits to the shelter than on benefits to themselves or their classmates. Alice specifically discussed ways that the grants helped the shelter:

> "I felt that if Puerto Seguro got the grant that they would use the money well to help people, and that would of course help people who would either get food, get winter clothing, specifically on these grants."

Because the grants had a direct tie to client services, she felt the shelter and clients would benefit. Andrea, in her interview, tended to mention almost nothing about herself but focused exclusively on the client and the organization. She had gained a significant amount of experience with the client, as she went on after the first iteration of the class to be a volunteer intern for the organization and to continue writing grants. Her responses about the effect of the project on clients were also more detailed than other students' responses. In her interview, for example, Andrea focused on the role that grants play for the organization:

> "Every nonprofit needs money and grant-writing—I've yet to come across a grant that's for overhead funds—but for projects and for updates and things that you just don't have the budget, like the $10,000 kitchen update, that you just don't have the budget to do that whenever you feel like it, you really need some kind of outside source to come in and provide you with that money all of a sudden in one lump sum to get you that project finished."

Andrea knew that the shelter had limited funds and often relied upon grants to make much-needed improvements or repairs. She was able to see how the money was used from the successful grant to make vital kitchen upgrades to remain compliant with FDA regulations. Michael identified benefits to the shelter as a key part of this grant-writing experience: "I also think that another major motivating factor should be, 'Are we actually getting something done for the client?'" Michael explained that he wanted to actually submit the grants, as he felt it was not enough to just generate text for the organization. He wanted to make sure that the project was finished and that the client actually benefitted. Alicia seconded the need to submit the grants and impact the client. It was impressive to see many of the students look beyond the benefits to themselves and appreciate that the client project was in fact benefitting the shelter.

Financial Benefits to the Shelter

Over the course of the three years we taught students to write grants in groups, we submitted some but not all of the grant requests they created, as some needs were more pressing and some students' writing was better than others'. We submitted a total of 17 grant requests. The shelter was awarded 12 grants over the last three years for a variety of upgrade projects totaling around $43,000. The projects were as follows: kitchen upgrade, plumbing upgrade, utilities support for clients, gas money for clients, temporary lodging for clients, shelving and lighting, chairs and tables, and opening the shelter an extra day during the week. All of the grants came from local foundations, and all had grant reporting expectations. Some of the students, particularly those who were interested in making grant-writing for nonprofits a career, helped Elisabeth complete the grant reporting.

Four grants that were submitted were not awarded, giving us a 70 percent success rate. Some of these grants came at critical times; the kitchen upgrade money came the week the stove quit working. One staff member mentioned that the grants kept the shelter open.

Morale-Boosting at the Shelter

The shelter received considerable publicity from these grants, and the community named the shelter best local organization of the year for 2014. Andrea, who had also interned for the shelter, indicated in her interview how the kitchen upgrade improved the morale of the volunteers and led to less bickering. The staff noticed how each of these projects lifted clients' morale and made the shelter experience better: in particular how tables and chairs gave more room and made the meal times more social events (and they were easier to clean). In our focus group session with shelter staff and board members, a participant reported that the grants "help us to treat them with dignity, and help them [clients] know that they are worth something instead of being beat down like that around the streets every day." Staff also reported clients helping more with the cleanup and putting away of chairs. As Andrea mentioned, all of these upgrades were not budgeted within the shelter's annual profit and loss but made serving ever increasing numbers of clients possible. Focus group participants acknowledged that the grants allowed the shelter to expand services as the grant funds fit into categories not covered by other existing funding.

Shelter Board and Staff Perceived Benefits

Record Keeping

In a focus group discussion with the board and staff, they raised several other benefits of this partnership that we had not considered. The chair of the board commented:

> "I think one of the things that the grant-writing—having the students do it for us—that's highlighted for us is we need better record keeping so that we have this information available. Particularly, the stories, the anecdotes, the number numbers, without having to go back and trying to pull it together in any one time."

When we started the first iteration of the project, we found that the shelter was not eligible for a number of grants simply because it did not have the appropriate data needed for reporting. For example, the shelter only recorded total visits and not total unique visitors, and did not keep track of veterans using its services. Andrea, who participated in the first class, noted in her interview that the shelter's record-keeping made writing grants difficult and had even dedicated time during her internship to helping redesign intake sheets:

> "First and foremost, the numbers and the record-keeping made this incredibly difficult to write because of the . . . Not bad record-keeping, just inconsistent I think is what we discovered—different numbers being kept in different places, confusion since we at that point in time we weren't really familiar with the record-keeping at the shelter and what went into each number, so what each numerical value represented. I remember that being the hardest thing to overcome because you have to have good record-keeping. If you're confused about the numbers I think that can come off in a grant and that will result in probably not getting funded since you're a little confused as to where your funding's actually going to be going."

The frequent and often frantic emails from the students brought attention to the issue of record-keeping at the shelter. With awareness raised about this issue, the board has sought solutions and this attention to statistics may enable future iterations of the class to be more competitive for larger, federal grants.

Students' Fresh Perspective

A staff member and a board member mentioned that students' writing was an asset to the shelter. One focus group participant thought that "they told a good story," while another focus group member more specifically mentioned a fresh approach to the plight of the homeless. This participant recounted, "These kids don't have it rote in their minds already." For many students, homelessness was a novel issue. Maddie even mentioned in her interview how surprised and sad she was that Census data indicated that a quarter of the people in our town fell below the poverty line. Civically engaging college students with writing grants for a homeless shelter may have in fact raised awareness of this issue within our community. As another focus group member explained, "We need every generation because it's an inter-generational community problem. We're all a part of it, but you don't always have those spokes going out to all of the folks." She thought the grant-writing class reached an essential but often out-of-touch generation.

From Maintenance to Growth

Another issue that was raised was that "the price is right": the students write for free, whereas a professional grant-writer may charge. For a small organization that is barely able to stay afloat financially, it is beneficial that the grant-writing is more of an in-kind donation and this helps maintain the shelter. One person in the focus group mentioned that at her previous nonprofit, the grant success rate was close to one percent. With the students' help, the shelter has been able to maintain a 70 percent success rate in the small foundation grants it pursues. The students benefit from the experience, but do not charge for this service. One reason the students may have been this successful is that the students are trained to problem-solve, and do so creatively, in effect helping the shelter plan strategically for next steps in improving services and the shelter facility. The first Frost grant was a good example of this, as it not only helped the shelter maintain food services but increased the shelter's capacity to store frozen meat donations, which helped decrease overall overhead for food costs. Kitchen renovation led to discovery of plumbing issues, which then became one of the next grants pursued and won for the shelter.

Finally, one focus group member mentioned that the grant-writing is "taking us to the next level." She further explained that these extra funds help the shelter grow and move in a direction to provide more services and help the shelter plan long-term to reach greater goals. In particular, money from the Wells Fargo grant helped the shelter experiment with opening another day of the week, and gave the flexibility to try different days, streamline services, and provide additional salary for employees. This helped the shelter expand services. Also, the plumbing renovation led to better water pressure for both showers and laundry. Both services have tripled since the renovation. Also, the director reports that clients frequently don't want to get out of the shower, a problem we have not had before.

Conclusions and Implications

As a result of this project, we see benefits to the community and to students through our sustained model of service-learning. We also see costs, particularly to the faculty involved in maintaining these relationships. Elisabeth continues to sit on the shelter board, attend meetings year round, and write grants even when the class is not running. She also participates in creating the annual budget, and reporting on grant implementation, and consults with board members throughout the year to make needed adjustments as grants are implemented. This involvement takes time but ensures successful projects. Sometimes, students also need more supervision in completing work for the shelter, and not all grants or flyers created are used. We feel that we are modeling civic responsibility for students and encouraging them to take these lessons with them wherever they end up as technical communication professionals. Though the level of civic engagement varied among the students, many appreciated the opportunity to give their time and talents to help the shelter in the community. Two students saw job opportunities in the nonprofit sector. The students were concerned, like Michael and Alicia mentioned in their interviews, about making sure the organization benefitted from the grants, even if that meant extending the work beyond the boundaries of the semester. Yet we realize that some students remain focused on the line on the résumé even with ample opportunities to connect to the community partner. In the following sections, we provide suggestions for program directors or instructors interested in starting similar service-learning partnerships.

Embrace the Chaos

Chaos is inevitable, particularly in service-learning projects engaging small community organizations. In order for teachers to help students learn to handle the complex needs of a real audience, students will need to see the organization's strengths and weaknesses, sift through extraneous information, and find ways to elicit the answers they need to complete the projects. At times in this partnership, specifically in the second iteration of the client project, we prioritized students' needs to the detriment of connecting them with the community. We wanted to shield them from some of the organization's internal conflict. Jared and Anthony both commented on how detached from the organization they felt. Our field trip in the third iteration helped with this. Also, we let students see some of the idiosyncrasies within the organization. We still believe in a very hands-on instructor approach, but we have taken steps to give students more opportunities to truly connect with the organization. From these findings, we assert that the more contact with the organization is involved, the better, even if some of those interactions prove awkward initially.

Pursue Deeper Relationships Between Instructor and Organization

From our findings, we conclude that deeper relationships between the instructor and the organization benefit these types of projects. We are able to uphold the reputation of our program (Cushman, 2002) through the final check of the proposals completed by the students. We also find ourselves discussing shelter needs *with* the community, as members of this community, rather than sitting on the outside telling the community what it needs. Elisabeth's membership on the board, and involvement in the finance committee for the shelter, give her an insider's look at the shelter's annual operations. What we have found from these deeper relationships, however, is that they cost time. Elisabeth spends quite a bit of time outside the semester maintaining the relationship and following-up with projects. In an effort to make the deliverables quality (Mathieu, 2005), Elisabeth sometimes fine-tunes what the students have written, or even, in some cases, works with students outside the semester to revise proposals. One should also note that not all grants written by students were submitted, and not all grants submitted were funded. Nonetheless, as one of the students mentioned, because there is a significant database of gathered information about the organization and because of Elisabeth's involvement with understanding shelter needs, the students are able to do more good for this organization than they might have if they had found their own clients. In light of this, we do recommend that programs and instructors strive for deeper levels of involvement and knowledge of community partners than the "hit-it-and-quit-it" model allows.

Model Community Involvement

We are embracing our university's mission to reach out to the community by working with the shelter and by expanding this project to now work with other community organizations. However, Elisabeth's involvement with the shelter is an essential part of keeping this partnership connected. This may, as Stoecker (2016) identifies, rely too heavily on individuals, but it has meant that there is less a sense of sending students "out" (Ornatowski & Bekins, 2004), and the students have reported a sense of working *with* the organization. The students have trusted the relationships that Elisabeth has established with the shelter, and this gives them confidence in helping the organization through grant-writing (as mentioned by three students). By placing ourselves at the intersection of university teaching and community need, we are modeling for students how to embrace local opportunities. This has led to more student involvement in other community activities this last year outside of the class boundaries. For example, several of our students organized a weekend volunteer effort at PSI in spring 2017 to open the shelter for an extra day each week. These students felt empowered to make connections, offer support, and build new ties to the larger community. We recommend that students are encouraged to forge their own relationships to the community and see beyond the bounds of the university.

We are happy that this project, according to the board and staff, is helping the shelter grow. Future support for the shelter could be to work with the shelter board and staff on a five-year strategic plan, but that has exceeded the scope of our time available. As we expand this project to involve more students at different levels and from different classes throughout the university, we may be able to expand the benefits to the shelter. We are also happy to report that our success with this project—and the publicity that we have received through local news stories—has created other grant-writing opportunities and has generated community interest in our classes. We plan to expand on these opportunities, and we hope to see our efforts have some effect on the vitality of our small community.

Note

1. A note on terminology. In this chapter, we use *client projects* and *service-learning* interchangeably, though we acknowledge that in some contexts, these terms may refer to different pedagogies. *Client projects* typically refer to class assignments in which students fulfill a service or provide a deliverable to a real world "client" outside the class. This client can generally be either a nonprofit or for-profit partner. *Service-learning* refers to assignments that ask students to volunteer services generally for a nonprofit organization or charitable cause. In our case, students are volunteering

proposal-writing services for a nonprofit client, which is an instance of overlap between these pedagogies. We acknowledge that not all assignments have this same overlap.

Discussion Questions

1) What are some techniques or checks that you could put in place to make sure that service-learning projects are beneficial for both students and the clients in the nonprofit organization?
2) One of the benefits and greatest challenges of working with a service-learning project is handling real audience expectations. Discuss what possible problems could arise for students in working with community partners in terms of audience and expectations.
3) What are some strategies for handling a bad experience with a client in a service-learning classroom?
4) What are some of the ethical considerations when working with real-world clients?
5) What would you do if some students in the class were not interested in the particular client or even had personal conflicts with the mission of the organization partnered for service-learning?

Further Reading

All website URLs accessed February 2018.

Deans, T., B. Roswell, & A. J. Wurr, (Eds.) (2010). *Writing and community engagement: A critical sourcebook.* Boston: Bedford/St. Martin's.

Holmes, A. J. (2016). *Public pedagogy in composition studies.* Urbana: NCTE.

McEachern, R. W. (2009). Problems in service learning and technical/professional writing: Incorporating the perspective of non-profit management. *Technical Communication Quarterly,* 10(2): 211–224. DOI: 10.1207/s15427625tcq1002_6

Walsh, L. (2010). Constructive interference: Wikis and service learning in the technical communication classroom. *Technical Communication Quarterly,* 19(2): 184–211. DOI: 10.1080/10572250903559381

Youngblood, S. A., & Mackiewicz, J. (2013). Lessons in service learning: Developing the service learning opportunities in the technical communication (SLOT-C) database. *Technical Communication Quarterly,* 22(3). DOI: 10.1080/10572252.2013.775542

References

All website URLs accessed February 2018.

Bowden, M., & Scott J. B. (2002). *Service-learning in technical and professional communication.* New York: Longman.

Cushman, E. (1999). The public intellectual, service learning, and activist research. *College English,* 61(3), 328–336.

Cushman, E. (2002). Sustainable service learning programs. *College Composition and Communication, 51*(1), 40–63.

Deans, T. (2000). *Writing partnerships: Service-learning in composition.* Urbana: National Council of Teachers of English.

Dubinsky, J. D. (2002). Service-learning as a path to virtue: The ideal orator in professional communication. *Michigan Journal of Community Service Learning, 8*(2), 61–75.

Eble, M., & Gaillet, L. (2004). Educating "community intellectuals": Rhetoric, moral philosophy, and civic engagement. *Technical Communication Quarterly, 13,* 341–354.

Grabill, J. T. (2012). Community-based research and the importance of a research stance. In L. Nickoson & M.P. Sheridan (Eds.), *Writing studies research in practice: Methods and Methodologies* (210–219). Carbondale: Southern Illinois University Press.

Huckin, T. (1997). Technical writing and community service. *Journal of Business and Technical Communication, 11*(1), 49–59.

Hughes, M. A., & Hayhoe, G. F. (2008). *A research primer for technical communication: Methods, exemplars and analyses.* New York: Routledge.

Jacoby, B. and Associates (1996). *Service-learning in higher education.* San Francisco: Jossey-Bass.

Kimme Hea, A. C., & Shah, R. W. (2016). Silent partners: Developing a critical understanding of community partners in technical communication service-learning pedagogies. *Technical Communication Quarterly, 25,* 48–66.

Kramer-Simpson, E., Newmark, J., & Ford, J. D. (2015). Learning beyond the classroom and textbook: Client projects' role in helping students transition from school to work. *IEEE Transactions on Professional Communication, 58*(1), 106–122.

Matthews, C., & Zimmerman, B. (1999). Integrating service learning and technical communication: Benefits and challenges. *Technical Communication Quarterly, 8,* 383–404.

Mathieu, P. (2005). *Tactics of hope: The public turn in English composition.* Portsmouth: Heinemann.

New Mexico Tech. *2015–2020 strategic plan.* Retrieved from www.nmt.edu/strategic-plans.

Ornatowski, C. M., & Bekins, L. K. (2004). What's civic about technical communication? Technical communication and the rhetoric of 'community.' *Technical Communication Quarterly, 13,* 251–270.

Sapp, D. A., & Crabtree, R. D. (2002). A laboratory in citizenship: Service learning in the technical communication classroom. *Technical Communication Quarterly, 11,* 411–431.

Scott, J. B. (2004). Rearticulating civic engagement through cultural studies and service-learning. *Technical Communication Quarterly, 13,* 289–306.

Stoecker, R. (2016). *Liberating service learning and the rest of higher education civic engagement.* Philadelphia, Temple University Press.

Weber, R., & Spartz, J. M. (2014). Engaging entrepreneurship in technical communication using client and service learning projects. *Programmatic Perspectives, 6*(1), 52–85.

6

AN INTERCULTURAL ANALYSIS OF SOCIAL MEDIA ADVOCACY IN DISASTER RESPONSE

Laura A. Ewing and Megan M. McIntyre

Introduction

In the United States, social media platforms are important and widespread parts of daily life. According to a 2016 survey by Harris Polls (commissioned by HootSuite), 83% of Americans have at least one social media account; 64% of Americans over the age of 12 have a Facebook account ("Hootsuite Survey Highlights . . .," 2016). Facebook and Twitter are not uniquely American experiences, though: 85% of Facebook's daily users are outside of the US and Canada (Facebook "Company Info," 2016), while 79% of Twitter's users are outside the US (Twitter "About," 2016). Both platforms are vast and sprawling. Facebook hosts 989 million daily mobile users and 1.51 billion active monthly users. Twitter's reach is not quite as enormous, but it is still immense, with 313 million monthly users (Twitter "About," 2016). Not surprisingly, given the vast number of users and the significant levels of regular engagement on both platforms, companies and organizations have also staked out space on Facebook and Twitter. There are nearly 50 billion organizations and companies on Facebook, and most active Twitter users follow five or more companies or organizations. The ubiquity of organizations and brands on Facebook and Twitter has led to increased interactions with users/customers. Nearly half of Americans (48%) have engaged with a company or organization on social media ("Hootsuite Survey Highlights . . .," 2016).

Given the extensive nature of social media participation, particularly in the American context, it is not surprising that social media usage pervades most consumer experiences, including responses to natural and human-made disasters; this pervasiveness also offers governmental and non-governmental organizations (NGOs) new and expanding opportunities to work as direct advocates for and with those affected by disasters. This usage is not global, however, and even those in regions – like Japan – without barriers to access sometimes avoid personal social media use. But, as we note later, the Japanese public is calling for a shift in social media use. In what follows, we offer background on social media and disaster response, review important cultural considerations that characterize American and Japanese contexts, analyze social media posts following two natural disasters (the August 2016 floods in southeastern Louisiana in the United States, and the 2016 Kumamoto earthquake in Japan), and finally, offer peda-gogical suggestions for students of technical and professional writing as they work across cultural contexts. These suggestions could be ideally employed as a service-learning course component, allowing students to integrate theoretical discussion with real-time practice. The research questions that drive our analysis include:

- How does each organization use social media?
- How does the organization position itself in its social media profile?
- What is the content of each organization's posts in the two months following the particular disaster, and how is information shared and with whom?

As we seek answers to this final question, we are looking, too, for specific kinds of social media advocacy, which we define as passive (sharing information), active (interacting with users), and directed (offering and/or pointing to ways of supporting others affected) ways of offering support to those affected by a natural disaster. Ultimately, the goal of our analysis is to better understand how social media in intercultural technical communication has begun to expand beyond US organizations; we note, however, that important cultural differences – in terms of the modes of advocacy and the visibility of social media advocacy – persist.

Social Media and Disaster Response

With the growth of platforms like Twitter (which only launched in 2006), governmental organizations began to take note of the potential power of social media communication in the face of disaster. As Liza Potts (2014) notes, this move to the social, mobile web creates new and important opportunities to connect users during times of great crisis. 2012's superstorm Sandy, which killed more than 230 people in eight countries and caused at least $75 billion in damage, saw a surge in disaster-related social media posts, including over 800,000 photos with geo-tagged locations (United States Department of Homeland Security (DHS), 2013). In a report following the disaster, the DHS (2013) noted that Hurricane Sandy "represent[ed] the first time a government agency officially used social media for response activities" (p. 7). Perhaps more important, however, the response to Sandy also allowed government agencies (including the National Oceanic and Atmospheric Administration and the Federal Emergency

Management Administration) and non-governmental organizations to engage in "multi-way information sharing and partnerships" with local officials, affected citizens and one another, which enabled coordination and discussion "across sectors, groups, organizations, and jurisdictions" even during the storm (DHS, 2013, p. 17). That is to say, for the first time, governmental and non-governmental agencies alike were able to use social media platforms to engage with, advocate for, and offer assistance to those affected by disaster.

As social media usage has grown in both governmental and non-governmental sectors, research in human-computer interaction and other technologically focused fields suggests a few important findings from the decade or more research into the role of social media in disaster response. First, various technological approaches predate and are used alongside social networking sites to reach citizens in times of disaster, including emergency response systems (Chen, et al., 2008), natural disaster management websites (Chou, et al., 2014; DHS, 2013), and crisis management information systems (Pan, et al., 2012). However, insofar as these systems operate from a centralized, "command and control" approach to disaster management, they may not be particularly effective in managing ongoing, widespread disaster responses (Nan and Lu, 2014). Unlike some other systems, however, social media platforms allow direct interactions and information sharing between agencies and affected citizens, and between agencies and other groups working within disaster-affected areas (Yenni, et al., 2016). These platforms also make space for both the dissemination of information and the accumulation of citizen knowledge and allow for the creation of flexible, shifting networks of organizations and individual users (Yates and Paquette, 2011). However, even with the introduction of multi-way information sharing via social media, Tapia and Moore (2014) noted that the amount of information coming from disaster response organizations during an incident can be overwhelming to citizens/consumers. The sense that too much information bears down on users is illustrated in both American and international contexts, though the basis of these concerns differs depending on the situation's cultural context.

Social Media and Intercultural Concerns

Despite being an international and cross-cultural phenomenon, it is important to acknowledge that social media (and users' relationships to the sites, spaces, and other users they encounter), exist as symbolic representations of culture. Amy Kimme Hea (2014) asserts that social media are not defined by the parameters of their platforms, but rather, "social media are symbolic representations, metaphors, articulations, assemblages of cultural systems of knowledge and power" (p. 2). The expectations users bring to social media have a direct impact on how these platforms are used and the persona created through these uses. Twitter, for example, through its concise 140-character structure, does not allow for explanations of context. While this certainly allows users to present an idea quickly, it also creates a situation where missteps are easy to make, and individuals or organizations can be easily embarrassed (Bowdon, 2014). In a culture that holds respect in high regard, such as the Japanese, this opens up a Pandora's Box of possible negative outcomes. Adding social media to disaster response practices further complicates Japanese communication practices and leads to concerns about the inability to control communication and adequately prepare employees to manage online interactions. The ideal professional relationship in Japan focuses on the need to work in harmony with others, and organizational behavior in Japan values collective needs over personal goals (Higashizawa and Hirai, 2014; Kim and Nam, 1998).

An important cultural distinction between Japan and the US comes from the context of their high and low cultural frameworks (High Context (HC) and Low Context (LC), respectively). To understand the variance between Japanese and American social media use, it is necessary to examine the role of identity in a HC vs. a LC culture. HC culture is one based on long-standing cultural cues. Within a HC society, most individuals share collectivist cultural beliefs and respond to cultural cues intuitively, thereby holding interpersonal relationships in high regard (Hall, 1976). Communication within professional organizations is influenced by the ideological beliefs inherent with culture and within a HC culture relies a great deal on non-verbal messages (Hofstede, 2001). In Japan, this is frequently seen when individuals meet and exchange business cards. The card itself is understood to be representative of the individual whose name appears on it and, therefore, is treated with respect (i.e., card always offered and accepted with both hands, cards are never placed in a back pocket). As such, a HC culture holds interpersonal relationships in high regard, using work hours to develop connections – not off-hours as in a LC culture.

In addition to these practical differences, Japanese customs hold the tradition of "saving face" in high regard. This need to save face is connected to the individual's desire to stay associated to his or her closely-knit community and avoid embarrassment (Ardichvili, et al., 2006). In modern contexts, this community extends to an individual's place of business and the loyalty he or she holds to an employer (Stedham, et al., 2008). In Japan, the HC culture is closely connected to its adherence to hierarchy. This hierarchy separates power (in the workplace, community, and even the family), in a way that ensures information flows in an agreed upon path with little divergence (Hofstede, 2011). Maintaining this hierarchy maintains the community structure and provides a clear identity for individuals. In a HC framework, identity is determined by boundaries – but a technology like social media breaks down boundaries, and as such, has the potential to threaten these community structures. LC cultures, meanwhile, do not adhere to such community associations and their identifying boundaries are limited only by the diverse context of their society.

While fairly standard in a LC culture like that of the United States, the use of professional social media applications is not prevalent in Japan's HC society.

Social media, which can be perceived as a fabricated network, does not allow such relations to exist in the same way they would in a face-to-face interaction. Moreover, social media changes organizational structure and business hierarchy by changing who is considered a co-worker. Business interactions may now occur via social media and cross traditional office-level boundaries. Therefore, workers find themselves negotiating professional relationships, projects, and plans with partners outside the traditional company structure including other offices, complementary companies, and contractors (Ferro and Zachry, 2014). Within Japanese business culture, then, there is an inherent distrust of these networks. The element of social media in business practices brings concerns about the inability to control communication and adequately prepare employees to manage online interactions (Higashizawa and Hirai, 2014).

Furthermore, social media breaks down the hierarchy that Japanese society holds in high esteem. An individual can contact an organization via Twitter to make a complaint or recommendation, but the company loses the initial opportunity to connect that client with a representative prior to the issue being made public – breaking down the traditional customer service route. Since the notion of saving face does not merely reflect on the individual, but on the group (or organization) as a whole, a business that opens itself up to commentary via social media also opens itself up to losing face (Stedham, et al., 2008; Forster, 2000; Kim and Nam, 1998).

In an organizational setting, in order to save face, the focus for the Japanese professional is to adhere to the accepted hierarchy of the organization. The American focus, alternatively, is to adhere to the needs of the organization with minimal concern for professional hierarchy (Luthans, et al., 1985; Kim and Nam, 1998). The Japanese employee, then, is concerned with how he or she may appear in the eyes of both supervisors and peers, and how his or her actions may impact them. Any action taken by the employee reflects directly back on co-workers – for better or worse. For the Japanese individual, then, there is a great risk for shaming not just oneself, but the organization as a whole if the hierarchy is broken down or misused. In the case of real-time communication via social media, the loss of face-to-face cues makes such errors easy and is therefore worrisome to the communicator concerned with his or her "face." Despite these concerns, social media use seems to be rising through the growth of small business ventures in Japan (Fackler, 2013; Erasmus, 2012); for the time being, however, the large, dominant organizations in Japan shy away from the real-time interactivity offered by various social media platforms.

As we will note later in our analysis of organizations' social media responses to disasters in the US and Japan, the limited usage of social media reported by Japanese responders and officials is evidenced by reactions to the 2016 Kumamoto earthquake. In the US, on the other hand, the emphasis on immediate response without regard to professional hierarchy is reinforced by the significant use of social media channels to provide information, establish ties to other organizations and individuals, and even to respond to individual users' questions and concerns in the aftermath of the 2016 floods in southeastern Louisiana.

Cultural Differences in Emergency Alerts and Engaged Disaster Response

In recent years, both the US and Japan have adopted Mobile Emergency Alert Systems to warn citizens of possible disaster situations. The US Federal Communications Commission implemented Wireless Emergency Alerts (WEAs) nationwide in 2008, notifying mobile network users of alerts involving imminent threats to safety or life, Amber alerts, and alerts initiated by the President (WEA, 2016). Similarly, the Japan Meteorological Agency began issuing Emergency Warnings in 2013, informing citizens of heavy rain, volcanic activity, and tsunamis (Emergency Warning System, 2016).

While there are certainly cultural barriers to adopting robust social media responses to local disasters in a Japanese context, employing social networking sites (SNS) as disaster management tools is very much on the radar of Japanese authorities. Various first responder groups active during the 2011 Tohoku earthquake and subsequent tsunami noted significant problems with information access and mobile reception. When the mobile network was available, disaster medical assistance teams reported that Facebook and Twitter were effective communication tools for locating victims. The teams requested that SNS response strategies be implemented before the next major disaster (Yamamura, et al., 2014). Following these after-action reports, telecommunication companies in Fukushima Prefecture and throughout Japan built stronger mobile infrastructures, including better emergency power sources. With this improved network infrastructure, SNS use among Japanese rose over 20% between 2012 and 2014, and new platforms (including the immensely popular LINE) were launched (Hiroyuki, 2016).

According to disaster response teams, these improvements were effective in keeping networks live in the immediate aftermath of the 2016 Kumamoto earthquake, but the SNS were not effectively utilized because responders reported a lack of consistent strategies. Information accuracy became a constant concern for first responders and aid agencies, with individuals retweeting or sharing posts instead of posting to a single hashtag or group and consolidating information. For example, if an evacuation center tweeted that it needed supplies, the message would be retweeted for hours, bogging down Twitter feeds long after the supplies had arrived. The same occurred for victims who had been rescued, but whose locations continued to be shared, thereby confusing rescue teams as to which victims still needed help (Takashima, 2016; Hiroyuki, 2016). Attempts to curtail this use were ignored, though possibly because the clarification tweets lacked concision and could be easily overlooked.

In response to this ineffective use, the mayor of Fukuoka, Kumamoto's northern neighbor, called for development of a SNS framework in his 2016 after-action report. Mayor Soichiro Takashima (2016) acknowledges that there were some SNS successes during the initial disaster response and in the days following:

> We learned from this incident that by using SNS to send out easy-to-understand messages to both residents and [government] employees during each of the relief and recovery stages. . . it could bring a sense of solidarity among the residents and the government to become a powerful driving force towards assisting the earthquake-hit areas.

To do this, however, he noted the necessity of creating a framework where information could be shared accurately and efficiently, pointing out that such a system needs to be "simple and unified nationwide" as well as fully developed, integrated, and trained on prior to a disaster. There is a need, expressed by Mayor Takashima and others, for more robust and consistent social media integration in Japanese disaster response. In the analysis that follows, a small sample of organizations in Japan and the United States were examined to gauge how social media were integrated during actual disasters.

Methodology

This analysis first examined how Japanese and American organizations position themselves on the two most popular social media sites, Facebook and Twitter. We then conducted an analysis of how engaged the organizations were in these social media spaces. To evaluate their engagement, we created an engagement scale drawn from the pedagogical taxonomy developed by Mehlenbacher and Dicks (2004). We then analyzed the themes/purposes represented in social media posts from the two months following the natural disaster. The coding scheme we utilized for this second analysis emerged from our initial engagement with the data; Hsieh and Shannon (2005) call this a "conventional approach" to content analysis in which "codes are defined during data analysis" and "are derived from the data" (1286).

The first cycle of analysis consisted of content references to each organization's social media presence on its homepage. If a social media presence was not indicated, organizations' sites were further searched for references to Twitter, Facebook, Flickr, Shutterfly, Google+, LinkedIn, YouTube, LINE, Pinterest, and Snapchat. Finally, we initiated a Google search for the company and its social media account (e.g., "Kumamoto Prefecture Japan Twitter"). English or global versions of Japanese homepages were not used, as often pages directed towards other languages also alter page design and information. Pages in Japanese were skimmed for familiar social media icons, then translated via Google translate. Additionally, when examining the Facebook, Twitter, and LINE accounts for these sites, we relied on the automatic translation provided by Bing or Google translate through the social media application.

To better understand the levels of social media engagement for each of the four organizations, we next conducted a content analysis of the social media profiles of all four organizations. This scale is based on the pedagogical framework presented by Mehlenbacher and Dick's (2004) study of faculty-student research. The degrees of engagement refer to how significantly social media content demonstrated professional communication between each organization and its audience (see Table 6.1).

The lowest degree of engagement is **Indication,** or using a social media tool (e.g., Twitter, Facebook) to provide basic information about the company. Organizations that use social media tools to **Inform**, providing consumers with updated information and news, achieve the next degree. This second engagement level differs from level one in that it consistently and reliably updates information, which may include (but is not limited to) links to new product pages, images of organizational activities, and retweets from various departments.

Administer, the third degree of engagement, dictates that an organization uses its social media presence to gain information from consumers. Organizations may do this through polling or crowdsourcing of information, but once the organizations collect this information, they do not follow-up the conversation with the consumer regarding his or her responses. For example, an organization may request feedback on a new logo, but the ways in which that feedback is used are not shared until a final decision is made (and shared, usually via level two engagement, **Inform**). Furthermore, the company does not ask responders why they made a particular selection or choice at this level.

TABLE 6.1 Content references and degrees of engagement via social media

Level	Content references for social media use
1 = Indicate (lowest level of engagement)	Social media provides organization information only.
2 = Inform	Social media disseminated updated organization information and/or news. Does not offer a means for consumers to respond.
3 = Administer	Social media are used to poll or crowd source information from individuals. Organization does not respond to consumers' responses via social media.
4 = Connect	Social media are used to communicate directly with individuals regarding organization news and/or information
5 = Coordinate (highest level of engagement)	Social media consists of real-time information sharing and helplines. Organization communicates immediately via social media with consumers regarding updates, resources, questions, etc.

The next level of engagement requires the organization to **Connect** with its audience directly. This level involves the organization responding to posted comments, though often to direct them to a different means of communication (i.e. requesting that a consumer contacts the organization via phone during business hours). An example of a company connecting also occurs via Twitter when a company quotes a tweet from a specific department or business partner, adding commentary and/or follow-up for its own followers.

Finally, the fifth and highest level of engagement involves an organization directly **Coordinating** with its audience via social media. This level requires the company to respond quickly and accurately to an individual's questions and reviews. At this level, posted concerns are, at least initially, managed through the social media application itself and provide users with the opportunity to co-ordinate with each other and the organization, chiming in with additional feedback and real-time advice. This level of engagement may be seen when an individual asks for technical support when making a donation and is met with troubleshooting responses from both the organization's own financial department and other donors who have dealt with the same issue.

For the second wave of analysis, we chose to conduct a thematic analysis of the data found in the content analysis. Since this examination concerned itself with the intricacies of cultural nuances, the thematic analysis allowed us to consider context and its impact on meaning in each social media post. We created an emergent coding scheme based on an initial examination of both American and Japanese social media posts on Facebook and Twitter.

Results and Analysis

Online Presence

To better understand potential cultural differences in how social media are deployed for disaster response, we examined social media responses from four organizations. This mixed methods analysis (content and thematic analyses) focused on two specific organizations in Japan – Kumamoto Prefecture (governmental) and the Nippon Foundation (non-governmental) – and two in the US – Federal Emergency Management Agency (FEMA) and the United Way of Southeast Louisiana. Kumamoto Prefecture was the location of the April 2016 earthquake and the Nippon Foundation is a non-profit organization "actively involved in supporting the recovery of areas damaged by the [Kumamoto] earthquakes" (Nippon, 2016). The official Kumamoto presence occurs through the Prefecture's mascot, Kumamon, a large friendly bear. Kumamon communicates via Twitter and Facebook and positions himself as the voice of Kumamoto and uses these platforms to share information about the region. The Nippon Foundation seems to conceive of its social media presence as a means to deliver news and events related to the organization. The Twitter feed also shares updates from the organization's blog and Facebook account. Both organizations position their online presence as a way for their audiences to find pertinent information regarding their respective missions.

In the American context, FEMA uses its social media biographies to humanize the organization. On both Facebook and Twitter, FEMA's bio reads, "Our story of supporting citizens & first responders before, during, and after emergencies. For emergencies, call your local fire/EMS/police or 9-1-1." The United Way of Southeast Louisiana, on the other hand, uses its bio/"About" sections to offer a succinct version of its mission statement: "United Way of Southeast Louisiana envisions equitable communities where all individuals are healthy, educated and economically stable." Both organizations, however, offer consistent biographical framing across platforms.

The Use of Social Media Platforms

Our analysis of social media presences also suggests that social media were indeed still more widely used in an American context. In the US, both governmental and non-governmental agencies participated on six platforms: Facebook, Twitter, YouTube, LinkedIn, Instagram, and Pinterest, and at least one of the organizations engaged on three other platforms: FEMA has a profile on Google+, though it appears largely dormant, and the United Way of Southeast Louisiana has active profiles on Shutterfly (an image sharing platform) and Snapchat. Japan, on the other hand, sees a significant difference between government and NGO social media use. Kumamoto Prefecture only utilizes an informational Twitter and Facebook page, which it shut down for four months following the earthquake, therefore no information was disseminated directly from the local government to the public via this medium. The Nippon Foundation participates actively on Twitter, Facebook, YouTube, and LinkedIn.

Further, an investigation of US organizations' websites suggested an emphasis on social media platforms, with the United Way prominently displaying links to social media platforms in the footer of all pages (see Figure 6.1).

On FEMA's website, meanwhile, social media profiles were more difficult to find. There are no links to social media profiles on the homepage nor in the footers of other main pages. Instead, links to some of FEMA's social media profiles were available on its "Social Media" page (fema.gov/social media). As of December

FIGURE 6.1 Footer on the United Way of Southeastern Louisiana's website

2016, this page included links to FEMA's main Twitter, as well as to the Twitter profiles of then-FEMA administrator Craig Fugate and Ready.gov, the US government's central website for disaster preparedness information. The "Social Media" page also contained links to FEMA's Facebook, LinkedIn, and YouTube accounts. Missing from this page, however, were links to the agency's Google+, Instagram, and Pinterest accounts, which were discovered via searches of those individual platforms.

The Kumamoto Prefecture's web page had no link to any social media presence. Through a Google search, we could find the informational Twitter feed for the Prefecture's official mascot, Kumamon. A second Twitter feed that appeared to be public relations for Kumamoto Prefecture was also found via Google, but this account was not verified as official and, therefore, not deemed appropriate for this analysis. The Nippon Foundation's web page linked to its Twitter, Facebook, and YouTube accounts, and a Google search returned a hit on the organization's LinkedIn profile.

The Degree of Social Media Engagement

After examining the organizations' social media use, we reviewed the applications they used and rated the level of engagement with their readers (1: lowest – 5: highest), with Twitter and Facebook being the most common (See Table 6.2 "Highest Level of Social Media Engagements Reached by American Organizations," and Table 6.3 "Highest Level of Social Media Engagements Reached by Japanese Organizations").

Based on our assessment, both FEMA and the United Way of Southeastern Louisiana fell into the final category, **Coordinate**, across multiple platforms. In fact, of the 807 combined posts by FEMA on Facebook and Twitter in the two months following the Louisiana floods, 351 were retweets or quoted tweets and 101 featured direct interaction with customers/users. On Facebook, these interactions took the form of direct responses to citizen/customer comments on posts. Two such interactions from FEMA's Facebook page are represented in Figure 6.2. In each of these interactions, a citizen responds to an informational post about flood relief with a specific question about her own situation. And in both cases, FEMA makes two conversational moves: first, the FEMA representative responds directly to the citizen's question; then, the FEMA representative points the citizen to an online resource. (In the first case, the resource is from the FEMA website; in the second case, the resource is from the Louisiana government site.)

The United Way of Southeast Louisiana tweeted and posted less frequently than FEMA in the months following the flooding. Between August 12 and October 12, 2016, it posted 182 times; 92 of these were flood-related. Despite fewer total posts, it too was engaged in direct communication with citizens/ consumers. Of its 182 total posts on Facebook and Twitter, 42 were retweets or quoted tweets, and six were direct interactions with citizens/customers. Both the

TABLE 6.2 Highest level of social media engagements reached by American organizations

	Twitter	Facebook	Google+	YouTube	LinkedIn	LINE	Flickr	Shutterfly	Instagram	Pinterest	Snapchat
GOV	5	5	N/A	5	1	N/A	N/A	N/A	3	1	N/A
NGO	5	5	1	5	1	N/A	N/A	1	3	3	3

GOV: FEMA

NGO: United Way of Southeast Louisiana

TABLE 6.3 Highest level of social media engagements reached by Japanese organizations

	Twitter	Facebook	Google+	YouTube	LinkedIn	LINE	Flickr	Shutterfly	Instagram	Pinterest	Snapchat
GOV	N/A*	N/A	N/A	N/A	N/A	N/A	N/A	N/A	N/A	N/A	N/A
NGO	2	2	N/A**	2	1	N/A	N/A	N/A	N/A	N/A	N/A

GOV: Kumamoto Prefecture

NGO: Nippon Foundation

*Kumamoto Prefecture's Twitter feed was silent for four months following the April 2016 earthquake.

**The Nippon Foundation has a Google+ account, but nothing is published.

FIGURE 6.2 Citizen comments and organizational responses on FEMA's Facebook page

level of interaction (the highest on the scale) and the sustained nature of the interaction suggest that FEMA and the United Way both view social media spaces as robust and significant ways to provide information and support to consumers/ citizens. In particular, FEMA consistently provided situational information via social media in addition to using its profiles to provide more generalized support and advocacy to those affected by the floods and other natural disasters.

The Kumamoto Prefecture's usage was notably lower with no issued social media communications. While the Nippon Foundation published 108 tweets regarding the earthquake, nearly 10% of these were repeat information, and the organization only posted three times on Facebook mentioning the disaster. Of the Twitter and Facebook posts, all were engaging with users at level two, to **Inform**, offering explanations of the disaster, requesting donations, and providing updates on continuing aftershocks. Of the 108 tweets, 53 contained links and/ or retweets to outside resources. Only a small number of tweets were intended for those living in the disaster zone: a tweet on May 13, 2016, provided local citizens with information regarding inspections in their neighborhoods (see Figure 6.3

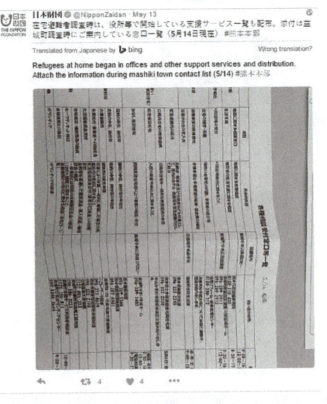

FIGURE 6.3 Nippon Foundation tweet providing local residents with inspection information

"Nippon Foundation tweet providing local residents with inspection information"); and a tweet on May 16, 2016, requested local citizens complete a damage survey (see Figure 6.4 "Nippon Foundation tweet requesting that local residents complete damage survey). One tweet did not translate well enough to discern its meaning.

After-action reports mentioned LINE groups used to disseminate information, but no links to these groups or active QR codes were found. The Nippon Foundation's YouTube page presented a video detailing the ongoing relief efforts, but the video was uploaded well after the eight-week timeframe of this analysis. YouTube posts made during the window of analysis provided viewers with organizational information on ongoing activities, engaging at level one. In general, then, Japanese organizations' social media profiles were not generally an integral part of disaster relief, response, or advocacy. Kumamoto Prefecture utilized no social media tools to reach or advocate for those affected by the disaster, and Nippon limited its use of social media almost exclusively to inform consumers/citizens about generally useful resources (see Figure 6.4).

FIGURE 6.4 Nippon Foundation tweet requesting that local residents complete damage survey

Prevalent Themes in Social Media Communications

Based on our analysis, we identified seven common themes: (1) connections to other organizations/businesses; (2) information on general/ongoing services; (3) information related to the disaster; (4) information related to another disaster; (5) organizational information; (6) "thank yous"/information on volunteering; and (7) information on fundraising and donation. Each post was reviewed for theme(s) and coded. Information related to the number of occurrences of each theme can be found in Table 6.4.

Information Related to the Disaster

As we note in Table 6.4, in the two months following the onset of flooding in southeastern Louisiana in August 2016, the local branch of the United Way

TABLE 6.4 Occurrences of particular themes in posts from disaster response organizations

CHECK MATHS

	JAPAN		USA	
Theme	Nippon Foundation	Kumamoto Prefecture	United Way of SE Louisiana	FEMA
Total number of posts	181 posts	0	182 posts	807 posts
Connections to other people or organizations	77 posts (41.7% of total posts)	0	68 posts (37.4% of total posts)	406 posts (50.3% of total posts)
Information on general and ongoing services	154 posts (90.5% of total posts)	0	16 posts (8.8% of total posts)	52 posts (6.4% of total posts)
Information related to the disaster	72 posts (42.3% of total posts)	0	91 posts (50% of total posts)	266 posts (33.0% of total posts)

(continued)

TABLE 6.4 Occurrences of particular themes in posts from disaster response organizations (*continued*)

CHECK MATHS

Theme	JAPAN		USA	
	Nippon Foundation	Kumamoto Prefecture	United Way of SE Louisiana	FEMA
Information related to another disaster	1 post (.005% of total posts)	0	0	385 posts (47.7% of total posts)
Organizational information	20 posts (11.7% of total posts)	0	3 posts (1.6% of total posts)	48 posts (5.9% of total posts)
"Thank-you" and information on volunteering	15 posts (.09% of total posts)	0	19 posts (10.4% of total posts)	16 posts (2.0% of total posts)
Information on fundraising or donations	24 posts (14% of total posts)	0	65 posts (35.7% of total posts	14 posts (1.7% of total posts)

posted a combined 182 times on Facebook and Twitter, the two platforms used most often by the organization. Of the 182 posts, 91 – or 50% – of these posts were coded as "Chosen Disaster Information"; in other words, half of the United Way of Southeast Louisiana's posts were specifically related to the August flooding. These posts included information about flood-related fundraisers (see Figure 6.5), information about flood recovery efforts and gratitude to existing corporate partners and other supporters who had given or participated in recovery efforts specifically aimed at those affected by the flooding.

A similar percentage of the Nippon Foundation's posts were part of this category: 72 – or 42.3% – of the Japanese NGO's posts were focused on the 2016 earthquake. Chosen disaster information made up a smaller percentage of FEMA's posts, with 266 – or 33% – of FEMA's posts coded as part of this category, and the Kumamoto Prefecture did not post at all in this or any other category.

Connections to Other Organizations or Businesses

The next most frequently seen code was for "Connections to Other People or Organizations"; this group of posts included posts thanking corporate partners (see Figure 6.6) as well as replies, retweets, and quoted tweets that brought other feeds' voices into the organizations' Facebook and Twitter feeds. These tweets were particularly noteworthy as they were the most easily identifiable examples of network building and called attention to relationships that existed offline but

United Way of Southeast Louisiana
September 12 ·

The 248-member St. Amant High School Band, one of the top marching bands in the state, suffered massive damage to its instruments, uniforms, band room and equipment when the Amite River overflowed its banks by 14 feet in August. Total damage: $284,000

We are proud to partner with Capital Area United Way, Sports Illustrated and the New Orleans Saints on this special opportunity to support the recovery of this educational institution.

Visit here to donate - https://www.unitedw... See More

HELP THE ST. AMANT BAND | United Way of Southeast Louisiana
The 248-member St. Amant High School Band, one of the top marching bands in the state, suffered massive damage to its instruments,...
UNITEDWAYSELA.ORG

Like   Comment   Share

10

2 shares

Write a comment...

FIGURE 6.5 United Way fundraising post

were not necessarily apparent. This category represented a significant number of posts for each of the three organizations that posted during the two months following the chosen disasters: for FEMA, in fact, this code represented the most frequent purpose for their posts, with 406 – or just over 50% – of their posts receiving this code. For the Nippon Foundation, 77 posts – or 41.7% – received this code; while this code accounted for 37.4% of the posts from the United Way of Southeast Louisiana in this period.

For the Nippon Foundation, this was the second most used code; many posts linked to information containing details on partnerships between the Nippon Foundation and other organizations or government entities. Similar to the United Way, the use of links and retweets demonstrated a network of trusted information sources; however, these sources were not widely varied, which indicates a relatively small network

Information on Fundraising or Donations

The third most frequent code associated with the United Way's posts (accounting for 35.7% of posts) was "Fundraising or Donations," and featured tweets, retweets, and Facebook posts related to fundraising events, fundraising needs, and donations (see Figure 6.5). For the United Way and FEMA, fundraising- and

FIGURE 6.6 United Way corporate thank you post

donation-related tweets were also the most likely to include video: three of the four Facebook posts (across both organizations) containing video were related to fundraising or donations, and the only tweet containing a video was related to fundraising or donations. The code was far less frequently assigned to Nippon (accounting for only 24 – or 14% – of posts) and almost non-existent in the FEMA data with only 1.7% of posts coded as fundraising or donations.

Information on General and Ongoing Services

While the number of posts for the Nippon Foundation was comparable to that of the United Way (181 posts to 182 posts, respectively), one key difference in the Nippon Foundation's use of social media communication was that it continuously connected posts back to ongoing work (i.e., the kind of work undertaken by these organizations when they're not responding to a specific disaster), and frequently included linked information. For this reason, all posts were dual-coded; 90.5% of the posts, found on both Twitter and Facebook, referenced ongoing business for the foundation, thereby making "General and Ongoing Services" the most frequent code for this organization.

Information Related to Another Disaster

This category noted the lowest code for both the Nippon Foundation and the United Way, garnering .005% and 0% of responses, respectively. FEMA, however, did post 385 references to other disasters. This discrepancy makes sense for two reasons: first, Nippon and the United Way of Southeastern Louisiana serve restricted geographic locations, while FEMA is a national federal agency that responds to fires, floods, hurricanes, droughts, and all other natural disasters that occur in the United States and its territories. For this reason, it is more likely to respond to a variety of disasters in geographically diverse locations. In fact, FEMA was responding to at least two other natural disasters in the United States in the same two-month period covered by this analysis. Second, as a federal agency, FEMA is responsible for ongoing, pre-disaster information efforts, which sometimes reference past or long-term natural disasters.

Organizational Information and "Thank Yous"/Information on Volunteering

In each of these categories, all three coded organizations posted the least. In the cases where these posts did occur, information frequently overlapped between the two categories with information about the organization coming at the same time as links to volunteering sign ups. Since the organizations all utilized the "About" section of the Twitter and Facebook accounts, most organizational information could be found there. Towards the end of the coding period, a small number of "thank you" posts appeared, addressing ongoing volunteer activities and plans for moving forward post-disaster.

Discussion

Though the Nippon Foundation and the United Way of Southeastern Louisiana used social media in sometimes overlapping ways, there was a stark difference in the ways that the two American and Japanese governmental organizations used social media in the aftermath of disasters in 2016. FEMA was a prolific user of social media. In the two months following the flooding in southeast Louisiana, FEMA posted on Twitter and Facebook 807 times. Of these 807 posts, about half were coded as "Connections to Other People or Organizations"; approximately one third of its posts were related to the flooding in southeast Louisiana, and 47.7% were coded as "Other Disaster," (which included posts about Hurricanes Matthew and Hermine, wildfires in the Western United States, and a deadly August heatwave). FEMA frequently used social media to share information, connect with other organizations, and raise awareness about disasters and other relevant issues. Such an approach stood in stark contrast to Kumamoto Prefecture's social media silence during and in the two months following the 2016 earthquake.

Overall, the results of our analysis indicated that both the Nippon Foundation and Kumamoto Prefecture were halted in their use of social media. The Nippon Foundation used social media applications in a limited way, while Kumamoto Prefecture did not use social media at all. Such a fact could be explained by some perceived risk of social media disrupting traditional Japanese organizational hierarchy, and the concern with unvetted information or misinformation (Bowdon, 2014; Hofstede, 2011; Stedham, et al., 2008; Ardichvili, et al., 2006). As such, the Nippon Foundation took a risk in posting at all, while the prefectural government chose to not place itself in a potentially embarrassing position. In contrast, both the United Way of Southeastern Louisiana and FEMA sustained an interactive social media activity.

One of the interesting observations was the fact that the NGOs in both countries showed a significant overlap in thematic content. Both the Nippon Foundation and the United Way used social media to build public networks and to share information about a current disaster. Sometimes, this network building took the form of thanking corporate partners (as in Figure 6.6) or in linking followers to other organizations' resources. Most often, though, this work took the form of retweets and quoted tweets in which the organizations brought another user or organization into the followers' feeds by sharing that other user or organization's exact message with their followers.

Another significant difference among the studied organizations concerned the type of advocacy they employed. The American organizations' use of social media aimed for more direct advocacy. Both the United Way of Southeastern Louisiana and FEMA promptly interacted with users via retweets, quoted tweets, and threaded replies. These practices were aligned with the Department of Homeland Security's (2013) recommendations and supported through legislative and administrative training protocols designed to maximize effective communication in the aftermath of a disaster. The Nippon Foundation, on the other hand, chose to advocate passively through its social media presence, offering information but no direct communication and little information focused directly on disaster victims. The Kumamoto Prefecture eschewed social media altogether in the aftermath of the 2016 earthquake. It should be noted, though, that Kumamoto Prefecture's decision to silence its Twitter feed was met with criticism, and many local citizens voiced displeasure over the verified Twitter feed not being used to share vital information (Oda, 2016). Though there could have been potential logistical and cultural challenges to implementing robust and interactive social media practices in response to the disaster, this citizen reaction suggested a growing appetite for more social media interactions in the Japanese context.

Limitations

While this content analysis provided insight into how the four Japanese and American organizations were using social media to communicate with customers, we recognize its limitations due to its small sample size. Our study provided a snapshot into intercultural social media use. Additionally, while this analysis did not include data for general social media use, prior research demonstrates continuous increase in social media use for Japanese individuals, organizations, and the government since 2010 (Okura and Kaigo, 2016; Sano and Sano, 2016; Lee and Phang, 2015; Acar and Muraki, 2011). Moving forward, a larger sample should be examined to gauge the use of social media in disaster situations and potential cultural similarities and differences that might exist in such contexts.

Conclusion

Using social media as tools to effectively advocate during disaster response falls in large part to technical communicators with expertise in digital communication. In the midst of a disaster, natural or man-made, it is vital that the voices of those impacted be heard to better employ immediate recovery action, as well as ongoing relief assistance. As natural disasters are an international phenomenon and as the same natural disasters sometimes cross national boundaries, students and practitioners in the field of technical communication need to understand and relate to multiple national and cultural priorities and interact with individuals from other cultures. Just as we consider cultural nuances within the American business contexts, so must we consider the diverse cultures existing outside of the United States as people communicate via online platforms. Social media invite all participates to cross linguistic and geographical barriers as they communicate (Kostelnick, 2011; Canagarajah, 2006), and it is against this ever-globalizing backdrop that we as scholars of technical and professional communication must consider how students might cross these cultural and physical borders as citizens and advocates with the help of social media.

The conclusions of this analysis assert the need for technical communication educators and practitioners to be aware of varying cultural contexts as expressed through global social media use (Canagarajah, 2006; Hall, 1976; Wurtz, 2005; Hofstede, 2001). While addressing this concept in a classroom setting is an excellent introduction, placing students in a service-learning context would provide the opportunity to see the real-world application of cultural contexts. Cultural contexts, such as HC and LC, vary greatly among countries that routinely do business together and are easily identified in what Richardson and Smith (2007) refer to as West and non-West relationships. Setting students up in remote global teams working across varying cultural contexts presents the opportunity for globalized writing practices concerned with the ability to build and maintain strong professional relationships, while being attentive to the differing cultural spaces in which communication occurs. While initially daunting to instructors, these remote introductions can be assisted by connections that already exist with international university partnerships and study abroad programs (i.e., Temple University in Tokyo, University Study Abroad Consortium Hiroshima University). Ferro and Zachry (2014) point out that if American students are taught to take cultural variables into account when communicating online, they are better equipped to evolve as site use changes and service needs progress.

Technical and professional communication classrooms are already embracing social media communication to demonstrate agency through writing and shifting the pedagogical focus from learning how to use a "site" (the application itself) to learning how to effectively employ a "service" (what the application does) (Ferro and Zachry, 2014). This same approach can be taken in disaster management training programs. Technical communication practitioners can develop a first responder that presents social media as a system of communicative devices, as opposed to a mere instrument, where first responders and affected groups have agency during and after a disaster.

The above analyses of governmental and non-governmental responses to recent natural disasters identified clues that demonstrated the similarities and differences seen across American and Japanese social media disaster response practices. The study found a significant discrepancy in governmental and non-governmental social media use, but also identified that the role of social media was changing in the Japanese culture as organizational roles evolved and as Japanese public officials began to recognize the potential communicative value of social networking sites in communicating with citizens, especially during a disaster. Moving forward, instructors of technical and professional communication could integrate intercultural contexts in the social media writing curriculum, demonstrating to students how their own personas could differ in various cultural contexts, which will ultimately raise students' awareness and provide them with the necessary tools to be effective communicators.

Discussion Questions

1) How might the differences between American and Japanese social media communication be illustrated in interpersonal communication practices?
2) What aspects of traditional professional writing are affected by cultural context? Why does this occur?
3) Considering how the Japanese concept of "saving face" influences social media use, how might communication be impacted by varying cultural contexts throughout America?
4) Referring to recent disasters, both natural and man-made, how could social media be employed to share critical information with citizens?
5) What are the dangers of engaging with technology during a disaster? How might local governments and first responders account for these dangers?

Further Reading

All website URLs accessed February 2018.

Bouvier, G. (2016). Social media and its impact on intercultural communication: The challenges for a discourse approach. *Journal of Communication Arts, 34*(3). www. tci-thaijo.org/index.php/jcomm/article/view/86005.

Faris, M. & Moore, K. (2016). "Emerging scholars and social media use: A pilot study of risk." *Communication Design Quarterly.* 4(2), 52–63.

Hofstede, G. (2011). Dimensionalizing cultures: The Hofstede model in context. Online readings in psychology and culture. http://scholarworks.gvsu.edu/orpc/vol2/iss1/8/

Jones, N. (2016). The technical communicator as advocate: Integrating a social justice approach in technical communication. *Journal of Technical Writing and Communication,* 46(3), 342–361.

Tombleson, B. & Wolf, K. (2017). Rethinking the circuit of culture: How participatory culture has transformed cross-cultural communication. *Public Relations Review, 43*(1), 14–25.

References

All website URLs accessed February 2018.

Acar, A. & Muraki, Y. (2011). Twitter for crisis communication: Lessons learned from Japan's tsunami disaster. *IJWBC Internaional Journal of Web Based Communities, 7*(3), 392–392.

Ardichvili, A., Maurer, M., Li, W., Wentling, T. & Stuedemann, R. (2006). Cultural influences on knowledge sharing through online communities of practice. *Journal of Knowledge Management, 10*(1), 94–107.

Bowdon, M. A. (2014). Tweeting an ethos: Emergency messaging, social media, and teaching technical communication. *Technical Communication Quarterly, 23*(1), 34–54.

Canagarajah, A. S. (2006). The place of world Englishes in composition: Pluralization continued. *College Composition and Communication. 57*(4), 586–599.

Chen, R., Sharman, R., Rao, H. R. & Upadhyaya, S. J. (2008b). Coordination in emergency response management. *Communications of the ACM, 51*, 66–73.

Chou, C.-H., Zahedi, F. M. & Zhao, H. (2014) Ontology-based evaluation of natural disaster management websites: A multistakeholder perspective. *MIS Quarterly, 38*, 997–1016.

Facebook Company Info. (2016). Retrieved December 13, 2016, from http://newsroom. fb.com/company-info

DHS (2013) Lessons learned: Social media and hurricane sandy. Department of Homeland Security (DHS). Retrieved February 6, from www.dhs.gov/sites/default/files/publications/Lessons%20Learned%20Social%20Media%20and%20Hurricane%20 Sandy.pdf

Japan Meteorological Agency Emergency Warning System. (2016). Retrieved December 28, 2016, from www.jma.go.jp/jma/en/Emergency_Warning/ew_index.html

Erasmus, A. (2012, April 19). Friday five: How social media works in Japan. *Edelman Digital,* Retrieved from http://blog.edelman.com.au/2012/04/20/friday-5-how-social-media-works-in-japan

Fackler, M. (2013, December 25). Start-Up Spirit Emerges in Japan. Retrieved February 07, 2018, from www.nytimes.com/2013/12/26/business/international/japanese-entrepreneurs-receive-tentative-embrace.html

Ferro, T. & Zachry, M. (2014). Technical communication unbound: Knowledge work, social media, and emergent communicative ractices. *Technical Communication Quarterly, 23*(1), 6–21.

Forster, N. (2000). Expatriates and the impact of cross-cultural training. *Human Resource Management Journal, 10*(3), 63–78.

Hall, E. (1976). *Beyond culture*. New York: Anchor Books.

Higashizawa, N. & Hirai, M. (2014). Understanding international labor and employment policy: A primer for multinational employers operating in a global economy (Japan). *Defense Counsel Journal, 3*, 263–271.

Hiroyuki, F. (2016, October 7). Information triage: Prioritization of the social media society following major disasters – three months after the Kumamoto earthquake. Retrieved December 11, 2016, from www.japanpolicyforum.jp/archives/society/pt20161007193412.html

Hofstede, G. (2001). *Culture's consequences: Comparing values, behaviors, institutions and organizations across nations* (2nd ed.) Netherlands: SAGE Publications, Inc.

Hofstede, G. (2011). Dimensionalizing cultures: The Hofstede model in context. *Online readings in psychology and culture, 2*(1). Retrieved from http://scholarworks.gvsu.edu/cgi/viewcontent.cgi?article=1014&context=orpc

Hootsuite survey highlights importance of social media across the customer journey. Retrieved December 2, 2016, from https://hootsuite.com/newsroom/press-releases/hootsuite-survey-highlights-importance-of-social-media-across-the-customer-journey

Hsieh, H. & Shannon, S. E. (2005). Three approaches to qualitative analysis. *Qualitative Health Research, 15*(9), 1277–1288.

Kim, J. Y. & Nam, S. H. (1998). The concept and dynamics of face: Implications for organizational behavior in Asia. *Organization Science, 9*(4), 522–534.

Kimme Hea, A. C. (2014). Social media in technical communication. *Technical Communication Quarterly, 23*(1), 1–5.

Kostelnick, C. (2011). Seeing difference: Teaching intercultural communication through visual rhetoric. In B. Thatcher and K. St.Amant (Eds.), *Teaching intercultural rhetoric and technical communication: Theories, curriculum, pedagogies and practices.* Amityville, NY: Baywood Publishing Co., Inc.

Lee, S. & Phang, C. (2015). Leveraging social media for electronic commerce in Asia: Research areas and opportunities. *Electronic Commerce Research and Applications, 14*(3), 145–149. doi: 10.1016/j.elerap.2015.02.001

Luthans, F., McCaul, H. S. & Dodd, N. G. (1985). Organizational commitment: A comparison of American, Japanese, and Korean employees. *Academy of Management Journal, 28*(1), 213–219.

Mehlenbacher, B. & Dicks, R. S. (2004). A pedagogical framework for faculty-student research and public service in technical communication. In T. Bridgeford, K. Kitalong & D. Selfe (Eds.), *Innovative approaches to teaching technical communication.* Logan, UT: Utah State University Press.

Nan, N. & Lu, Y. (2014). Harnessing the power of self-organization in an online community during organizational crisis. *MIS Quarterly, 38*, 1135–1157.

Nippon Foundation (2016). Response to the 2016 Kumamoto earthquake. Retrieved December 10, 2017 from www.nippon-foundation.or.jp/en/what/projects/kumamoto

Oda, S. (2016, April 19). Beloved mascot Kumamon's absence since quakes spurs Japan Twitter traffic. *Japan Times.* Retrieved from www.japantimes.co.jp/news/2016/04/19/national/beloved-mascot-kumamons-absence-since-quakes-spurs-japan-twitter-traffic/#.WGYIrvl97IU

Okura, S. & Kaigo, M. (2016). Who leads advocacy through social media in Japan? Evidence from the "Tsukuba civic activities cyber-square" *Information, 7*(4), 66. doi: 10.3390/info7040066

Pan, S. L., Pan, G. & Leidner, D. (2012). Crisis response information networks. *Journal of the Association for Information Systems, 13*, 31–56.

Potts, L. (2013). *Social media in disaster response*. New York: Routledge.

Richardson, R. M. & Smith, S. W. (2007). The influence of high/low-context culture and power distance on choice of communication media: Students' media choice to communicate with professors in Japan and America. *International Journal of Intercultural Relations, 31*(4), 479–501.

Sano, K. & Sano, H. (2016). The effect of social media on customer satisfaction and relationship strength in a service with high perceived risk in Japan. *Celebrating America's Pastimes: Baseball, Hot Dogs, Apple Pie and Marketing? Developments in Marketing Science: Proceedings of the Academy of Marketing Science*, 435–439. doi: 10.1007/978-3-319-26647-3_88

Stedham, Y., Yamamura, J. H. & Lai, S. C. (2008). Business ethics in Japan and Taiwan: Relativist and utilitarian perspectives. *Asia Pacific Business Review, 14*(4), 535–551. doi:10.1080/13602380801987554

Takashima, S. (2016). *2016 Kumamoto earthquake report on Fukuoka city's disaster relief activities in the areas affected by the disaster*. Fukuoka City, Japan: Mayor's Office.

Tapia, A.H. & Moore, K. (2014). Good enough is good enough: Overcoming disaster response organizations' slow social media data adoption. *Computer Supported Cooperative Work, 23*, 483–512.

Twitter "About" (2016). Retrieved December 13, 2016 from https://about.twitter.com/company

Wireless Emergency Alerts (WEA). (2016, October 25). Retrieved December 28, 2016, from www.fcc.gov/consumers/guides/wireless-emergency-alerts-wea

Wurtz, E. (2005). A cross-cultural analysis of websites from high-context cultures and low-context cultures. *Journal of Computer-Mediated Communication,11*(1). Retrieved from http://jcmc.indiana.edu.ezproxy.lib.usf.edu/vol11/issue1/wuertz.htm

Yamamura, H., Kaneda, K. & Mizobata, Y. (2014). Communication problems after the great east Japan earthquake of 2011. *Disaster Medicine and Public Health Preparedness, 8*(04), 293–296. doi: 10.1017/dmp.2014.49

Yates, D. & Paquette, S. (2011) Emergency knowledge management and social media technologies: A case study of the 2010 Haitian earthquake. *International Journal of Information Management, 31*, 6–13

Yenni, T., Pan, S. Ractham, P. & Kaewkitipong, L. (2016). Digitally enabled disaster response: The emergence of social media as boundary objects in a flooding disaster. *Information Systems Journal*. doi: 10.1111/isj.12114

7

MONITORING AND MANAGING ONLINE COMMENTS IN SCIENCE JOURNALISM

John R. Gallagher

Introduction

With the rapid rates and large-scales of writing on the World Wide Web (web), audience participation has emerged as an expectation in 21st century journalism. While this phenomenon is partially due to easy-to-use social media interfaces (Arola, 2010), it is also a consequence of print journalism's economic collapse. News websites rely on website traffic, such as page-views and duration of page-views, to generate revenue rather than paid subscriptions from readers. News websites aim to boost these metrics by offering comment sections and other forms of audience participation, such as social media forums.

Within this context, web-journalists have an increased number of responsibilities. The decline of print advertising and economic subscription models encourages organizations to place editorial and readership concerns on writers who manage participatory audiences in an attempt to control the conversation (Santana, 2014), especially because comments can have an effect on readers' perception of content (Lee, 2015). In addition to writing articles, journalists curate and advocate their writing by monitoring online comments, choosing to delete vitriolic comments, and respond to comments they perceive as genuine or productive. Journalists publish content across social media platforms and respond to inquiries at odd times of the day and any day of the week.

As technical communicators, science-based web-journalists contend with the consequences of these situations. They are often hired on an ad hoc basis, commonly referred to as freelancing or, in terms more *apropos* of e-commerce, as a "gig" in the "gig economy." While their jobs are similar to earlier instantiations of print science journalists, the requirement of being an editor or manager of audience participation leads to an affective type of labor associated with being a web-writer and specifically a web-journalist.

This chapter advocates for documenting the ways that web-journalists contend with reader comments because it enables technical and professional communication (TPC) scholars to better understand the balancing act online writers maintain when engaging a readership while maintaining authoritative control over their texts. These journalists thus confront a vexed relationship between civic engagement and scientific credibility. The strategies I present in this chapter are useful for TPC scholars because the strategies recognize the value of reader participation while coping with the necessity to remain true to facts of reported science. This balance is especially salient given the 2016 presidential election in the United States, during which misinformation, disinformation, and propaganda deliberately proliferated.

To do so, I investigate how such journalists contend with comments. My guiding research question for this chapter is as follows: "What kinds of strategies do online journalists report for negotiating with participatory audiences?" While scholars have investigated comments themselves from a variety of disciplines (Cho and Kwon, 2015; Coe, et al., 2015; Quinn and Powers, 2015), relatively little work has explored how individual journalists contend with participatory audiences outside of organizational structures. This chapter addresses this phenomenon through five one-to-one interviews with science-oriented journalists. Science journalists are encouraged to monitor their comments more than sports or commentary-oriented writing because the former type of writing is less opinionated; their writing is based on objective information. The writers in this chapter must, thus, carefully monitor false comments made about scientific findings.

In this chapter, I first foreground the contexts of the writers' organizations by labeling them "all-edge adhocracies," which extends Clay Spinuzzi's *All Edge* (2015). To Spinuzzi's concept of adhocracies I add the element of *affective labor* to working within an adhocracy on the web. Using the work of Jennifer H. Edbauer (2005) and others, I locate this chapter at the intersection of science web-journalism, adhocracies, and affective labor. The second section lays out my methodology: five case studies of professional web-journalists. After describing my methodology, I identify the following strategies that these science web-journalists use to advocate for civic engagement and control over their texts: (1) ignoring; (2) establishing forums; (3) correcting/updating; and (4) textual listening. I conclude with implications for online writers who wish to contend with participatory audiences.

Adhocracies in a Digital, Content-Driven Economy

In the freelance web-economy, referred to as the "gig economy," science journalists partake in "all-edge adhocracies" (Spinuzzi, 2015), or organizations that appear unified but are comprised of adjunct workers. All-edge adhocracies is a two-part concept. First, adhocracies are "rotating teams of specialists who come together to swarm a project, disperse at the end of it, and reform in a different configuration for the next project" (p. 1). Second, all-edge means "able to rapidly link across organizational boundaries" (p. 2) that temporarily connect specialists across organizations rather than just within an organization" (p. 3). Spinuzzi notes, "*Projectification* [sic] is the organizing principle of adhocracies" or the idea that projects, rather than bureaucracies, guide people within such organizations (p. 31; italics in original).

While Spinuzzi focuses on nonemployer firms across both off and online projects, I extend and reorient all-edge adhocracies to web-journalism. In all-edge adhocracies on the web, writers are hired on a freelance basis. They may categorize themselves as journalists for an online newspaper or magazine, such as *Wired* or *Forbes*, but they are not full-time employees. These organizations largely maintain their brand through the social media presence of their part-time writers. Individual writers maintain the organizations' social media presences, which in turn extend an organization's "front-stage" appearance of "unity, stability, and competence" (Spinuzzi, 2015, p. 53).

The collapse of organizational influence, coupled with the rise of an individual ideology buttressed by social media corporations, has led web-journalists to take on multiple roles that exceed traditional notions of writing—or what Lisa Dush (2015) has described as seeing writing as content. Dush defines content as follows:

> "...digital assets, conditional in their shape and value, that are assembled within and pushed out to networks, where human and machine audiences will assess them, assign value to them, consume them, appropriate and repurpose them, extract from them, and push them into other networks. Said differently, as a set of characteristics, content is conditional, computable, networked, and it is—or will be—commodified."
>
> (p. 178)

The assets to which Dush refers are writing, such as journalist's article, as well as the ecosystem that surrounds that article: infrastructures, analytical data, and comments.

I use Dush's approach to content for three reasons. First, it grounds the economic nature of what web-writers and, specific to this chapter, web-journalists perform for work. "Content producer" is an economic-oriented term for writers' labor when producing content on the web. Second, the term better captures the variety of activities that writers might be assigned. Third, content is a common label for writing in the 21st century World Wide Web. Pairing all-edge adhocracies with content usefully captures the wider variety of meanings and responsibilities of writing. Writing is a broader term in these contexts than in other types of adhocracies. This has led writers to become content producers who *distribute* content to their followers on social media, write on an *ad hoc* basis, and manage feedback from their participatory audiences.

This last role, managing online audience participation, places journalists in the position of monitoring online comments of their articles. This role is extraordinarily complex because journalists need to eliminate off-topic and vitriolic comments while encouraging civic exchange and engagement. They take on the role of editor in a similar situation to the "letter-to-the-editor" genre while harnessing the participatory role of new media by promoting observant comments. In managing participatory audiences, web-journalists consequently negotiate a type of affective labor.

Affective Labor in Online Adhocracies

When monitoring and managing content for online adhocracies, web-journalists must contend with affective labor. While I cannot give a full account of affect or relationality in the scope of this chapter, I will define affective labor within the circumstances of managing participatory audiences for web-journalists. I first want to define my use of *affect*: I use affect to describe the powerful emotional, embodied, and excess that accompanies writing in the context I described in the previous section.

Jennifer H. Edbauer's "(Meta)physical graffiti: 'Getting up' as affective writing model" (2005) provides some useful definitions and descriptions that can be applied to online adhocracies. While her focus is on graffiti and composition studies, Edbauer simultaneously produces an account of affect beyond the boundaries of the classroom (p. 134–6). For Edbauer:

> "...writing scenes are overwhelmingly populated by bodies: shocked, angry, delighted, and feeling-full bodies. Although many models of composition focus upon the signifying dimensions of writing, they often fail to account for writing's experiential aspects."
>
> (p. 133)

Edbauer's claim that affect permeates writing scenes helps clarify her exigency:

> "Because the body-of-sensation is always stubbornly present in scenes of writing, there can be no affectless compositions. In order to more fully answer the question of what writing does, therefore, we need a model that takes affect's operations into account."
>
> (p. 133)

Edbauer's account of affect emphasizes the emotional and embodied nature of writing, as aspect that elaborates on the social forces involved with producing writing.

I want to extend Edbauer's keen observation that the "body-of-sensation" is "stubbornly present" to the work of web-journalists in online adhocracies. While it is cliché of writers to use the phrase "don't read the comments," the requirements of being a writer in such adhocracies prevent such advice from being taken. Using affect, then, helps describe the persistent range of emotional and bodily responses to reading, managing, editing, and ignoring comments and audience participation. Considering affect explicitly foregrounds excesses of writing activities and content production freelance web-journalists encounter.

Adding this notion of affect to labor helps to designate the range of sensations and embodiment that Edbauer highlights as *work*. Web-journalists, in managing comments and content, experience affect as a phenomenon required by their job and, in an era of social media prominence, profession. As Michael Hardt (2007) writes in "What affects are good for," affective labor entails "the corporeal and intellectual aspects of the new forms of production, recognizing that such labor engages at once with rational intelligence and with the passions or feeling" (Hardt, 2007, p. xi). Hardt connects work, understood through enlightenment logic, to feelings, sensations, and excesses that this logic cannot connect (p. xi). As Hardt writes, ". . .affective labor highlights not only the common qualities [workers'] products share but also the fact that in all these activities the body and the mind are simultaneously engaged, and that similarly reason and passion, intelligence and feeling, are employed together" (p. xi). Affective labor framed in these terms helps to depict a wider range of work with which web-journalists engage.

Ken Hillis, Susanna Paasonen, and Michael Petit (2015) pick up on Hardt's work in order to move affective labor into online and digital contexts. For them, affective labor is a direct point of concern in our networked, digital age. They note, "A consideration of affect is further present in work that engages the concepts of immaterial and affective labor" and then go on to observe, "In the business models of sites such as Amazon, Google, and Facebook that rely on advertising income, and which work to naturalize the attention and experience economy, the various layered exchanges of users add up to virtual value" (p. 7). In the context of this chapter, Hillis, Paasonen, and Petit's view of affective labor brings to light the function of discursive information as value in e-commerce and social media environments. The virtual value of a discursive attention economy, based on metrics, comments, and virality, has value in terms of capital: layered exchanges can be used to measure economic viability of a journalist's article, e.g., more and higher-quality comments often lead to a favorable reception. Likewise, the affordances of a particular platform's template, such as "likes" on Facebook or "retweets" on Twitter, can add economic value to articles. Layered exchanges on social media—and the web more generally—provide monetary incentive to monitoring and managing the affective labor associated with such comments and affordances. It motivates adhocracies and the individuals within them to engage layered exchanges in such environments. Affective labor highlights that people are responsible for producing such discourse and the labor involved with monitoring it on the web.

When taken together, the framework of affective labor and online adhocracies assists with contextualizing the case studies I present shortly. While none of the activities my participants engage with are radically new, the scale and speed of managing comments has no direct print precursors. Web-journalists engage readers directly, repeatedly, and frequently in ways that print journalists simply never experienced. And they perform all of these roles without the organizational backing and security that journalists experienced before the economic collapse of the print newspaper industry.

A Case Study Methodology

My five participants (four female and one male) live in North America: the US and Canada. I have chosen pseudonyms for them: Matt Grimes, Rosa Kennedy, Tracy Monroe, Maggie Skinner, and Lola Upton. Participants were found from a snowball sample from my previous work (Gallagher, 2015) and are part of a larger study of the way that web-writers develop strategies for contending with readers and other participatory audiences. I have chosen these five participants because they already have participatory audiences and, as science journalists, contend with comments while adhering to the scientifically grounded information in their work. My guiding research question from the *larger study* was as follows: "In what ways do web-writers contend with their participatory audiences?"

I interviewed participants during the summer of 2015; semi-structured interviews lasted between 25–75 minutes. I asked participants extensively about their conceptions of audience and self-reported ways of negotiating online response, which frequently took the form of comments. For instance, I asked the following pair of questions: "Do you classify or categorize comments in any particular way when you encounter them? If so, can you describe those categories, their key features, and how you might have developed them?" The purpose of these interviews was to identify the self-reported strategies participants had for contending with participatory audiences.

I then transcribed the interviews. I followed up with participants via email once and then on an ad hoc basis. To keep my participants' identities confidential, I will not explicitly state which participant writes for which organization(s) because this might allow readers to discover participants' identities. However, together, they have written for *Huffington Post, Forbes, Psychology Today, Wired*, and *U.S. News & World Report*. They have published for a variety of other news websites, professional trade publications, and academic journals.

All participants maintain an active web presence and curate their own blogs. Tracy Monroe and Matt Grimes have published books with reputable publishing companies. I have chosen these participants because they actively considered their participatory audiences, which also means they have such audiences; in other words, they already have a participatory readership. None of my participants are employed full-time by the organizations for which they write. While they have other full-time positions, their writerly roles are part of online adhocracies. All are college-educated. In the following descriptions, I briefly highlight participants' relationship to comments while offering some context to that writer-audience relationship. In particular, I aim to describe how each writer contends with participatory audiences and monitors comments.

Matt Grimes

Grimes is a medical doctor who writes for an award-winning blog and a variety of well-known news organizations. Grimes told me, "I've been blogging for ten years and writing for various media outlets." About comments, he remarked that they are ". . .generally only incredibly on-board or the opposite. It's very polarizing. Effusive praise or calling people names." He sees value in the comments for his readers ("I do see value for my readers") but recently turned off comments (within six months from the time of our interview) on his personal blog, although comments on some of his more public work are still functional. He did so because "the negative comment will skew interpretation," despite feeling "guilty about turning off the comments." He still encourages readers to engage in discussion but re-routes them to an online forum such as Facebook. He views venues off his personal website as productive sites of engagement: "Facebook is different from the comment section. People tend to engage one another there." These views demonstrate a vexed relationship to comments, one that reflects recent shifts in eliminating comment sections on scientific writing on the web.

Rosa Kennedy

Kennedy is a committed environmental journalist and writes for a variety of online news organizations and blogs. She told me, "I started writing online in 2003 when I signed on to work on [Presidential candidate John] Kerry's [2004] campaign." This was her first experience with participatory audiences, via comments, because, as she recalled, "I had to figure out who was an anarchist and who was a real commenter and who was a concern troll." A concern troll is someone who feigns interest, typically by asking a question, only to attack an online exchange or derail an ongoing debate. Kennedy is "always writing towards the lurkers rather than the commenters" because "they greatly outnumber the commenters." She tends to conceive of her audience as "people reading the comments but not asking questions." Kennedy tries to avoid overt influence by commenters and "being pulled in one direction by the commenters."

Tracy Monroe

Monroe is a journalist and educator who writes about science writing. She writes regularly about health sciences, including childrearing, childbirth, and vaccinations. She teaches journalism. She maintains a regular blog and professional advice column. In order to combat the myth of a vaccine-autism connection, she needs to develop strategies for engaging commenters who do not believe her work. I believe she is the most rhetorical of the five participants I present in this chapter. With respect to anti-vaccine readers and commenters, Monroe told me, "you really need to listen to their argument so you can deconstruct it." She has developed forums for refuting standard arguments of anti-vaccine readers/commenters. Monroe believes her acumen as a question-posing journalist helps her to contend with and monitor deleterious comments.

Maggie Skinner

Skinner started out as an independent blogger in 2004 and eventually wrote for multiple professional science societies. For various science websites, Skinner is "required to monitor" her comments, a labor that is uncompensated though it is an "expectation that probably falls under the category of 'duties as assigned.'" This is because there is a "fairly substantial literature about the effects of comments." She "almost quit over comments" at a major online news magazine. Although according to Skinner, comments are not as vitriolic as emails: "email commenters show a scarier side of commenters because it takes time and effort to send that email." She has been compared to "the whore of Babylon" by a commenter. It's never one comment that bothers Skinner; it's the accumulation of them over time because, for her, "they chip away at you." Skinner has a two-tiered system that involves a yellow card and a red card, although she admits there is a third category of comment that she labels "completely batshit crazy with no connection to reality." This third type of comment, which is generally incoherent and/or off-topic, she ignores and deletes it if she can. This two-tiered system acts as a warning system and is her way of "making a public statement about comments" that are "over the line." The system "really seems to help" although she warns that writers must be "really clear about consequences," i.e., reader response, when choosing to delete comments.

Lola Upton

Upton is a science writer who mainly tries to inform and, secondarily, educate. When I asked her about the distinction between these ideas, she told me that informing was "providing information" whereas education was "taking the next step." She elaborated on this "next step" by telling me that educating means that the reader "understands information," "why it is important," and what "readers can do right now." She explained educated readers would "react" in some way, which could mean a range of activity from donating money to "talking about the issue over coffee." As a science writer who sees herself as situated within a "print model," she wants to keep the conversation surrounding comments on-topic and focused on "the science." For this reason, she believes "comments are too personal" and too frequently attack journalists. Her ideal goal with respect to comments is "to have an online conversation" about the topic, but she has not experienced that ideal very often. Upton believes that writing on the web, like print writing, is "goal-oriented and always seeks to engage readers in some way." Engagement takes many forms for her and, thus, "context is important." For Upton, "comments make you forget there is a lost art to not giving a shit about what people think about you." She believes that individuals need to have their own view of themselves and "not view themselves through the lens of others."

Procedures

I transcribed these five interviews and searched for patterns using grounded theory (Strauss and Corbin, 1998). I read through transcripts identifying places where participants reflected upon managing comments. After I identified preliminary patterns, I then examined participants' texts (various publications) for the previous six months to look for patterns that were exhibited in texts as well as stated by participants.

Analysis: Textual Strategies

This section addresses the strategies that my participants self-reported as using while managing their comments. Some of these self-reported strategies cannot be verified because there is no discursive evidence; I must, therefore, rely on the accounts provided to me by my participants. In other cases, discursive evidence can be recovered within the texts themselves. These are strategies that cut across the five case studies.

Ignoring

All writers discussed the act of ignoring comments. By this, participants did not mean avoiding comments. All participants *read* comments, obviously some more carefully than others. They processed comments in some form or another and then decided not to respond; all of them told me that responding to comments was a learned experience. They were not adjusted to this type of response, were not formally trained for it, and did not believe that responding was a primary tactic. For these reasons, I foreground ignoring comments as a strategy because it best reflects my participants' perspectives. TPC scholars may view the practice of reading and then ignoring certain comments as a strategy for developing on-topic and purposeful civic engagement because they may need strategies for contending with the *opposite* of civic engagement, i.e., trolling and vitriolic comments. My participants had three broad categories of comments they ignored, e.g., (1) overly positive, (2) not helpful, and (3) insincere. These categories are based on their perceptions.

First, participants ignored the "thanking" comments or "effusive praise." All four female participants discussed ignoring the thanking comments while Grimes labeled this type of comment as effusive praise. While positive comments were "nice," they did not serve any purpose, from the perspective of my participants. Grimes ignored comments because comments are often binary. He told me, "Only two [types of comments] for the most part: agreeable, congratulations, and warmth. Or you're an idiot. Not much of an in-between." Grimes' sentiment reflected the views of the other participants as well. Kennedy, Monroe, Skinner, and Upton ignored positive comments because they did not call for a response.

Second, participants ignored comments they perceived as not helpful. All five reported ignoring comments that were perceived as bloviating. Grimes told me he ignored comments that "pontificated without questions, which are most comments." Kennedy, Monroe, and Skinner told me, independently of each other, that most comments were for other commenters. Upton told me that although comments were often authentic, regardless of whether they were good or bad, most commenters were "after attention." Kennedy echoed this sentiment by telling me that some commenters just "want a microphone."

Third, they ignore "insincere comments" (Monroe) or comments that did not seem genuine to the participant. Perception of a comment's tone was key for ignoring comments. Many commenters ask questions, but participants needed to decide which questions were really statements, sarcastic questions, or rhetorical questions. With respect to commenters who posed false or insincere questions, Kennedy labeled this type of commenter "concern trolls." I inquired about this term:

> GALLAGHER: "And what is a concern troll?"
> KENNEDY: "They act as through they're really worried but really trying to plant doubts."

She further elaborated on concern trolls as category of commenter: "I had to figure out who was an anarchist and who was a real commenter and who was a concern troll." Concern trolls, often men, would try to insert themselves into a conversation for the opportunity to explain, despite the expertise of female journalists. Grimes, a man, did not mention this type of insincere question-posing.

Establish Forums

While some off-topic comments were "interesting" (Grimes, Monroe, and Skinner) or "constructive" (Kennedy, Monroe, and Skinner), the participants all saw productive but off-topic comments as better suited for a discussion forum not directly attached to their writing or article. This was the second most commonly reported strategy, behind ignoring comments. Skinner told me, "Let [comments] be on Facebook or Twitter," and Grimes told me he set up discussion forums via a link to a social media platform, e.g., Facebook. Monroe also set up forums for intense discussions not directly on her professional writing. This sentiment was significant because it showed that these writers were not interested in sharing their authority or authorial *ethos* with pseudo-anonymous commenters. Simultaneously, these authors recognized the function of spaces for participatory audiences; forums allowed for greater engagement and readers to discuss a particular text. Creating forums separate from a web-journalist's text is thus a strategy that accounts for the significant role of participatory audiences while retaining authorial power.

Correcting and Updating

The most traditional (but not the most common) strategy that participants mentioned was the act of issuing a "correction" or "update." Based on reader comments, these journalists used relevant comments to help them edit. If a comment pointed out a spelling error, a factual error, or a usage error, then participants changed their texts to account for the comment. While this strategy is similar to what print journalists encounter, it is different due to *who* offers the editorial feedback. Participatory audiences become the source of editorial feedback, although all participants expressed that such audiences only have influence in the case of objective concerns with their writing.

Correcting and updating was a frequent occurrence. Upton "dives into comments when something is factually inaccurate or the reader misconstrued what [she] wrote." Upton told me that "commenters are so focused on their reaction to a small word or phrase" that they do not finish reading. The only time Kennedy edited her work in response to a comment was ". . .to make notations about updates." Kennedy told me that she left these comments up out of respect to the commenter. Skinner updated her work to issue a clarification statement based on comments or to correct "a minor typo." She was "not required to disclose" that she corrected minor typos. Grimes echoed Kennedy's and Skinner's perspectives in that he did not change his work in any major way. When I asked him about any pieces he'd edited or changed based on comments, he said, "Not unless someone has pointed out an error, spelling, or something like that." He mentioned that he would "update the original post" to indicate a change was made. While he wouldn't change his articles in any significant way, he did state, "I'll add information but won't change." Monroe would make updates in terms of spelling and information "objective in nature." The frequency of correcting and updating, based on comments, provides evidence that participatory audiences possess influence on the way writers revisit and revise their texts, however minor that role may be.

Textual Listening

Textual listening, as a concept, is meant to highlight the ways that web-writers, in this case web-journalists, read and skim through concatenations of public audience participation in order to make determinations on how and when to respond. I use *textual* to emphasize the discursive nature of listening for these writers; they had to interpret tone and sincerity in alphabetic text. I use *listening* for two reasons in the context of this chapter. First, participants used this word when discussing their comments. They mentioned reading comments, but they tended to discuss audience participation as an act to which they could listen. They referred to aggregates of comments as conversations—while voicing a desire to "keep the conversation going" (Kennedy, Monroe, and Skinner). I understood their use of listening to be a stance of openness, echoing Krista Ratcliffe's (2006) concept of rhetorical listening, towards the comments they deemed genuine and sincere. Second, listening seemed to capture my participants' behavior accurately: they did not respond to all of the comments but contended with the ongoing conversation of participatory audiences by "looking through" the comments to determine "what's of value and what needs to be ignored" (Skinner). Textual listening highlights the oral nature of participants' actions in a textual web-environment.

Textual listening involved determining which comments deserved a response through a consideration of tone. Participants listened for sincerity and a genuine tone through the identification of questions posed by commenters and subsequently deciding if those questions were authentic or simply rhetorical/sarcastic. As Kennedy told me, "There are people who ask fake questions or just want to prove you wrong. And then there are people who ask real questions and those people are the best because, as a reporter, you can give people a voice."

All participants mentioned in their interviews that questions were a source of consternation. Grimes and Upton did not respond to questions in their comments because they perceived the commenters' minds as already made up. As Grimes said, "My writing is an area of deeply-held convictions. . . It's a personal offense people take if you disagree with their opinion. Even if commenters ask questions, they don't want their minds changed. Their questions aren't real." Upton believed commenters "jump down [to] the comment section" without reading the entire text. Commenters for her were so "focused on their reaction or a small word or phrase" that they did not finish reading. In other words, Grimes and Upton did not respond to questions because they did not deem their comments to be sincere.

Of the five participants, Monroe was the most rhetorical and active with textual listening, due primarily to her efforts to debunk the anti-vaccine movement. She carefully read the question(s) in a comment, determined if it was sincere or not, and then carefully crafted responses to "anti-vaxxers," i.e., people who were against vaccinations. While all participants wanted to change people's beliefs, Monroe knew that she could change their mind with carefully written responses. While some commenters were "of course batshit crazy," many of the comments Monroe received were from concerned parents who, though skeptical, "remain in the purview of being convinced to vaccinate their children."

Textual listening is, in my estimation, an oral trope that usefully describes the process of reading through not one text but rather a multitude of short comments from a public participatory audience—and then determining which comments require a response based upon a level of sincerity as determined by the journalist (not the commenter). In the context of web-journalism, it helps to capture the labor associated with monitoring comments that requires objective, scientific claims in order to maintain the veracity of the author's statements.

Conclusions and Implications

Most broadly, the strategies participants presented in this chapter are useful to TPC scholars because they demonstrate that professional writers can have an ongoing role in the circulation of online texts and building communities. Writers imbedded in online communication practices may have a varied set of responsibilities, both coerced and self-initiated. Coupled with the obligation of reporting scientific findings and publications, the writers in this chapter demonstrate that 21st century online communication practices can impose two different purposes: to create a community by monitoring, managing, and responding to comments, while simultaneously retaining control and authority over those texts.

The specific strategies I have documented give insight into the ways that individual web-journalists continue to write *after* the production of a text. While these strategies may not be generalizable to groups of online writers, they assist with documenting the diverse roles that 21st century web-writers may experience—activities that may be required of writers, despite the possible ways this work may not initially fall under the auspice of "writing" or even "labor." While these four strategies have some parallels to the work of print journalists, especially correcting and updating, they are different because the online activities of monitoring and managing comments and reader responses are more fluid and frequent than in print.

With the task of monitoring comments coming frequently and in close proximity to a writer's initial text, writers in situations similar to my participants might consider the work of being a 21st century web-writer as requiring oral modes of communication within text-based online forums and contexts. From my conversations with these writers, I have understood that a journalist's labor does not conclude with the publication of an article. Their writing circulated, and as it circulated, it often required additional attention and tending. Very rarely did my participants mention the role of an editor. While having an editor came up occasionally, these participants, from my point of view as an outsider, tended to view themselves as autonomous writers and journalists circulating their work and managing their audiences.

I believe this chapter, thus, has three implications. First, professional online communicators of science have labor associated not only with the production and dissemination of their writing but also with work associated with being *speakers*. They may address and invoke an audience, to borrow a phrase from Ede and Lunsford (1984). Like speakers, they manage audience perceptions of their writing and how their writing is received (Goffman, 1956). They may also imagine audiences (Litt, 2012) based on their interactions with commenters while developing an emergent sense of participatory audience. The writers in this chapter illustrate oral modes of communication, i.e., ignoring and listening, that may be employed when writers attend to the circulation of their writing.

From a broad perspective, then, my participants help to put pressure on distinctions between writing and speaking in the context of circulating web-writing. To remove some of the conceptual boundaries between speaking and writing may help shed light on the diverse roles that my participants experience. The act of writing an online article is different in its purpose than acts of back-and-forth of online commenting, for instance. From a perspective that views writing and speaking as similar, writing and speaking are simply communicative acts mobilized for different purposes on the web. This approach is helpful for civic engagement because it helps to remove artificial divisions between online and offline community activism and organization. The work of online and offline advocacy, from this perspective, is intimately related.

Second, if participatory audiences are a foundation of 21st century web-writing and communication, then sometimes these audiences may need to be ignored while others may need to be cultivated. As I hope to have made clear throughout this chapter, comments are not entirely useful or productive. From the viewpoints of my participants, they are more often negative, off-topic, or overly positive ("thank you!"). Nevertheless, there are useful comments that allow conversations to continue. The effort to find these comments, engage with them, and highlight them for other readers is an important act of building an online readership and community. Cultivating some types of audiences while discouraging vitriolic audiences may be helpful for encouraging productive, civic engagement.

Lastly, the strategies I've presented here could be integrated into classroom contexts where comments need to be read and analyzed. While Grabill and Pigg (2012) have rhetorically analyzed engagement in comments within science forums, TPC scholars need teaching strategies for managing and monitoring comments as a form of advocating certain positions in an organization, website, or social media community. In doing so, we might remind our students of the time-consuming and affective labor that community advocacy requires.

Discussion Questions

1) What kinds of managing and monitoring strategies have you encountered that are similar to the ones presented in this chapter? Different? What are some reasons for these similarities and differences? What are some additional strategies?
2) While this chapter focuses on science journalists, what other professions and occupations might encounter similar types of affective labor?
3) What are some gendered aspects of affective labor?
4) Which strategies presented in this chapter do you think are most useful? Least useful?
5) This chapter focuses on writers in North America. To what extent do you think these strategies are effective for contexts outside North America?

Further Reading

All website URLs accessed February 2018.

Bergstrom, K. (2011). "Don't feed the troll": Shutting down debate about community expectations on Reddit.com. *First Monday, 16*(8). http://firstmonday.org/ojs/index.php/fm/article/view/3498/3029
Carlson, M. (2014). The robotic reporter. *Digital Journalism, 811*(December), 1–16.
Clerwall, C. (2017). Enter the robot journalist users' perceptions of automated content. *Journalism Practice, 8*(5), 519–531.
Faciloscope. http://faciloscope.cal.msu.edu/facilitation. Software designed by Michigan State University for managing online comments.
Kennedy, K. (2016). *Textual curation: Authorship, agency, and technology in Wikipedia and chambers's cyclopædia.* Columbia: University of South Carolina Press.

References

All website URLs accessed February 2018.

Arola, K. L. (2010). The design of Web 2.0: The rise of the template, the fall of design. *Computers and Composition, 27*(1), 4–14.
Cho, D., & Kwon, K. H. (2015). The impacts of identity verification and disclosure of social cues on flaming in online user comments. *Computers in Human Behavior, 51,* Part A, 363–372.
Coe, K., Kenski, K., & Rains, S. A. (2014). Online and uncivil? Patterns and determinants of incivility in newspaper website comments. *Journal of Communication, 64,* 658–679.
Dush, L. (2015). When writing becomes content. *College Composition and Communication, 67*(2), 173–196.
Edbauer, J. H. (2005). (Meta)physical graffiti: "Getting up" as affective writing model. *Journal of Advanced Composition, 25*(1), 131–159.
Ede L., & Lunsford, A. (1984). Audience addressed/audience invoked: The role of audience in composition. *College Composition and Communication, 35*(2), 155–171.

Gallagher, J. R. (2015). Five strategies internet writers use to "continue the conversation." *Written Communication, 32*(4), 396–425.

Grabill, J. T., & Pigg, S. (2012). Messy rhetoric: Identity performance as rhetorical agency in online public. *Rhetoric Society Quarterly, 42*(2), 99–119.

Goffman, E. (1956). *The presentation of self in everyday life*. Edinburgh: University of Edinburgh.

Hardt, M. (2007). What affects are good for. In P. T. Clough & J. Halley (Eds.), *The affective turn: Theorizing the social*. Durham: Duke University Press.

Hillis, K., Paasonen, S., & Petit, M. (2015). "Introduction." *Networked affect*. Cambridge: MIT Press.

Lee, M. (2015). The persuasive effects of reading others' comments on a news article. *Current Psychology, 34*(4), 753–761.

Litt, E. (2012). Knock, knock. Who's there? The imagined audience. *Journal of Broadcasting & Electronic Media, 56*(3), 330–45.

Quinn, K., & Powers, R. M. (2015). Revisiting the concept of "sharing" for digital spaces: An analysis of reader comments to online news. *Information, Communication & Society, 419*(4), 442–460.

Ratcliffe, K. (2006). *Rhetorical listening: Identification, gender, whiteness*. Carbondale: Southern Illinois University Press.

Santana, A. D. (2014). Controlling the conversation. *Journalism Studies, February 2015*, 1–18.

Spinuzzi, C. (2015). *All edge: Inside the new workplace networks*. Chicago: University of Chicago Press.

Strauss, A., & Corbin, J. (1998). *Basics of qualitative research: Techniques and procedures for developing grounded theory* (2nd ed.) Thousand Oaks: Sage.

8

JOURNALING AND BIBLIOTHERAPY PARTICIPATORY DESIGN AS A HEURISTIC FOR PROGRAM DEVELOPMENT

Joshua M. Rea, Peter Cannon,
Alysia Sawchyn, and Katie L. Walkup

Technical Communication Methods for Vulnerable Populations

Faculty, librarians, and graduate students from multiple departments at the University of South Florida (USF), including the School of Information and Rhetoric and Composition, have been working to build a bibliotherapy library at the Drug Abuse Comprehensive Coordinating Office (DACCO) women's residential drug and alcohol rehabilitation center in Tampa, Florida. This project was initially funded by several grants, including ones from the American Library Association (ALA) and the Library Services and Technology Act (LSTA), and is already well underway. After much of the work toward the library's installation was carried out, we began to discuss how composition and technical communication might be useful within the center.

We see incorporating technical communication methods in the DACCO library as a way to serve the vulnerable population within the center. Researchers in technical communication have been making a push toward civic engagement and social advocacy for some time (Eble and Gaillet, 2004; Jones, et al., 2016; Jones, 2016; Rose, 2016). Technical communicators are uniquely positioned to help implement communicative practices within the center that can help the women develop reflective and meta-cognitive skills as well as develop employable skills (one of the main goals of DACCO). However, implementing many methodologies can be difficult, if not impossible, because of the constraints of the center as well as the Health Insurance Portability and Accountability Act (HIPAA). For instance, when discussing building an electronic writing application for use in the center, we ran into several roadblocks, not least of which was the lack of internet access and the need (both legally and ethically) for the women's writings to remain private, as they are part of therapeutic endeavors.

With these restraints in mind, we decided to engage in participatory design strategies (Blythe, et al., 2008; Moore and Elliott, 2016; Rose, 2016), building programs continuously in concert with, and with feedback from, both the center's administrators and patients. We began to iteratively attempt different programs with input from all involved to improve them with each iteration, after input from methods such as focus groups and surveys. Through this process, we settled on the development of a journaling program to meet both the needs of the population and goals of the center.

The journaling program that we have developed consists of voluntary, workshop-style sessions. This chapter will detail the iterative processes that led to the development of these sessions, our rationale and planning for the sessions, as well as our experiences with the first of them. Here, we will cover both the theoretical framework from which we approach the project and the practices and results we observed.

The following will detail our initial attempts at implementing a journaling program within the bibliotherapy library. First, we will give an in-depth look into the context of these efforts, expanding on the details of the bibliotherapy library and the theories behind its implementation. Then, we will review the composition and technical communication theory that leads us to believe journaling would enhance this program. This work will be grounded within a lens of feminist disabilities studies (FDS), especially as the DACCO residents are a special population entirely made up of women who many might consider disabled[1]. After the theories are established, we will follow with a discussion of participatory design and the way that we incorporated this methodology to develop programs within the center. We will then provide an overview of our determinations regarding the best practices and limitations of implementing the journaling program, including required technologies and infrastructure. Finally, we will discuss the implications of this project and the possibilities for future research and praxis, both for this specific program and for others. We will then show the values of adapting journaling theories and pedagogies, from writing studies to therapeutic environments, using the DACCO library as a context in which to explore these connections and their relative success.

The Bibliotherapy Center: Bringing Books to Residential Treatment Facilities

A multidisciplinary team at USF has been working for some time to provide a library and library services for the female residents of the DACCO. The facility is the largest comprehensive treatment program in Hillsborough County, serving over 4,000 people a year with over 260 employees and an annual budget of approximately $15 million. Specifically, the female long-term residential treatment program is an 80-bed facility that is approximately six months in duration (DACCO, 2014). This program, which houses about 300 women a year, provides treatment for substance abuse and any co-occurring mental health disorders while also focusing on providing employment skills for when the residents eventually take their leave of the center. The population is racially and ethnically diverse; many clients are economically disadvantaged or politically disenfranchised, and most have been targets of physical, mental, or sexual abuse. While the program is non-secure, residents are restricted from leaving without prior approval. During their six-month stay, they lack access to the internet or reading materials due to treatment restrictions.

The lack of reading materials provided librarians with an opportunity to serve this population. In many incarceration environments, libraries are a "normal zone," acting as a portal to the outside world and the wider community (Lehman and Locke, 2005; Ljødal and Ra, 2011). Thus, efforts were begun to provide library services and a bibliotherapy program to this population.

At the heart of this project is the idea that for every reader there is a book, guided by Ranganathan's *The Five Laws of Library Science* (1964). The library operates as a partner to the patients' treatment plans, proceeding under Ranganathan's five core values:

1. Every reader her book.
2. Every book its reader.
3. Books are for the use of the patron.
4. The library is a vehicle of empowerment.
5. The library is a place of human dignity.

In conjunction with these core values, the library offers four service promises to the center and its residents that focus on providing therapeutic outcomes, collaborative treatment processes, and viewing library services as part of the treatment process. These service promises are circulation, reference services, health literacy (i.e., providing patients with the skills to find health information), and bibliotherapy.

Bibliotherapy is a recognized therapeutic form that can be used as an adjunct to substance abuse treatment programs (Schutt, et al., 2013; Fanner and Urquhart, 2008). Bibliotherapy can be performed using affective treatment techniques, cognitive-behavioral therapy (CBT), and visual-based techniques. Affective bibliotherapy relies on fiction aiding the patients; by empathizing with a story's character, the patient undergoes catharsis, leading to insight and behavioral change. CBT relies mainly on self-help books, working to correct negative behaviors by offering positive alternatives. Finally, visual-based materials use mediums such as graphic novels and incorporate both affective and CBT methods. The library at DACCO incorporates all three methods, providing non-fiction self-help books, affective young adult fiction books, and therapeutic-based graphic novels (Shereff, et al., 2016).

The implementation of the bibliotherapy program allows multiple avenues for therapeutic outcomes. It provides the residents with the opportunity to reflect inwardly and connect with the books in the library and with the community that the books represent. This can lead to positive, productive thinking and correction of negative behaviors, and has certainly proved to be effective in previous implementations. However, we see a gap in its potential for *outward* expression; while there can be group sessions and other opportunities for discussion, reading is often a personal and intimate experience that focuses on the consumption of information. Thus, journaling can work as an effective partner to the bibliotherapy program by allowing the residents the opportunity to outwardly reflect on their reading, their thoughts, and their personal experiences, and would further develop their set of employable skills.

Participatory Design and (Re)Conceptualizing the Project

The study team's technical communicators were new to DACCO and had to learn about the facility's residents, administrators, and policies. Though we wanted to gather more robust data, including details from patient experiences, facility administrators were skeptical about our motives. Moore and Elliott's (2016) case study may illuminate a possible cause of this skepticism: too often study designers do not know how to ask for or use citizen knowledge. Salvo (2001, p. 275) suggests that dialogue is key to mediating these participatory problems. Similarly, facility administrators were adamant that we would not have access to patients or their journals for research purposes. We were told that this project would need to work within or as an adjunct to the existing bibliotherapy library. Moreover, resident participation would be entirely voluntary. We would not be guaranteed time with the residents. While at first we were discouraged from providing our services under these conditions, we remembered Spinuzzi (2005, p. 165) and the importance of locating knowledge within all participants' interpretations of the project. Similar to Rodrigo & Ramírez (2017), this project did not start out as a participatory design study, but we realized that we would need to adopt a mindset of participatory design as we moved forward. We needed to include all stakeholders in designing this project for the treatment center, and we had to work with facility staff, within facility policies. We needed to receive training from both DACCO and its bibliotherapy library. Input from residents, administrators, and librarians would be considered in revising the project design. Before we could access DACCO and its residents, we had to become part of DACCO ourselves.

Guided by existing technical communication research on participatory design, we sat down once more with our stakeholders. Rather than thinking about the intervention we wanted to test, we asked facility administrators and library personnel what they needed. Then we listened. Facility administrators needed more resources to support their residents' recovery and professional development, including workshops, books, and music. Library personnel needed evidence of the bibliotherapy program's efficacy to meet their service promises and to obtain further funding. By working with librarians, we could support their argument that bibliotherapy and journaling had helped DACCO residents. Once we had collected this evidence, we could use our expertise to apply for more funding, which would serve the facility administrators. DACCO's personnel needed our skills as teachers, researchers, and grant-writers. Certainly the project demanded more of our participation and expertise than we originally anticipated.

Additional Therapeutic Tools: Journaling and Narrative Construction

The creation of the journaling program began with the construction of the DACCO library and the development of its collection and services. An initial focus group comprised of the residents was held on March 1, 2016. Most of the respondents preferred information related to alcohol and other drugs (AOD) addiction treatment, spirituality, self-care, and achieving balance in life. Program preferences included creative writing and poetry workshops for the residents as well as interactive health reference programs for both residents and their families.

The first workshop involved the delivery of health literacy instruction. While it was unrelated to the other, more creative programs being developed at the library, its implementation was important for understanding how future workshops would function. It became immediately apparent that the library program space had its limitations. First, as an outside space, the unusually hot Florida spring and summer weather made large industrial fans a necessity. Fortunately, the initial grant allowed for their purchase and installation. Cooling the program participants, however, meant having the fans at higher speeds and in close proximity. This created noise concerns and issues with papers flying about. Second, even though the outside space was covered and relatively free from sunlight, many of the respondents felt that they could not see the information from the computer that was projected onto a screen. In all, the service satisfaction survey of the participants found that they overwhelmingly enjoyed the program, but there were a few comments about the outside conditions.

The next program was a poetry workshop developed by a USF English graduate student. This workshop was held in June of 2016 and addressed many of the concerns from the previous program. There were 22 participants and each one submitted a service satisfaction survey. Even though it was summer, programmatic space was still an issue so the workshop had to be held in the same location as before. This time, instead of relying on a computer and a projector for the program content, materials were copied and distributed to the participants. The fans were evenly distributed and set to the next lowest speed. This allowed for cooling while affording an opportunity for the participants to hear the workshop leader. Survey respondents enjoyed the workshop but felt that the combination of heat, the fans, and the mix of papers made it somewhat difficult to be creative.

A two-part fiction workshop was next. Again, the satisfaction surveys were consulted in the development of this program. Many of the previous survey respondents requested a fiction workshop as part of the library's original programming but grant obligations had made scheduling difficult. It was decided that these workshops would be held inside and split up into two sessions.

It was after these iterative steps in developing a usable writing program for the DACCO residents, and with input from all of the stakeholders involved, that we came to the idea of journaling as a solution. Specifically, we wanted to implement a program that would help residents connect their readings to their experiences. Thus, we began to research the pedagogical value of such a program in order to begin building new workshop sessions, as we detail below.

Journaling has long been used in the classroom in both technical communication and composition courses[2]. The process provides what Brodkey (1989) called an "authentic reason to write" (p. 128) that authorizes students' own discursive practices. Furthermore, according to Newton (1991), who writes specifically about journaling in response to reading, the journal is "a particularly effective way for students to track their individual meaning-making efforts over a period of time," helps students "develop and assess their own learning strategies," and "gain valuable insights about themselves," (p. 477–478) as well as insight into why they respond to certain texts the way they do. Journaling can also be seen as a step toward creating a community of writers (Harris, 1989) and can help writers understand and validate personal experiences, as well as connect those experiences to others. Especially with reflective, reader-response journaling, writing allows reflection on the readings and connection with the authors through a dialogic response system. Finally, journaling can also help develop basic communication and writing skills; it is often said that writing every day will help one become a better writer.

Journaling and narrative have also been found to be useful and important tools in therapeutic situations. Charon (2009) discusses the idea of journals as narrative medicine, arguing that "narrative medicine reminds us that illness unfolds in stories" (p. 120) and admitting that "it gradually has become clear to me now with the help of narrativists from far outside mainstream medicine that medicine is practiced on an unstable gap between the body and the self" (p. 122); this gap between the body and the self can be filled by journaling and narrative.

Furthermore, an interview with James Pennebaker reveals the following:

> From a therapeutic perspective, one tool that is really beneficial is giving students just the awareness that writing about an experience, even if it's only for five or ten minutes, can be beneficial, and having them do that occasionally, and not as a graded assignment, for the first five or ten minutes of class can show them how beneficial it is – that it is a really

powerful coping tool. The other perspective, speaking as not a psychologist but as a teacher, is that students really do need to be taught to write."

(Moran, 2013, n.p.)

Indeed, according to Pennebaker, constructing narratives can oftentimes be more productive than traditional therapy: "There's a big difference between pouring out your emotions about a trauma and constructing a story or narrative about it" (Moran, 2013, n.p.).

Journaling and narrative construction can also help in therapy, and in disability studies more generally, by giving writers tools to understand their unique realities and identities. According to Block and Weatherford (2013), "narratives provide avenues for multiple realities to be shared," and "our stories are left incomplete if we omit the metaphoric and symbolic codes we use in narrating our subjective and personal realities" (p. 498). For Block and Weatherford, those with disabilities have unique experiences, and the best way to understand them at a personal level is through the construction of personal narrative and the articulation of their lived experience. They tell us that "the experiences of these individuals are best told through the lived narratives of those who live in distinct bodies and because of those differences face unique challenges" (2013, p. 501). Here, we see the importance of the journaling process for self-understanding and meta-cognitive awareness of one's experiences and identity. This also answers calls in Feminist Disability Studies to "understand human diversity, the materiality of the body, [. . .] and the social formations that interpret bodily differences" (Garland-Thomson, 2011, p. 15). Writers would be able to interrogate such topics as "the status of the lived body, the politics of appearance, the medicalization of the body, the privilege of normalcy, multiculturalism, sexuality, the social construction of identity, and the commitment to integration" (Garland-Thomson, 2011, p. 16) on their own terms and in relation to their own experiences. Finally, narrative has been understood as an important tool in social justice work, as it can help vulnerable populations articulate their struggles (Jones, et al., 2016).

In the context of the DACCO library, specifically, journaling would help accomplish the center's goals in several ways. It would serve as an important counterpart to the bibliotherapy process, allowing residents to reflect explicitly and externally, rather than internally, on the texts that they read. It would imbricate them within a network of writers, including the authors of the books they read and one another. Furthermore, journaling would allow the development of meta-cognitive awareness and for the construction of personal narratives that would help residents understand their unique experiences and connect those experiences to their readings, allowing them to better understand why specific texts resonate with them. Finally, it would help to develop their writing skills, giving them the chance to work on an employable skill that would be useful beyond the context of the center.

We find that technical communicators are uniquely equipped to implement such a program. The discipline brings several important aspects to the table. Teachers of technical communication, specifically, often have experience in working with basic writers, the level at which many of the DACCO residents find themselves. Many technical communication teachers are also experienced with and knowledgeable about journaling pedagogies, including their importance as a reading response mechanism and as a tool to develop meta-awareness. Though it is not a technique that is traditionally used in technical communication classes, most technical communication teachers are knowledgeable about writing pedagogy more broadly, especially composition, where journaling has certainly found homes. Adapting this pedagogy, then, would answer Palmeri's (2006) call to adapt our discourses to special populations. Furthermore, technical communicators are experienced with usability issues and with technology, giving us the ability to both critically and pragmatically work closely with the specific details and challenges of the program's implementation; these challenges and our answers to them will comprise much of the remainder of this chapter.

Adapting Theory to a Restricted Environment

Once we realized the theoretical and therapeutic value of adapting journaling pedagogies for this context, we had to begin thinking realistically about what it would look like in the center. We consider this treatment center a restricted environment, so we had to take into account the requests of administrators, who required that residents not be able to access the internet or interact with anyone outside the center. We were also concerned by the needs of the residents, who have been diagnosed with clinical or subclinical mental health disorders. Given these circumstances, we could not implement an existing computer or mobile writing program and conduct usability tests afterwards. While usability tests have since been conducted, usability must begin at the project's nascence. Drawing on multidisciplinary theories and methodologies, we used actor-network theory (ANT) to determine the unique needs of the population and speculative usability to consider criteria that would meet those needs.

These realizations about usability are not new; Palmeri (2006) argues that usability discussions that do not take into account people with disabilities *before* the creation of an interface, technology, etc., marginalize those populations. Because of this, "we technical communication scholars must also critically intervene in broader usability discourses in which people with disabilities are often absent or marginalized" (Palmeri, 2006, p. 59). Nathaniel Rivers and Lars Söderlund (2016) refer to this way of thinking about usability as "speculative usability." Rivers and Söderlund (2016) allow us to not only think of usability as a pre-creation concern, but also tell us that usability must move beyond traditional models which focus closely on the relationship between a user and an object in a one-on-one, context-free, imaginative situation. Instead, we must think of the contextual factors that occur when an object is used. The object and user are both actants within a network of other actants[3], and the network itself must be taken into account more holistically when thinking about the usability of an object. Understanding usability in this way allows for "an increased inventional capacity for usability testing, which ought to be able to *both* narrow the scope of an object in order to assess its usefulness for specific tasks *and* intensify and multiply the usefulness of objects" (p. 3, emphasis in original). In keeping with this model of usability, Spinuzzi (2009) points out that discussions of interface usability must move beyond metaphor and into an ecological understanding of user experience. As we envisioned user, administrator, and project director needs as an ecology, we drew heavily on Latour's (2007) actor-network theory to conduct preliminary usability tests.

Tracing the connections of residents, administrators, and researchers was not easy. We knew that we could not interrogate the tens or hundreds of relationships that residents, our intended consumers, had made. Even though we wanted to help the population, we were concerned about the ethics of prying into the residents' lives. In keeping with our ecological model of usability, the librarians we were working with decided to conduct informal focus groups to determine residential and administrative needs. Then we would adapt our new technologies in response to residents' feedback. Our residents, then, helped develop their own journaling technology. Their ideas became part of a conversation between designers, libraries, researchers, and administrators. We began this conversation by building usability into the program itself (Cannon, et al., 2016).

We also realized that conducting surveys as part of usability testing gave us the opportunity to conduct research about user salience. We could not forget that the purpose of the project was to help residents gain self-efficacy. As they evaluated the usefulness of the application, we wanted them to also question their own thoughts and feelings over time. We drew upon a modified Comprehensive Model of Information Seeking (CMIS), a popular model from information science. The CMIS determines user connections, experiences, and beliefs. In this project, it functions to elicit both usability and salience information from residents (Johnson, et al., 2001).

Space and Place Theory for Usability

Space and place theory are also important for helping us to understand the unique needs and materiality of the DACCO library. DACCO has a very strict set of constraints and also what we see as a prescient need that we can meet, creating what Jenny Rice (2012) calls a "crisis of place" into which, as we have laid out previously, we see technical communicators as well-equipped to intervene. The connection between journaling, the lived experience of the residents, and DACCO itself, show the ways in which "spaces are textualized (as well as how texts themselves are spatialized)" (Rice, 2012, p. 10). A textual-spatial ecology is already in place within the bibliotherapy library, and implementing our journaling program will intervene meaningfully into this ecology. Keeping the space of the library in mind, then, is important as it will both inform and be informed by the new journaling program. As Rice (2012) explains, "we always write from a place, and our writing itself create spaces" (p. 12). As we discuss implementation and usability, then, we will also be bearing in mind space and place theories and thinking about both the ways that the space of DACCO is composed and will be recomposed, as well as how the space will affect the composing practices that occur within it.

Speculative usability, the CMIS, and space/place theory allow us to think about the action of the journaling technology in relation to the entirety of the DACCO library. The library has a very specific set of constraints and of actants that must be taken into account when thinking of the best way to implement a journaling program. The other actants here include the other residents who may be in the library, the librarian, and the books themselves, among others. The constraints of the center include a lack of internet access and privacy concerns, both of which deeply narrow the field of applications that could be used for journaling.

We were able to set up several criteria for a functionally useful journaling application. First, the application should be able to replicate physical writing in digital space. There are two main reasons for this: first, according to Sharp and Hargrove (2004), handwriting is more likely to arouse the affective capacities of writers than computer input, and thus offers far more in terms of expressive capability; second, some residents may be unwilling or unable to use keyboards, though we did not want to limit users who write more effectively in computer-mediated spaces. To compound the issue of computer vs. handwriting modalities, residents should also be able to verbally record entries in case they do not feel comfortable writing or typing.

Usability issues for storage of journal entries also touch on residential needs of confidentiality and privacy. Ideally, entries should not be able to be accessed by others, either on paper or within the application. Team members were adamant that as researchers and as advocates, we should not share these residents' narratives unless ethically required, or unless the resident specifically requested that someone else be able to access their entries. This need for confidentiality caused several issues, especially in terms of the functionality of current applications that could be used for journaling. Entries cannot be stored on a cloud system (this criteria is reinforced by the lack of internet storage), but they should be locally-stored so that, if they wanted to, residents could take their entries with them when they leave DACCO to further reflect on or add to. However, these locally-stored entries would have to be inaccessible to anyone other than the resident that wrote them, and their doctor if the resident gave them permission.

Thinking about the space of the library and the other actants within it leads to the development of further criteria. Residents should be able to move about during the journaling process; there should be an environment of mobility and interaction, both with other residents and with the books in the library. The journaling process should not, then, be a secluded and isolated one where the residents have to sit at a station that is somewhat sequestered off from the rest of the room. They could certainly do this if they wanted to, but the technology used should at the very least *allow* for mobility throughout the library area. This mobility would allow for interactive situations that would help better foster a sense of community, as well as further encourage residents to get books while they write and connect their readings with their narratives and experiences.

At this time, the development of such an application is underway. We have applied for and received additional funding from the Institute of Museum and Library Services to further develop an application for personalizing mental health literacy services, and our research team has moved forward by beginning the journaling program with one-on-one, pen-and-paper group sessions. These sessions still required quite a bit of design work, which will be discussed in the next section.

Implementation: Beginning a Journaling Program

The implementation of a journaling program in a restricted environment was a challenge to us. Traditional designs for community-based library services do not operate well in restricted environments where access to the internet is controlled or non-existent. We often forget how much we rely on technology in the profession and how many applications require internet connectivity. This single challenge required decisions regarding how the journaling program would be delivered and what kind of information architecture (IA) needed to be constructed.

We decided that the best place to conduct the journaling program was in the library's activity-based section as it focused on the resident. This space comprised of a 709 sq. ft. covered, outdoor area, which allowed the residents to spend time outside while protected from the elements by a 31.5 ft. deep overhang. Here is where the residents spend their time reading and participating in group therapy sessions. Tables and chairs were provided for residents to work on writing assignments.

We developed an hour-and-fifteen-minute-long lesson plan for the group journaling sessions based on previous workshops held at the facility. In the months preceding our case study's program, our researchers had the opportunity to hold several creative writing groups through the existing library. In these creative writing groups, participants read contemporary short stories together, discussed them, and then wrote their own stories and shared these with the group. The original lesson plans for these groups were often over-scheduled; that is, the participants were very eager to speak about the stories, often in the context of their reactions to the texts, and also in sharing their own writing. As a result of the therapeutic environment, we believed it best to devote more of the time to sharing, allowing everyone who wished to contribute or share an opportunity to do so. We also observed in the creative writing sessions that the DACCO residents demonstrated a wide range of comfort in their interactions with texts. Most noticeably from these earlier sessions, the participants' reading comprehension varied greatly. We used this information in the creation of our plans for the journaling program. Thus, rather than asking participants to read *and* respond to texts, we asked them to work based off memory. This would not only allow more time for the women to participate in the discussions and sharing, if they chose to do so, but would also allow the women to respond to whichever texts they were most comfortable engaging with.

For the purposes of this journaling program, we decided that, at least for initial sessions, a scaffolded set of prompts would be the best approach: we asked the residents to write about an experience that they'd had, then write about a book that they had read, and finally to write about how the experience and the book were related. These prompts worked to ask the residents to both express their narratives and to think critically about how the experiences and stories of others were similar to their own. After the writing was completed, we allowed twenty minutes for residents to share their writing (or a summary of such) if they wished to do so.

Implementation of library services in a restricted environment required the cooperation of many different stakeholders, including counselors, administration members, librarians, and the residents. Naturally, the librarians were the first individuals we enlisted in our attempt to offer the journaling sessions since they were able to determine the needs of the residents based on their prior satisfaction surveys. Next, the counselors were approached since we had to determine whether the journaling sessions would be consistent with the overall treatment plans of the residents. Engagement with the counselors required that the overall structure of the sessions be developed enough in order to explain them to the counselors, yet flexible enough to allow change based on their input. After we obtained input from the counselors, administration officials had to be convinced that the journaling sessions would advance the therapeutic goals of DACCO and that the residents were not at risk if they participated. Finally, the residents had to be on board with the journaling sessions. Working in a treatment center such as DACCO meant that anything could become a trigger and that no two residents had the same triggers. Therefore, the residents had to be assured that they would get something out of the library services journaling sessions.

The librarians at DACCO developed a survey as part of their programmatic evaluation process that was handed out to the residents that would allow us to improve future sessions. The survey also helped us form initial thoughts about the journaling application that would be developed, in a manner that would be responsive to the needs of the residents. These surveys were, at this point, quite simple, asking the residents if they enjoyed the activity, if they would like to participate in more writing activities, if the activity helped them be creative, if the information was interesting, and what type of writing activities they would be interested in in the future. The initial simplicity of these surveys allowed the librarians to first ensure that the residents were interested in the program and that it was fulfilling their needs; they will continue conducting surveys as we continue with the program, making sure that the program meets the expectations of the library and the residents. The results of these sessions and surveys will be discussed in the next two sections.

Journaling Session Results: Observation and Feedback

We held the first hour-and-fifteen-minute journaling session at DACCO on December 2, 2016. The library provided ruled composition notebooks and pens/pencils for about thirty participants (most were present for the entire lesson, but due to the scheduled nature of DACCO, several arrived late and/or left early); the journals and utensils were theirs to keep and, ideally, continue using for journaling.

The initial session plan was comprised of three, twenty-to-twenty-five-minute segments: 1) a welcome/introduction; 2) a series of writing activities; and 3) optional sharing. However, this plan was modified during the actual session to better engage participants. The goal for this journaling session was to increase the efficacy of the bibliotherapy program at DACCO by promoting conscious attention and written reactions to participants' interactions with library books. Our belief was that such activities would also improve participants' writing skills through practice—thus aligning with one of DACCO's goals of vocational training—while providing a therapeutic outlet for DACCO residents. What follows is an account of the journaling program as it was implemented.

The journaling session was held outdoors on a covered patio, and participants were seated at large tables with the session leaders seated near the entrance to the space. During the first portion of the session, the session leaders introduced themselves and the activities' intended objectives. Many participants were familiar with one of the session leaders, the librarian for the bibliotherapy center at DACCO, and some had met the other one, who orchestrated previous writing (though not journaling) sessions at the facility. The women were very enthusiastic and eager to answer the initial questions: 1) "Who enjoys reading?"; 2) "What are some books participants have enjoyed lately and why?"; 3) "Who likes to write/has journaled before and how was the experience?"; and 4) "Why might someone write about what they've read?" The purpose of these questions was to provide the session leaders with an understanding of participants' prior experience and to have participants verbally externalize to a group about the very internal process of reading. The women were quick to demonstrate meta-cognitive awareness, both in regards to why they enjoyed the books they read and their previous journaling experience. Additionally, it was observed that in addition to sharing their answers, the women were quick to offer feedback and suggestions to other participants: "If you liked X book, you should read Y." It seems reasonable that this sort of discussion and recommendation happened outside the context of the journaling session, which suggested this particular population already verbally reflected on the DACCO library reading materials. The questions were posed rather informally; however, all the women raised their hands to speak and waited to be acknowledged by the session leaders before sharing their answers and experiences. This was likely due to how most DACCO sessions were formatted and to the facility's emphasis on structure.

The remainder of the session alternated between guided writing time and voluntary sharing. Though the initial plan was to first do several writing activities and then share about all of them at the very end, it appeared some participants had difficulty focusing or were uninterested in the activities and spoke among themselves during the writing portion of the session. Because this group of women seemed more attentive while we or the other participants were speaking and sharing, we decided to alternate between writing activities and sharing. We gave participants three writing prompts: 1) to journal about a particular book or part of a book they found moving; 2) to journal about a personal experience; and 3) to journal about how the two (the book and the personal experience) related to one another.

In response to the first question, participants asked the session leaders to repeat and be more specific in the writing prompt; some of the women either a) hadn't read any books they could remember in detail or b) were concerned that they would be doing the exercise "incorrectly." Rather than present ourselves as the arbiters of "correct" journaling practices and also perhaps isolate the women who weren't readily able to describe particular book passages, we opened up the prompts, saying participants could write about whatever they felt moved to express, if no books came to mind. This, of course, led to blurring of responses: some women wrote about their personal experiences in response to the first prompt and so wanted to know "what to write about" for the second—whether to continue writing more or to write about something else. So though the bulk of the session was less organized than we had anticipated, we believe that the process of constructing personal narratives is often a messy process, and so we decided it was better to move all participants in the general direction of journaling than claiming a "best way to do it" and become rigid and alienating those women whose experiences did not fit neatly into our plan.

Participant Feedback

During the final few minutes, the librarian passed out an optional survey that asked participants to rate on the Likert Scale their experience of the session through a series of statements. Table 8.1 details the twenty-six collected survey responses (percentages rounded to the nearest tenth).

The results of the twenty-six collected surveys showed that participants found the session to be a positive one overall. Their responses of enjoyment in the

TABLE 8.1 Survey results

	I enjoyed today's writing activity.	I would like to participate in more writing activities.	Today's writing activity helped me be more creative.	The information was interesting to me.
Strongly Agree	11 participants (42.3%)	10 participants (38.5%)	11 participants (42.3%)	9 participants (34.6%)
Agree	15 participants (57.7%)	12 participants (46.2%)	10 participants (38.5%)	15 participants (57.7%)
Uncertain	0 participants	4 participants (15.4%)	3 participants (11.5%)	2 participants (7.7%)
Disagree	0 participants	0 participants	1 participant (3.8%)	0 participants
Strongly Disagree	0 participants	0 participants	1 participant (3.8%)	0 participants

session and interest in the information, in particular, demonstrated an engagement in the construction of personal narratives alongside the texts they were reading through the DACCO library and that the materials were appropriate to the community setting. Due to facility restrictions and ethical concerns, we left the journals with the participants for them to continue journaling in their spare time at the facility. Since the journaling session was a component of their (often court-ordered) treatment program at DACCO, the contents of the participants' writing was considered private and not to be included in this case study.

Discussion of Results: How to Best Meet Participants' Needs

Our aims in implementing a journaling session as part of the library services at DACCO were to help participants improve their writing skills, increase their self-awareness, and provide another therapeutic opportunity. We were concerned in particular with meeting Rice's (2012) crisis of place, and creating a session that would both meet the needs of the DACCO population while fitting into the institutional constraints. To respond to these constraints and needs, we worked closely with the participants to craft programs that would best benefit them, incorporating technologies and tools that would be most useful. Indeed, the participants were familiar with the provided tools, some commenting that they remembered using the same types of notebooks in early grade school. In this way, the participants were interacting with and responding to the materials and practices on an emotional level; rather than being simply tools to achieve an intended outcome, the notebooks appear within the institution as hallmarks of an earlier time in the women's lives.

During the first portion of the journaling session, many of the women were extremely enthusiastic and outspoken about the library services. They described the experience of reading while at DACCO as at least one of the following: a positive activity to pass the time; as a form of escapism; or as a cathartic act, reimagining alternatives to their own lives. All the women had previously kept a personal journal and found it beneficial; many said that it helped them process their emotions and/or the events of their lives. Connecting the two activities, then, by journaling about their reading as it related to their personal lives, allowed participants to articulate and acquire new self-knowledge in a more formal and fixed manner than speaking or thinking and thus to gain a more clear understanding of their experiences (Moran, 2013).

During the second portion of the session, which mixed writing and sharing, some women spoke among themselves during the allotted journaling time and fewer were interested in sharing what they'd written. There were a number of possibilities for this waning desire to share throughout the session, though it is worth noting that "waning desire to share" in this instance was merely a contrast to the beginning Q&A when almost all thirty participants wanted to share. Additionally, some side conversations became louder during the later writing times, which made it difficult for at least one other participant to focus on her journaling.

One possible reason for the decreased participation was that the women were all in various stages of withdrawal after serious substance abuse, which impedes concentration for any prolonged period of time and deteriorates attention span. Another possibility might have been a respectful group dynamic. The women were generally very supportive and empathetic toward one another, often referring to one another as "sister." Many of the women seemed quieted after sharing—even the group of side conversations were resumed at an even lower volume—and it seems that the DACCO population was particularly well-suited to a nonacademic version of Harris' (1989) ideal writerly community: one that "allows for both consensus and conflict" (p. 20) and is bound by a limited and specific place. Despite their differences in life experience and reading levels—which were the subject of their sharing—and investment in the journaling session, the participants were united in their desire to support one another.

Overall, the journaling session proved effective in helping the women to articulate their experiences and practice writing, moving from the discussion of experiences to creating a constructive narrative. Most said they enjoyed the activities and were happy to keep the notebooks, and it appeared that several planned to continue journaling regularly, though not necessarily about what they'd been reading. In the future, ideally, these bibliotherapy and journaling sessions would meet regularly, perhaps with women doing the writing activities beforehand and then using the actual meeting as a time to share. As with all service-learning initiatives, allowing for flexibility and adapting to meet the needs of the target population is key to bringing our services to the community in a helpful manner.

Implications and Further Research: Encountering Challenges of Funding and Ethics

As in many community writing activities (Grabill, 2007), scholar-advocates face many problems. Despite our not having the time or funding to further develop an electronic application, our work in participatory design was not in vain; we obtained further funding to create this technology in 2017. Our efforts may have been stymied in this area, but our research team was more determined than ever to deliver quality bibliotherapy and therapeutic journaling services to this special population. These actions lead to new directions of research for two members of our team; we expanded the reach of bibliotherapy and therapeutic journaling to include mental health literacy, or an individual's recognition and response to their mental well-being. Since all of the residents of this center have been diagnosed with mental health concerns, mental health literacy is especially needed in this population. Our efforts with participatory design led to new research with mobile health (mHealth) technologies, specifically the opportunity to pursue technology's impact on user health ecologies. Indeed, we continue to engage with stakeholders at the center to design new programs and technologies for use in the center, with the goal of eventually making these programs self-sustaining.

As our research team uncovers the possibilities of adapting journaling pedagogy within this context, we continue to develop an application that meets the specifications requested by the treatment. We have considered questions of practice in this research journey (Rude, 2009), among them technology design, information infrastructures, and application perpetuity. While as scholars of technical communication, we may be equipped to design technology and help users find the information they are looking for, we have discovered that the bridge between research and practice is difficult to navigate. Our current mental health intervention, requiring mental health librarians in the treatment center, cannot continue without funding. We have learned to request funding for technology and tools, not labor. The more computers and materials we can obtain for this treatment center, the greater chance our intervention has to endure, either after funding dries up or the research team moves in other directions. Thus, we are designing technologies and materials for an age of funding austerity.

Clearly, the next steps in researching the possibilities of adapting journaling pedagogy within this context are to develop an application that meets the constraints described above and secure the technological tools needed to implement the journaling application through grant funding (a process that is already underway). These very practical applications of our research lead the field to question program design and advocacy in an age of austerity and an electronic journaling application would make the journaling program more self-sufficient and sustainable, as the residents could then freely journal with only very minimal group sessions. After implementation, several options would become available for further research with the specific context of DACCO.

We have also considered the limitations of ethical usability testing in this treatment center. While our clients have so far been generous with their time and suggestions for improving the mental health intervention in this center, we are hesitant to conduct full tests of accessibility, usability, and privacy; our ability to do robust usability testing, and especially to report such, are limited by HIPAA and our own Institutional Review Board (IRB). To include the personal stories of the participants in this case study, including their responses during the journaling programs themselves, would be to infringe upon patient privacy and complicate the ethics and responsibilities of working with vulnerable populations. This presents difficulties for us as researchers and scholars who would like to make our work accessible to others who are similarly interested in questions of literacy and mental health, or working with other marginalized groups. Less altruistically, this also presents difficulties of acquiring funding, as the merit of a particular project is often linked to its demonstrable, or publishable/published, impact. We implore fellow practitioners to not be dissuaded or daunted by these constraints, as the work of technical communication must concern itself with advocating for vulnerable groups.

Additionally, the treatment center administration is also hesitant to let users participate fully in the development of usable technologies. Our research in this context can thus serve as a heuristic for how those in the field can engage in participatory design with populations that have similar constraints. Our usability tests have evolved similarly; we have adapted treatment center usage statistics, conducted mini-focus groups within workshop sessions, and relied on anecdotes and other qualitative user data. We continue to adapt conventional usability testing to fit within this setting.

Further research for our team includes further study of the connection between journaling and bibliotherapy. While our research must adapt to respect residents' privacy concerns, we would like to look at meta-cognition in this treatment center, and examine meta-cognition's role in both mental health literacy and self-efficacy. These research areas span many fields, including technical communication and rhetoric of health and medicine. Our goal as technical communicators is to help these users achieve self-efficacy within the context of this treatment center. Our goal as scholars of rhetoric and health medicine is to examine self-efficacy itself, and determine its development.

We believe our work at DACCO is one of social justice, advocating for increased resources in the forms of bibliotherapy and guided journaling for vulnerable populations. Though this case study is specific to the needs of this particular location, the difficulties we've encountered and detailed above are by no means unique to our situation. Rather, we stress that the ubiquity of these challenges means that adaptation and responsiveness to the specific needs of each site and population is a crucial component of any writing endeavor that works within the community. It is by taking such a position in our research that we can best work *for* the populations, rather than ungainly imposing our theoretical frameworks and models upon them.

Conclusion: Responsible and Responsive Advocacy for Technical Communicators

The DACCO center has already been given the tools for relatively new, innovative forms of therapy through the implementation of a bibliotherapy program. Implementing a journaling program has already allowed residents to further understand and articulate their experiences, understand why readings resonate with them and how the readings connect to their situations through responsive readings, develop a community of writers inside and outside of the center, develop meta-cognitive awareness of their writing and reading processes, and develop their writing as an employable skill. The program thus serves several important therapeutic goals and helps to accomplish the major goals of the DACCO treatment center.

Our initial implementation of a journaling program has taken the form of face-to-face sessions where residents write in a pen-and-pencil journal. As we continue to do more of these sessions, we look to do two things: 1) explore available technological options to move the journaling process from pen-and-paper, continuing to think about the constraints of the situation and conducting surveys with the residents to choose options that best fit the center's goals and the residents' needs; and 2) work to phase out the face-to-face sessions and make journaling a self-sustaining, regularly occurring process within the center, which could still be assisted by staff if need be.

After the process of implementing the program is complete, usability tests will be performed to judge the efficacy of the technology, and the possibility of exploring the entries will be further researched. Hopefully, this further research will allow for an even deeper understanding of the connections between bibliotherapy and journaling, and, even more broadly, an understanding of the possibility of journaling as a heuristic for articulating personal experiences and developing meta-cognitive awareness in therapeutic settings. Our initial usability surveys have already showed that the residents are eager to participate in the program and that it has helped them think more deeply and creatively about their reading and their experiences. We hope that this trend will continue as the program develops more fully, as meeting the needs of the residents is our main goal; since its inception, the bibliotherapy library has sought to help the residents understand their narratives and improve their mental health literacy, and journaling will serve as a key component in helping residents to do so.

This project provides one example of the ways in which we can use our expertise as technical communicators to assist vulnerable populations. Indeed, we see this as a social justice concern. Our methods and experiences can provide examples of some of the many concerns that occur when advocating for and working with vulnerable populations; our work when designing for these populations must be responsible and reflexive, and must always be in the best interest of those we serve. Thus, we have showcased here some of our ethical concerns in undertaking this project, such as participants' need for and right to privacy, which complicated the way we would normally proceed, and the ways that we responded to these issues.

Examining this project can thus provide technical communicators with ways in which we can advocate for vulnerable populations (and especially for mental health literacy) and work with them to design, develop, and provide valuable and beneficial services, doing so in a reflexive, responsible, and responsive manner. Participatory design is a useful way to approach clients who have unique physical, spatial, and ethical constraints. Thus, we would recommend that technical communicators engage in this practice to best determine the needs of the populations that they serve. Understanding the usefulness of participatory design can also be useful in the classroom, as we can further encourage our students to participate in civic engagement and advocacy by using participatory design strategies in the situations that they are asked to work with. This chapter should serve as a heuristic for how to engage in this methodology in concert with a real client in order to develop programs and communicative practices that uniquely match a client's most prescient needs.

Notes

1. The DSM 5 defines addiction itself as a disorder, regardless of any co-occurring conditions these women may have. It is worth noting that we contest the assumption that addiction is a disability, which aligns with one of FDS' main goals: to trouble the category of disability itself.
2. The technique is also used in disciplines such as Creative Writing, Literature, and Philosophy, among others.
3. Rivers and Söderlund explicate actor-network theory (ANT), the theoretical base of their essay, quite well. For more, however, see Latour (2007).

Discussion Questions

1) How can participatory design techniques be used to ensure that the needs of vulnerable populations are met?
2) What other writing and communication techniques can technical communicators use to help develop programs for clients?
3) In what other ways can researchers present as much information as possible while navigating ethical and legal concerns?
4) What is the best approach to take when initial research does not pan out because of unforeseen circumstances or consequences?
5) What other methods can technical communicators use to build programs for and with clients?

Further Reading

Cannon, P., Walkup, K. L. & Rea, J. M. (2016, September). mHEaL and mHealth in a restricted environment: Design and usability for an offline mental health literacy application. In *Proceedings of the 34th ACM International Conference on the Design of Communication*. Silver Spring, MD: ACM.

Garland-Thomson, R. (2011). Integrating disability, transforming feminist theory. In *Feminist Disability Studies*. Ed. K. Q. Hall. Bloomington, IN: Indiana University Press, p. 13–37

Palmeri, J. (2006). Disability studies, cultural analysis, and the critical practice of technical communication pedagogy. *Technical Communication Quarterly, 15*(1), p. 49–65.

Shereff, D., Palmer, R. & Cannon, P. (2016). Every reader her book: Creation of a therapeutic library at a women's residential treatment facility. *Journal of Hospital Librarianship, 17*(1), 42–52.

Spinuzzi, C. (2005). The methodology of participatory design. *Technical Communication, 52*(2), p. 163–174.

References

All website URLs accessed February 2018.

Block, B. A. & Weatherford, G. M. (2013). Narrative research methodologies: Learning lessons from disabilities research. *Quest, 65*(4), p. 498.

Blythe, S., Grabill, J. T. & Riley, K. (2008). Action research and wicked environmental problems: Exploring appropriate roles for researchers in professional communication. *Journal of Business and Technical Communication, 22*(3), p. 272–298.

Brodkey, L. (1989) On the subjects of class and gender in "The Literacy Letters." *College English, 51*(2), p. 125–141.

Cannon, P., Walkup, K. L. & Rea, J. M. (2016, September). mHEaL and mHealth in a restricted environment: Design and usability for an offline mental health literacy application. In *Proceedings of the 34th ACM International Conference on the Design of Communication*. Silver Spring, MD: ACM.

Charon, R. (2009). Narrative medicine as witness for the self-telling body. *Journal of Applied Communication Research, 37*(2), p. 118–131.

Eble, M. F. & Gaillet, L. L. (2004). Educating "community intellectuals": Rhetoric, moral philosophy, and civic engagement. *Technical Communication Quarterly, 13*(2), p. 341–354.

Fanner, D. & Urquhart, C. (2008). Bibliotherapy for mental health service users Part 1: A systematic review. *Health Information & Libraries Journal, 25*, p. 237–252.

Garland-Thomson, R. (2011). Integrating disability, transforming feminist theory. In *Feminist Disability Studies*. Ed. K. Q. Hall. Bloomington, IN: Indiana University Press, p. 13–37

Grabill, J. T. (2007). Writing community change: Designing technologies for citizen action. Cresskill, NJ: Hampton Press.

Harris, J. (1989). The idea of community in the study of writing. *College Composition and Communication, 40*, p. 11–22.

Johnson, J. D., Andrews, J. E. & Allard, S. (2001). A model for understanding and affecting genetics information seeking. *Library and Information Science Research, 23*(4), p. 335–349.

Jones, N. N., Moore, K. R. & Walton, R. (2016). Disrupting the past to disrupt the future: An antenarrative of technical communication. *Technical Communication Quarterly, 25*(4), p. 211–229.

Jones, N. N. (2016). The technical communicator as advocate: Integrating a social justice approach in technical communication. *Journal of Technical Writing and Communication, 46*(3), p. 342–361.

Latour, B. (2007). *Reassembling the social: An introduction to actor-network theory*. Oxford: Oxford University Press.

Lehman, V. & Locke, J. (2005) Guidelines for library services to prisoners. The Hague, IFLA Reports.

Ljødal, H. K. & Ra, E. (2011). Prison libraries the Scandinavian way: An overview of the development and operation of prison library services. *Library Trends*, (3), p. 473.

Moore, K. R. & Elliott, T. J. (2016). From participatory design to a listening infrastructure: A case of urban planning and participation. *Journal of Business and Technical Communication, 30*(1), p. 59–84.

Moran, M. H. (2013). Writing and healing from trauma: An interview with James Pennebaker. *Composition Forum, 28*.

Newton, E. V. (1991). Developing metacognitive awareness: The response journal in college composition. *Journal of Reading, 34*(6), p. 476–478.

Palmeri, J. (2006). Disability studies, cultural analysis, and the critical practice of technical communication pedagogy. *Technical Communication Quarterly, 15*(1), p. 49–65.

Ranganathan, S. R. (1964). *The five laws of library science*. Bombay, New York: Asia Pub. House.

Rice, J. (2012). Distant publics: Development rhetoric and the subject of crisis. Pittsburgh: University of Pittsburgh Press.

Rivers, N. & Söderlund, L. (2016). Speculative usability. *Journal of Technical Communication, 46*(1), p. 125–146.

Rodrigo, R. & Ramírez, C. D. (2017). Balancing institutional demands with effective practice: A lesson in curricular and professional development. *Technical Communication Quarterly, 26*(3), p. 314–328.

Rose, E. J. (2016). Design as advocacy: Using a human-centered approach to investigate the needs of vulnerable populations. *Journal of Technical Writing and Communication, 46*(4), p. 427–445.

Rude, C. (2009). Mapping the research questions in technical communication. *Journal of Business and Technical Communication, 23*(2), p. 174–215.

Salvo, M. J. (2001). Ethics of engagement: User-centered design and rhetorical methodology. *Technical Communication Quarterly, 10*(3), p. 273–290.

Schutt, R. K., Deng, X. & Stoehr, T. (2013). Using bibliotherapy to enhance probation and reduce recidivism. *Journal of Offender Rehabilitation, 52*, p. 181–197.

Sharp, W. G. & Hargrove, D. S. (2004). Emotional expression and modality: An analysis of affective arousal and linguistic output in a computer vs. paper paradigm. *Computers in Human Behavior, 20*, p. 461–475.

Shereff, D. Palmer, R. & Cannon, P. (2017). Every reader her book: Creation of a therapeutic library at a women's residential treatment facility. *Journal of Hospital Librarianship, 17*(1), 42–52.

Spinuzzi, C. (2005). The methodology of participatory design. *Technical Communication, 52*(2), p. 163–174.

Spinuzzi, C. (2009) Light green doesn't mean hydrology!: Toward a visual rhetorical framework for interface design. In S. Miller-Cochran & R. L. Rodrigo (Eds.). *Rhetorically rethinking usability: Theories, practices, methodologies*. Cresskill, NJ: Hampton Press, p. 69–87.

9

RÉSUMÉ DESIGN AND CAREER ADVOCACY IN A GOODWILL CAREER CENTER

Derek G. Ross

Introduction

Résumés are an integral part of the job application process, and could be considered the single most important piece of technical documentation that job seekers ever create: After all, in most cases, no résumé means no job. Despite a résumé's obvious importance, however, agreement on what constitutes an "effective" résumé is limited, with many different types of designs proposed in many different venues, from technical communication textbooks to a wealth of online job search tools.

Since the Fall of 2012 I have volunteered as a writing coach, or "résumé doctor," at a Goodwill Career Center. In that time, I have worked extensively with visitors to the center to help them prepare résumés and job letters. Additionally, I have worked with Goodwill Industries to develop, in conjunction with a graduate class in document design at my institution, materials for a résumé writing class, résumé templates, and additional job application materials which have been shared across all 50 counties served by Goodwill in my area.

I started working with the Goodwill Career Center as a way to become more involved in my local community, and in the time I have volunteered there I have been conducting research on the perceptions of résumés from multiple perspectives: job seeker, potential employer, and Career Center employee.[1] My work with the center led to several research questions:

RQ1. Do job seekers' perceptions of the value and design of résumés differ from potential employers' perceptions of the value and design of résumés?

RQ2. What are common "mistakes" made on résumés by job seekers as compared to the types of résumés advocated by potential employers and communication professionals?

RQ3. What is the role of a technical communication professional as a volunteer in a career services organization, and how might we best serve our communities as advocates?

In answering these questions, I consider research on various organizational strategies for résumé design and discuss the importance of engaging with local, on-the-ground organizations. I intend this chapter to serve as a locus for discussing ways for technical and professional communicators to become more involved with their local communities, to discuss ways that our expertise might better serve our communities, and to consider how civic engagement can help inform our own research and teaching practices.

Goodwill, Career Advocacy, and Résumé Design

Goodwill and Career Advocacy

Reverend Edgar J. Helms founded Goodwill in 1902 as both a social enterprise and industrial program. In its earliest iteration, Goodwill collected used goods and clothing from those with means, then employed those in need to repair and resell the items. Goodwill's modern mission stays true to its work-related roots, "Goodwill® strives to enhance the dignity and quality of life of individuals and families by helping people reach their full potential through education, skills training and the power of work" (Goodwill, "About Us," 2017, par. 1).

In 2016, Goodwill helped more than 313,000 people find employment, and helped over 31,000 people earn some type of credentialing. Over two million people "received Goodwill services in-person to build their career and financial assets" (Goodwill, "About Us," 2017, "Our Results" section). Some of the services job seekers use come in the form of Goodwill's Career Center—a full-service employment-aid agency that helps visitors find and apply for jobs, teaches basic computer and communication skills, and provides both a full-time and volunteer staff to help clients achieve employment.

Goodwill's Career Center serves a valuable role in supporting jobs in our community, and their use of a volunteer force makes it an excellent space for academics to enact Cushman's (1996) call for professional rhetoricians to "bridge the university and community through activism" (p. 7). In her model, "activism" can be as simple as facilitating social change through the micro-transactions of "empower[ing] people with our [own] positions" (p. 14). Working with a non-university run Career Center allows academics to serve as Eble and Gaillet's "community intellectuals" (2004, *passim*). In so doing, we bring our multiple literacies (rhetorical, social, technological, ethical, and critical—see Cargile Cook, 2002) to bear on valuable, real-world problems that ultimately contribute to the localized good of our home communities.

Volunteering in an organization devoted to the practice of communication also enables the sort of advocacy perspective Rose (2016) describes regarding human-centered design. Those using the center often come from "resource-constrained contexts" (p. 433) as their need often stems from a lack of training on the types of writing practices that facilitate job acquisition, and, in many cases, use of the Center is motivated by a need for access to computers and internet access (see also Toftelande-Trampe, 2017). Our role in connecting our academic institutions with public organizations dedicated to serving resource-constrained publics is valuable: Career advocacy becomes a tool for helping enact social change while also contributing to professional knowledge.

When we connect with publics who might not otherwise have access to our resources and knowledge, we take something valuable away from the experience. As Cushman notes, community activism cannot be purely altruistic, as it is our status, position, and resources, conferred by our academic institutions, that allow us to bring our specialties to bear (1996, p. 19), and so an exchange must take place. We help with the sorts of writing valued by the community, and our actions in the community facilitate our classrooms and our academic writings (see Clark, 2004). Volunteering with a non-academic-based Career Center also has the potential benefit of providing increased credibility in the technical communication classroom and increasing our ability to understand community partner needs in service learning partnerships (see, for example, Kimme Hea & Wendler Shah, 2016). As Randazzo (2016) points out in her article on student's sources for résumé advice, for example, students often may not value a teacher's suggestions because teachers seem so divorced from the "real world" of non-academic job seeking. Working with local job seekers, Career Center employees and volunteers, and, occasionally, potential employers, then, has the benefit of keeping us plugged in to industry trends and the realities of the job search process.

Résumé Design

An overview of textbooks and papers offers a wealth of information regarding the creation of an effective résumé. A survey of textbooks in technical communication suggests that résumés for entry-level job applicants should be either chronological or functional, with chronological being the most common and preferred for new graduates or those with low experience (Dobrin, et al., 2008; Gurak & Lannon, 2013; Johnson-Sheehan, 2012; Markel, 2012; Tebeaux & Dragga, 2010). Schullery, et al.'s 2009 research on résumé design shows that 71% of the employers they surveyed (employers from U.S. and multinational companies that recruited on their university campus) preferred chronological résumés (2009, p. 170). Designing functional résumés which emphasize relevant experiences and skills, for both new graduates and experienced professionals, however, may be more effective (Anderson, 2007; Lannon, 2008) as relevant experience is prized (Ross & Young, 2005).

Schullery, et al.'s 2009 examination of employer preferences for résumé design suggests that only 7% of employers prefer paper résumés (p. 163), as opposed to electronic-only formats. They note, however, the value of having a traditional, paper-based résumé as well (p. 174). Several textbooks suggest that, should a traditional résumé be required, it should be printed on white or off-white paper (Dobrin, et al., 2008; Gurak & Lannon, 2013; Lannon, 2008; Tebeaux & Dragga, 2010).

On length, some authors note that résumés should be one-page long (Gurak & Lannon, 2013; Lannon, 2008; Tebeaux & Dragga, 2010), though two may be appropriate given relevant information or to cut down on clutter (Anderson, 2007; Dobrin, et al., 2008; Gurak & Lannon, 2013). Blackburn-Brockman & Belanger's study on résumé length suggests that two-page résumés may be ranked as more favorable by recruiters, even if they claim to prefer only one page.

In terms of content, authors suggest listing objectives and education (Dobrin, et al., 2008; Gurak & Lannon, 2013; Johnson-Sheehan, 2012; Lannon, 2008; Markel, 2012), relevant experience (Dobrin, et al., 2008; Gurak & Lannon, 2013; Johnson-Sheehan, 2012; Lannon, 2008; Markel, 2012) and relevant interests, activities, and awards (Dobrin, et al., 2008; Gurak & Lannon, 2013; Johnson-Sheehan, 2012; Lannon, 2008; Markel, 2012). As some authors have noted, all information should be related to the work sought (Tebeaux & Dragga, 2010), and the fields one chooses depend on the type of résumé developed (Anderson, 2007).

Résumés should be designed using a professional, consistent font (Dobrin, et al., 2008) and use generous margins and white space (Anderson, 2007; Markel, 2012; Tebeaux & Dragga, 2010). Résumés should adhere to the basic design principles of "balance, alignment, grouping, consistency, and contrast" (Johnson-Sheehan, 2012, p. 329) and be clearly organized (Markel, 2012).

Stylistically, information should be arranged to emphasize strengths (Dobrin, et al., 2008), use unique fonts, text, or bullets to emphasize relevant information (Anderson, 2007; Gurak & Lannon, 2013), and be clear, concise, and well-proofread while adhering to proper language use (Anderson, 2007; Gurak & Lannon, 2013; Johnson-Sheehan, 2012; Lannon, 2008; Markel, 2012).

Taken together, textbooks and papers offer a general sense of what a résumé should look like. Potential employer and potential employee perceptions of what the résumé needs to look like, and what it needs to accomplish, however, do not always agree; an issue I discovered during the course of this research.

Methods

My intent in conducting research on perceptions of résumés was to determine where potential job seeker and potential employer expectations might differ, and to establish how technical communication professionals volunteering in career services organizations might best serve our communities. To answer my research questions, I conducted semi-structured interviews with two key personnel at a Goodwill Career Center, conducted surveys with visitors to the Career Center seeking help with résumé design, worked with Goodwill's own research into what employers look for in effective job applications and résumés, and considered my own observations and experiences as a volunteer with Goodwill.[2] This multi-part approach allowed me to gain a more robust picture of perceptions of résumés than if I had used only one approach with one demographic. It also allowed me to make connections between perceptions and descriptions offered by potential employers, employees, and professional communicators.

The initial interviews with two Goodwill employees were conducted in 2013 and consisted of questions on use of the Center, visitor needs and expectations, and prior background working with résumés. These interviews provided context for understanding how the Center serves the community and how professional communicators might best serve their communities as advocates and helped situate the other research components.

Surveys of Career Center visitors were conducted between 2013 and 2016. The bulk of the surveys came from 2014–2015. Though the final data set was fairly small, (21 completed surveys), the surveys themselves showed internal cohesion with regard to answers, and supported my own observations of the way visitors would talk about the résumé in our one-on-one writing sessions.

The bulk of the employer surveys were distributed through the East Alabama Society for Human Resource Managers' email list in 2015 with the rest being completed in-house (at Goodwill) from employers conducting job fairs. Twelve potential employers completed surveys for the Goodwill Career Center location at which I volunteered.[3] Comparing the two sets of surveys allowed me to establish differences in perception between potential employers and job seekers and set up a comparison of perceptions regarding the construction of a proper résumé between those actively engaged in the job search and placement process, and textbook descriptions of the documents involved.

In addition, data from textbooks and papers on résumé design[4] were collected in an Excel spreadsheet, then mapped using the Gephi data visualization platform,[5] as were the anonymized responses from both the Career Center visitor surveys and employer surveys.

Results

Employee Interviews

The two formal interviews I conducted with employees I use primarily to contextualize other data, to help paint a picture of the Career Center, and to discuss how career advocacy works. Both interviews were lengthy, the first taking 25 minutes, the second 52 minutes. In the semi-structured interviews, both respondents clearly identified the value of the Center in providing a space for job seekers to find help in everything from résumé design to interviewing techniques, as well as serving as a sort of jobs clearing-house and technology center. Both employees spoke of their desire for more staff, as they both saw the face-to-face value of the Center as one of the most valuable aspects they could provide. The primary themes evident in both interviews were both this simple, and this complex: both interviewees identified the Center as a place that should (and does) show caring concern for all that seek to use its services; a place that should (and does) help visitors work with often unfamiliar technologies and genres to accomplish the goal of finding a job; and that this is work that benefits from face-to-face interaction, so more caring professionals are always needed.

When I asked who used the Career Center, I was told:

> "Well, our main purpose is for job searches, so we, you know, obviously have a lot of unemployed people, um, but also underemployed, who are looking for a better job, and then we have people who maybe have what they consider a good job but they're also looking for additional income. Um, in addition to that we have people that come in that maybe just need to update their résumé, they come for computer classes, it's, most of it is related to job search, but we also have groups that utilize the Career Center, the training room, um, local employers for job fairs, local organizations, companies that use it for meeting space, for orientation, so just, really, the main thing is job search, but it's open to the community."

The role of the center as a place of education, service, and advocacy is perhaps most clearly articulated in one employee's somewhat lengthy description of a single older woman's visit. I was told:

> "I don't want anybody walking out that door feeling more down than they were when they walked in here. So, if they see a smile, and if they feel encouraged, and, an example of that would be, um, if we sat down and helped somebody with a résumé, and like, kind of as an example, a 61-year-old lady that was here walked in one day, sat right there on that computer, she'd worked with a textile company 34 years, never needed, never done, had never needed a résumé. But she had, you know, the plant closed before she was able to quit, stop working, she tried retail, that wasn't working too well, pay wise and hours wise, so she realized she needed a résumé. She's 61, she came in, said, 'I've never had a résumé, can you help me with one, and, oh, by the way, I've never used a computer.' So we sat down with our résumé writing program, in an hour-and-a-half we had a résumé, gave her a hardcopy, set up an email address, saved it to her email, so that she would have that for what she needed, um, and, um, you know, I guess that, when she left here, I didn't, you know, I'll be honest with you, I did most of the typing, because she's never used a computer. But my thinking was, when she left here, was I wanted her to go home and say, 'look, I did a résumé today,' I didn't want her to go home and say, '[Employee] at the Career Center did a résumé for me.' So that's our goal, is for them, when they leave here to have more confidence, and feel like they accomplished something."

This narrative captures the essence of what it means to both work at and use the Center—in an hour-and-a-half, a Center employee has helped someone use unfamiliar technology, created a digital presence for that visitor, helped create a résumé, and empowered that visitor to take part in a modern information economy.

The value of a career advocate in the Center is apparent in one employee's response regarding helping clients design more effective résumés:

> "Being able to have somebody to bounce ideas off of, and get some direction on what their résumé should look like, what kind of information, because you do it, when you're looking for a job you do the same thing over and over and over again. And it's so hard to put 100% into every single job application that you do in a day, in a week, in a month, and 18 months, that it gets really frustrating and you will find yourself getting into a lurch where you're doing the same thing over and over and over again, and a lot of times that opens you up for mistakes, so having somebody outside to really give you their undivided attention and give you new ideas, fresh ideas, I think, honestly, I think that's probably the most important thing."

The visitors seem to appreciate this considerate approach, and while I did not specifically interview visitors on their perceptions of the Center, as my primary focus for the project was on résumé design, I did notice a certain familiarity between many of the visitors and the staff: it was obvious that many visitors used the Center on a regular basis. This was also my experience as a volunteer. As of the time of this writing, I still have regular clients that check back with me from time to time as they improve their résumés and have worked with clients to develop and refine interviewing skills. My observations suggest that, in general, those that use the Center on a regular basis are similar demographically to those that chose to take part in this study, described in the next section.

Career Center Visitors

The survey distributed to Career Center visitors was designed to collect information on visitors' perceptions of the role of a résumé, what they felt were the most important parts, how long a résumé should be, how much time they think an employer spends looking at a résumé, if there are different ways to organize a résumé, and how important a résumé is to the job application process. The 21 visitors to the Center that were willing to fill out my survey ranged in age from 21 to 68, were comprised of White/Non-Hispanic, Latinx/Hispanic, and Black/African Americans, reported yearly earnings from less than $10,000 per year to over $60,000 per year, and ranged in education from High School Graduate/GED to Bachelor's and Professional degrees. To summarize the following data, the largest category of responses to each question suggests that, from a job seeker point of view, the résumé is a tool to show skills, the most important parts deal with experience, it should be one to two-pages long, there are multiple ways to organize a résumé, and the résumé is an important part of the job search process.

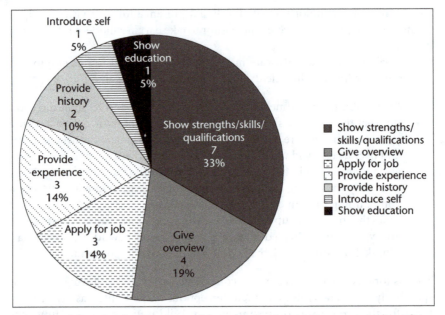

FIGURE 9.1 Job seekers' perceptions of the role of a résumé. Data suggest that job seekers are not viewing the résumé as a rhetorical object, but only a display object: an object designed only to show information, not motivate action.

Role of a Résumé

Respondents did not fully agree on the purpose of a résumé. While data show that 33% of the job seekers I surveyed primarily view the résumé as a tool to show skills, there was some disagreement as to its overarching purpose (Figure 9.1).

Most Important Part of a Résumé

When asked specifically about the most important parts of a résumé, job seekers felt that the most important parts were those that showed experience (32.43% of coded responses), skills (16.22%), and education (16.22%) (Table 9.1).

Length of a Résumé

Job seekers agreed that résumés should be between one and two-pages long, with eight (38%) agreeing that a résumé should be only one page, seven (33.3%) agreeing that it should be one to two pages, and four (19%) believing that a résumé should be two-pages long. Two respondents had other answers: One noted that a résumé "used to be 1" page, and another that it "depends on the type of résumé, if it is federal or private" (Figure 9.2).

TABLE 9.1 Perceived important components of a résumé

Mentioned part of résumé	Number of occurrences[1]
Experience	12
Skills	6
Education	6
Qualifications	3
Descriptions	2
Keywords	1
Time on job	1
Words	1
Name	1
References	1
First page	1
Job history	1
Summary	1

1 Out of 37 mentions, not 21 individual responses. A response indicating, "work experience, education, and skills" is coded as having one mention of "experience," one of "education," and one of "skills."

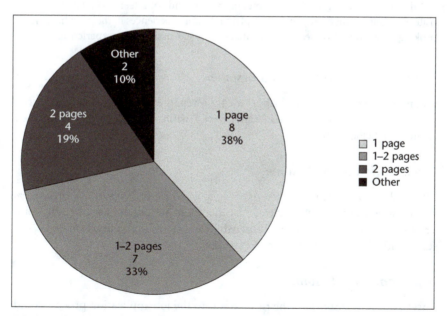

FIGURE 9.2 Perceived résumé length. Respondents agree with generally recognized standards of length, such as those put forward in textbooks. The question was open-ended (respondents provided their own page lengths). This suggests a certain amount of shared résumé lore.

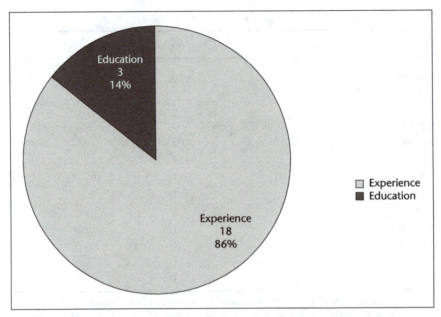

FIGURE 9.3 Perceived value of experience vs. education on a résumé. The majority of respondents agreed that presentation of "experience" is more valuable than presentation of "education." This suggests that Center employees and volunteers would benefit visitors by helping them unpack and explain relevant experiences in their job history. Looking ahead, this also speaks to potential employers' desire to see experience.

Experience vs. Education in a Résumé

When asked which is more important on a résumé, experience or education, 18 respondents (86%) selected "experience," while only three (14%) selected "education" (Figure 9.3).

Organization of the Résumé

When asked, "Is there more than one way to organize your résumé?" 18, or 86% of respondents, overwhelmingly agreed that there are different ways to organize a résumé, one (4.76%) said "no," and two (9%) offered ambiguous answers: "not sure," and "depends on the type of experience."

Importance of a Résumé

Answers to how important the résumé was to the job application process could be generally categorized as either "important" or "not important," with 18 respondents writing some version of "important" (85.71%), one writing "not important" (4.76%), one writing "not sure" (4.76%), and one (4.76%) writing that a résumé "helps to pinpoint main points" (Figure 9.4).

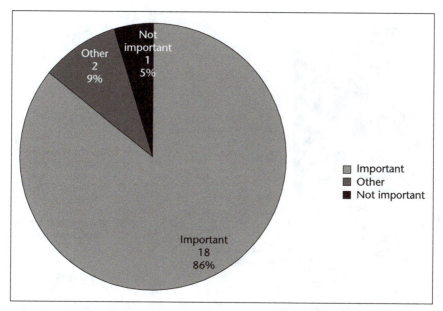

FIGURE 9.4 Perceived importance of résumé to job search process. Respondents overwhelming agreed that the résumé is important. That some do not, however, shows that Center employees and volunteers cannot take the perceived importance of job application materials for granted.

Perception of Potential Employer Time Spent on Résumé

Job seekers could not agree on how long a potential employer might look at their résumé, with answers ranging from seven seconds to 30 minutes, with the bulk of the answers suggesting under five minutes (Figure 9.5). Averaging the 15 estimates with definitive time periods[6] suggests that job seekers believe potential employers spend an average top-end time of 5.31 minutes per résumé. Averaging all 21 answers, which include six answers with no set time, suggests that job seekers believe a potential employer spends an average top-end of 3.8 minutes.

Employer Surveys

The first thing the 12 potential employers noted looking for in a résumé varied widely, including everything from missing phone numbers to qualifications. The most common thread in these responses, however, was a desire to see relevant work experience and job history, with four answers each (one answer contains both responses). The remaining responses were split regarding education, skillsets, and other factors, such as completeness.

Potential employers noted that the most common mistakes they saw on an application or résumé involved editing and completeness, with five (41.7%) noting surface-level grammatical errors. When asked what the most important factor on

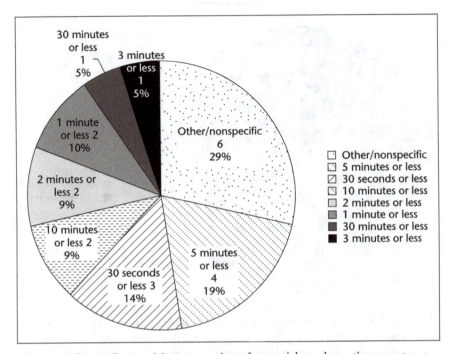

FIGURE 9.5 Career Center visitor perception of potential employer time spent on résumé. This is an area with almost no agreement, but far-reaching rhetorical implications. If visitors think a potential employee spends large amounts of time considering their résumé, there is the potential that their design reflects this perceived time on task.

a résumé was, potential employers overwhelmingly noted the importance of related qualifications and experience, with seven of the answers mentioning those facets. Five answers suggested that job history was most important, three education, and one noted that the most important factor on a résumé was "ease of reading."

With regard to preparing for an interview, reported here because of its relevance to discussions with job seekers, almost all suggested some form of general preparedness. Three (25%) noted the value of being positive, suggesting that the most important thing a job seeker could do would be to "have a positive attitude," be "upbeat," and "relax." Four (33.33%) noted the value of dressing appropriately, and five (41.7%) reported the value of knowing something about the company to which one is applying, including being able to ask questions or describe how one fits in.

Discussion: The Role of the Career Advocate in a Career Center

Job seekers' perceptions of how long a potential employer will spend on their résumé, as well as what it is supposed to accomplish, vary greatly. Almost all responses regarding the role of the résumé suggest that it is viewed as demonstrative, rather than performative: something that shows information, rather than doing rhetorical work like impressing or convincing, even though potential employers specifically noted their attention to surface-level errors. This suggests several interesting areas of focus for a career advocate in a Career Center: teaching genre expectations, presenting relevant experience, editing, and instilling confidence in the job seeker.

Genre Expectations Described in Textbooks

First, career advocates would do well to spend time discussing common résumé formats. As the literature review shows, while examples offered in textbooks are similar and one can make coherent connections regarding desired intent between textbooks and paper, the actual language used to describe résumés varies widely. Mapping design advice from seven textbooks and five papers using Gephi shows only 12–13 points of specific linguistic agreement. Condensed, these can be described as follows: use either a chronological or analytical résumé, create a computer-scannable version if needed, use either one or two pages, be concise and balanced, use action verbs and past tense, have generous margins and good white space, and print it out on white paper (Figure 9.6).

While this is good advice, it is relatively generic, so it becomes the job of the career advocate to paint a picture of these common genres for job seekers and to help job seekers refine any existing work. Textbooks, for example, may suggest that two-page résumés might be preferred by some employers, but it becomes the advocate's job to work with clients to refine their material to present it in the most effective, attractive, concise way possible. This level of refinement speaks, in part, to the issue of time spent by potential employers on each résumé: While textbooks and papers put the time anywhere from a few seconds to just under a minute, one for-profit résumé consultation company documents the actual time, measured using eye-tracking, at six seconds (Evans, 2012), a significant difference in time from the generous estimates proposed by job seekers. Thus, an employer's need to rapidly scan for the information they need must be supported by effective design.

The Career Center I volunteer with follows a genre-oriented, practical model of résumé introduction, so visitors get a sense of what a résumé, in general, should look like. How they are read, including the résumé's role as a visual introduction to the job seeker, the time a potential employer might spend on a résumé, and even the simple value of *having* a résumé, however, cannot be overlooked when working with new job seekers. One Center employee told me that, "the majority of the people that have come in here have not had a résumé, or have not had a résumé made recently." Thus, they may be unfamiliar with genre expectations or need to be reminded. As the other Center employee

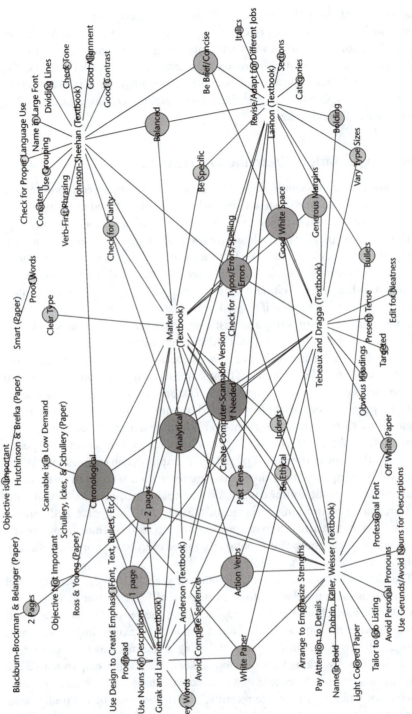

FIGURE 9.6 Résumé design terms from textbooks and professional papers mapped by number of related connections (larger nodes have more connections). Data suggest relatively few shared design considerations, at least at a semantic level.

I interviewed noted, it would be incorrect to assume that all job seekers even understand the value of a résumé:

> "Someone walks in and, and they want to go to work in retail, they want to go to work in food services, and we start talking about résumés, and they may say, 'well, why do I need one of those?' And we explain to them, this day and time, maybe McDonalds is hiring five people and they used to get 50 applications, um, now they may get 100, 200, but the bottom line is, we want you to be, let's say they narrow it down to ten people, and they're looking for five. You know, and they've got five that have résumés, and five that don't, that may not guarantee you the job, but it gives you a leg up. It sets you apart from those that don't have it. And it shows that you have taken the time, that you are very serious about it, um, you've taken the time to do it, and it tells you, it gives you one more opportunity to show them something about yourself."

So the career advocate needs to set the stage for what potential employers want to see, even so far as basic application materials go.

Experience Section on a Résumé

Second, the career advocate serves an important role in helping job seekers determine how best to organize their résumé. While the job seekers I surveyed overwhelmingly indicated that they understood that résumés could be formatted in multiple ways, my experience working with job seekers suggests that that understanding may not transfer over to their actual designs. In many instances, for example, I have worked with job seekers who are looking for work that differs from their current job. They may have experience doing related work, but the jobs they have may not directly correlate. This is problematic when the one thing that employers generally agree on is a need to see relevant experience—a need supported by the employees I interviewed and repeated in textbooks as well. When asked what successful résumés (résumés resulting in jobs) had in common, one Career Center employee stated:

> "Uh, I think, I think something that looks like it's well thought-out, it's not just thrown together. The main thing I think is having relevant work experience. And of course education, depending on what the requirements are. Um, but I think the main thing is the relevant work experience, because, let's face it, right now employers can be very, very picky. They've got a huge, you know, group to choose from, because so many people are looking."

This need to show relevant experience appears to be generally understood by job seekers; indeed, this is the one area where both job seekers and potential employers consistently overlap in their expectations of what needs to be presented on a résumé (Figure 9.7). That need, however, may not translate to their own designs.

The career advocate must help the job seeker determine how best to express relevant experience on a résumé. In many cases, the approach that we have taken with visitors to the Career Center is to introduce them to the functional résumé as an alternative to the more traditional chronological résumé. In short, the functional résumé, also often called an "analytical" résumé, or a "skills-based" résumé, asks for job seekers to front-load their résumé with a list of relevant skills, as opposed to simply outlining specific jobs they have held. To do this, we often ask job seekers to, in essence, code their own job experiences. For example, I worked with one gentleman who had worked in the fast-food industry for several years. He no longer wanted to work in the food industry and was seeking employment in management or reception. None of his jobs, at first blush, would suggest that he had relevant skills. When we dug into his experiences, however, we discovered that in his many years in fast-food, he had not only cooked food, but had also trained employees; managed training meetings, stock intake, and scheduling; dealt with finances; and more. To build the functional résumé, we had him list everything he had done at each job he had held, then categorize each action: communication, management, finances, training, etc. Though it took an admittedly long time to build a satisfactory functional résumé, we eventually developed one which showed his skills in management and communication, all based on many years' worth of experiences. I have worked similarly with others, and, anecdotally, I know that this approach has the potential to work. I have had several job seekers come back to tell me that they received interviews or jobs after reworking their résumés to more effectively illustrate their functional skillsets, rather than the places they held jobs.

Editing

When asked about the biggest problems people had with their résumés, one Career Center employee told me that, "Ok, well, a common thing that we see is it's too long, um, and a pet peeve of mine, I know I'm OCD, but it just drives me crazy that somebody would do a document that told a story about them and not get the spelling correct." Another employee, when asked what the biggest impediment was to clients getting hired responded, "Communication. Expressing themselves in the interviews or in writing on the job application and their résumés, any of those areas, like most people would need a little work." Potential employers echo this, noting that surface-level grammar issues are among the most common mistakes they see in résumés.

Attention to detail extends to phrasing—we should help our clients achieve a professional voice on their résumé. We cannot, nor should we, hide lack of experience, and lying on a résumé is *verboten*. Many of our clients, however, are

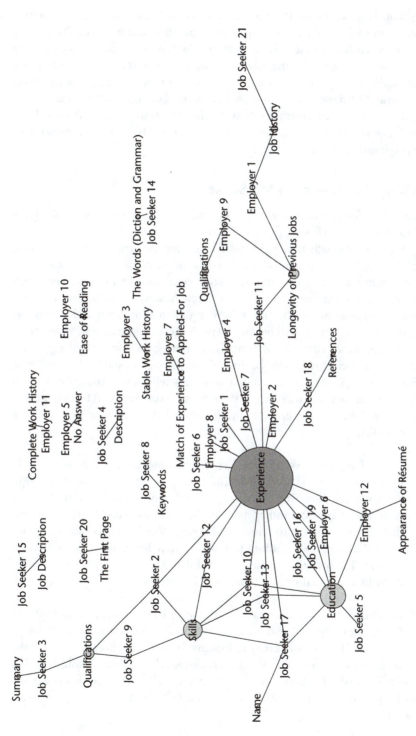

FIGURE 9.7 Mapped network of potential employers' and job seekers' responses to questions asking them to indicate the most important components of a résumé. Incoming node size is controlled by number of related connections (larger nodes have more connections). Data suggest that both potential employers and potential employees believe the résumé should prioritize experience. For Center employees and volunteers, then, presentation of experience should be a primary concern.

exceptionally good at what it is they actually do, be it machine operator, forklift driver, short-order cook, house painter, medical intake specialist, etc. Those skills do not necessarily translate to being wordsmiths, however, and that is a valuable distinction. If the résumé is the gateway to an interview, then we owe it to those we champion to help them get that interview. From there, their job depends on their own ability to speak the appropriate language (both literally and figuratively) and to be able to demonstrate relevant skills. In editing for professionalism, however, we must offer constructive feedback that builds confidence, rather than simply critiquing mistakes.

Instilling Confidence in Job Seekers

Looking for a job can be a daunting task, and, in many cases, those looking for jobs are doing so with few supportive resources. As a result, the job search process becomes an emotionally trying process. As has been my experience volunteering at the Career Center, those looking for jobs often come in with little or no experience in résumé design, an observation confirmed by my interviews with employees. Those that have done their research, however, may be overwhelmed by competing evidence of the "right" way to design a job letter and résumé, as suggested by my analysis of technical and professional communication textbook and research paper advice. Additionally, searching "résumé" online yields a staggering number of results at the time of this writing: 585,000,000. In offering clarity, however, it may be all too easy to simply tell clients "the right way" to design a résumé without listening to their story. To do so would be doing them a disservice. One employee, for example, offered the following example of a returning client:

> "A gentleman that would come in here every morning, and he would walk in the door with his head down and a sad look on his face, and he'd sign his name as a returning customer, and we'd say 'Good morning, how are you?' and 'Oh, just another day.' Or, 'Oh, not too good.' Or, you know, then the more he got to know us he'd say, 'What's so good about it,' you know. But we finally got him to a point where he would walk in and say, 'I know, I know, it's a good day.' And then he got to a point where he'd come in and actually have a smile on his face."

As this employee noted, with regards to the way visitors should be greeted and treated, "the one thing that we think that they should see when they walk through the door is a smile, because if they're looking for work, chances are it's not the best day that they've ever had." Another employee told me that, "I would say that a lot of people, whether they can admit it or not, really need a confidence boost when they come in here, because if it was easy to find a job, they probably wouldn't be here."

Confidence is an important part of the job search process. As noted regarding potential employer expectations, applicants should be upbeat, be prepared to answer questions, and dress for success. All three of these facets relate in some way to the way job seekers enact confidence. Similarly, I argue that confidence plays an important role in the writing process. It has been my experience that résumé writing is often treated as a formulaic endeavor: design the page, plug in the information, and submit to potential employer. But, as I hope has become evident over the course of this chapter, not all job seekers are alike, just as not all employers are alike. To that end, the role of the career advocate should be to enact the general principles of good and ethical technical and professional communication: listen to our clients to determine their needs and expectations, carefully consider the audience for the designs we enact, then help those that we work with best articulate the information they are working with for their potential audiences. In thinking about the human side of the equation—in instilling confidence—we provide a best-practices model for human-centered communication.

Conclusion

The purpose of my research study was to answer a few key questions that would help potential community advocates work more effectively with local career centers, specifically regarding help with design of résumés. My three driving questions were designed to get at differences in perceptions of résumé design, because my work with visitors to the Career Center suggested that potential employers, potential employees, and even academic experts do not necessarily share a common vision when it comes to résumé design.

The first question I asked sought to determine if—not necessarily how, though that became an important facet of the data I collected—job seekers' perceptions of the value and design of résumés differ from potential employers' perceptions of the value and design of résumés. To this, we can safely answer, "yes," job seeker's perceptions differ from potential employer's perceptions, and they do so in the following respects: while potential employers are looking for a rhetorically sound document that is error-free, shows job history and relevance to the applied-for position, and indicates a match for the job at hand, job applicants primarily view the résumé as rhetorically inert, as purely demonstrative. While both groups agree on the need to provide experience, potential employers want to see that experience contextualized against the advertised job.

Question two tried to determine common "mistakes" made on résumés by job seekers as compared to the types of résumés advocated by potential employers and communication professionals. This question is more difficult to answer concretely, though taking potential employers' responses, job seeker interviews, and my own experiences into context provides a holistic answer. In short, while communication professionals do not necessarily agree on the way we *describe* good résumés, in that different scholars focus on different aspects, and use similar-but-different language to describe the final product, I suspect that readers of this chapter could synthesize that information into a genre-identifiable, well-formatted document with some degree of consistency. Experts want to see something that is well edited, effectively designed, and specific to the task at hand. Job seeker résumés often differ from these expectations, in that they may be poorly designed, contain numerous errors, and are non-specific. This may be due to a lack of understanding of the value of the résumé in the first place, or viewing the résumé as a simple list of skills, as opposed to a performative document. So, the most common mistakes made on résumés are those that result in a general, poorly edited document not targeted to a specific audience—recall, potential employees noted that the most common mistakes they saw on an application or résumé involved editing and completeness.

Last, I hoped that this work could help determine the role of a technical communication professional as a volunteer in a career services organization, and how we might best serve our communities as advocates. Here, I return our attention to the value of instilling confidence, of providing a strong background in audience analysis and document design, and of providing a supportive, human-centered approach to communication. Agboka (2013) has argued that technical communicators should "redefine localization as a user-driven approach, in which a user (an individual or the local community) identifies a need and works with the designer or developer to develop a mutually beneficial product that mirrors the sociocultural, economic, linguistic, and legal needs of the user" (p. 44). The way volunteerism works at the Career Center supports this approach: we serve as experts who are willing to listen to a client's situation and provide contextualized advice, rather than simply pointing them toward a set example and saying, "Do this." Examples have real value, of course, but being willing to make adjustments as circumstances dictate is one of the best things we can do as career advocates.

My own process of working with a client has evolved based on my experiences and interviews and now follows this basic format: First, once I have greeted the client and they have given me their résumé (if they brought one), and any supporting documents, I turn those face-down on the table between us and ask a series of questions determined to scope out their needs and expectations. These questions include asking where they work now, where they would like to work, what their dream-job might be, what skills they have that they are most proud of, what kind of environment they would like to work in, and others in a similar vein. Only after we have talked about their work history and the sorts of skills they have acquired over the years, along with where they would like to work, do I turn their résumé over to assess it. At this point, I ask if I can be brutally honest with them because time is limited. I have not yet had someone say "no" and had many answer that this is why they are here in the first place. They want to know why they aren't getting jobs. I then critique their résumé against what they want to show (based on our conversation) and what they are actually showing. From there we move to different formats as warranted, and I share with them a series of examples, including two types of résumés (analytical and chronological), job letter examples, sheets with action words on them, and more, again, as needed. We usually end with the client either moving to the Career Center's computers to continue work, where I often come by to help, or having them head home. I find that this process offers a good mix of structure and opportunity for creating unique résumés ideally suited to an individual client's needs. Hopefully, along the way I can offer some help and provide openings for their voices to come through. Does this process work? Anecdotally, I have heard that it does, and many clients seem pleased with the outcome.

Working with Nonprofits

Working with nonprofit organizations is a difficult, but rewarding, task. When we serve as career advocates in our communities, we take on an important role that sets us as a bridge between academics and non-academics. To that end, I offer the following suggestions for those seeking to make this a part of their lives:

1) Remember that the organization with which you are working follows a different organization structure from your own, with its own chain of command, and its own rules and regulations. Abide by them and make sure that you discuss your process and work with those around you.

2) Remember that those with whom you are working, employees and clients alike, are not students. When sharing your work with employees, listen to their stories and build those experiences into your own framework, and when working with clients, remember that they are there for a very direct purpose: to help improve their chances of getting a job. Many are on short timeframes, so there is no time for lecturing. Instead, listen to their needs and help accordingly.

3) Last, though the previous points already say this, listen. Listen to the nonprofit for its needs and expectations, and the clients for theirs. Try to find the points of intersection between your own knowledge and experience and theirs, and the gaps—both yours and theirs. Take that practical knowledge back to your classrooms and use it to help contextualize your own research, writing, and teaching.

In conclusion, as I discovered in my research, textbooks and professionals offer a cacophony of competing voices on what constitutes good résumé design. Based on those findings, it is my argument that our job must be to listen to the job seeker, consider who the ultimate audience of their résumé will be, and help them form a job search strategy that is not simply formulaic, but specifically targeted toward their intended profession. This means counseling job seekers on the differences between chronological and functional résumés, the value of a job letter, the different types of résumés they might need during their job search, and helping them create the documents most valuable to them at that time. A professional communicator—or Career Center employee—working as a career advocate can offer great value by taking a humanistic approach that cuts through the different, often competing voices, to help job seekers consider audience and purpose.

Notes

1. All data gathered in this study were collected with Institutional Review Board approval.
2. A draft of this chapter was also shared with current Goodwill Career Center employees for member-checking (see, e.g., Creswell & Miller, 2000; Lincoln & Guba, 1985).
3. These surveys were created and distributed by Goodwill, so not all the questions were directly relevant to the résumé writing process. I report results on four questions: the first thing they look for on a résumé, the most common mistakes seen on an application or résumé, the best advice they could give someone preparing for an interview, and the most important factor on a résumé.
4. The textbook and academic paper analysis portion of this project began in late 2012 with the help of a research assistant. Books and articles included in the analysis are Anderson, 2007; Blackburn-Brockman & Belanger, 2001; Dobrin, et al., 2008; Gurak & Lannon, 2013; Hutchinson & Brefka, 1997; Johnson-Sheehan, 2012; Lannon, 2008; Markel, 2012; Schullery, et al., 2009; Smart, 2004; Tebeaux & Dragga, 2010; and Ross & Young, 2005.
5. Gephi is open-source, data visualization software that allows researchers to examine complex data relationships while facilitating visual play, thereby potentially enabling new ways to come at existing problems. Additionally, Gephi enables multimodal Social Network Analysis (mSNA), a variant of SNA that considers nodal modes (multiple communication artifact types, along with location, for example) in addition to social interactors (Ghani, et al., 2013).
6. For example, taking the top end of each estimate, I marked "less than 5 minutes" as 300 seconds.

Acknowledgements

I am grateful to Kendall Erlandson and Ayshia Green-Calloway for many long hours of conversation about the job search process. Additionally, this chapter would not have been possible without the help of my research assistants, Aubrey Wood and David Kistler, and the support of the many individuals working with—and visiting—Goodwill.

Discussion Questions

1) How does our understanding of technology and technological expertise affect the way we help others learn? Would working with people who had no experience with computers change the way you interact with them?
2) How might the relatively simple micro-transactions of helping someone write more effective workplace documents work as activism?

3) What makes the résumé such a conflicted document? Why do people interpret a document so common to our lives so differently? What does your answer suggest to you about the nature of working with others on technical and professional documents?

4) In this chapter I argue that one of the most important things that an advocate can do is listen to the advocated-for. How might listening to someone's story affect the way you perform advocacy or enact your own expertise?

5) Pretend that you are working with a client on a job letter and application package. They tell you that though they have held several odd jobs over the last few years they cannot find one that they like that really uses their skillsets. How would you go about working with them to craft a document that might improve their chances of getting a better job? What sorts of questions would you need to ask them to get started?

Further Reading

All website URLs accessed February 2018.

Clark, D. (2004). Is professional writing relevant? A model for action research. *Technical Communication Quarterly, 13*(3): 307–23.

Cook, K. (2002). Layered literacies: A theoretical frame for technical communication pedagogy. *Technical Communication Quarterly, 11*(1): 5–29.

Cushman, E. (1996). The rhetorician as agent of social change. *College Composition and Communication, 47*(1): 7–28.

Randazzo, C. (2016). Where do they go? Students' sources of résumé advice, and implications for critically reimagining the résumé assignment. *Technical Communication Quarterly, 25*(4), 278–297. https://doi.org/10.1080/10572252.2016.1221142

Ross, C. M., & Young, S. J. (2005). Resume preferences: Is it really "business as usual"? *Journal of Career Development, 32*(2), 153–164.

Ross, D. G., & Parks, M. (2017). Mutual respect in an ethic of care: A collaborative essay on power, trust, and stereotyping. *Teaching Ethics. Forthcoming*

Willerton, R. (2015). *Plain language and ethical action: A dialogic approach to technical content in the 21st century.* New York, NY: Routledge.

References

All website URLs accessed February 2018.

Agboka, G. Y. (2013). Participatory localization: A social justice approach to navigating unenfranchised/disenfranchised cultural sites. *Technical Communication Quarterly, 22*(1): 28–49.

Anderson, P. V. (2007). *Technical communication: A reader-centered approach* (6th Ed). Boston: Thomson Wadsworth.

Blackburn-Brockman, E., & Belanger, K. (2001). One page or two?: A national study of CPA recruiters' preferences for résumé length. *The Journal of Business Communication, 38*(1): 29–57.

Cargile Cook, K. (2002). Layered literacies: A theoretical frame for technical communication pedagogy. *Technical Communication Quarterly, 11*(1): 5–29.

Clark, D. (2004). Is professional writing relevant? A model for action research. *Technical Communication Quarterly, 13*(3): 307–23.

Creswell, J. W., & Miller, D. L. (2000). Determining validity in qualitative inquiry. *Theory into practice, 39*(3): 124–130.

Cushman, E. (1996). The rhetorician as agent of social change. *College Composition and Communication, 47*(1): 7–28.

Dobrin, S.I., Keller, C.J., & Weisser, C. R. (2008). *Technical communication in the twenty-first century.* Upper Saddle River: Pearson Prentice Hall.

Eble, M. F., & Gaillet, L. (2004). Educating "community intellectuals": Rhetoric, moral philosophy, and civic engagement. *Technical Communication Quarterly, 13*(3): 341–354.

Evans, W. (2012). Eye tracking online metacognition: Cognitive complexity and recruiter decision making. *TheLadders.* Retrieved October 24, 2016, from https://cdn.theladders.net/static/images/basicSite/pdfs/TheLadders-EyeTracking-StudyC2.pdf

Ghani, S., Kwon, B. C., Lee, S., Yi, J. S., & Elmqvist, N. (2013). Visual analytics for multi-modal social network analysis: A design study with social scientists. *IEEE Transactions on Visualization and Computer Graphics, 19*(12): 2032–2041.

Goodwill Industries International, Inc. (2017). "About us." Retrieved September 28, 2017, from www.goodwill.org/about-us

Gurak, L. J., & Lannon, J. M. (2013). *Strategies for Technical Communication in the Workplace* (2nd Ed.) Upper Saddle River: Pearson.

Hutchinson, K. L., & Brefka, D. S. (1997). Personnel administrators' preferences for résumé content: Ten years after. *Business Communication Quarterly, 60*(2): 67–75.

Johnson-Sheehan, R. (2012). *Technical Communication Today* (4th ed.) Upper Saddle River: Pearson.

Kimme Hea, A. C., & Wendler Shah, R. (2016). Silent partners: Developing a critical understanding of community partners in technical communication service-learning pedagogies. *Technical Communication Quarterly, 25*(1): 48–66.

Lannon, J. M. (2008). *Technical communication* (11th ed.) New York: Pearson Longman.

Lincoln, Y. S., & Guba, E. G. (1985). *Naturalistic Inquiry* (Vol. 75). California: Sage.

Markel, M. (2012). *Technical communication* (10th ed.). Boston: Bedford/St. Martins.

Randazzo, C. (2016). Where do they go? Students' sources of résumé advice, and implications for critically reimagining the résumé assignment. *Technical Communication Quarterly 25*(4): 278–297.

Rose, E. J. (2016). Design as advocacy: Using a human-centered approach to investigate the needs of vulnerable populations. *Journal of Technical Writing and Communication, 46*(4): 427–445.

Ross, C. M., & Young, S. J. (2005). Résumé preferences: Is it really "business as usual"? *Journal of Career Development, 32*(2): 153–164.

Schullery, N., Ickes, L., & Schullery, S. E. (2009). Employer preferences for résumés and cover letters. *Business Communication Quarterly, 72*(2): 163–176.

Smart, K. L. (2004). Articulating skills in the job search: Proving by example. *Business Communication Quarterly, 67*(2): 198–206.

Tebeaux, E., & Dragga, S. (2010). *The essentials of technical communication.* New York: Oxford University Press.

Toftelande-Trampe, R. (2017). Crossing the divide: Implication for technical communication user advocates. *Technical Communication, 64*(2). Retrieved May 18, 2017 from www.stc.org/techcomm/2017/05/10/crossing-the-divide-implications-for-technical-communication-user-advocates

Introducing Advocacy Techniques in a Classroom

PART THREE

Introducing Advocacy Techniques in a Classroom

10

INCLUSIVE PRACTICES IN THE TECHNICAL COMMUNICATION CLASSROOM

Jessica Edwards

Understanding Systemic and the Structural Inequalities in Education

For many people, even those who study language and writing, broaching the topics of racism and race can be a challenge. As a southern, African American woman, four generations removed from slavery, one generation removed from sharecropping, I saw and continue to see first-hand how systems of oppression impact my family and others like me, particularly via education. For instance, my grandparents, children of the 1920s and 1930s, were proponents of formal education. They did not attend high school or middle school—however, not because they did not want to, but because there were no high schools in our region of the state to educate African American people. The lack of access to formal education shaped the choices that my grandparents were able to make for themselves and for their families, which certainly impacted their future job possibilities and their social mobility. My story is not a unique one for people of color in the United States as systemic problems in education continue to manifest themselves. Although the 1954 Supreme Court decision, as well as other policies, were put in place to make education more equitable, day to day operations were slow to match the directives. Mujic (2015) noted that "access to education in the U.S. has improved for demographic groups across four important categories: race, class, ethnicity, and gender. But progress on these fronts has been slow and contentious" (p. 1). The writer goes on to say that "historically, local, state, and federal leaders have instead used education as a tool to control minority populations" (p. 1). This control, from lack of access to limited resources, contributes to poverty and continues a cycle of oppression that is hard to break without intentional conversations and structural changes.

Moreover, the Yale Child Study Center reports how Black and Brown students are stereotyped as early as preschool and that implicit bias allows disparities in preschool expulsions (Brown, 2016). Brown (2016) shares the following:

> The study asked more than 130 preschool teachers to watch video clips of children in classrooms. The teachers were told to look for signs of "challenging behavior."
>
> The children in the videos were actors, and the clips did not actually show any challenging behaviors. But the teachers didn't know that. They were anticipating trouble. And as they scanned the video clips, looking for signs of that trouble, they spent more time looking at black children than white children, according to equipment that tracked their gaze.
>
> The teachers spent even longer looking at black boys.
>
> (p. 2)

This study gets at how engrained bias is and how educators begin to shape the ways in which children are reprimanded at an early age. For my grandparents, then, it was access to education and blatant bias. For students today, it is more covert bias and limited access. These moments that I describe are systemic problems that may change in appearance, over time, but continue with the same discriminatory results. In other words, institutional problems infiltrate the lives of those who are disenfranchised and also affect those who are not. It is the educator's responsibility to not only advocate for safe spaces to address the racial histories that shape us all in education, but to think about how studying diversity and learning about the experiences of others can help to achieve advocacy and action.

I strategize ways to meet challenges with pedagogies and practices that advance conversations about diversity, particularly in higher education. These practices have the potential to translate to workspaces and workplaces, and as an artist-scholar, I am committed to thinking about and pushing practices that may help teachers take on conversations about diversity and about race. After conducting focus groups of 15 faculty and students interested in writing studies and conversations about inclusiveness at the University of Delaware (UD), in this chapter, I examine the pulse of thinking about inclusivity and strategies therein using Nelson-Laird's (2014) diversity framework as a lens to add useful conversations about effective classroom practices, about teaching with tension, and about difference. I asked both students and faculty members questions about diversity, about their own practices to engage diversity, and how they understand what it means to advocate for diverse practices and ideas. I also provide assignments, which were inspired by my research, that instructors may use or adapt for their classes to promote inclusivity by engaging difference in productive and explicit ways.

In doing this research, I call for developing antiracist agendas, particularly in the technical communication classroom. I argue that teaching about diversity in technical communication classrooms contributes to the development of active citizens.

A Conversation

In the Fall of 2015, the United States was erupting with different, yet similar narratives about racial and sexual discrimination on college campuses and on the streets. With the violence against Black and Brown bodies and public displays of shootings in constant rotation on social media, the topics of both race and racism were unavoidable. Even more, college students from over 75 institutions created specific demands. According to Demands.org (2015), students published these technical lists to work toward an "end to systemic and structural racism on campus" (p. 1). Students used technical communication, through the creation of several technical documents in the form of a demands list, to voice specific problems: colleges and universities are more diverse, and yet resources to fully engage diverse and safe practices are few. To extend student demands, as artists, teachers, and scholars, we should work to chip away at structural racism on college campuses by advocating for more thoughtful and diverse spaces. Our class discussions should help students to develop language about race and racism, connect ideas across perceived boundaries, apply knowledge to begin to situate ideas, and reflect about best practices to begin to counter systemic problems that will translate into professional spaces beyond college. In many ways, our work has the potential to help students better advocate for themselves and for others as they consider language practices and history more carefully. Students have started the process by using technical communication as a vehicle. It is important to consider how technical communication can continue to help advocate for diverse needs. Doing so may help us, as scholars and those who are committed to social justice, better connect diversity and advocacy in an effort to push against structural oppression.

Scholars like Sapp and Crabtree (2002) remind us that our scholarship and teaching is connected to our communities and that universities should make better community connections to "develop more actively responsible citizens who possess democratic values" (p. 413). As workplaces, college campuses have a duty to provide spaces where students are challenged, as well as protected; some understanding of race and racism will help encourage more diverse thinking, which, in turn, will lead to more responsible practices. Despite evidence recently printed by Moyer (2016) that diversity policies have little to do with progressive change, there are studies and research that show the importance of intentional practices in the classroom to promote diversity. According to hooks (1994), inclusive teaching disrupts the dominant model of education, and "any radical pedagogy must insist that everyone's presence is acknowledged. That insistence cannot be simply stated. It has to be demonstrated through pedagogical practices" (p. 8). hooks's point encourages a valuing of education to challenge ideas and chip away at systemic practices, thus, building advocacy into the core of teaching practices.

Furthermore, Williams and Pimentel's (2014) edited collection, *Communicating race, ethnicity, and identity in technical communication*, provides important scholarship, from considerations of race and ethnicity in social media to social justice issues in technical communication. One scholar in the collection, Medina (2014), examines how race has been left out of writing conversations and how language practices via social media—namely, Twitter—could offer useful information about language diversity, particularly for Latinos. This work informs teaching about diversity for technical writing classrooms because it marries social justice and advocacy, which helps students rethink their relationships to media.

Additionally, Savage and Mattson (2011), in "Perceptions of racial and ethnic diversity in technical communication programs," surveyed technical communication program directors about diversity. The survey results provided useful recommendations for enhancing diverse practices in technical communication programs, one of which includes implementing a more diverse curriculum. My work helps to bring more tangible options to the forefront.

Moreover, Jones and Walton's essay, "Using narratives to foster critical thinking about diversity and social justice" (forthcoming 2018), provides a definition of diversity research and pedagogy related to social justice; they also share a heuristic that may allow for more explicit pedagogy that considers social justice in technical communication. Jones and Walton put forth the need for more narratives that may help us understand just why individual stories matter for effective communication. They define social justice research in technical communication, noting that it:

> investigates how communication, broadly defined, can amplify the agency of oppressed people—those who are materially, socially, politically, and/or economically under-resourced . . . As such, our definition of social justice is broad and encompasses action-oriented research and pedagogy that can inform and integrate civic engagement, participatory research and action research, and minority studies.
>
> (p. 337)

Jones and Walton's definition helps me to think through the possibilities of technical communication with an eye toward social justice as they bring in ways in which diversity, or explicit conversations about social, material, and economic paradigms, matter for our classrooms and our pedagogy.

Taken together, these writers help to situate writing studies in general and technical writing studies in particular as fields and subfields that have great potential to promote a more diverse curriculum. My work adds to the conversation, using Thomas F. Nelson-Laird's diversity framework, and suggests practices that may help students and professors to begin or continue useful pedagogies and promote active citizenship.

Theoretical Framework

Published in the *Association of American Colleges & Universities* periodical, Nelson-Laird's (2014) report, "Reconsidering the inclusion of diversity in the curriculum," offers a diversity framework that encapsulates a varied approach to getting at diverse practices in the classroom; the report also serves as the major guide for articulating my focus group data. Nelson-Laird's approach is understood through nine basic categories: purpose/goals of a course; content; foundational perspectives; learners; instructor(s); pedagogy; classroom environment; assessment/evaluation; and adjustment. After each category, Nelson-Laird offers an inclusivity continuum that "illustrates how the [category] can vary from not inclusive to fully inclusive" (p. 1). The nine categories and the continuums provide a useful way for faculty and students to measure inclusiveness and diversity practices.

Nelson-Laird notes that the framework "allows for flexibility in which elements a faculty member chooses to address, and in which order (as decisions about one element will affect decisions about the others)" (p. 2). The malleable nature of Nelson-Laird's approach models the function of diversity itself. In other words, difference in approaches offers a new and often healthy way of adjusting to and meeting the needs of a multicultural population.

For my study, faculty and students were asked questions related to their experiences and thoughts about diversity at the UD, as well as what they would like to see happen with classroom practices. Student responses contributed to the conversation by providing a counter to professor feedback, showing the nuances of discussion about diversity, as well as the different and often similar conceptions of diversity. The results of the focus group helped me to develop several assignments related to diversity and advocacy that can be used in different contexts in university technical communication classrooms.

Method

In using a qualitative approach to understand the pulse of diversity and inclusion on the university's campus and to offer suggestions for engagement, I conducted three focus groups. Participants responded to a university-wide e-mail, which asked them to enter a research focus group session to provide feedback about diversity, teaching, and campus life. Of the 15 people who responded and participated in all three focus groups, five were university professors who taught writing and communication from the fields of Education, Biological Sciences, English, and Food Science, and ten were students from various disciplines who had taken or were planning to take technical communication courses. Both faculty and students identified as African American, Latinx, and White. I recorded all of the focus group sessions using a small microphone.

For the purposes of this study, I analyzed the recordings using three of the nine categories from Nelson-Laird's theory: foundational perspectives, content, and pedagogy. I chose these three categories because they are, for me, most transferable across disciplines and communities; they can provide ideas for how one might approach developing a critically diverse curriculum. Also, foundational perspectives, content, and pedagogy can arguably be three of the hardest parts of engaging diversity, teaching advocacy, and promoting inclusive practices because they establish connections between the personal, the professional, ways that encourage community engagement in thoughtful and productive ways.

I asked questions about teaching, classroom practices, and future thoughts about engaging diversity to faculty; similarly, I prompted students to discuss what they believed teaching about diversity looked like, as well as what kinds of assignments they believed may be useful to foster inclusion in the classroom (a complete list of questions asked of faculty and students can be found in Appendix A).

Below, I synthesize faculty/student answers and provide discussion related to Nelson-Laird's framework for achieving more diverse and inclusive classroom practices. I find the results of the data to be rich, encouraging, and useful to help scholars think about the possibilities of the technical communication classroom.

Category 1. Defining Diversity: Foundational Perspectives

According to Nelson-Laird's 2014 diversity/inclusivity framework, foundational perspectives are about how "the background characteristics of students and faculty affect their understanding of events, issues, and concepts. A course that includes diverse foundations or perspectives draws on theories that help explain how human differences influence our understanding of a course topic" (p. 4).

In all of my focus groups, I asked participants to first define "diversity" in order to get at some foundational approaches to both thinking, learning, and teaching. When asked what diversity meant, each professor group overwhelmingly pointed to the idea of differences. For professors, diversity was grounded in understanding the audience as well as the context for a situation. One professor noted that "diversity is like a critical approach. So, the goal is to make the familiar unfamiliar and make the unfamiliar familiar." This professor was invested in articulating the care with which one needed to explain diversity. By positing diversity as a critical approach, the professor made known the need for understanding difference. The professor went on to say that:

> "Critical diversity is kind of like difficult so the goal of education would be to achieve diversity. Without different perspectives, there would be no education . . . Alternate points of view can be disturbing for students. Part of diversity is about, for me, is about freedom. Again, people cannot be free unless they know something else."

This professor made some important points by first defining diversity as a core part of education and then arguing for alternative views to be at the forefront of the learning process. The professor's point about diversity as freedom was particularly interesting because it got to a transformative conversation that connected both policy and action. When one is free, it can be inferred that a person is able think, teach, and talk through challenges without being confined by them. Freedom is important to consider for the development of consciousness about difference, mostly because it allows for choice, for idea development, for agency. The need for critical thinking strategies to help foster such freedom, then, is important because it encourages self-acknowledgment, along with thinking through difference, similarities, and possibly the importance of informed action.

Another professor noted that when asked to define diversity, they:

> "immediately thought about things that it should not be, which is an add-on to a syllabus or a faculty. Just the token day when/where kids dress up and do things to just add on. I wish that it wasn't that way. I think of difference as a richness that we can draw from. That is a meaningful kind. Some of our schools have the potential to experience diversity in a way that they have not done so before. So, I am thinking about institutions that could help encourage diverse experiences."

This particular professor expressed concern about how diversity often became something extra, as not a part of the fabric of change. In many ways, this professor acknowledged disconnects between policy and action. The professor also pointed to the importance of at least thinking about how institutions could foster more diverse practices to move beyond simplifying the diversity in critical spaces. For example, in addition to policies that speak to diversity, institutions may involve students and faculty more by holding public forums, developing a social media presence dedicated to diversity, and even promoting more diverse programing by strategically bringing in speakers.

Rather than being an add-on, another professor claimed that, "In [my] field, [diversity] is essential. In my field, students are not as racially diverse, but must be prepared to embrace and teach diverse learners. The demographics of our country are changing drastically and we need to prepare our students for what they will encounter." Again, the idea of racial diversity and awareness thereof was a huge point for professors as concern was expressed about the need for more diversity both in the classroom, as well as in a programmatic way. The professor brought up the fact that students who were not racially diverse needed to be sensitive to and aware of diverse people and learners because they will encounter racially diverse people throughout life, whether on the job or in other public spaces.

Professor definitions of diversity seemed to strike a consistent tone, one that argued for more collaboration and connection between what was said about diversity and what was actually done. In addition to the need to actually define what diversity might mean in a specific way, the professors agreed that racial diversity and awareness therein was important for students to understand to achieve freedom: freedom in language and freedom in knowledge. All professors, in some way, brought up the classroom, too, as a way to engage diversity without being prompted to do so. The ways in which the classroom comes across as a building block and not simply lip service to policy, strikes me as a powerful way to think through meaning making about diversity and to actualize it for student learning and development.

When students were asked to define diversity and to talk about its meaning, their responses varied, but each spoke powerfully to the need for understanding foundational perspectives. First, I asked students to define diversity. One student noted that they understood diversity as "races and different types of people coming together or being separated based on their race, gender, or ethnicity, or even where they come from." The student went on to say that diversity was "people being not discriminated, but different types of people either coming together or being separated, so it could be good or bad." This student saw diversity as intertwined, in many ways, with segregation, as both a negative and positive idea that could add to or take away from a situation. Several students began to chime in, noting that diversity was "different ways of doing things," "different cultures, races, ethnicities blending together," and even "different personalities and different viewpoints."

After the chorus of student definitions, I presented them with a definition that I prepared about diversity. The definition was as follows: "Diversity is acknowledging race, class, and gender and taking strategic steps to include inclusive practices in classrooms, workplaces, and social spaces." I then asked students to engage with the prepared definition and to tell me what they thought in relation to their own ideas. One student said that "my ideas connect with this definition . . . I think of diversity in that it can be good or bad. In the 1900s, diversity was bad because people got different types of treatment based on their race . . . some people think that diversity is bad." The student went on to specify: "bad as in race and gender. When we learned about education in the 1900s and African Americans had special schools and women could only go at certain times. People were not working together to accomplish things." This student's perspective about diversity after engaging the definition says something about his/her historical understanding. Furthermore, the student's point about diversity being "good or bad" gets to a slippery connotation that is often connected to diversity as an "add-on" or as something that is viewed as forced rather than a resource or useful addition.

Another student posed the following question after engaging with the prepared definition: "Can you have diversity without talking about it? There are people who see diversity in a negative way. Some people see it in a deeper root." A student answered the question by saying that we should be "careful with words that you use because you do not want people to feel like a rare case. It is important to acknowledge similarities as well." This particular engagement was fascinating because it seemed that students were collapsing conversations about race, racism, and diversity into one sweeping idea. The "deeper root" for the student who posed the question shows that there was some history associated with the word "diversity" that few want to talk about. The next student, who brought up an empathetic tone with noting the need to look for similarities, also seemed to gloss over the fact that "rare cases" were what made diversity so important. The function of language here, as a way to make meaning and to understand, seemed to break down in translation as students wanted to talk about diversity, they wanted to share how they had seen it play out (or how they have not viewed it), but did not quite have the language to fully express the history that shapes them.

Overall, students made tangential connections between diversity and history, but struggled to pin down a clear point, despite being provided with a definition. Thus, they brought up the need to not only provide definitions in a classroom, but to explain the history of language use and society over time to increase understanding. It can be inferred that more directed discussion about race and diversity would be useful to help students contextualize the ideas.

According to Nelson-Laird's (2014) continuum, a foundational perspective is all about exposing different ideas and then moving toward examining those ideas in a productive way (p. 2). Understanding the perspectives of both students and teachers, then, matters greatly in one's ability to begin to address the lack of diverse practices in any setting. In these focus groups, foundational ideas about diversity provided a good sense of what it might mean to begin to engage with diversity on campus, because we see how foundational ideas influence how diversity is viewed. While professors saw diversity as a huge part of the educational experience, students saw the idea of diversity as something that could be "both positive and negative" and revealed the need for more instruction and explanation about the topic. Taken together, it can be gathered that more strategic planning is needed to help build on student foundational perspectives about diversity and to support professor efforts in doing so. The foundational perspectives from both students and professors helped me to develop some strategies that educators may consider thinking about and encouraging conversations in the classroom about diversity and difference.

Category 2. Engaging Diversity through Content

Course content is a big part of the thinking process as professors develop classes and as staff prepare for retreats and other functions. For Nelson-Laird's (2014) framework, content speaks to "the subject matter covered, the way it is ordered, and the materials used to present it. In courses that include some diversity, the content includes subjects that are ignored in traditional courses or alternative perspectives on traditional subjects. In more inclusive courses, the content reflects the experiences of multiple cultural groups from their own as well as other perspectives" (p. 2). When engaging focus groups about the function of diversity on campus, as well as the promotion of diversity in classrooms, a theme related to content development was brought forth to understand more about what and how professors engaged diversity and how students had encountered it.

When asked about practices that they engage in related to diversity, both professors and students shared ideas about developing content. One professor noted that:

> "In my methods class, we are talking about critical pedagogy and examining power structures. I find it important for my students to have some historical understanding of institutional racism and structured forms of oppression. It doesn't fit into the course necessarily, but without that context, students have a hard time understanding how it fits with the structure. Understanding neighborhoods, lending practices have helped them engage with issues of race. I have always had students identify as Queer so those students help to bring that up."

This professor stressed the importance of providing background information for students in a specific way. Conversations and particular points about institutional and systemic racism are, for this professor, an important part of content development, even if it goes outside of the realm of study for the course. Thus, before engaging what the professor deemed as the core of the methods course, the content must contain some discussion or reading about the function of racism in society. Making those important distinctions seem, to me, a wonderful way to help students make meaningful connections as to why diversity is encouraged and regarded as needed not only in academia and in workplaces, but in society in general.

One student noted that:

> "professors in my History classes and stuff talk about diversity. They don't talk about it in my Math class. Most students know what diversity is and what it means, but don't know how to connect it back. Like, in my History of Education class, [my teacher] never talks about separation, but that class talks about how diversity is good."

This student made known some disconnects that he/she noticed in classes across his/her university. By highlighting a specific class, the student made known that there could be more effort with infusing information about diversity into each subject. Such comments make a large point about the importance of content development with an eye toward making connections within and outside of classes.

Using Nelson-Laird's (2014) continuum, we understand that content in inclusive courses "reflects the experiences of multiple cultural groups from their own as well as other perspectives" (p. 3). Content development becomes just as important as foundational ideas because it helps to actuate or build on what students may already understand. What comes out from professors in this section is that context is central for student engagement. Conducting a short survey at the beginning of a semester, for instance, about student understanding related to diversity would help a professor see just where students are in their development. Then, professors can add to student understanding. Student comments about the need for more connections across the curriculum are important, too, as they speak to a life skill that students should develop: the ability to recognize diversity and difference as a resource, which provides a window for advocacy.

Category 3. Engaging Diversity Through Pedagogy

In Nelson-Laird's (2014) diversity/inclusivity framework, pedagogy is all about thinking through:

> the theories and scholarship (e.g., theories of student development and learning) that inform these processes and methods. More inclusive pedagogies account for the fact that not all students are the same, but rather have varied learning needs. At its most inclusive, pedagogy will demonstrate a focus on the learning of diverse students through the interplay of theory and instructional process at a highly developed level.
>
> (p. 4)

Pedagogy, then, must be a strategy that infuses the foundational with theory and specific content in order to be effective. Effective pedagogical thinking and practice take into account ways to engage students in meaningful ways.

In one focus group, a professor spoke of pedagogy in terms of engaging students to allow them to feel more comfortable talking about diversity and race relations. The professor noted the following as it related to pedagogy: "I use this thing call Polleverywhere.com to get some understanding about [what students might find] difficult to understand. If you notice race and talk about race that makes you racist . . . I am trying to model for them that noticing race is not bad and that creating an environment is important. If you provide an open space, students will call you on it if you do not talk about it." Using Poll Everywhere, a live interactive audience participation tool, which could be set up in a way that encourages students to be anonymous to ask and engage questions, this professor welcomed explicit acknowledgment of race as an identity marker to help students become more comfortable with engaging the environment. Since users can respond anonymously using Poll Everywhere, it may help them to feel more comfortable with asking questions, which, hopefully, would translate to classroom-rich discussions about race and difference.

Another professor spoke of pedagogy in this way:

> "History is important. With my own kids, they are steeped in history . . .
> When my kids were young, they asked why is it that everywhere we go that
> Black people are always at the bottom. Why wouldn't they think that way.
> I use readings and I work to capture the imagination. I talk a lot about
> myself and how I perceived things as I grew up in a very radicalized society
> as opposed to my husband. We very often don't see things the same way
> and . . . that can influence teaching."

This professor's approach draws from personal experience as a way to make connections with students; a professor who is able to bring in personal experiences has the potential to help students understand difference in a more engaged way. Doing so may help students to consider their own lives and to make connections between what they see and what they hear. In the appropriate context, personal stories may help students to view diversity as a resource for more dynamic engagement.

Moreover, one professor spoke of the idea of a free classroom. The professor said students:

> "come up with the topic at home and we come and discuss as I try to
> engage them in the personal. For example, we have this next topic about
> amnesty education. They have been working on them on the web. It's
> about whether or not illegal people should be deported, should we work to
> have educational freedoms. So, very quickly, they become engaged because
> it is their view."

This professor worked to make sure that students were part of the development process, thus involving them more closely in the writing process. This professor went on to say that after students come up with the topic for discussion:

> "They become immediately a big part of the conversation. I encourage
> them to bring in computers to class. They can find something that relates
> to the topic and that becomes a lot of how I run the class. Surveys, articles,
> hopefully they will have future questions. I will help, it is nice for them to
> have other ways as well."

The idea of a free classroom, as the professor suggests, is a pedagogical tool that pulls from Paulo Friere's theory of a more inclusive classroom, one that does not subscribe to the banking concept of education. This professor's approach speaks to the possibilities of the classroom as a student-driven place, one that values student voices by providing them with an active role in the teaching process.

For my study, student voices were clear as they worked to articulate points about how pedagogy shaped their thoughts about diversity. Students spoke of making more effort to use language more consciously. One student said he/she would like to "see more talking about [diversity]. Most of my classes, it's like brushed over. Even if it was one class to talk about diversity and how it affects certain things, I feel like students would understand. So, like, I knew the definitions, but haven't been able to make in-depth connections about how it affects us." This student made known the importance of providing students with information about diversity by simply "talking" about it. Just talking helps students have better footing to advocate for diverse practices and people. The student went on to suggest that students saw the word "diversity" and tended to not think critically about what it meant.

Another student suggested that pedagogically, it would be useful to have students develop "timelines to look at things over time . . . it may be helpful to see how things were then and now. Understand how the past influences in the present." This student pointed to the need for a more historical view of diversity over time to better connect the conversation. By suggesting a mapping approach to the situation, the student called for more specificity around the subject to make pedagogy about diversity more useful to student development.

Nelson-Laird (2014) suggests that to achieve a pedagogy that is inclusive, one must not only use varied techniques, but they must also make sure that the techniques are equity oriented (p. 5). The focus groups helped to bring out points about equity, in fact, as both students and professors made some reference to the need for more direct approaches to teaching difference and to understanding diversity. Professor strategies about student-centered engagement, historical lessons, and question development coincided with what students were calling for: the need for more meaningful engagement in the classroom. The focus groups were able to bring out key points about clarity in definition, specificity with the use of content, and direct action as it related to pedagogy.

Limitations of Research

My sample size for this research project was relatively small. Drawing from only five professors and ten students from different backgrounds, the results were varied, but were not as varied as they could have been with a larger sampling of participants. Another limitation of my research is that my framework is not a heuristic that comes from technical communication studies. In spite of these two points, using Nelson-Laird's (2014) framework as a lens, the analysis of the research allowed useful results that have implications for the teaching of technical communication, particularly as it relates to considerations of diversity as well as grooming active and aware students. Use of the framework also adds an interdisciplinary spin that, I argue, should happen more often to move toward transformative work in diversity studies.

Discussion and Implications

Professors need flexibility when thinking through and engaging diversity as they make crucial decisions about how to enter important, often sensitive conversations. Flexibility is also important when thinking about teaching students to advocate for themselves and for others. These conversations must be had to help challenge students in ways that will promote a more meaningful engagement with differences in race, class, gender, or creed. As professors begin and continue conversations about diversity and race in the technical communication classroom, they may be able to help students achieve learning outcomes that not only recognize diversity, but connect both advocacy and social justice for transformative results.

The focus group research solidified the need for candid discussions about race, diversity, and difference as not only part of the classroom fabric, but as part of what the college promotes, supports, and honors in order to better support active citizenship. When students are equipped with the tools to make the unfamiliar familiar, they will be able to use these skills in life beyond the classroom as more socially informed doctors, lawyers, teachers, and overall citizens. The rich feedback from professors and students spoke to the need for more directed engagement with inclusion and difference in order to provide the best education for students who will become participants in an increasingly diverse world. Professors were able to speak to the need for more student ownership of learning, whereas students alluded to the need for more "talk" about the subject of diversity in the classroom.

The three sample assignments in Appendix B about history, design, and analysis all complement the focus group research by providing specific ways that both students and professors may go about engaging with more inclusive practices that teach technical writing while also advocating for social awareness. More specifically, Assignment #1, "Uncovering institutional histories to meet diverse needs: Designing and communicating history in technical communication," meets students where they are while also asking them to further investigate constructed stories and histories to discover diversity on their college campus. Assignment #1 is closely tied to analysis on foundational applications to teaching as noted in my analysis on foundational ideas. Assignment #2, "Active participation beyond the classroom: Developing diverse content in technical communication," helps students to identify a professional organization's proposal for technical communication via design. Students are asked to create content that is not only clear and focused, but that considers diversity. By asking students to develop content for a real, diverse audience, they engage in content development which is key takeaway from my analysis on content development. Lastly, Assignment #3, "Considerations of design: Advocacy, analysis, and report writing in technical communication," asks students to visit archives and old collections to understand how technical communication has changed and how it has also remained similar. With this assignment, students create their own peda-gogical moves by comparing design principles, cultural and social histories as well as kairotic truths to help contextualize a document. By doing research about practices, theories, and designs, students are encouraged to make connections that promote more engaged citizenship.

In a time when socially constructed issues cause multiple problems with engaging difference, we, as instructors, artists, educators, professors, and those who care, need responsible and equitable language use and practices more than ever. In addition to language practices, we need action, i.e. assignments and strategies to help to model what we say and aid us in teaching students how to advocate for diverse practices beyond the classroom space. There must be efforts, both institutionally and in the classroom, that go beyond paying lip service to diversity and diverse practices to more intentional and engaged approaches. After conducting this research and thinking about the technical communication classroom as a space to encourage advocacy for diversity and diverse practices, I am reminded of how this work has to be intentional, multifaceted, and outreach driven to continually consider the connections between the university and the community. My hope is that conversations continue about the need for more directed, focused, and direct approaches in order to prepare for and engage in more responsible practices.

Discussion Questions

1) In groups of two to three people, brainstorm a positive current event (within the last two years) related to diversity or diverse practices from a racial/cultural group other than your own. What is important to consider about the current event? How did you learn about it?

2) Write a paragraph description of what diversity may mean for a popular organization like Twitter. Think about why diversity is so important and how you may go about convincing your readers of its importance. What did you come up with? How did you get started?

3) Respond to an image, video, or meme by taking note of audience and how different audiences might receive the message communicated. How does diversity come into play here? Why might it be important to consider difference when creating information for mass audiences?

4) Bring in your college mission statement (or your department's mission statement). How does the statement address inclusion? What specific information is there to convince you? What is missing? How would you rewrite the statement?

5) List five diverse and influential scholars in your field of study. Talk through their contributions. If you are unable to name five people who represent diversity, think through just why that may be so.

Further Reading

All website URLs accessed February 2018.

Beetham, G. Addressing passive racism in the academy. *Inside Higher Education*. Retrieved from www.insidehighered.com/blogs/university-venus/addressing-passive-racism-academy

Espinosa, L., Gaertner M., & Orfield, G. (2015). *Race, class, & college access: achieving diversity in a shifting legal landscape*. Los Angeles: American Council on Education.

Facing History and Ourselves. (2017). Free resources for teachers. Retrieved from www.facinghistory.org

Johnson-Eilola, J., & Selber, S. (2012). *Solving problems in technical communication*. Chicago: University of Chicago Press.

Teaching Tolerance. (2017). Free resources for teachers. Retrieved from www.tolerance.org/classroom-resources

References

All website URLs accessed February 2018.

Brown, E. (2016, September 27). Yale study suggests racial bias among preschool teachers. *Washington Post*. Retrieved from www.washingtonpost.com/news/education/wp/2016/09/27/yale-study-suggests-racial-bias-among-preschool-teachers/?utm_term=.9f692a90a52f

Jones, N., & Walton, R. (2018). Using narratives to foster critical thinking about diversity and social justice. A. Haas & M. Elbe (Eds.), *Key theoretical frameworks for teaching technical communication in the 21st century* (pp. 336–375) Colorado: Utah State University Press.

hooks, b. (1994). *Teaching to transgress*. New York: Routledge.

Medina, C. (2014). Tweeting collaborative identity: Race, ICTs, and performing latinidad. In M. Williams & O. Pimental (Eds.), *Communicating race, ethnicity, and identity in technical communication* (pp. 63–86). Amityville, NY: Baywood Publishing Company, Inc.

Moyer, J. (2016, January 5). Workplace diversity policies 'don't help' – and 'make white men feel threatened.' *The Washington Post*. Retrieved from www.washingtonpost.com/news/morning-mix/wp/2016/01/05/workplace-diversity-policies-dont-help-women-minorities-and-make-white-men-feel-threatened/?utm_term=.d6d677c8c4d7

Mujic, J. (2015, October 29). Education reform and the failure to fix inequality in America. *The Atlantic*. Retrieved from ww.theatlantic.com/education/archive/2015/10/education-solving-inequality/412729

Nelson-Laird, T. F. (2014). Reconsidering the inclusion of diversity in the curriculum. *Diversity and Democracy*. Retrieved from www.aacu.org

Sapp, D. A., & Crabtree, R. D. (2002). A laboratory in citizenship: Service learning in the technical communication classroom. *Technical Communication Quarterly*, *11*, 411–431.

Savage, G., & Mattson, K. (2011). Perceptions of racial and ethnic diversity in technical communication programs. *Programmatic Perspectives*, *3*, 5–57.

The Demands. (2015). We the Protestors. Retrieved from: www.thedemands.org

Williams, M., & Pimental, O. (2014). *Communicating race, ethnicity, and identity in technical communication*. Amityville: Baywood Publishing Company, Inc.

APPENDIX A

Focus Group Questions

Questions Asked of Professors

- What does diversity mean to you and how does that meaning shape your thinking/approaches to teaching?
- What are your thoughts and perceptions about diversity on the university's campus?
- What practices do you engage in to promote diversity in your classroom/ workspace?
- What practices would you like to explore in your classroom/workspace?
- What happens when you cannot visibly see ethnic diversity in your classes? How does your approach change? Or does it remain the same?
- If charged with making programmatic changes related to diversity on campus/in your department /in the classroom, how would you go about measuring student understanding?

Questions Asked of Students

- What is diversity?
- How might you define it?
- What do you think about my prepared definition of diversity?
- Prepared definition: "Diversity is acknowledging race, class, and gender and taking strategic steps to include inclusive practices in classrooms, workplaces, and social spaces."
- What does diverse teaching look like at the university?
- What are some examples that you can think of?
- What should be the goals of a diverse classroom?

- What assignments may be useful in communicating diversity or engaging diversity with peers?
- What has been or could be a useful assignment that would help peers engage diversity in the classroom?

APPENDIX B

Assignment Examples for Technical Communication Courses

Assignment #1 Uncovering institutional histories to meet diverse needs: Designing and communicating history in technical communication

Purpose: To practice critical thinking and rhetorical awareness by developing an infographic.

Context: Our conversations about writing genres, responding to texts, and even recognizing constructed histories all help us to consider and prepare for writing situations that we may face in the job world. As a genre, infographics are quickly becoming a legitimate and respected way to provide information to advocate for a particular issue and/or to market a product. For this assignment, we will practice developing a skill that will help us consolidate what we've been learning by working to meet the needs of incoming student users as well as thinking about the needs of diverse users.

Assignment: In teams of two to three, scholars should identify one building on campus to create an infographic that provides specific and important facts about the building. More specifically, each team will create an infographic that will inform incoming student users about the history of the chosen building as well as how the building connects to diversity.

In addition to including sufficient data and creating a visually engaging document, each infographic must meet the following requirements:

- Provide clear changes to original template.
- Use icons and graphics.
- Integrate a combination of images and words.
- Include citations throughout or at the bottom of the document.

Please create your infographic with a user-friendly online infographic creator such as:

- Piktochart
- Easel.ly

A few places that would provide reliable, timely data to help you create your infographic are as follows:

- Data.gov
- Pew American and Internet Life Project Surveys
- School Archives (look for school events held there and older photos of the building)
- Library

Assignment #2 Active participation beyond the classroom: Developing diverse content in technical communication

Purpose: The purpose of this assignment is three-fold: to connect concepts learned in the technical communication classroom about diversity; to best show knowledge of course objectives; and to demonstrate rhetorical awareness and critical thinking.

Context: *Technical Communication*, the Society for Technical Communication's (STC) journal, publishes articles and book reviews about technical writing theories and practices. *Technical Communication* includes both quantitative and qualitative research while showcasing the work of some of the field's most noteworthy writers (http://techcomm.stc.org). STC recently put out a call for scholars to help them convey the theme "Social Media Practices in Technical Communication." This assignment has been adapted to engage the theme in meaningful ways.

Assignment: With conversations about diversity and diverse practices in mind, teams should create an inclusive design based on the theme "Social Media Practices in Technical Communication." The theme-related illustration should appear in the form of a diagram, a drawing, a collage, specifications, instructions, a cartoon, a comic strip, or even a brief narrative. When brainstorming about the design, teams might consider one of following questions:

- How are technical communicators using social media to promote diversity? How is social media changing the field to consider diversity? Or changing the profession to include more diversity?

- How are technical communicators thinking about diversity? How are they engaging difference with respect to race, ability, gender, or sexuality?
- How might we guide the direction of social media and encourage effective and ethical practices?

In addition to designing a document, teams will also develop a short proposal to accompany the document. Once each team has created both a design and a proposal, teams will present their ideas to the class in a short pitch presentation. Teams will then choose the best project; once a winning team is chosen, that team's work will be submitted to the editor of STC for possible publication in *Technical Communication*. Visit www.stc.org/techcomm/propose-a-cover-illustration for more information about the journal and the call for illustrations.

Details: All students are responsible for the content of the proposal and the design. Therefore, groups should appropriately manage portions of the assignment.

Assignment #3 Considerations of design: Advocacy, analysis, and report writing in technical communication

Purpose: This assignment has been created to help scholars hone critical thinking and rhetorical awareness skills by analyzing a professional or technical document and creating a recommendation report.

Context: Professional and technical documents come in many forms and have been around for some time. We are quite familiar with professional documents in modern day, but what about those before the 1960s? This assignment will give scholars a chance to analyze documents prior to 1960 to delve more into cultural trends as well as historical and political shifts that shape how we view material.

Assignment: After considering our class discussions about analysis and ethics, each scholar should choose one piece of professional/technical writing published in 1960 or earlier. Then, each *scholar should compose a two-page internal report, in memo format,* that analyzes the professional document and notes how the information presented could be adapted to fit 21st century standards. Scholars should include a note of transmittal to accompany their internal report.

Details: Each scholar should choose one professional or technical document and analyze it to show critical thinking and rhetorical awareness. In order to perform a solid analysis, each student should consider *audience, purpose, context, design* and *ethics*, all topics that we have covered in our course. Then, scholars should make a recommendation as to how they see the professional/technical document being adapted or changed to fit 21st century standards and advocate for why they deem that change important.

Texts before 1960 that can be found in Special Collections:

- *The Crisis Magazine*
- Sears & Roebuck catalogs from 1897, 1956–1957, and 1966–1967
- Illustrated Catalogue, Henry Heil Chemical Company (1891)
- *The Young Craftsman* (1943)
- Illustrations of Paper Mill Machinery (1921)
- Illustrated Catalogue, Chemical Apparatus (Eimer & Amend, 1907)
- Catalogue of Ventilating Grates (Edwin A. Jackson & Brother, 1904–1905)
- The Indian Rotary Aero Motor (Hendee Manufacturing Co., ca.1915)
- *National Geographic* issue

Other texts before 1960 to consider when using search tools:

- Memos and reports from major disasters (choose a small portion of the whole)
- Images of medical documents or apparatuses
- Letters, notes, images used to galvanize or move an audience to act
- Maps or menus related to travel or restaurants, respectively.

11

COMMUNITY-ENGAGED LEARNING IN ONLINE TECHNICAL COMMUNICATION CLASSES

A Tool for Student Success

Ann Marie Francis

Introduction

Since the 90s, trends in education have seen a push in service-learning, which requires students to work with community organizations as part of the course requirements. When Huckin (1997) explored service-learning as a component of technical communication classes, he outlined the pedagogical benefits of the approach. One benefit of service-learning Huckin found was to promote civic engagement, which, in turn, led to increased student motivation. Huckin's favorable conclusions of community-based teaching approaches were supported by others who applied service-learning pedagogy to their technical writing classes (Stone, 2000; Dubinsky, 2001; Scott, 2004). When Matthews and Zimmerman (1999) integrated service-learning in their technical writing class, they noticed that for their students, the service-learning projects helped provide "benefits in the form of development of civic values, improved academic learning, and motivation to accept responsibility for their own learning" (p. 391). Scott's (2004) findings were equally positive. He found that the "emphasis on civic responsibility can be motivating to students, leading them to look beyond their career preparation or their success in the course, and promoting them to engage with others in community problem solving" (p. 289). These studies inspired me to implement service-learning in my technical communication classes. Although these previous publications focused on face-to-face classes, I taught online technical writing courses, which I knew would add different challenges.

The implantation of service-learning pedagogy in an online class is often called *service eLearning*, a term first adopted by Strait and Sauer (2004). The term can cover a variety of service-learning scenarios: face-to-face classes with online service-learning components; online classes with face-to-face service-learning components; online classes with online service-learning components; or any other variation. While the research on service eLearning in technical writing courses is still fairly limited, especially in online technical communication classes, it is beginning to emerge. In a recent study, Soria and Weiner (2013) compared the outcomes between the sections of online technical writing courses taught with and without the service-learning component. Overall, their results were promising:

> "The data suggests that service-learning in online technical writing courses helps students to make connections to the 'real world,' encourages students to connect with their audience(s) and develop a sense of purpose for writing tasks, connects students to future employment, and develops deep learning with course materials."
>
> (p. 189–190)

Bourelle (2014) also successfully implemented service eLearning in an online technical writing class, and while she faced some challenges, she concluded that the approach provided transferrable skills and helped students become "responsible citizens who care about their community" (p. 262).

While there was considerable research on the pedagogical benefits of service-learning and eLearning in technical communication classes, there was limited research on the students' perceptions of service-learning. Noticing the gap, I decided to explore students' views of service-learning, specifically in online technical communication classes, and see if their attitudes change as they work through the semester and the service-learning projects. Specifically, I wanted to explore the following questions:

- How do students perceive service-learning in an online technical communication class?
- How do the perceptions change over the course of the semester?

To accomplish this goal, I implemented service eLearning in my online technical communication class and used reflective journals to study the students' perception of service-learning, the relationship between student motivation and service-learning projects, and student attitudes over the semester. This chapter outlines the course, the implementation process, and the results of the study.

The Course

English 2010 Technical Communication at the University of North Georgia is a service course that introduces students to the basic elements of technical and professional communication including organization, style, and mechanics. Students learn to produce communication that is typical in the business world:

letters, emails, descriptions, blogs, proposals, technical descriptions, and instructions. This 2,000-level course requires students to have completed freshman composition one and two and a literature survey class as course pre-requisites. While the university does offer an English degree with a writing and publication concentration, the course tends to attract non-English majors, including students majoring in psychology and environmental spatial analysis. In response to the impact of technology on the business world, the university moved English 2010 from a traditional face-to-face format to a completely online format in fall of 2013. In addition, the course name was changed from "Technical Writing" to "Technical Communication" to reflect the importance of other types of communication used in business, specifically electronic communication.

Implementation of the Service-Learning Component

Choosing the Right Assignment

The first step, after making the commitment to implement service eLearning in my online technical communication class, was to determine what assignments should be required as part of the service-learning component and the best type of community partners for my class. I started by outlining the types of documents I could have students produce that would benefit organizations, as well as represent vital course concepts. The key when considering what type of work to have students produce is to make sure the assignments meet course objectives; the service-learning assignments must supplement learning. I considered the course objectives as I came up with several assignment ideas that I felt would benefit nonprofit organizations and reinforce the class concepts: correspondence, manuals, handbooks, blogs, proposals, grants, videos, and infographics. I knew I could not require that many assignments in a one-semester course, so I grouped similar deliverables together so I could work with each organization to pick the assignments that would best directly meet their needs.

Finding Community Partners

Once I had an idea of what assignments would be required, I worked on securing community partners before the semester started. To locate community partners, I originally sent emails and made phone calls to organizations I thought could benefit from the project. While I did get some interest, it was very limited and none of the organizations that I called ended up working with the class. What worked best was word of mouth. I talked to friends and posted on social media that I was looking for organizations to work with and explained briefly what I planned to do. When I explained the plan for the students to work with community organizations, people were quickly able to identify friends and colleagues they knew who would benefit from working with the students. I asked for contact information only after the friend initiated contact with the organization's contact person and indicated that they would be interested in the project. At that point, I reached out with a phone call, explained the project, and discussed ideas of how to make it work for their individual organization.

Negotiating the Workload

As I approached potential community partners, I quickly realized that the organizations were concerned about the time commitments. They wanted to verify that they were not expected to teach the students how to do the assignments and that the time they invested would be beneficial for the organization. I specified that I wanted to have one contact person from each nonprofit that the students would be able to email with questions but that the questions would be strictly related to the organizations' wants and needs; I would answer all questions about the class. I also provided a list of potential general assignments with room for the organization to provide input so the assignments could be catered to meet the specific needs of the nonprofit.

When talking to the contact person for the organization, I identified ways to adjust the different course assignments to meet the needs of the organization while still meeting course objectives. For example, the "Increased Awareness Assignment" discussed below required students to incorporate student research, along with information from the organization, and highlight the mission of the organization; the information was used to create some type of visual document designed to increase the general public's awareness of the organization and its purpose. The details for the assignment varied for each group; some organizations wanted infographics while others wanted brochures. As a result, each student group was given a different assignment prompt based on the needs of their specific organization.

Preparing Students for Service-Learning

The first week of class, I had students read information on service-learning and answer a discussion question related to the information they had read. In addition, they completed a journal entry about their thoughts on the service-learning aspect of the course. After reading their responses, I created an FAQ document to address some of their concerns. I also addressed the questions and concerns in the discussion threads and the service-learning information sheet. The first time I taught the class, I did not continue the theme of service-learning in the discussion threads that were ongoing throughout the semester, but the second time I did. The discussions were not limited to service-learning, obviously, but I wove service-learning into the discussions throughout the semester. As we explored different elements of technical writing, I brought in the service-learning aspect and made the direct connection between each lesson and the service-learning projects. The discussion board format of the online class provided a place for the students to compare struggles and successes and get feedback from their peers. It was important to continue the discussion instead of presenting information on service-learning once and moving on, as it provided a continued opportunity for students to discuss their concerns with others, especially others outside of their group. While the reflections also allowed students to express their concerns, any response was limited to the instructor's feedback. The online discussions provided the benefit of feedback from the students' peers.

Connecting Students and Nonprofits

The students selected their organization the second week of class. Waiting until the second week provided two benefits: students had time to get familiar with the idea of service-learning, and the initial drop-add period ended, which prevented students from picking an organization and then dropping the course. I wanted students to have input on the organization they worked with because, as Nielsen (2016) suggested, students would be more motivated when they had a connection to the organization in service-learning projects. I was not comfortable letting the students locate their own partner because of the time restraints and the struggle of assigning groups and having the groups work together to find an organization. So I let them pick from one of the four organizations that agreed to be part of the project. At the start of the week, I provided students with an overview of each organization, including the organization's name and mission, general information provided by the organization, the website and any social media sites, and potential assignments.

The class was divided into groups as defined by the community partners the students selected. The size of the groups varied slightly, but most groups had four students; no group had more than five students or fewer than three. I provided students with a specific day and time when the group selection would open. Using the group features in the learning management system, I created groups with a limited number of slots. Students selected the organization they wanted to work with on a first-come-first-served basis, and those who had strong preferences for a specific organization tended to get online early and select their groups.

The organizations varied in their purpose and mission, providing a range of interests for the students to select from. For example, one organization provided supplies for diabetes patients in third world countries; another supplied books to children whose parents were incarcerated. Other organizations' missions included support for epilepsy patients, work to end suicide, and funding for oversees missions. After learning about each organization, the students selected the community partner they wished to work with based on their personal preferences. I had a few students comment that they were glad they were allowed to select their organization because one or more of the organizations did not appeal to them for a variety of reasons.

Making Initial Contact

The next week of the class, students made their first contact with their community partner. They were required to send a formal introduction outlining why they selected the organization, what specifically appealed to them about the nonprofit, and what they had to offer to the organization. Again, this assignment changed between the two semesters that I taught the course. The first semester, I did not ask students to include what skills they had that would benefit the projects and the organization; instead I asked them to write a formal introduction and include whatever information they felt their community partner would benefit from knowing. I realized, though, that requiring students to include specific details about their skills forced them to consider their strengths and explain what they brought to the table. As a result, instead of feeling they were in over their heads, they had a chance to consider what knowledge and skills they had that would benefit the projects. To help facilitate the introductions, I organized the discussion during the second week of class centered on skills needed for technical writing and which of those skills the students already possessed. The students felt more comfortable with the project when they realized that they had many of the skills that were necessary to be successful with their nonprofit.

Staying in Touch with Students and Community Partners

To help manage the class, I asked students to copy me in on emails sent to their community partner. This practice helped me to address situations as soon as they arose and to ensure that all communication was appropriate and complete. That request did result in quite a few emails, but it allowed me to step in when there was something that needed to be addressed and to help translate if there was a question that was not clear. In addition, it reinforced the idea that I was the instructor and that they needed to ask me questions related to the class. Quite a few times, I received emails that asked if the question would be appropriate for the community partner or if I could help the students figure out a better way to word the question so it would sound professional. The emails also helped ensure that I had all the information from the nonprofits when I was evaluating the students' work. In addition to overseeing communication between the students and the nonprofits, I also kept in contact with the community partners throughout the semester. Every week or two, I sent updates to each organization outlining the current project, any concerns the students had, what to expect from the students, and when to expect it.

Completing Tasks and Assignments

The first two assignments that the groups worked on were individual assignments. The first assignment primarily consisted of letters written for the organization, including letters soliciting donations and thanking for donations. The second assignment worked to produce visuals that would increase community awareness about the organization and/or the organization's mission. For this project, some students created an infographic for the organization that could be included on the organizations' webpage; other students created a brochure, one of which was later included in utility bills for the local area to advertise an upcoming event. Each student in the group completed the assignment for their community partner, resulting in the organization having several variations of the project. The organization could then select the document(s) that best met their needs. The final project was a collaborative assignment that required the group to work together to complete the larger assignment, resulting in one collaborative document for the organization, including a proposal or grant. One organization asked the students to design a procedural manual to document all the steps and necessary forms for its annual festival, an event that had been taking place for years without any standard documented policies. The final assignment also required more contact between the students and the organization to determine the exact needs of the organization and how the students could work to meet those needs.

In relation to the service-learning aspect of the course, the rest of the semester was not very different from non-service-learning courses, especially those that utilized collaborative student projects. Aside from teaching the course material, I primarily managed groups, dealt with conflicts, and interacted with the contact person for each organization. I also used the semester to implement a research study to explore the students' perceptions of service-learning and determine if those perceptions changed over the course of the semester.

Method

The purpose of the study was to explore students' perceptions about service-learning, so I designed a qualitative study to examine students' views. Using reflective journals at different points in the semester, I was able to evaluate the students' perceptions of service-learning and determine if their perceptions and attitudes towards service-learning changed as they worked on service-learning projects.

Procedure

Because my research question focused on students' perceptions and attitudes, I conducted qualitative research using journal entries to collect data. Students were required to write five reflections throughout the 15-week semester as part of the course requirement. For each journal entry, students were given a journal prompt with specific questions they were asked to answer (see Appendix A for a copy of the journal prompts). The qualitative method is effective when researchers want to "gain an understanding of underlying reasons and motivations" (Park and Park, 2016), which is exactly what I wanted to do. In addition to providing an insight into students' attitudes, the journals provide a place for the students to write reflections on their experiences, a step many consider a critical part of the service-learning experience (Deans, 2000; Dubinsky, 2006; Hatcher and Bringle, 1997; Jacoby, 1996). As Hatcher and Bringle (1997) explain, "When students contemplate their service activities, there is potential to reformulate assumptions, create new frameworks, and build perceptions that influence future action" (p. 153). The reflections for this class, which combined were a minimum of 2,000 words per student, served two purposes. First, they worked to help students see the connection between their work and the community, to consider how their work moved beyond the confines of the classroom, and to explore how the work could have affected the students, both positively and negatively. Second, the reflections served as the basis for the study by allowing a place for students to comment on their perceptions of service-learning and the way they felt while working on each assignment.

To help reduce professor influence, students earned full credit for all reflections that were completed on time and met the minimum requirements. Throughout the semester, students were encouraged to be honest in their reflections. Before each journal assignment was due, students were reminded that they were being graded only on completing the work and that the goal was to have students share their thoughts. In addition, each journal prompt included a statement that reminded students that I wanted them to be honest about their feelings towards the projects. Although some professor influence might have been present, all effort was made to have students write honest, reflective feedback.

To ensure student confidentiality, pseudonyms were used for all reflections and information provided in this chapter. In addition, any identifying remarks were omitted including indicators of gender, race, age, or major, as were any comments that were not relevant to the purpose of the survey. Otherwise, the comments are presented exactly as written; no grammar, spelling, or other errors were corrected.

Participants

The study for this chapter was conducted on two sections of English 2010 that were offered in the spring of 2014 and fall of 2015. A total of 30 students in two sections were enrolled in the courses after the initial drop/add period. Of those students, 20 (67%) were male and 10 (33%) were female. All students were juniors or seniors, with an average of 84.67 earned credit hours before the class started. The students were enrolled in a variety of degree plans; 16 (53%) were majoring in environmental spatial analysis, six (20%) were majoring in psychology, and the remaining students were majoring in nursing, math, physics, or general studies. All the students who submitted journals agreed to have their reflections used in the study and signed the appropriate documentation as required by the university's Institutional Review Board guidelines.

Measures

The students completed five reflections throughout the course, referred to as journals. The first journal entry, which was completed the second week of the semester after the idea of service-learning had been introduced but no assignments were completed, asked students to share their initial perceptions of service-learning, to examine their reactions upon learning the class would include service-learning, and to share any concerns they may have had. The second journal entry was completed after students submitted their first service-learning assignment and asked students to consider how they approached the assignment compared to how they had approached non-service-learning assignments in the past, the time they spent on the assignment, and their feelings about the quality of their work. The third journal entry was completed after students finished a substantial assignment to be given to their selected organization; the journal prompt asked students to consider the various elements of the assignment, especially the fact that there was no or very little face-to-face interaction with their community partner. As a result, students could provide input on the process of completing the assignment and offer ideas of what they would do differently if given the option.

The fourth journal entry was a little different because it was completed after students submitted an assignment that did not require them to work with their community partner. Rather, it was based on a fictional case study and asked students to explain how they approached the non-service-learning focused assignment compared to how they approached the service-learning assignments. Specifically, I asked students to discuss the time spent on the assignment, the attitude about the assignment, and any concerns they had while doing the work.

The fifth and final journal entry was completed as the last requirement of the class. The students completed a collaborative project for their organization before completing the final journal entry. The journal asked students to reflect on the service-learning process as a whole. Students were prompted to consider if the service-learning aspect affected their approach to the course and how they learned the material. In addition, students were asked if they would recommend a course with service-learning elements to other students.

Results

I analyzed the content of each journal entry to determine if the student had a positive, neutral, or negative view of service-learning. Students who indicated that they enjoyed the projects, found the project rewarding, or used words including "beneficial," "motivating," and "advantageous" were classified as having a positive view of service-learning. Students who indicated that the service-learning project was not positive, was too stressful, or was too time consuming were classified as negative. Words students used that were negative included "worthless," "frustrating," and "annoying." Journals were labeled neutral when they included words such as "indifferent," "neutral," and "ordinary."

Based on the analysis of the journals, students started the semester with both excitement and trepidation about the service-learning requirements. Of the 30 students, 22 submitted the first journal entry. The most common concern upon hearing that it was a service-learning class was that it would require more time than a traditional course, which would result in scheduling issues, with over half the class addressing scheduling demands in their first reflections. Twelve out of the 22 students (55%) indicated that they were concerned that the service-learning part would take too much time. For example, Daniel commented that he was "worried that these organizations, in their zeal for support of their causes, would ask too much of us on a day-to-day basis" and even questioned "where the line would be drawn to say how much is too much, how I would go about communicating this to the nonprofit organization, and at what point my grade in the class would be affected if I were to draw such a line." He was not alone. Aimee noted, "I am taking a very heavy course load this semester (in fact, the heaviest one I have ever taken), and I am selfishly concerning of how service-learning will work with that." Robin was so concerned about the time it would take that she considered dropping the class: "I even talked to my advisor about dropping the class but I need it to graduate so here I am."

Although the majority of the class expressed concerns about how much time the service-learning component would take, almost half of those who completed the journal also admitted they were looking forward to the work. Ten students (45%) confessed that they were excited about the prospect of working with a nonprofit organization. For some, like John, the first reaction was positive: "My first thoughts were of excitement and anticipation." Aimee agreed; she admitted that she had been hoping to volunteer with a nonprofit for a while but hadn't found the time. Now she was going to be forced to help an organization, something that left her "very excited" because it was a "good use of her extra time." However, not all students agreed. Of the 22, six (27%) did not see the purpose of a service-learning class. Jessica was frustrated that the class was using service-learning and did not understand why any class would require a service-learning approach, noting that "the idea of having a service-learning project when taking a college class is not right." William was not opposed to the general idea of service-learning, but he did not see the purpose of it in a technical writing class: "I am not real sure how that will benefit me or hurt me. I still do not understand why this class is called Technical Communication when I don't see anything technical about helping nonprofits."

Even though there was some trepidation about working with nonprofits, eight of the 22 students (36%) admitted that they would probably take the assignments more seriously because their work would be given to their selected organization. John explained, "Where I might have sent in something that ticks the boxes of the assignment, knowing that they will be read by people making decisions based on what they read will encourage me to reach deeper in to the material and try to connect with the reader in a more sincere way." Nathan also felt that working with a nonprofit would encourage him to spend more time on the assignments, noting that "I don't always worry about editing but will have to if someone other than the teacher will read what I write." Five students (23%) indicated that they were uncertain that they would have the ability to produce documents that meet the quality that would be expected in a professional environment. All five students expressed the same basic concern, which Jessica explained quite simply: "I do not feel like I am in a place yet in my career where I can properly help these organizations."

The first assignment the students did in conjunction with their organization was to write a letter. Each organization had different needs, so the letter assignment was adapted to the needs of the organization. The second assignment was a visual rhetoric assignment that required students to create a visual for their organization. Again, the visual created varied with each organization. After submitting their first and second assignments, the students wrote their second and third reflections, which indicated that they felt motivated by the projects. Of the 24 students who submitted the second and third reflections, 22 (92%) of those students made comments about feeling motivated to do a better job because the work was for a nonprofit organization. Daniel said that the assignment gave him "a greater sense of purpose" and noted that for him the "personal choice aspect of working with the nonprofit organizations will be the biggest motivator as we continue with these projects." AJ agreed, saying that while he did not spend additional time on the assignment compared to what he would have done for other classes, he was more focused because he wanted to represent the organization "in a positive and respectful manner." In addition, he admitted that he seldom proofread his assignments before submitting them, but in this instance he asked a friend to review the draft, which helped him catch some minor errors. Upon completing the assignment, John found it was "much more rewarding and reflective of what a student can expect once they leave the classroom setting." While several students commented that they spent more time than originally planned on the assignment, none of the students provided negative comments about the service-learning component in the second and third reflections.

The third assignment required students to create a blog with corresponding links and illustrations for a fictional company. The students were given a case study that discussed a decision by their company that led to a negative environmental impact for the community. The students were required to write the blog with the general public as their intended audience. The journal prompt for the third assignment asked students to consider how they approached the case study assignment and what feelings they had when working on the assignment.

Of the 22 students who submitted the reflection after the third assignment, 18 (82%) chose to compare the assignment to previous assignments that were designed for their selected organization, and all concluded that the service-learning assignments had benefits that the case study did not. Aimee noted that "when you are using a fictional company, you can only imagine who your target audience is because an actual audience does not exist." Paige questioned the case study approach and commented that she had not anticipated that she would prefer the service-learning projects at the beginning of the semester, but after working with her nonprofit, she found the case study to be "meaningless," "uninspired," and "mundane." Daniel, on the other hand, highlighted the benefits of creating a document for a fictional company, pointing out that there was "less pressure in the small details of the project as I wasn't worried about it affecting any real-world situation." However, he also acknowledged that there was a shift in the purpose: "I felt like my work on this project wasn't worth as much as the previous projects." Four students (18%) preferred working on the case studies. They argued that the assignment was "more like a school assignment should be" and "better for people who aren't sure what they are doing." Another student observed, "The assignment was not stressful but it was not as enjoyable either. It felt like a waste of time after doing the other assignments that were going to a real company."

The final assignment of the course required students to work in groups to produce a proposal, grant, or similar document for their community partner. Like the other assignments, the focus of the assignment varied based on the organizations' needs. Projects included creating complete documentation to run an annual weekend fundraiser, creating a proposal for increasing revenue for the nonprofit organization, and writing and submitting a grant proposal for additional funding. Sixteen students submitted a journal at the end of the course, which asked them to reflect on the service-learning process as a whole, instead of focusing only on the final assignment. All 16 students responded with positive comments about service-learning, and 14 students (88%) stated they would either recommend a service-learning class to others or would opt to take another service-learning class if one became available. Ten students (63%) made specific comments about their work having a purpose. Peter reported, "writing for someone else [other than the instructor] meant that my work did something and helped someone instead of sitting on a desk." In addition, students noticed a change in their attitudes. Jessica saw a shift in her confidence level. She asserted:

> "I did not think I was ready to write for an actual organization when the class started. I thought it would be a failure and I would look like a fool. I wanted to drop the course but I am glad I did not because I feel like I did something that was useful and I know I wouldn't have felt comfortable offering to write letters for a company before this class. Now I know I can do it and will try to help others with the stuff I learned in this class."

Daniel compared the approach he took when working on the service-learning assignments and traditional assignments:

> "I didn't like the idea of service-learning at first. I wanted to just do my work and have it graded. But after talking to Rebecca [the contact person for his community partner] about what she needed, there was a reason to do the work . . . I spent more time on the work to make it perfect because I knew someone was actually going to use it."

Paige agreed and added, "I didn't care that the assignments took more time since they were going to be used by a real company." Overall, the students agreed that they took their service-learning assignments more seriously than the assignment that did not have a service-learning component.

Limitations

The data for this study was collected through reflections, and there is always the potential for bias in reflections. Students have been known to reply to journal prompts in a positive manner to gain favor with the instructor (Anderson, 2010), which can obviously skew the data. In addition, the reflections were required as part of the course grade, which could have impacted what students included in their responses. In an effort to encourage students to provide thoughtful feedback throughout the course, the journal prompts asked open-ended questions about the service-learning experience and prompted students to share their personal thoughts and experiences. To help avoid professor influence, students were given full credit for the reflections as long as they met the minimum requirements for each response. In addition, students were reminded to be honest before each reflection was due. Based on the reflections and the willingness of students to share their concerns from the first journal entry, it appears that students were honest in their responses, but there is always the chance that they may have felt the need to provide positive responses.

Benefits of Service-Learning in a Technical Communication Course

From the students' comments, it is evident that, overall, the students who participated in the study felt the service-learning component of the online technical writing class was beneficial. The study indicates that service-learning in an online technical writing class helps keep students motivated to produce higher quality work. There were several things the students indicated that they did differently with the service-learning assignments, including dedicating more time to the assignments, soliciting peers for editing, and reviewing and revising documents before submission – all steps that instructors of technical writing ask their students to do for all assignments. The reason for the increased motivation was clear: students felt a duty to produce better work when the assignment was being delivered to a person outside of the academy. While none of the students were enthusiastic about writing for a local nonprofit organization, all students who completed reflection journals indicated at least once that they worked harder to produce quality work for the service-learning assignments. As the students progressed through the course and worked with their community partner, they also saw an increase in confidence, which was another direct benefit of incorporating service-learning pedagogy in the online technical writing class.

In addition to increased motivation to produce quality work, the journals also showed a distinct shift in perceptions of service-learning from the start of the class to the end of the semester. Most students started the semester questioning the idea of service-learning for a variety of reasons. Students were skeptical about the time requirements, their ability to complete the work to the standards for an outside organization, and the necessity of service-learning requirements. These findings parallel the limited studies of student perception of service-learning in face-to-face classes (Cooke and Kemeny, 2014). Because of the uncertain feelings students have about service-learning, it is important to clearly explain the expectations and requirements early in the class. Since many students are unaware of what service-learning is, instructors need to introduce the idea of service-learning, explain what service-learning entails, and outline the differences between a class that utilizes service-learning and one that does not. While it often seems self-explanatory, if students are not familiar with the approach, they will not be comfortable with the course. In an online environment, it is especially important to ensure that a clear explanation is given and that students are assured that the assignments will not require more time than assignments in a non-service-learning course. It is the uncertainty that seems to cause the most stress for students. When instructors clearly outline the requirements and provide avenues to discuss, ask questions, and reflect, this uncertainty is reduced.

The idea of extra course demands because of service-learning assignments is not the only thing that causes students stress. Students also need to know how the service-learning assignments are associated with the course objectives. A key part of service-learning is the reciprocal benefits: the assignments must both benefit the organization and meet course objectives. While I would argue that instructors typically work to make sure the assignments help students learn key course concepts, students don't always see the connection. If students do not understand the connection between the work with the community partners and their learning, they will not be as motivated to do the work. Instead they will feel as though they are doing community service with no benefit to their learning. Instructors need to clearly show students how the service-learning work relates to the course. Providing the overall course objectives and then connecting those objectives to specific assignments can seem tedious to some, but the students appreciate having a clear connection between the assignments and the course goals. In addition, it helps students see that the skills they are learning are transferrable to their future careers and other classes.

The study also supports the idea of service-learning as a positive tool for student engagement in an online class. The findings indicate that students felt a purpose and increased motivation when completing the service-learning assignments in an online class, similar to the responses given by students who completed service-learning projects in face-to-face classes (Darby, et al., 2013). That motivation can be seen in the online class discussions. As the service-learning components were brought into the class discussions, the students posted more frequently and provided more in-depth responses to their peers. Beyond the class discussions, students in the online class reported feeling a connection with the assignments and a sense of civic engagement, which led to motivation and increased focus on the coursework. When asked how the case study (the non-service-learning assignment) compared to their previous assignments, students admitted feeling more motivated and/or working harder on the assignments that were for the nonprofit; they also reported that they enjoyed the work more.

An unexpected result of incorporating service-learning in my class was the retention rate. After the initial drop-add period, only two students dropped the course. I also received comments from students, both in the journals and in personal communication, that they had considered withdrawing but felt a duty to their organization and remained in the class. Johnathon ended the semester by observing, "I felt an obligation to the organization." That obligation encouraged the students to remain in the class for the duration of the semester and to complete all assignments. This connection between service-learning and student retention is one that should be explored, especially since along with an increase in service-learning pedagogy, there is a push nationwide to offer more online classes. Sixty-three percent of the institutions that responded to a survey by the Babson Survey Research Group reported that online learning was a critical part of their long-term strategic plan. The same study found that enrollment in online classes increased 3.9% from 2013 to 2014, with 28% of students taking at least one online class while working on their college degree (Allen and Seaman, 2016). Although there are more online classes, including composition courses, being offered and more students are taking those classes, studies show that retention rates are declining for distance learning courses (Dietz-Uhler, et al., 2007; Gaytan, 2013). Researchers have not found one specific reason for this decline, but studies indicate that time management, personal problems, and family/work commitments were more common reasons given by students than complaints about the online format, teaching style, or technical problems (Fetzner, 2013). The results of this study indicate that service eLearning in an online technical writing class may help improve retention rates and course completion. While the study did not focus on retention, the preliminary results seem to indicate a connection.

Conclusion

Incorporating service-learning pedagogy in my online technical communication classes proved successful. Over the course of the semester, the students' perception and attitude about service-learning became more positive. The students were hesitant about the approach at the start of the semester, but as they worked with the community partners and produced work for their organizations, the students became more comfortable with the idea. By the end of the semester, most students indicated that the experience was positive and said they would recommend a service-learning class to their peers. In addition, they cited benefits of working with community partners including increased motivation, civic engagement, and an opportunity to see the connection between their academic work and their future careers.

As the instructor, I also received unexpected benefits as I watched students work for their organizations. The increased motivation led students to work harder and spend time on each step of the writing process, including revising and editing – steps that are often ignored by students. In addition, the class interactions were more active as the service-learning assignments were discussed. Students appreciated having an audience for their work other than the instructor, and they worked harder to make sure their final products met the needs of their organization, resulting in better assignments and overall higher course averages.

Fortunately, the benefits were not limited to the students and instructor. The nonprofit organizations also provided positive feedback about the experience. In email communications, many noted that while they could not use everything the students produced, they found it worthwhile and appreciated the work the students submitted. While the students felt a sense of civic engagement, several spokespersons for the different organizations also said they felt a connection to the community by working with the students. When asked about participating in future classes, each organization that responded to follow-up emails indicated that they would like to be included in future service-learning projects with technical communication students.

Discussion Questions

1) Often organizations feel that students will not be able to produce the level of work that they require. How would you respond to someone who doesn't want to work with students for that reason?
2) What do you feel is the most important element to successfully incorporate service-learning into a college course?
3) What assignments can you design that would work for a technical writing class as well as benefit a nonprofit organization?
4) How would you as an instructor respond to students who feel that service-learning should not be part of the college curriculum and/or that the

assignments are not related to what should be studied in a technical writing course?

5) As a student yourself, what specific recommendations would you make for an instructor to help students who are new to service-learning?

6) How do you anticipate that service-learning in an online class would differ from service-learning in a face-to-face class?

Further Reading

Bourelle, T. (2012). Bridging the gap between the technical communication classroom and the internship: Teaching social consciousness and real-world writing. *Journal of Technical Writing and Communication, 42*(2), 183–197.

Holmes, A. (2016). *Public pedagogy in composition studies.* Urbana, Ill.: National Council of Teachers of English.

Jacoby, B. (2015). *Service-Learning essentials: Questions, answers, and lessons learned.* Hoboken: Jossey-Bass.

Jones, N. (2016). The technical communicator as advocate: Integrating a social justice approach in technical communication. *Journal of Technical Writing and Communication, 46*(3), 342–361.

Nielsen, D. (2016). Facilitating service-learning in the online technical communication classroom. *Journal of Technical Writing and Communication, 46*(2), 236–256.

Soria, K. M., & Weiner, B. (2013). A "virtual fieldtrip": Service learning in distance education technical writing courses. *Journal of Technical Writing and Communication, 43*(2).

References

All website URLs accessed February 2018.

Allen, E., & Seaman, J. (2016). *Online report card: Tracking online education in the United States.* Retrieved from http://files.eric.ed.gov/fulltext/ED572777.pdf

Anderson, C. (2010). Presenting and evaluating qualitative research. *American Journal of Pharmaceutical Education, 74*(8), 1–7.

Bourelle, T. (2014). Adapting service-learning into the online technical communication classroom: A framework and model. *Technical Communication Quarterly, 23*(4), 247–264.

Cooke, C. A., & Kemeny, M. E. (2014). Student perspectives on the impact of service learning on the educational experience. *Schole: A Journal of Leisure Studies & Recreation Education, 29*(1), 102–111.

Darby, A., Longmire-Avital, B., Chenualt, J., & Haglund, M. (2013). Students' motivation in academic service-learning over the course of the semester. *College Student Journal, 47*(1), 185–191.

Deans, T. (2000). *Writing partnerships: Service-learning in composition.* Urbana, IL: National Council of Teachers of English.

Dietz-Uhler, B., Fisher, A., & Han, A. (2007). Designing online courses to promote student retention. *Journal of Educational Technology Systems, 36*(1), 105–112.

Dubinsky, J. M. (2001). *Service-learning and civic engagement: Bridging school and community through professional writing projects.* Paper presented at Teaching Writing in Higher Education: An International Symposium, Coventry, UK.

Dubinsky, J. (2006). The role of reflection in service learning. *Business Communication Quarterly, 69*(3), 306–311.

Fetzner, M. (2013). What do unsuccessful online students want us to know? *Journal of Asynchronous Learning Networks, 17*(1), 13–27.

Gaytan, J. (2013). Factors affecting student retention in online courses: Overcoming this critical problem. *Career & Technical Education Research, 38*(2), 145–155.

Hatcher, J. A., & Bringle, R. G. (1997). Reflection: Bridging the gap between service and learning. *College Teaching,* (4), 153.

Huckin, T. N. (1997). Technical writing and community service. *Journal of Business and Technical Communication, 11*(1), 49–59.

Jacoby, B. (1996). *Service-learning in higher education: Concepts and practices.* San Francisco, CA: Jossey-Bass Publishers.

Matthews, C. & Zimmerman, B. (1999). Integrating service learning and technical communication: Benefits and challenges. *Technical Communication Quarterly, 8*(4), 383.

Nielsen, D. (2016). Facilitating service learning in the online technical communication classroom. *Journal of Technical Writing and Communication, 46*(2), 236–256.

Park, J., & Park, M. (2016). Qualitative versus quantitative research methods: Discovery or justification? *Journal of Marketing Thought, 3*(1), 1–7.

Scott, J. B. (2004). Rearticulating civic engagement through cultural studies and service-learning. *Technical Communication Quarterly, 13*(3), 289–306.

Soria, K. M., & Weiner, B. (2013). A "virtual fieldtrip": Service learning in distance education technical writing courses. *Journal of Technical Writing and Communication, 43*(2), 181–200.

Strait, J., & Sauer, T. (2004). Constructing experiential learning for online courses: The birth of e-service. *Educause Quarterly, 27*(1), 62–65.

Stone, E. (2000). Service learning in the introductory technical writing class: A perfect match? *Journal of Technical Writing and Communication, 30*(4), 385–98.

APPENDIX A

Journal Prompts

Journal #1 Prompt

The class is just starting and you have learned that the course will work as a service-learning class, which means that instead of writing assignments for the instructor, you will be writing for a nonprofit organization. The work you will do will be used by an organization for professional purposes. For your first journal entry, you are to consider what your first thoughts are. What did you think when you heard the class was a service-learning class? What are your expectations? What concerns do you have?

Considering the above questions, write at least 400 words. Remember to be honest; you are not being graded on what you say, but rather that you complete the assignment.

Journal #2 Prompt

You have now completed your first assignment that called for you to work with your organization. You introduced yourself to your contact person and you also wrote a letter. At this point, you should be starting to get an idea of how the service-learning aspect of the class will work. You will do typical class assignments, but they will center around an actual nonprofit.

Think for a minute what you did for this assignment because it was for an outside organization and not a case study. ("Pretend you work for XYZ Company and they need a letter...") Did you approach the assignment a little differently? Did you spend more time on it or less time? Did you edit it more carefully? Do you feel that you were able to produce a quality document for the organization?

Considering the above questions, write at least 300 words. Remember to be honest; you are not being graded on what you say, but rather that you complete the assignment.

Journal #3 Prompt

You completed a big project for your organization. One challenge that you may have faced is that you did not meet anyone from the organization face-to-face. While it seems like it would be rare to have such circumstances, it is really quite common. Technical writers often do not meet the people they work with and are often required to complete work for clients they never meet.

That being said, what are your thoughts? How do you feel the project went? What challenges did you face that you did not expect? What would you do differently in the next project?

Considering the above questions, write at least 400 words. Remember to be honest; you are not being graded on what you say, but rather that you complete the assignment.

Journal #4 Prompt

The last assignment you completed was not for your organization. Instead, you worked on a case study that was based on a fictional company and a fictional situation. The assignment was directly related to technical writing but not directly related to an actual organization. Think about how you approached this assignment compared to the last assignments that were going to be sent to your organization for possible use with their clients. What did you do differently? How did you feel about the assignment? How much time did you allocate for this assignment compared to previous assignments?

Considering the above questions, write at least 400 words. Remember to be honest; you are not being graded on what you say, but rather that you complete the assignment.

Journal #5 Prompt

You have completed three assignments for your organization; the first two have already been forwarded to the contact person and the last one will be shortly. For your final journal entry, you are asked to reflect on the service-learning process. How did it affect your approach to the class? Did it change your learning at all? Would you recommend it for other students?

Considering the above questions, write at least 500 words. Remember to be honest; you are not being graded on what you say, but rather that you complete the assignment.

12

TEACHING PROPOSAL WRITING

Advocacy and Autonomy in the Technical Communication Classroom

Diane Martinez

Introduction

Proposal writing is a common core curriculum element of many technical and professional communication (TPC) programs. The genre is used extensively in almost every discipline, including engineering, science, and business, as well as in government work and the non-profit sector. The skills-based approach to teaching proposal writing separates context and language thus limiting students' understanding of TPC to only technique (Miller, 1991); however,

> when professional communications are studied and taught as a social practice, then the literacy we teach will become not just the ability to read and write professional documents but the ability to question and act on shared problems through language.
>
> (Miller, 1991, p. 69)

One way for students to "question and act on shared problems through language" is to teach them about advocacy and to effectively advocate through the proposal writing process.

Jones (2016) proposed that "technical communicators must be aware of the ways that the texts and technologies that they create and critique reinforce certain ideologies and question how communication shaped by certain ideologies affects individuals" (p. 345). Instructors of TPC have the perfect opportunity to demonstrate these concepts in action and move students toward a critical stance themselves by teaching the proposal writing process using projects that are important to the students. When students identify and work toward solving a problem that they currently experience, or in the case of graduate students, see others experience, they are acting as agents of change, and they have the opportunity to engage on a personal level to solve a problem and transform their world in a positive way through TPC. Through the proposal writing process, students participate in an activity that legitimizes the field in their own eyes and empowers them and possibly others in the process, as called for by Jones.

To get students to the point of engagement, however, requires them to think critically not only about their own views of the world but to consider and value the views of others. This is, in part, how Jones (2016) defines social justice. Proposal writing is inherently a process that acknowledges some sort of problem and can lead students to critically analyze ideologies that shape and sometimes govern communities, as well as identify hierarchies of power and populations that are underserved, marginalized, or otherwise oppressed. Thus, when proposal writing is taught as more than a skills-based class and incorporates elements of advocacy and social justice, students learn how to write their "'selves' into the world" (Miller, 1991, p. 69), which reinforces the idea that "texts and technologies have an impact on the human experience" (Jones, 2016, p. 345).

When teaching advocacy and about advocacy, educators must be aware of how much autonomy they give students. "Autonomy" is a broad term that has many definitions and characterizations (Dworkin, 1988; Tomhave, 2015), and college students are in the position of developing autonomy, that is, learning where they stand on issues (Tomhave, 2015). To allow students to develop their own stance on issues, teachers should not indoctrinate students into accepting their own perspective on certain matters. Guidance can be given toward critical thinking about a subject but that guidance should not imply a particular position on the matter; students have to figure out their own position and why they believe as they do. As Tomhave pointed out, "good teaching does not simply involve letting students determine where they stand. It also involves learning what counts as proper reasoning and evidence for the position that [they] develop" (p. 177). The proposal writing process promotes student autonomy and critical thinking; students are guided to "develop the skills necessary to evaluate evidence and argumentation" (p. 177). The whole point of writing a proposal is to change an existing condition; thus, students learn through the proposal writing process to develop as autonomous individuals and advocate for a particular position.

In this chapter, I discuss the types of advocacy that teachers may bring to the classroom (Bomstad, 1995; Tomhave, 2015) and the degree to which these types of advocacy may support or be problematic to student autonomy (Dworkin, 1988; Kupperman, 1996; Tomhave, 2015) when teaching the proposal writing process. Afterwards, the chapter is divided into two sections. In the first part, I cover how proposal writing assignments can be used to help undergraduate students advocate through inquiry, critical thinking, problem solving, and professional communication. In the second part, I discuss how a graduate-level proposal writing course that includes theoretical foundations in social justice and cultural studies in TPC can be used to teach students about advocacy for others by analyzing requests for proposals (RFPs), understanding the rhetorical nature of proposals, and learning about the complexity of the proposal writer's role. In the conclusion, I discuss how students find their own voices and comfort levels in terms of being an advocate, as well as address ongoing concerns regarding autonomy.

Advocacy and Autonomy in the Classroom

Bomstad (1995) identified three ways teachers may introduce advocacy in the classroom: 1) disclosure; 2) advocacy through inquiry; and 3) partisan advocacy. Through disclosure, teachers simply reveal their position on an issue. Advocating through inquiry has broad meaning but generally refers to using argument as a "tool of our investigation, a means for examining a position" (p. 200). Partisan advocacy, the most intrusive and possibly punitive type of advocacy in the classroom when it comes from an instructor, is where teachers present their position on an issue with intent to persuade or convince students that it is the right position rather than allow them to discover or learn about an issue on their own.

Each type of advocacy has implications in regard to student autonomy. Autonomy in a general pedagogical sense means letting students figure out where they stand on particular issues. But determining where they stand on an issue involves more than opinion; students in higher education have an obligation to evaluate various possibilities before settling on one perspective (Tomhave, 2015).

If one goal of higher education is to graduate students who can think for themselves and base decisions on sound evidence, knowledge, and shared understanding, then the most helpful type of advocacy that teachers can bring to the classroom would be advocating through inquiry. When taught this form of advocacy, students inquire to learn about various perspectives of a problem or issue, and through their own developing reasoning abilities, use the information to make up their own minds. In the end, they will become partisan advocates when they write their proposal because not only will they want to convince their audience to agree with them, but they will also be informed partisans by that time, which is one of the end goals of the proposal writing assignments described in this chapter.

Undergraduate Proposal Writing and Advocacy

Costa (2016) stated that grant writing can be used to teach "basic professional communication skills that are seldom included in the general curriculum, despite their importance in the workplace . . . this includes the ability to write for business purposes, rather than composition" (para. 3). It is true that proposal writing can be used to teach many aspects of professional communication; however, it is advisable to analyze how proposal writing is taught. In a traditional sense, TPC is often seen as practical writing where technical documents use practical discourse as a means to get things done (Miller, 1989). This instrumental view of technical writing "assumes that knowledge is an object—a portable commodity generally called information—and defines writing as a technique of information processing" (Miller, 1991, p. 58–59). By teaching advocacy in the proposal writing process, students learn of the "social implications of writing and the social responsibilities of writers" (Miller, 1991, p. 59) because they will act as agents of change and not as mere "technicians of the word" (Miller, 1991, p. 58).

In my undergraduate technical writing courses, a full-length unsolicited proposal that addresses an issue on campus or in another community that a student encounters (workplace, for instance) is a semester-long project that is achieved through the completion of smaller assignments. The course is based on the foundation that the best way for students to learn about the nuances, power, and social implications of technical communication is to work on a problem that is addressed through the exchange of various technical documents with the culmination of the project being a full proposal. The learning outcomes of the proposal writing assignments are to have students work directly with stakeholders to shape effective technical discourse, conduct primary and secondary research, and produce effective technical documents. Skills that students are expected to develop during the proposal writing process include effective writing practices for various audiences, critical thinking, and problem solving. Students are guided to achieve these goals and skills through a series of assignments that lead up to the full proposal (see Table 12.1). Ideally, along with meeting the learning objectives and developing these skills, students will see the fruition of their work if their proposal is accepted and implemented by their primary readers, thus

TABLE 12.1 Series of assignments

Assignment	Audience
Brainstorming	Class
Memo proposal	Teacher
Email to primary reader asking for an interview	Primary reader or decision maker
Research Primary research: interview Secondary research	Primary reader with considerations for secondary readers (the teacher, for instance, in regard to assignment requirements)
Progress report	Teacher
Writing the problem statement	Primary reader with considerations for secondary and tertiary readers
Writing the solution statement	Primary reader with considerations for secondary and tertiary readers

giving them satisfaction for their work and a sense of what it means to be an advocate.

Identifying problems that students can feasibly address during the semester project is an initial act of autonomy and advocacy in the proposal writing process. Students, either individually or in small groups, work on a unique problem or issue they identify as needing to be fixed. It is important to make the distinction here that what I am writing about in this chapter is not service learning for no other reason than I am not taking that approach to my pedagogy; therefore, when speaking of "the community," I am not referring to a ubiquitous entity that is in need of civic hospitality (Ornatowski & Bekins, 2004); I am referring to any environment in which students find themselves and want to institute change for a particular issue.

For students to see the proposal writing process as a legitimate means for instituting real change and not as just a class exercise to learn how to write in a particular format, they have to be invested in the topic they choose to write about, which means they have to choose something they actually care about. A good way to facilitate this investment is to share successful proposals from previous classes (or ask other instructors for examples if this is the first time running the class in this manner) prior to initiating a class brainstorming activity. After seeing what other students have accomplished through this same assignment, students brainstorm ideas for problems that exist on campus or in their workplaces, living, or recreational spaces, which give them the opportunity to voice their positions on issues that concern them. Common topics include: the quality and variety of cafeteria or vending machine food; prices of food, books, or parking; the absence of childcare facilities for students with children; and ways the university can be more environmentally friendly or conserve energy. In terms of autonomy, teachers collect ideas from the class and act as guides where, based on their experience and institutional knowledge, they let students know what projects are too complex to address in one semester or are already in process at the institution (e.g., proposing a new freeway, new building, or parking garage), but they remain neutral, meaning they do not voice or show their opinion or position on any topic.

An illuminating result of this class brainstorming activity is that students start to notice how much their position on certain issues is based on personal experience only or single anecdotal evidence from friends because sometimes other students will voice contrary experiences and/or opinions. For example, some students bring up parking issues only to find out that there are parking lots available to them that they did not know about, or when broaching the issue of textbook prices, students share their "secrets" for how to find the best prices of books online or through other avenues besides the campus bookstore. In terms of autonomy and advocacy, voicing diverse opinion and experience is a valuable classroom exercise as long as one perspective is not valued over another, either by the teacher agreeing or disagreeing with anyone or letting a group of students override the voices of other students. In fact, this open classroom brainstorming sometimes helps students think through possible solutions, and it prepares them for what they may encounter during the research phase of this project.

Tomhave (2015) argued that "it is not enough to have true beliefs. Our obligation as educators entails also giving students the skills necessary to justify those true beliefs, turning them into knowledge" (p. 177). The research phase of the proposal writing process helps students sort through what they know or what they hold as a belief and discover other perspectives on an issue. The following steps in the proposal writing process help students reach that level of reflection and critical thinking.

After brainstorming, students write a memo proposal to the instructor to identify the problem they choose to work on and explain the change they would like to see and reasons why the change is needed. This memo formalizes their initial perspectives and beliefs on an issue or how they see things as they currently exist and their initial ideas about how to solve the problem. They also identify the decision-maker for their project, as much of the correspondence about their project will be with this person and not the instructor. The purpose of this assignment is for students to clearly articulate the problem they will address for the proposal assignment and document what they already know or think they know about a topic, which helps them identify a research focus. As part of their research, it is critical that primary research in the form of interviews be part of the proposal writing process. Talking in person with stakeholders responsible for a budget and for meeting the needs of an incredibly diverse population (e.g., cafeteria administrator) is an eye-opening experience that can illustrate the complexity of an issue for students because it shows them that while the change they wish to see may be warranted, a solution may have more dimensions than they initially realize.

As teachers help students prepare for their interviews and other research, they must be aware of the level of autonomy they give students and help them find a comfortable and equitable stance for advocacy as they learn to advocate through inquiry. Advocacy for the purpose of inquiry means to use argument as a means for proposing,

> an answer to the unsettled question, looking for supporting reasons for that answer, and checking the reasons themselves for relevance, presuppositions and strength of support. It also involves looking for considerations or other arguments that would refute the point of view and argument under examination.
>
> (Bomstad, 1995, p. 200)

For many students, the interview may be the first time they speak with someone in a decision-making position to learn about an issue of importance to them, and the experience can be intimidating for some students while others may see it as a means to confront administration and tell them what they need to do. The purpose of the interview, however, is to help students use inquiry to learn more about an issue and to "draw on the shared knowledge of the community to make sense of an experience" (Miller, 1991, p. 61) so that they can advocate for a particular solution in the final proposal; thus, the interview exposes students to the perspectives, concerns, values, and responsibilities of others—the knowledge they need to assess a situation more fully.

Teachers can help students prepare for the interview by using inquiry to develop interview questions and by prompting them to write questions that solicit information rather than confront (see Appendix A for assignment). For example, students who would like to see more diverse dishes served in the cafeteria may initially frame confrontational questions like "Why don't you offer . . . ?" Teachers, however, can guide students to conduct secondary research about other universities' cafeteria offerings and conduct surveys in several classes to find out what dishes other students might like to see in the cafeteria. They can also be guided to look up the ingredients needed to make the most popular dishes reported on the survey. Now students can develop questions with wider context other than their own personal experiences or preferences and inquire rather than confront, such as asking questions like "A large number of students have asked to have X on the menu regularly, but it has never been served. What would it take to serve dishes like X on a regular basis?" The reason students were prompted to look up ingredients is because they are often focused on the end product—the meal—whereas food service managers are concerned with behind-the-scenes issues, such as ingredients that are readily available from commercial vendors, price, shelf life, and the culinary ability to authentically prepare meals, which are some of the issues that may arise during the interview. Consequently, students who use inquiry and multiple perspectives to guide their research, both primary and secondary, are still advocating for changes they want, but they do so through informed rather than blind advocacy, which in turn helps them develop feasible solutions.

After students conduct their interviews and the bulk of their other research, they will benefit from writing a progress report. Progress reports require students to parse the proposal writing process into manageable steps that clearly show what they have accomplished and outline the remaining workload. They also develop a plan to complete the outstanding work on time.

Thio (2005/2006) stated that "a key challenge in tertiary education is to ensure that students appreciate and grasp the core principles and concepts of a discipline. However, higher education must transcend the mere acquisition of knowledge and extend toward developing critical thinking and application skills" (p. 108). As stated earlier, one goal of the proposal writing assignment is to have students write effective proposals. To achieve this goal, students must now think critically about their research and apply the knowledge they have gained to develop an informative and persuasive problem statement and feasible solution that will be accepted by their primary reader(s).

The problem or need statement provides the basis for the proposal and justifies the need to find a solution for a particular issue. Writing a problem statement requires students to analyze information from the interview and synthesize material from secondary sources; thus, they are using shared knowledge to critically examine the issue or problem from various perspectives. They also incorporate their own ideas. It should be reiterated to students that they are writing a proposal for a change *they* want to make, and while they are using primary and secondary research in their proposal, they are using it to support *their own ideas* about why this problem is important and needs to be fixed. They compose this section of the proposal in a persuasive voice intended to convince the primary reader(s) that the problem is indeed a problem and one worth solving. Even though students sometimes see persuasive writing as a means of placating their primary reader(s), writing the problem statement is actually a form of advocacy because they are taking a stance on an issue; an informed stance formed from the evidence collected in the research phase. In fact, the problem statement should show progress from the memo proposal where they first identified the issue they are working on. That progress should be in the form of how they now view and articulate the problem; it should have more dimensions and perspectives built in, which come from their interview(s) and secondary research. A widened perspective on an issue means students are "analyzing how shared assumptions are put into practice within organizations and disciplines and how these communities themselves function in the larger public context" (Miller, 1991, p. 69). And through their understanding of the way things are currently functioning within a community, students further their critical thinking and application skills to solve the problem.

The solution in a proposal is presented in several sections: the solution or project description, implementation plan, and budget. When writing these sections, students learn about feasibility. A feasible solution solves a problem and can be implemented ideologically, practically, and fiscally. Feasibility is often a new concept to students because their initial view of possible solutions usually takes only their personal experiences into account; that individualistic viewpoint, however, should evolve into solutions that now consider multiple perspectives because they place their experiences into a larger context based on what they learn from their research. This evolution is an important step because students who take the confrontational route in the proposal writing process (despite guidance from the instructor) often view feasibility as a way of "giving in" because they have to consider others' responsibilities, perspectives, and, well, people who may not entirely agree with them. Conversely, those students who do consider other perspectives in the proposal writing process learn fundamental lessons about autonomy and advocacy: the importance of not merely acquiring knowledge but critically examining and applying knowledge they have gained (Thio, 2005/2006) and how texts can reinforce hegemonic practices, even their own (Jones, 2016). Students who use inquiry as a means toward advocacy usually adjust their thinking on a subject and modify their initial solution into something that is equitable for a wider community of people and not centered solely on themselves. Modification is not viewed as defeat—quite the contrary. Students who advocate for change by applying knowledge gained from the proposal writing process see themselves as developing autonomy and agency because they now place their knowledge and experience in a larger context, and they are acting as informed partisan advocates by participating in personal and collective social change (Jones, 2016).

Graduate Proposal Writing and Advocacy

In my undergraduate proposal writing course, students write unsolicited proposals for problems they identify in one of their immediate environments. In the graduate course, students work on proposals that serve populations in a larger context where they respond to an RFP or private organization's funding opportunity that addresses concerns for populations on a university, city, county, state, or national scale. One goal of a graduate proposal writing course is to teach theory alongside practical writing skills. As Smith (2010) stated:

> Theoretical work is essential to keep a movement on the path toward its goals, while adapting to changing circumstances. Not paying attention to the deep structure of society and to long-term principles, by contrast, almost always leads people and organizations to conform to the system, even if they start out in militant opposition.
>
> (p. 622)

To achieve this goal, I incorporate readings on social justice, civic responsibility, and cultural studies in TPC (e.g., Agboka, 2013; Barclay, 2010; Charmaz, 2005; Cleary & Flammia, 2012; Jones, 2016; Jones, et al., 2016; Miller, 1979; Miller, 1989; Rose, 2016; Thralls and Blyler, 2002; Walton, 2016) in order to help students:

- understand the political and humanistic aspects of technical communication;
- appreciate that technical communicators are in a position to advocate for oppressed groups (Jones, 2016);
- critically examine their own role in the proposal writing process; and
- recognize the rhetorical nature of RFPs and proposals (see Appendix A for assignment).

A social justice or civic responsibility lens can be used in many TPC courses, but such perspectives are especially relevant in a proposal writing course because proposals are rhetorical documents that are usually perceived as a means for philanthropic activities; however, RFPs and proposals can be vehicles for maintaining existing power structures and keeping marginalized and disenfranchised populations on the margins and without power. In my graduate course, students learn how to read RFPs to understand the practical aspects of how to compose winning proposals, but they also learn to read RFPs through a social justice lens to "analyze relationships between human agency and social structure" (Charmaz, 2005, p. 508). Consequently, when students write their own proposals, they apply theory they learn in the course and take into consideration the underlying social constructions, power hierarchies, and unequal distribution of resources that create oppression. By bringing these matters to students' attention, they are poised so that they do not unknowingly further discriminate or disadvantage anyone in their own writing, and they are able to recognize such discrimination when it is being done by others. This theoretical background also gives students foundational knowledge to become critical participants in future proposal writing endeavors, such as when working for or negotiating with a funding agency. Furthermore, because TPC has roots in industrial contexts where writing in the field is generally associated with "efficiency, expediency, and streamlining processes" (Jones, 2016, p. 344), a social justice perspective demonstrates to students the political, social, and humanistic side of technical communications (Jones, 2016).

Proposals that follow an RFP can be complex, and the format for large-scale projects varies greatly; therefore, in this chapter, I focus only on the research that goes into writing the problem/needs statement and solution section of a proposal. These two sections of a proposal are crucial not only from a funder's perspective, but they are also the two most vulnerable sections for overlooking and writing over the very community of people the proposal is meant to serve.

Because students are asked to operate within a larger context, they often start thinking about who they want to represent when writing the required proposal for the class by identifying a target population that they see as being marginalized, disenfranchised, or discriminated against—a group of people that they want to advocate for, such as refugees, people with disabilities, or minority populations. During these initial conversations, however, the following terms are usually interjected in regards to discrimination and advocacy:

- Race
- Socioeconomic status
- Religion
- Gender
- Sexual orientation
- Disability
- Ageism
- Refugees and migrants
- Children
- Poverty

- Illness
- Certain bodily conditions (pregnancy)
- Educated and uneducated
- Equality
- Social justice
- Oppression

Collecting these terms and asking students to define them or deconstruct their meanings and connotations is an initial lesson in advocacy because in order for students to understand who they want to help and how they can help, they have to break apart these seemingly monolithic, but definitely complex, concepts that are often used when talking about advocacy. It is also a good place to introduce theory. For instance, when speaking about disability, students may identify a certain type of disability and discuss aspects of discrimination associated with that disability; however, even though students can usually see unequal distribution of resources or issues of access, they may not know much about disability theory and distributive justice, for instance (Barclay, 2010), which, if they were informed on those topics, would give them a fuller, more critical, perspective of the problem—and population—that they wish to advocate for. This is not to say fragmentation makes the terms more understandable, but through research and discussions about the definitions and multiple meanings of these words, students are introduced to various perspectives and theories about "norming" or domination and subordination (Tatum, 2010) and privilege (Johnson, 2010); thus, students can explore the terms above by examining how "values, characteristics, [and] features of the dominant group" are used to evaluate others (Kirk & Okazawa-Rey, 2010, p. 12). For example, they can explore cultural values, taught responses, and stereotypical gendered practices for situations like medical clinical trials, the use of the word "minority," and equality for LGBTQ populations (Kirk & Okazawa-Rey, 2010). From these discussions, students should start to understand the foundations of oppression and need for social justice in multiple contexts. And just as important, they may begin to understand the responsibilities and complication of their role as proposal writers.

Reading the RFP is crucial to writing successful proposals. From a skills perspective, students are taught reasons why proposals fail, reasons that are often associated with not adhering to the technical instructions in the RFP and vague or ambiguous writing. For example, in *A Guide for Proposal Writing* by the National Science Foundation (2016), successful proposals are "always readable, well-organized, grammatically correct, and understandable" (n.p.); project summaries are "written clearly and concisely" (n.p.); and narratives are "explicit," specific, and detailed. The *Guide* further notes that "careful writing should allow you to describe, in the limited space available, enough about your project to give the reviewers a clear idea of exactly what you plan to do and why your plan is a good one" (n.p.). Furthermore, final advice before the proposal is submitted includes the suggestion that administrative details, which includes things like page count, are important and should be followed exactly as stated in the program announcement.

The *Guide* also offers advice on writing about a target audience in the problem or needs statement:

> The target audience of the grant should be clearly explained in terms of demographic characteristics, size, and special characteristics or problems/challenges faced by the group. The project design should be developed in a manner which will effectively assist the target group in addressing those special problems or challenges. The disparity between the educational sophistication of the project and the educational naiveté of the audience (e.g., a software package which is primarily being used for research that is proposed to be used in a developmental mathematics class) is usually noted by the reviewers and can be one reason for declination of funding.
>
> One of the goals of the Foundation is to increase the participation in science, mathematics, engineering, and technology of women, underrepresented minorities, and persons with disabilities. If your project is going to provide learning opportunities for women, underrepresented minorities, and persons with disabilities, explain exactly how this is going to be done. The proposal should explicitly identify components that will result in increased participation by and/or success of these groups. There must be a focused plan, explaining in detail how your project will accomplish this.
>
> ("Thinking About the Target Audience," n.p.)

From a theoretical perspective, the solicited description of the target audience can be read as being somewhat superficial in the way a target audience is defined (demographics, size, special characteristics, problems and challenges of the group). Since my course incorporates social justice, students expand their concept of those they wish to serve through their proposal writing activities and use a more humanistic approach to understand and describe target populations by reading about the background, purpose, and focus of cultural studies in TPC (e.g., Longo, 1998; Thralls and Blyler, 2002; Scott, et al., 2006). Equally important, students should explore their role as the proposal writer, which in many ways can be compared to the scholarly researcher as mentioned in Thralls and Blyler (2002). For example, Karsh and Fox (2014) provide multiple ways that need can be documented in a proposal, such as finding "economic and demographic statistics," "census data," current "research, trends, and literature," "anecdotal evidence," and "focus groups" and reviewing needs for past programs, newspaper articles, and data from police precincts, health departments, and schools (p. 140). Alongside readings about *how* to write a problem or needs statement, students are introduced to participatory research in TPC where "the researcher and the participants together define the problem that the research will address, the way knowledge will be gathered, and the uses for that knowledge, of which the participants continue to be the owner" (Thralls and Blyler, 2002, p. 203). When students learn about participatory research, they can be more critical about reading RFPs where oftentimes problems or needs in a community are defined and described by funders and not by people in the community; thus, students can reflect on ways that they can include the community to identify and describe what they need. For instance, when speaking about people with particular disabilities, students may use a single person's anecdotal evidence as the basis for their interest in the topic and for the solution they want to propose. It would be beneficial, though, for students to talk to a variety of other people who live with the disability, and they might even learn a great deal from a shadowing experience, too. Likewise, funders may be the only voice in determining how funds can be spent; therefore, students should explore ways to include people in the community during the proposal process. Inclusion or participation of people from the target audience can be something along the lines of asking people from the community to identify solutions for problems in their communities or serve as members on a board associated with the community project. In other words, the study of cultural studies in TPC, such as participatory research, provides students with foundational knowledge to critically examine who determines what the target population needs, who benefits from the proposed project, and who is actually empowered in the process (Thralls and Blyler, 2002) because sometimes target populations that are meant to be served are kept at a disadvantage (Silva, et al., 2013). It is important that students understand that the proposal genre itself is not an act of advocacy. Advocacy comes about through careful, deliberate, and genuine engagement and the fullest participation with the community that the proposal project is meant to serve.

Theoretical background from cultural studies in TPC can be used to help students scrutinize the wording of RFPs for issues associated with power and empowerment. For instance, the Appalachia Regional Commission (ARC) (www.arc.gov) is a federal agency committed to "innovate, partner, and invest to build community capacity and strengthen economic growth in Appalachia" (ARC, "About ARC," n.d., para. 1). Since 2000, it has had a two-pronged mission for the most "distressed counties" in Appalachia that includes a capacity-building program and a telecommunications and information technology program. Both programs are designed to stimulate economic growth in these regions (ARC, "Distressed Counties Program," n.d.). On its website, ARC has identified goals for these programs and defined ways that its programs are supposed to help these regions. By using cultural studies in TPC as a lens when reading through the website, students may start to question the rhetoric itself:

- Why is economic development a common solution for pulling distressed communities out of their suffering?

- Who defines the "economic goals" that are supposed to help "Appalachian communities reach socioeconomic parity with the nation"? (ARC, "Leadership Development and Capacity-Building," n.d., para. 1)
- Do the people in these regions want economic development? What about natural reclamation or preservation?
- Do local "elected officials, businesspeople, and other local leaders" (ARC, "ARC Members, Partners, and Staff," n.d., para. 3) fairly represent people in these distressed counties? Are those people selected to participate in the project the people who are indeed distressed or suffering?

It is through examination of case studies like this one that students can see the rhetorical nature of RFPs in terms of social hegemony as well as the complex role of the proposal writer; a role that has many angles. However, by exposing students to cultural studies in TPC, instructors may force students to think beyond data and research sources (e.g., government websites and statistics) when they define and describe target populations, problems and challenges, and most certainly solutions.

Voices of Advocacy

Proposal writing can be taught as a genre course; however, in order for students to understand that TPC is rhetorical and has social implications and humanistic characteristics, they have to be taught more than genre and skills. According to Miller (1979), as teachers, we should be offering students more than mere instruction about the skills needed to compose technical documents:

> Our teaching of writing should present mechanical rules and skills against a broader understanding of why and how to adjust or violate the rules, of the social implications of the roles a writer casts for himself or herself and for the reader, and of the ethical repercussions of one's words.
>
> (p. 52)

Proposal writing assignments as described in this chapter help students understand the social implications of their role as an author of technical documents and that they are acting as agents of change, not merely as transcribers of information (Slack, et al., 1993). For undergraduate students, the fact that they have to interview other people and learn about the responsibilities and values of others regarding an issue that they consider important helps them appreciate multiple perspectives and shared knowledge because social problems generally cannot be solved without either one. Furthermore, this assignment gives them first-hand experience with developing a stance on an issue that involves more than only personal opinion or personal experience. For undergraduates, realization about their developing autonomy and their work as advocates often comes toward the end of the process because they are usually focused on the final product. When given the opportunity to reflect on their experience, however, they usually talk about how much work it takes to enact change and that a feasible solution is not as easy to develop or implement as they originally thought when they consider perspectives other than their own. In the graduate course, students are in a constant state of reflection as they learn about social justice and cultural theories and how those concepts can be applied to their proposal from start to finish. Consequently, their sense of advocacy and autonomy is evidenced throughout the semester because they integrate their reflections into their own problem/needs statement and solutions.

One thing that both undergraduates and graduates talk about at the end of the class is "voice." Going into the course, undergraduate students conceptualize voice as them asserting and inserting their original ideas into a document that I am going to teach them to write. Through the interview process, most especially, students most often encounter personable people who actually care about their experiences and do not mind change if the solution is feasible. The concept of feasibility, students learn, is sometimes one where they have to work within existing structures, which are not always negative; however, sometimes it does mean creating a whole new paradigm, which can be a challenge. Either way, a common comment from students is that the class taught them two important things about having a voice: 1) they learned the technicalities of using different professional genres, which they appreciate and feel empowered by; and 2) their voice is stronger and heard when they write in the perspectives of others besides themselves no matter what the solution may be.

When graduate students discuss voice, because of the nature of their course, voice is collective or communal, not personal. They are asked to focus on concepts like participation and community engagement, so they soon realize that one of their roles as a proposal writer is to ensure the voice and agenda of the community is written into the proposal, not the voice and ideas of only one person or entity, such as themselves or a funding agency. Graduate students, like undergraduates, often realize at the end of the term that proposal writing is about people and communities. To return once again to Miller (1979):

> Under this communalist perspective, the teaching of technical or scientific writing becomes more than the inculcation of a set of skills; it becomes a kind of enculturation. We can teach technical or scientific writing, not as a set of techniques for accommodating slippery words to intractable things, but as an understanding of how to belong to a community. To write, to engage in any communication, is to participate in a community; to write well is to understand the conditions of one's own participation—the concepts, values, traditions, and style which permit identification with that community and determine the success or failure of communication.
>
> (p. 52)

As a consequence of learning about advocacy in the proposal writing process, students realize that through inquiry, critical thinking, problem solving, and technical writing they can activate their own agency and advocate for the changes they would like to see in the world.

A constant challenge for instructors when teaching advocacy and about advocacy is the importance of finding a balance of autonomy in the classroom. As educators, it is our responsibility to guide students through the learning process, but we also want to empower them to think *for* themselves—and *about* others. Integrating social justice into the curriculum is one way to help students become informed advocates who see their experiences within a larger context; it also instills a sense of confidence about using technical documents for practical and critical purposes to make their world a better place for themselves as well as others.

Discussion Questions

1) Discuss the term "advocacy." What is the dictionary definition? In what ways have you seen advocacy in action? In what ways have you advocated for yourself or someone else? Has anyone ever advocated for you, either personally or for a group you belonged to? Describe your experiences.

2) Identify technical and professional documents that are used as some form of guidelines for business relationships, such as specific laws, contracts, user agreements, employee handbooks, airline policies and procedures, etc. How is power and authority written into these documents? Discuss how these technical and professional documents affect us, govern our behavior and decisions, and characterize us as citizens, a party in a contractual bond with another, an employee, or a user of a service or product. Discuss how this conversation relates to the proposal writing process. This exercise is beneficial to do at the beginning and end of a proposal writing course.

3) Conduct your own independent research to find definitions for: privilege, empowerment, oppression, social justice, reductionism, essentialism. Once you think you have a clear understanding of the terms, reflect on and describe how you have seen these concepts in action. In your own words, write a definition or modify an existing definition for these terms based on your research and reflections. Share your definitions with the class.

4) Read Thralls, C. and Blyler, N. (2002). Cultural studies: An orientation for research in professional communication. In L.J. Gurak and M.M. Lay (Eds.) *Research in Technical Communication* (p. 185–207). Westport, CT: Praeger. Select an RFP and read through it carefully. Based on the concept of participatory research, analyze where the funder encourages involvement from people in the target population to define problems within a community, develop solutions, and participate in implementing the proposed program. Share your analysis with the class.

5) After conducting an interview with the primary reader for your proposal, summarize the most important points or highlights from the interview. What, if anything, did you learn about the topic of your proposal that you did not already know going into the interview? Describe how that information has changed your thinking about the problem you are working to solve or the solutions you are considering. If you did not learn anything new from the interview, has just the interaction with your primary reader during this interview changed your thinking on the problem or solutions? In what ways, and why?

Further Reading

All website URLs accessed February 2018.

*   Blogs are a great way for college students to learn about the numerous and diverse issues of social justice and about contemporary and historical perspectives on these issues. *Social Justice*, a scholarly journal that has been in publication since 1974, maintains a regular blog at www.socialjusticejournal. org/debates
*   Aaron Barksdale from the *Huffpost*, October 28, 2015, compiled "16 Thought-Provoking Social Justice Blogs on Tumbr." www.huffingtonpost.co.uk/ entry/16-thought-provoking-social-justice-blogs-on-tumblr_us_562f8638 e4b06317990f591d
*   Teachers may find Melinda D. Anderson's article, "Teaching MLK's Life— The Man, Not the Myth" in *The Atlantic*, January 18, 2016, thought-provoking in terms of determining their approach to teaching about social justice and advocacy.
*   Alex de Waal's (Ed.) *Advocacy in conflict: Critical perspectives on transnational activism* (London: Zed Books Ltd, 2015) discusses legitimate advocacy.
*   Jon Greenberg's website, Citizenship and Social Justice (http://citizenshipand socialjustice.com), provides helpful lists of news stories, websites, films, and other resources related to citizenship, social justice, and advocacy.

References

All website URLs accessed February 2018.

Agboka, G.Y. (2013). Participatory localization: A social justice approach to navigating unenfranchised/disenfranchised cultural sites. *Technical Communication Quarterly*, *22*(1), 28–49.

Appalachian Regional Commission. (n.d.). Retrieved from www.arc.gov.

Barclay, L. (2010). Disability, respect and justice. *Journal of Applied Philosophy*, *27*(2), 154–171.

Bomstad, L. (1995). Advocating procedural neutrality. *Teaching Philosophy*, *18*(3), 197–210.

Charmaz, K. (2005). Grounded theory in the 21st century: Applications for advancing social justice studies. In N. K. Denzin & Y. S. Lincoln (Eds.), *The SAGE Handbook of Qualitative Research* (pp. 507–536). Thousand Oaks: Sage Publications.

Cleary, Y., & Flammia, M. (2012). Preparing technical communication students to function as user advocates in a self-service society. *Journal of Technical Writing and Communication, 42*(3), 305–322.

Costa, J.T. (2016). Grant writing as a pedagogical tool. *Business Education Innovation Journal, 8*(1), 50–55.

Dworkin, G. (1988). *The theory and practice of autonomy.* New York: Cambridge University Press.

Johnson, A.G. (2010). The social construction of difference. In M. Adams, W.J. Blumenfeld, C. Castañeda, H.W. Hackman, M.L. Peters, & X. Zúñiga (Eds.), *Readings for Diversity and Social Justice*, 2nd Ed. (pp. 15–20). New York: Routledge.

Jones, N.N. (2016). The technical communicator as advocate: Integrating a social justice approach in technical communication. *Journal of Technical Writing and Communication, 46*(3), 342–361.

Jones, N.N., Moore, K.R., & Walton, R. (2016). Disrupting the past to disrupt the future: An antenarrative of technical communication. *Technical Communication Quarterly, 25*(4), 211–229.

Karsh, E., & Fox, A.S. (2014). *The only grant-writing book you'll ever need*, 4th Ed. New York: Basic Books.

Kirk, G., & Okazawa-Rey, M. (2010). Identities and social locations: Who am I? Who are my people? In M. Adams, W.J. Blumenfeld, C. Castañeda, H.W. Hackman, M.L. Peters, & X. Zúñiga (Eds.), *Readings for diversity and social justice*, 2nd Ed. (pp. 8–14). New York: Routledge.

Kupperman, J.T. (1996). Autonomy and the very limited role of advocacy in the classroom. *The Monist, 79*(4), 488–498.

Longo, B. (1998). An approach for applying cultural study theory to technical writing research. *Technical Communication Quarterly, 7*(1), 53–74.

Miller, C.R. (1979). A humanistic rationale for technical writing. *College English, 40*(6), 610–617.

Miller, C.R. (1989). What's practical about technical writing. In B.E. Fearing & W.K. Sparrow (Eds.), *Technical writing: Theory and practice* (pp. 14–24). New York: MLA.

Miller, T.P. (1991). Treating professional writing as social praxis. *Journal of Advanced Composition, 11*(1), 57–72.

National Science Foundation. (2016). *A guide for proposal writing.* Retrieved from www.nsf.gov/pubs/2004/nsf04016/nsf04016_5.htm

Ornatowski, C.M., & Bekins, L.K. (2004). What's civic about technical communication? Technical communication and the rhetoric of "community." *Technical Communication Quarterly, 13*(3), 251–269.

Rose, E.J. (2016). Design as advocacy: Using a human-centered approach to investigate the needs of vulnerable populations. *Journal of Technical Writing and Communication, 46*(4), 427–445.

Scott, J.B., Longo, B., & Wills, K.V. (2006). Why cultural studies? In J.B. Scott, B. Longo, & K.V. Wills (Eds.), *Critical power tools* (pp. 1–17). Albany: State University of New York Press.

Silva, D.S., Smith, M.J., & Upshur, R.E.G. (2013). Disadvantaging the disadvantaged: When public health policies and practices negatively affect marginalized populations. *Canadian Journal of Public Health, 104*(5), 410–412.

Slack, J.D., Miller, D.J., & Doak, J. (1993). The technical communicator as author: Meaning, power, authority. *Journal of Business and Technical Communication, 7*(1), 12–36.

Smith, C. (2010). Social struggle. In M. Adams, W.J. Blumenfeld, C. Castañeda, H.W. Hackman, M.L. Peters, & X. Zúñiga (Eds.), *Readings for diversity and social justice*, 2nd Ed. (pp. 620–625). New York: Routledge.

Tatum, B.D. (2010). The complexity of identity: "Who am I?" In M. Adams, W.J. Blumenfeld, C. Castañeda, H.W. Hackman, M.L. Peters, & X. Zúñiga (Eds.), *Readings for diversity and social justice*, 2nd Edn. (pp. 5–8). New York: Routledge.

Thio, L. (2005/2006). Facilitating independent inquiry, critical thinking and writing: An integrated teaching methodology applied in human rights education. *International Journal of Learning, 2*(8), 107–114.

Thralls, C., & Blyler, N. (2002). Cultural studies: An orientation for research in professional communication. In L.J. Gurak and M.M. Lay (Eds.), *Research in technical communication* (pp. 185–207). Westport, CT: Praeger.

Tomhave, A. (2015). Advocacy, autonomy, and citizenship in the classroom. *Teaching Ethics, 15*(1), 173–189.

Walton, R. (2016). Supporting human dignity and human rights: A call to adopt the first principle of human-centered design. *Journal of Technical Writing and Communication, 46*(4), 402–426.

APPENDIX A

Sample Assignments

Assignment 1. Undergraduate Interview Question Assignment

Learning outcomes for this assignment:

- Understand the rhetorical nature of language, especially as it pertains to scientific and technical writing.
- Organize documents coherently.

The purpose of this assignment is to prepare you for the personal interview with the primary reader of your final proposal.

Briefly explain the topic of your proposal. In other words, what is the problem you are addressing, who does it affect, and why does it need to be solved now?

Identify the primary reader of your proposal; include the person's title and organization he/she works for. Explain what you know about this person at this time. Based on the research you have conducted so far, would your primary reader be receptive or resistant to changing the current situation or current operations regarding the problem you are working on? What is your rationale for this supposition? How does this information affect the way you will word your interview questions?

Compose seven questions that you think your interviewee will be able to answer for you. Questions might be along the lines of helping you under-stand the problem more thoroughly or understand it from his/her perspective, exploring what this person knows about the subject outside of his/her context or community, and asking what solutions he/she would be willing to consider. The main things for you to think through are as follows:

1) What do you want and need to know about the subject?
2) What information can this person provide you with regarding the subject?
3) What is the best way to get the information you need and would like to get from this person?

Compose both open and closed variations of each question. Sequence the questions in a progressive order.

Assignment 2. Graduate Funder Research and Evaluation Assignment

Learning outcomes for this assignment:

• Identify appropriate funders.
• Understand the technicalities and nuances of RFPs.

The purpose of this assignment is to document your research process of finding funding for your program/research project, research and report on the funder, and analyze the RFP in light of the social justice, advocacy, and cultural studies readings.

Funder Search

In this section, describe your funding search as a way to document where you started, what threads you followed, brilliant moments of enlightenment about where to find funding or how you stumbled upon the perfect funder, and what RFP (and funder) you finally decided on.

Funder Research

In this section, describe the funder. Write this section as an informative piece where you describe and/or explain to co-workers what they need to know about this organization/agency. The research on the funder should not come just from the funder site; research what others say about this organization for as far back as you can find (newspapers or philanthropic journals, for instance).

RFP Analysis

Read Thralls, C. and Blyler, N. (2002). Cultural studies: An orientation for research in professional communication. In L.J. Gurak and M.M. Lay (Eds.) *Research in Technical Communication* (p. 185–207). Westport, CT: Praeger.

By now, you have closely read your RFP several times. For this assignment, re-read the RFP paying careful attention to the rhetoric in the RFP and any other company documents you used to research the funder, such as company mission statement or promotions of other programs they fund or have funded. Based on what you read regarding cultural studies in TPC, most especially participatory research in Thralls and Blyler, how are individuals or groups from the target population represented rhetorically in the RFP? What about the funder, especially in terms of power? Include discussion on linkages (Thralls and Blyler) as you see them in your funder's materials and the RFP. Use citations from both the RFP and the articles to support your conclusions. Also consider your role as the researcher/proposal writer. Discuss your role as a researcher/proposal writer for this project. What is the role of individuals from the target population, if any?

13

OPEN-SOURCE TECHNICAL COMMUNICATION IN THE CLASSROOM

Digital Citizenship, Communities of Play, and Online Collaboration

Robert M. Rowan

Sowing the Seeds: Cultivating Collaboration on the Web

The internet and its complementary technologies are no longer "rapidly becoming" a global repository for the sum of human knowledge. It is accomplished. Now, after two-plus decades of astounding growth, the internet has upended our entire civilization's relationship with information, both as a concept and in the particulars. Perhaps its most special quality is the fact that the internet is designed to be open to contributions from all of us. This presents a wonderful and diverse set of opportunities for technical communicators of all levels and backgrounds to participate, collaborate, and advocate with and for one another. This chapter explores the technical communication classroom as a platform for focusing students' writing and research skills through the lens of *digital citizenship*. Advocacy does not *only* mean directly challenging injustices or the status quo. It also includes the logistical and back-office support (such as technical communication services) that any sustained participatory work or movement requires. Other chapters address direct political and social action; this chapter is about how we can prepare our students to take up such advocacy. We will examine some ways in which technical writers, who are specialists in cultivating and managing information, can apply their skills to the tumultuous global bazaar of collaboration and interests that is the World Wide Web.

Many of our students already engage in the work of technical communication in communities of play. In this chapter, we will walk with our students through *their* world, illuminating the ways in which they already perform (or may wish to perform) intellectual labor for pleasure, satisfaction, and fun. Students are encouraged to choose and contribute to projects, collections, wikis, or other sites that interest them personally, not necessarily professionally or scholastically. The other chapters in this book have addressed many different ways for technical communicators to contribute to the world; this chapter is meant to provide an onramp or preface to more intensive forms of activism by starting where our students are (cognitively and socially) rather than where we want them to be. In other words, we will ask them to make contributions to communities of play in which they are already invested and engaged.

My own approach to technical communication pedagogy includes an extended metaphor of technical communication as teaching—the moves and skills we use in teaching and in technical writing are similar, if not identical, and this metaphor will occasionally shine through in the sections to follow. Both "fun" and the "tech-comm-as-teaching" metaphor are deliberate and tested pedagogical choices aimed at improving the likelihood of skills transfer. I developed the metaphor and related course materials over several years of Introduction to Technical Communication courses in an attempt to solve a multi-part problem: students coming into the class usually knew little if anything about technical communication, even though they had interacted with it all their lives. Based on surveys and questionnaires I gave out throughout the course, students usually had a very narrow idea of the kinds of workplace writing they would be asked to produce, and "writing" was often just a substitute word for dreaded "essays," a school thing that would soon be blessedly left in the past. (See also Bergmann and Zepernick, 2007.) I needed a way to connect something they were familiar with (but didn't universally dislike) to the work I was asking them to do. Additionally, students showed a tendency to think of their technical communication audiences as being duplicates of themselves, with the same baseline knowledge and understanding of the world, which often got in the way of clarity and understanding.

The knowledge work that technical communicators and teachers both perform is very similar. First, we determine what the reader or student needs to know (what we might call learning objectives). We then gather information on our subject and shape that information for the audience by organizing, sorting, summarizing, and otherwise distilling it. We present it to the audience through classroom instruction, writing, multi-modal offerings, or other means, and then assess how and whether the audience took up the information. When we can't assess the audience's understanding directly, we build self-check tools into the materials so that the audience can verify their own understanding. This doesn't just apply to procedural discourse, but to a wide variety of technical communication documents (with some variations, naturally).

Teaching and learning are two activities that our students have observed and performed for many years. They have extensive experience with both, even if they may not always understand our pedagogical purposes. Further, my surveys and discussions with students revealed that they nearly always had strong ideas about what "good" and "bad" teaching looked like. Every one of them had also engaged in their own teaching of others, like all humans do. Those two components (have been taught and have taught) provide a strong and familiar foundation onto which we can scaffold a positive and thoughtful approach to technical communication—one in which the audience is real, not imaginary like an essay, and in which the writers (our students) have now been de-centered slightly. If they're taking the metaphor seriously, then they will typically try to see their writing from the reader's perspective instead of relying solely on their own perspective. This can (and often did, in my classes) help students to see confusing, obscure, incomplete, or in-group references in their writing and to make corrections.

When we ask our students to write workplace documents, they have few experience-based models to draw on, so research into genres such as resumes, reports, memos, and other document types is helpful. When we ask our students to write online, however, they have far more experience—and not all of it is positive. This is another piece of the multi-part problem mentioned earlier. As wonderful as the internet is, its relative anonymity can encourage or allow people to be aggressive, mean, sarcastic, and speak in in-group slang while deliberately excluding outsiders. These aren't desirable traits for our work, so the tech-comm-as-teaching metaphor once again shows its worth. The online contributions we ask our students to make, when put through the filter of teaching, invites them to model their best practices (kind of like asking them to give a presentation in business attire). When they're contributing to one of their own communities of play, we want them to be able to switch roles from "one of the gang" to "professional writer/teacher" (or at least to lean in that direction). Fun is still part of the equation, but we also want our students to stay mindful of their obligations to make positive and productive contributions.

In the next section, I will examine "open-source" as it relates to the internet and to the practice of technical communication as an act of digital community-building. I will then consider the role of play in learning and the role of participatory communication in play. I will also discuss how I implemented one specific open-source project in my own course and the results. The appendices provide a student self-analysis instrument, a set of sample discussion questions, a collaborative project from my own classes, and a list of resources and readings.

The World (Wide Web) Is Our Garden

Open-source technical communication is not yet a formally recognized term, but the practice has been in place since the beginning of the internet. In computer programming, *open-source* refers to software that is designed, written, tested, debugged, and revised collaboratively by members of an online community rather than by a corporation or other institution. This open-source software or its underlying source code is typically made publicly available rather than sold. Well-known examples of open-source software include Linux (operating system), Firefox (web browser), Apache (web server software), and LibreOffice (productivity suite). There are many hundreds more, both common and obscure.

Open-source software needs documentation and instructions too, but that's only one possibility among many. The nature of the internet itself is strongly and inextricably influenced by the open-source concept. Cultural, literary, civic, governmental, scientific, engineering, and educational endeavors of all kinds now have some form of user-editable presence on the web, including wikis, fan sites, blogs, YouTube channels, research projects, hardware design projects, and more. Newer software tools, sometimes called Web 2.0 tools, allow participants to easily add, edit, or extend online documentation and other information resources. Creating a new space within the global commons and inviting others to join is trivially simple. Collaborative projects and sites have flourished, making it easy to contribute to nearly any area of interest. The open-source model of decentralized knowledge creation and distribution is a form of activism: it starts with an individual, grows from a basic respect for knowledge, and blossoms as a desire to work with other people to gather, develop, test, refine, and share information on a particular topic. Online participation is both an act of technical communication *and* an act of digital citizenship, in which we bring our best skills and strengths to bear on a global resource which greatly needs our attention.

Kimball (2016), in "The golden age of technical communication," points to "the historic growth of the *performance* of technical communication . . . the vast, under-recognized landscape of technical communication as enacted by nearly everyone in the world who communicates about or through technology" (p. 2). Technical communicators are far more common than our field's program enrollments and society memberships might indicate. The "golden age" Kimball refers to is contingent upon recognizing technical communication as immense, growing, and massively decoupled from any specific institution:

> "At no time in human history have more people, or a greater proportion of living people, been involved in helping to accommodate each other to technology and to accommodate technology to their own ends. They instruct, they demonstrate, they hack, they modify, they tweak—they engage in brilliant and mundane acts of sabotage and *bricolage*—and almost compulsively, they share with the entire world how to do what they did."
>
> (p. 12)

Technical writing serves to instruct, to inform, to guide action, and to move the reader toward a desired result. Moreover, this kind of work is as natural and human as a parent teaching a child; technical communication as a field cannot claim ownership of it, but we can offer our expertise to help promote best practices as a facet of engaged citizenship. Next, I will look more closely at some of this in-the-wild technical communication.

Are We Having Fun Yet? Or, Working at Play

Our students will almost always have an established identity as a member of a community of play, providing a solid foundation to scaffold onto when discussing engagement and collaboration. An increasingly common and diversely populated pastime is playing video games. *Play* can mean many things, from hobbies, to games, to intellectual pursuits, and more; the specific articles and choices discussed here were selected because of the richness of the scholarly work lately being done and because I have abundant experience with this type of play. Further, user-written and web-hosted supplements for games and hobbies are not just allowed but increasingly necessary and expected.

Hunter (2011) analyzed the writing practices and interactions of players on WoWWiki, a site created for and by players of the online multiplayer game *World of Warcraft*. Contributors engage in all of the activities of writing that a composition teacher might wish for: composing, collaborating, self-organizing, giving and responding to constructive feedback, research on various topics, citing (usually hyperlinking) of sources, editing existing articles, and more. WoWWiki has tens of thousands of articles written by players for players, and it's just one site of many for *Warcraft* and its games, books, and lore.

Other games and players have their own wikis and similar repositories of knowledge. Hunter cites Squire and Steinkuehler's 2005 study of Lineage players: "[player clans] have their own social organizations, mores, folkways, web sites, history, and collective identities" (p. 41). More important:

> "[gameplay] is a thoroughly literate activity involving manipulation of texts, images, and symbols for making meaning and achieving particular ends. If the ends–conducting sieges and defending castles–are not valued literacy activities, then the means surely are: researching equipment, making maps, managing resources, investing currencies, building models, designing strategies, debating facts and theories, and writing. Tons of writing."
>
> (Squire and Steinkuehler (2005); as cited in Hunter 2011, p. 42)

Mason (2013) notes that "modern online gaming is an intensely social activity" (p. 220). The games themselves are often deep and rich with lore and play-work to be done. Much of that work is intentionally presented (by game developers) as requiring collaborative effort.

Printed game manuals, which were once a standard (and sometimes beautifully designed) accompaniment to any new computer game, are now usually minimalist cards or sheets with basic installation information and little more, chopped in the name of profit margins. Mason writes that "the demise of print manuals may arguably make gamer-created manuals more necessary and valuable than ever before, creating, in Miller's (1984) terms, a social situation that calls for a rhetorical response" (p. 220). Video games are not everyone's favorite pastime, of course, but they are part of a much larger sphere of life activity that drives fans and experts alike to create, collaborate, and share their knowledge and experience—without prompting from a boss or writing instructor. (See also Colby and Colby 2008; Hau and Kim 2011; Poor, 2014; Zhong, 2011.)

Citizenship and civic engagement often carry a connotation of weightiness or seriousness that may limit the room we give ourselves to play, or to think of our play as a valid contribution. Burgess, et al. (2006), Roozen (2008), Stedman (2012), and others have argued that "bona fide citizenship is practiced as much through everyday life, leisure, critical consumption and popular entertainment as it is through debate and engagement with capital 'P' politics" (Burgess, et al., 2006, p. 1). Literate activities take place in far more venues than just the classroom or the workplace, and "success" is rarely measured on a single common axis. Roozen worked with a student, Charles, who wrote for his school paper, composed and delivered standup routines in comedy clubs, and performed other successful literate activities concurrently with his sub-par performance in Roozen's Rhetoric 101 course. Stedman examined remix literacy (such as fan fiction) and described an effective remixer as one who "will show proficiency using the technical skills and tools needed for a task, an astute understanding of the expectations and generic considerations of a chosen discourse community, and a well-practiced system for internally and externally evaluating the quality of a given text" (p. 109). In each of these studies, the writer and literate performer deliberately alters their relationship with the institution (such as school or the publisher of a fan-worthy work) and brings intellectual labor to bear on works of their own choosing. They, students, want to participate and so they do; they don't need us to command it of them. (See also Getto, et al., 2011; Kahne, et al., 2013; Lessig, 2008; Ray, 2013; Simmons and Zoetewey, 2012; Wolff, 2013).

Classroom Implementation: The Open World

The class project in Appendix C, "The Open World," is designed to introduce students to the discussion of technical writing as a socially-situated act of digital citizenship (though those specific terms are of course not required), and then to give students the opportunity to perform legitimate (live, published) technical communication within online discourse communities they are already familiar with or interested in. In this section, I will describe how the main exercise (finding and contributing to an online collaborative project) typically ran. My students were juniors and seniors and most of them were computer science majors. The course was taught using a learning contract (sometimes called a grading contract), in which students are assured a baseline grade as long as they turn in all assignments and meet a minimum standard of quality in their work (Danielewicz and Elbow 2009). Students are also asked to perform a self-analysis of their research and writing through a variety of instruments (Boiarsky, 2008; Prior and Shipka,

2003; Yu, 2008). The learning contract minimizes the reliance on a rigid rubric and emphasizes the work being produced as legitimate even if it contains some flaws. The Open World project may work best if assessed in this same spirit.

The first few projects in the course covered typical technical communication topics such as genre analysis, document design and visual rhetoric, and instructions and documentation. The Open World project asks the students to find an online, open-source project that interests them and that they can make a contribution to, using the skills they have practiced in the previous projects. The tech-comm-as-teaching metaphor was introduced at the beginning of the semester, so students were familiar with it and had typically made at least some progress in conceiving of their audiences as more than just me or an imaginary echo of themselves. I have tried to make the project as open and accommodating as reasonably possible, though I exclude comments in discussion forums, posts on social media, and recipes on cooking sites. These genres typically don't offer much room to make a substantial contribution or to show off one's writing chops.

Students' initial responses to the project were mixed but generally positive. Some students were nervous about posting on a live site; some were open to the prospect; some had already made contributions of one kind or another. More than once, after the project was done, students commented that they hadn't thought about making such contributions before but would do so again. Our class discussions included encouragement for the nervous students, some brainstorming sessions about types of sites that might accept contributions as well as how to tap into their own interests for public participation, and reminders and examples of how different websites would present their posting requirements or contributor guidelines. We also revisited and reinforced the idea of teaching as a useful guide for how to approach the job of writing for a community they belonged to. The computer science majors in particular had a tendency to act as gatekeepers in their writing, using jargon and obscurity to maintain an in-group slant (Margolis, et al., 1999; Barker, et al., 2002; Klawe, 2002; Barker and Garvin-Doxas, 2004; Beyer, 2008; Levy, 2010). The tech-comm-as-teaching metaphor was developed in no small part with these students in mind. In my experiences over ten semesters, this pedagogical tool was both helpful and effective in encouraging students to be more mindful and understanding of their audiences' needs and expectations (Rowan, 2015).

The Open World is designed as a project for individual work, in the sense that students each select and produce their own topic and contributions. However, it's a participatory and discussion-driven project as well. Brainstorming exercises, informal workshopping or peer review, and periodic check-ins with students can all be used during class to encourage productive sharing of ideas and resources, and to make sure that no one feels left behind or overwhelmed. Tasks 1 and 2 were usually handled as discussion items or pre-writing work; I've broken them out here for instructors who may want to see a longer paper trail of the students' work and thought process. Tasks 3 and 4 were the core components of the project, and students were asked to choose one or the other. In most classes, about 80% of the students opted for Task 4, making a direct contribution to a live site. Task 3 is not intended to go live (sent to the site's administrators) unless the student really plans to follow through, which is why some students found that option more comfortable. The project lasted for about a month, and at least some time was set aside for in-class work (our class was equipped with computers for each student). This individual project ran concurrently with a group-based project on a similar theme, not addressed here, and if the individual project were offered by itself it could potentially be condensed to two to three weeks if needed.

Not all computer science majors play video games, but a lot of them do. As I had anticipated, many students chose various computer or console games as their topic of interest. In these cases, we usually had very little difficulty finding relevant communities of interest for them to look at. Finding something that they could contribute, however, was a greater variable. Newer games, or games with newly added features or expansions, often had lots of untapped potential. Older games tended to be covered pretty thoroughly by existing community-generated documentation. Students sometimes had to either get creative about their contributions (coming up with a subject or an approach that hadn't been addressed before) or fall back to their second or third topic choice.

Some students chose other areas of interest, such as sports, music, literature, or other activities. Non-game topics included the Chicago Blackhawks, fantasy football, Bruce Lee, various musicians and their music, golf, genealogy, programming languages such as Python, an array of TV shows and films, podcasts, Debian (an open-source operating system), Jeeps, fitness and exercise, and many others. As with video games, many of these topics had already been written about in detail, but there were plenty of sites and articles that needed edits, clarifications, or a modest amount of additional content. To accommodate this, I devised a point system for how students contributed. Edits and cleanup work were worth one point, one or two paragraph entries were worth two points, and full articles (three or more paragraphs) were worth three points. To get credit, students needed to rack up five points' worth of contributions. Students were not restricted to making contributions to only one website (or only one topic, for that matter). Occasionally students found it necessary to contribute to more than one site, and every now and then they would work with more than one topic or community of interest.

Students were required to complete a reflective exercise called the "Genre Understanding Sheet" (the GUS, Appendix A) for Task 3 or Task 4. For the students who made online contributions, I had them make a basic document with a link to each page they'd worked on, how many points each one was worth, and a brief description of their contributions. I suggested, but didn't require, that they take before-and-after screenshots of their edits and include these in the link document, just in case something unexpected happened with their edits.

Grading Task 3: For the proposal, I looked at how well (how clearly and how tactfully) they explained their proposed changes or improvements. I checked their research listed in the GUS to confirm that they had dug deeply enough into the problem to provide a worthwhile solution or content. I also carefully reviewed the proposal's format, grammar, and mechanics since I had emphasized the importance of these elements in class. Mock-ups and samples were helpful in getting a clearer visual perspective on what the student wanted to do, but unless they had glaring errors I graded them gently. We had spent some time on visual design in class, but not enough that I felt I could demand a high level of rigor there. As long as the proposal's design and logic were sound, the samples were understandable, and the GUS documented their labor sufficiently, the task would receive credit.

Grading Task 4: For students who contributed to an article on a wiki-type website, the first thing I did was to check the article's revision history (usually found under a History tab at the top of the page). Once I had confirmed that the edits they described had taken place within the date range for our project, I evaluated the content itself for grammatical and mechanical fitness and conformity with the site's style. I also reviewed their source list in the GUS and did my best to verify the information they had added. If their edits or additions were accurate and largely error-free and their GUS responses were reasonably detailed, they would receive credit.

Parting Thoughts

The World Wide Web is a critical part of the fabric of our lives now; barring some cataclysm, there's no going back. When we or our peers or our students participate civically or culturally online, we engage *as and with* citizens of the world. In the technical and professional writing classroom, we should encourage and empower this engagement by working with our students to improve their chosen forms of communication, not simply for the students' own sake but for the benefit of the communities of interest and play they participate in. We already take this pedagogical approach with students' writing in the workplace and the academy, and have done for many years; now we are ready for the logical next step of creating citizen technical communicators. Just as importantly, it's in our own best interest as teachers to ensure that good technical writing flourishes on the web, no matter the subject. Online communities can provide living examples of writing and are often written for a particular (and real) writing situation rather than for a case study or artificial scenario. By studying the written works of these communities and encouraging our students to make their own contributions, we support our students' interests and elevate the quality of work to the whole community's benefit. This is the practice of digital citizenship at a grassroots level. Moreover, strengthening our engagement with online communities will tend to strengthen our appreciation for the internet as a vital global resource—one which must remain neutral and open to all.

Additional Online Resources

Open-Source Projects and Sites

- Wikia, hosts user-created fandom wikis of all types (www.wikia.com)
- GitHub, hosts software and coding projects and documentation (www.github.com)
- Writing Commons, a free peer-reviewed writing textbook (www.writingcommons.org)
- Challenge.gov, an open-source project of the US federal government to innovate and solve problems for various government agencies (www.challenge.gov)
- Write the Docs, offers conferences and local meet-ups on topics related to software documentation (www.writethedocs.org)
- Instructables, hosts how-to guides, demonstration videos, and other documentation for do-it-yourself projects (www.instructables.com)

Net Neutrality and Internet Policy Organizations

- The Electronic Frontier Foundation (www.eff.org)
- The Center for Democracy and Technology (www.cdt.org)
- The Software Freedom Law Center (www.softwarefreedom.org)
- Creative Commons (www.creativecommons.org)
- Free Software Foundation (www.fsf.org)
- Access Now (www.accessnow.org)
- Public Knowledge (www.publicknowledge.org)
- The Internet Society (www.internetsociety.org)
- Digital Citizenship (www.digitalcitizenship.net)

Discussion Questions

Understanding Digital Communities
What communities do you belong to in addition to work and school? These could be based on an interest, an activity, a hobby, a game, a shared belief system, or any other common element. Are these communities local, regional, national, or global? Have you contributed anything written to those communities? Do you want to? What sort of standards of quality would you expect to be held to in making your contributions?

Technical Communication and Digital Citizenship
What role, if any, should practitioners of technical communication take in promoting or improving digital citizenship? What about teachers of technical communication? How does the technical communicator's role in the workplace,

or the demands of the business world generally, complement or conflict with the idea of open and participatory citizenship on the web or through other media?

Technical Communication and Teaching

Instructor Note: Consider explaining and discussing your own teaching process, from researching and writing the course plan to assessing student work, mapping those activities onto the work of the technical writer as you go.

Think about the last time you successfully taught something to another person. How did you do it? What tools or techniques did you use? Teaching one another is something we all learned to do at a very early age. We do it naturally, which means we might need to stop and think about the working parts. How would these tools or techniques compare to some of the methods used in good technical communication? How can you use those tools or techniques to guide your own technical communication work?

Sharing versus Plagiarizing in a Digital Community

Instructor Note: The GUS (Appendix A) refers to "web text" as a catch-all for copied or borrowed material. This acknowledges the reality of reusing material on or from the web, while reinforcing the idea that writers should be mindful and respectful of their sources.

In academic settings, plagiarism means copying someone's work without giving them credit, or trying to pass someone else's ideas off as your own. On the web and in the workplace, however, the rules for copying other people's work change (along with the reasons for doing the copying). Many online sources offer written material or images of all kinds that are meant to be copied or used differently than copyrighted or scholarly works would be. For example, we can easily find samples of business letters or legal forms online and modify them to suit our needs. This can be considered an acceptable form of copying, depending on how the author or owner of the item has chosen to share it. How can we navigate the differences between acceptable sharing and copyright violations or plagiarism? What tools and resources are available to help us with this?

Further Reading

All website URLs accessed February 2018.

Burgess, J., Foth, M., & Klaebe, H. (2006). Everyday Creativity as Civic Engagement: A Cultural Citizenship View of New Media. In *Proceedings of Communications Policy & Research Forum*, Sydney, Australia.

Kimball, M. (2016). The Golden Age of Technical Communication. *Journal of Technical Writing and Communication.* 47(3), 330–358. http://dx.doi.org/10.1177/0047281616641927

Lessig, L. (2008). *Remix: Making Art and Commerce Thrive in the Hybrid Economy.*

Mason, J. (2013). Video Games as Technical Communication Ecology. *Technical Communication Quarterly*, 22(3), 219–236. http://dx.doi.org/10.1080/10572252.2013.760062

Simmons, W. M., & Zoetewey, M. W. (2012). Productive usability: Fostering civic engagement and creating more useful online spaces for public deliberation. *Technical Communication Quarterly, 21*(3), 251–276. http://dx.doi.org/10.1080/10572252.2012. 673953

References

All website URLs accessed February 2018.

Barker, L., Garvin-Doxas, K., & Jackson, M. (2002). Defensive Climate in the Computer Science Classroom. *SIGCSE 2002*, 43–47. https://doi.org/10.1145/563340.563354

Barker, L., & Garvin-Doxas, K. (2004). Making visible the behaviors that influence learning environment: A qualitative exploration of computer science classrooms. *Computer Science Education, 14*(2), 119–145. http://dx.doi.org/10.1080/089934004123 31363853

Bergmann, L. S., & Zepernick, J. S. (2007). Disciplinarity and transfer: Students' perceptions of learning to write. *WPA: Writing Program Administration, 31*(1–2), 124–149.

Beyer, S. (2008). Gender differences and intra-gender differences amongst management information systems students. *Journal of Information Systems Education, 19*(3), 301–310.

Boiarsky, C. (2008). Teaching engineering students to communicate effectively: A meta-cognitive approach. *International Journal of Engineering Education, 20*(2), 251–260.

Burgess, J., Foth, M., & Klaebe, H. (2006). Everyday creativity as civic engagement: A cultural citizenship view of new media. In *Proceedings of Communications Policy & Research Forum*, Sydney, Australia.

Colby, R. S., & Colby, R. (2008). A pedagogy of play: Integrating computer games into the writing classroom. *Computers and Composition, 25*(3), 300–312. http://dx.doi.org/ 10.1016/j.compcom.2008.04.005

Danielewicz, J., & Elbow, P. (2009). A unilateral grading contract to improve learning and teaching. *College Composition and Communication, 61*(2), 244–268.

Getto, G., Cushman, E., & Ghosh, S. (2011). Community mediation: Writing in communities and enabling connections through new media. *Computers and Composition, 28*(2), 160–174. http://dx.doi.org/10.1016/j.compcom.2011.04.006

Hau, Y. S., & Kim, Y. G. (2011). Why would online gamers share their innovation-conducive knowledge in the online game user community? Integrating individual motivations and social capital perspectives. *Computers in Human Behavior, 27*(2), 956–970. http://dx.doi.org/10.1016/j.chb.2010.11.022

Hunter, R. (2011). Erasing "property lines": A collaborative notion of authorship and textual ownership on a fan wiki. *Computers and Composition, 28*(1), 40–56. http:// dx.doi.org/10.1016/j.compcom.2010.12.004

Kahne, J., Lee, N. J., & Feezell, J. T. (2013). The civic and political significance of online participatory cultures among youth transitioning to adulthood. *Journal of Information Technology & Politics, 10*(1), 1–20. http://dx.doi.org/10.1080/19331681.2012.701109

Kimball, M. (2016). The golden age of technical communication. *Journal of Technical Writing and Communication, 47*(3), 330–358. http://dx.doi.org/10.1177/0047281616641927

Klawe, M. (2002). Girls, boys, and computers. *SIGCSE Bulletin, 34*(2), 16–17. https://doi. org/10.1145/543812.543818

Lessig, L. (2008). *Remix: Making Art and Commerce Thrive in the Hybrid Economy*. New York, NY: The Penguin Press.

Levy, S. (2010). *Hackers: Heroes of the Computer Revolution*. Sebastopol, CA: O'Reilly Media, Inc.

Margolis, J., Fisher, A., & Miller, F. (1999). Caring about connections: gender and computing. *Technology and Society Magazine, IEEE, 18*(4), 13–20. https://doi.org/10.1109/44.808844

Mason, J. (2013). Video Games as Technical Communication Ecology. *Technical Communication Quarterly, 22*(3), 219–236. http://dx.doi.org/10.1080/10572252.2013.760062

Miller, C. (1984). Genre as social action. *Quarterly Journal of Speech, 70*, 151–167.

Poor, N. (2014). Computer game modders' motivations and sense of community: A mixed-methods approach. *New Media & Society, 16*(8), 1249–1267. http://dx.doi.org/10.1177/1461444813504266

Prior, P., & Shipka, J. (2003). Chronotopic Lamination: Tracing the Contours of Literate Activity. *Writing Selves/Writing Societies: Research from Activity Perspectives.* 180–238.

Ray, B. (2013). More than just remixing: Uptake and new media composition. *Computers and Composition, 30*(3), 183–196. http://dx.doi.org/10.1016/j.compcom.2013.07.003

Roozen, K. (2008). Journalism, poetry, stand-up comedy, and academic literacy: Mapping the interplay of curricular and extracurricular literate activities. *Journal of Basic Writing, 27*(1), 5–34. www.jstor.org/stable/43443853

Rowan, R. (2015). Technical communication as teaching: A grounded theory study of cognitive empathy and audience engagement among computer science majors in a technical communication classroom (Doctoral dissertation). Retrieved from http://ir.library.illinoisstate.edu/etd/426

Simmons, W. M., & Zoetewey, M. W. (2012). Productive usability: Fostering civic engagement and creating more useful online spaces for public deliberation. *Technical Communication Quarterly, 21*(3), 251–276. http://dx.doi.org/10.1080/10572252.2012.673953

Stedman, K. D. (2012). Remix literacy and fan compositions. *Computers and Composition, 29*(2), 107–123. http://dx.doi.org/10.1016/j.compcom.2012.02.002

Wolff, W. (2013) Interactivity and the invisible: What counts as writing in the age of Web 2.0. *Computers and Composition, 30*, 211–225. http://dx.doi.org/10.1016/j.compcom.2013.06.001

Yu, H. (2008). Contextualize technical writing assessment to better prepare students for workplace writing: Student-centered assessment instruments. *Journal of Technical Writing and Communication, 38*, 265–284. http://dx.doi.org/10.2190/TW.38.3.e

Zhong, Z. J. (2011). The effects of collective MMORPG (Massively Multiplayer Online Role-Playing Games) play on gamers' online and offline social capital. *Computers in Human Behavior, 27*(6), 2352–2363. http://dx.doi.org/10.1016/j.chb.2011.07.014

APPENDIX A

A Self-Analysis Tool for Students

Genre Understanding Sheet (GUS)

The GUS is a tool to help you actively think about what you're learning while you work on the assignment (not just at the end). Be specific and detailed in your explanations below and describe how you arrived at each answer. In other words, answer the follow-up question "How do you know this?" for each item. Avoid vague, over-used terms such as "professional" or "formal." Save your answers in a separate document with your name and the assignment name.

1. Genre Name or Description. Remember that many genres are hybrids without a formal name.
2. Writing Purpose. What is the communication task you're trying to accomplish with this document? Is this genre suitable for the task you're working on?
3. Audience Needs: Who are your primary audiences? What do your audiences want or need from this document? How will this document get used by your audiences? What kind(s) of persuasion are you using with each audience to encourage them to accept your message or to trust you as a reliable source of information?
4. Content. What is your content (the facts, figures, images, and details)? Is this genre a good fit for the content you're trying to deliver and the audiences you're trying to reach? If you're deliberately breaking a genre's conventions or expectations, explain why and describe the results you wanted to achieve.
5. Research. Describe *and document (list sources for)* the research and other knowledge-work you performed for the assignment. "I Googled it" is not sufficient—be more thorough.

   a. List and describe your genre research below. Copy headings and repeat for each source.

      i. Author(s)
      ii. Title or description
      iii. Useful because
      iv. Reliable source because
      v. Link

   b. List and describe your content research below (including images).

      i. Author(s)
      ii. Title or description
      iii. Useful because
      iv. Reliable source because
      v. Link

   c. List and describe your audience research below.

      i. Author(s)
      ii. Title or description
      iii. Useful because
      iv. Reliable source because
      v. Link

6. Trajectories. When producing this type of document, what tools, prior knowledge, and other genres are usually involved? Where will it go (and how will it travel) once it leaves your hands? How does this info (about trajectory) affect your design of the document?

7. Ethics. What ethical, legal, or cultural considerations did you take into account when working on this assignment? "None" is the wrong answer. Ethical issues are often subtle and easy to overlook (our assumptions can blind us here), but that doesn't make the issues less important.

8. Web Text. If you copied text from another source into your document (web text), explain what the copied text means and why it's a better choice than something you could say yourself.

9. Teaching. What teaching skills or activities did you use while working in this genre? Does thinking about it from a teacher's perspective help you produce better work? Why or why not?

10. Self-Analysis. What made this genre easy or challenging for you to work with? What would you do differently next time? What new discoveries did you make? How could you connect this work to writing or other activities you've done before, in school or elsewhere?

11. Group Contributions. If this was a group assignment, describe the *content* and the *research* provided by each group member.

APPENDIX B

The Open World

Task 1: Finding Sites of Interest

Outcomes: You will be able to distinguish between websites that are open to public collaboration and those that are not; for collaborative sites, you should be able to identify the site's rules, scope, and contact information.

<u>The Work</u>
Choose one of your communities of interest, where your interest could be a game, a hobby, a sport, or some other topic or activity you enjoy. Select three or more websites for that interest. At least one of those sites should be one that allows members to contribute their time and expertise online in some way. Analyze these sites to better understand how they work and what they expect of their contributors.

Write an evaluation of three websites that are relevant to your selected community of interest and address the following questions:

- Who runs the site? This could be individual people or an organization. How do you contact them?
- What is the site's general area of interest?
- What is the site's specific area of interest? Does the site exclude certain topics or types of content?
- Is the site a reliable source of information? Describe in detail how you determined this.
- If the site accepts content contributions from the community at large, does it have a set of rules or guidelines for those contributions? What are they? Could you abide by them?

Grading

I want to see evidence of critical and objective thinking (presenting research and observations). You should also produce a tidy and internally consistent document in an appropriate format.

Task 2: Evaluating Sites and Their Purposes

Outcome: You will be able to read a website critically and determine whether the site is a suitable, reliable place for collaboration to occur.

The Work

Using your list from Task 1, evaluate each website to decide if it would be a good candidate for your time and energy in making a contribution. Address the following items (and any others you feel are relevant):

- How long has the site been around?
- Has it seen much recent activity?
- Does the main page have any obvious errors or performance problems?
- Does the site have a style guide of any kind? It might be titled "How to Contribute," or "Rules for Posters," or "Formatting Guide," or something else—or it might not exist yet.
- If the site belongs to or is primarily sponsored by an organization, is that organization one that you know anything about?
- Is it an organization that actually does what it purports to do? Some sites and organizations, just like some people, are not what they appear to be. Sometimes these sites are satirical, but sometimes they're intentionally pushing disinformation on some specific topic (e.g. climate change is a hoax, tobacco is good for you, vaccines cause autism, and so forth). Typically, such sites are not open to user contributions.
- Do you recognize any of the people on the "About Us" (or similar) page?
- For the above questions, do any of your answers cause you to change your mind about potentially contributing to the site? If so, why?

Grading

I want to see evidence of critical and objective thinking (presenting research and evaluations). You should also produce a tidy and internally consistent document in an appropriate format.

Task 3: Proposing Improvements to a Collaborative Site

Outcomes: You will be able to identify areas for improvement or contribution on a collaborative site, and write a clear, concise proposal that explains your potential writing contribution. You will be able to distinguish between a writing contribution and a programming or technological contribution. This is of special importance if your first instinct is to offer programming help.

<u>The Work</u>
Select a collaborative website or project that's part of your community of interest. Put together a one to two-page proposal for a writing contribution (not a programming or technological contribution) you'd like to make to that site or project. Include a sample or mock-up if you think it will help. The proposal does not actually need to be sent to the site's administrator to receive credit. Only send it if you plan to perform the work described in your proposal.

Audience(s): The site or project's administrator or manager. Find out who that is.

Genre(s): Business letter or email. Research how these should be laid out. Samples of the proposed work. Research your options for preparing and presenting suitable samples as well.

Content: Describe the contribution you're offering, explain how it would benefit the site's users, and provide some details about your method for producing it (such as what research you'll do, which topics you'll cover, how you'll organize the material, and how long it would take you to complete your work). Be positive throughout—do not offer criticism about why the site is terrible and needs improvement, even if that's true. If you include sample material, explain it in the proposal. Don't expect the reader to figure it out on their own.

<u>Grading</u>
I want your proposal and sample materials to include accurate content, effective persuasion, an appropriate degree of formality, and good grammar and mechanics. You should also produce a tidy and internally consistent document in the genres described above.

Task 4: Making a Contribution to a Digital Community

Outcomes: You will be able to select a suitable site for collaboration, find and understand the site's rules or requirements, conceive and design one or more contributions for that site which adhere to the site's rules and expectations of quality, and post your contribution to the site.

<u>The Work</u>
Select a collaborative site from your list in Task 1 (or a different site if you wish). Study the site carefully, looking for contributions you could make. Some sites, especially wiki-based sites, may flag topics or articles needing additional work. Your contribution could be a new article or additions and improvements to

existing articles or documentation. Collaboration on the web often means editing or adding to someone else's work. It also means that someone else can add to or edit (or damage or erase) your work later on.

Warning: Some sites may hold contributions for review, and it's possible that your contribution may be deleted, modified, or rejected. That's the nature of collaboration. Allow at least a few days of lead time before the work is due, just in case you run into problems. In addition to providing a link to the page(s) you've worked on, you can also take before-and-after screenshots of the edits you've made as a way of documenting the work you've done.

Audience(s): The site's regular readership, including people with different skill or knowledge levels than your own. Remember that the audience is not "people exactly like me."

Genre(s): Research this site and determine how you should design your contribution to fit seamlessly among the site's other content. If the site has a style guide, read it and follow it.

Content: The information you want to contribute, backed up by research and written or composed with the needs of the genre and the audience in mind. Cite your sources (including audio, video, and image files) in the same way that the rest of the site does.

Example 1: World of Monsters just released an expansion that includes several new dungeons. Your favorite fan site, WoMHead, doesn't have a walk-through for Creepy Keep yet, and you're planning to go through the dungeon with your guild mates over the weekend. Take notes (or record your visit with video capture software), look for corroborating or supplemental information on other sites, and write a walk-through or other guide for this dungeon. Review WoMHead's rules for writing and formatting, and be sure to follow them. Remember that your audience may include less experienced players, so don't leave them out by using too much jargon, slang, or other insider language.

Example 2: You downloaded a small utility program called Zoop from a collaborative programming and software design site called HubGit. You like Zoop and use it a lot, but you noticed that it didn't come with any documentation. Write a user guide for the program and upload it to HubGit. You can (and probably should) contact Zoop's authors and let them know what you're planning. Find out if they have any user documents you can improve on. They may also be working on a new version of Zoop, in which case you could write a user guide for that instead. Be sure to address the needs of both novice and advanced users of Zoop. Upload your user guide to the appropriate location on HubGit.

Example 3: Your home town doesn't have an entry on AllCitiesWiki, despite its prominence as home to the world's third largest corn cob. Research the posting rules for AllCitiesWiki and the details on your town (do not just go by memory). Create an entry worthy of its subject. When writing about specific geographic locations, keep in mind that people from elsewhere may not be familiar with local terms, customs, or landmarks. Write your entry in a way that would be interesting and useful to locals and to people from other regions or countries.

Grading

I want you to produce accurate, well-researched, and relevant content. Your additions or edits should meet the target site's guidelines for contributions. If formal guidelines are not present on the site, you should do your best to match the style of other major articles or works on the site. Grammar and mechanics should be as close to flawless as you can possibly get.

Notes for Instructors

Depending on time and student experience level, you may want to expand the definition of "contribution" to include infographics, podcasts, videos, or other multi-modal works.

Contribution length is a variable for Task 4, so a point system may be useful: 1 point for minor cleanup work, 2 points for adding a paragraph or two, and 3 points for a full-length (3+ paragraph) article. Assign a total of X points as time allows. Drafting and revision is recommended, especially for longer contributions. Wikis are a common destination for this exercise, and most wiki articles have a History page. Use this to cross-check what was updated and when.

14

SOCIAL MEDIA AND ADVOCACY IN THE TECHNICAL AND PROFESSIONAL COMMUNICATION CLASSROOM

A Social Justice Pedagogical Approach

Sarah Warren-Riley

Introduction

Scholars have long argued that technologies are never neutral (Selfe & Selfe, 1994; Slack & Wise, 2015; Scott, 2003). In addition, scholars engaging in technical and professional communication (TPC) and public rhetorics scholarship have argued for the importance of paying close attention to the role of mundane (everyday, seemingly inconsequential) texts in the shaping of overall societal practices (Grabill, 2014; Rivers & Webber, 2011). As technologically mediated communication continues to increase and permeate everyday life, it is important to recognize how these two arguments become easily intertwined. On the one hand, online and social media texts have certainly become the mundane texts that we engage with daily and, as they are both crafted through and shaped by technologies, they are of course, never neutral. On the other hand, as mundane texts, these communication practices often become naturalized (nearly invisible) and, therefore, remain largely uninterrogated (not unlike the technologies used to create them). Additionally, I would argue that it is crucial to recognize that through our interactions with these mundane texts, which advocate in their own ways, we often advocate positions whether we intend to or not. For example, the uncritical liking and sharing of posts that are enacted in social media spaces often advocate in ways that we often do not fully intend or realize.

Building upon previous research on social media (Dadurka & Pigg, 2011; Vie, 2014; Verzosa Hurley & Kimme Hea, 2014), in this chapter I will outline a pedagogical approach that engages the concept of advocacy as a lens through which to teach technical communication students to interact with and create texts in a more thoughtful, critical, and socially just way. I argue that, as teachers of technical communication, it is essential to help students to recognize both the power of mundane texts and the way that these texts often advocate positions for various stakeholders. Further, I argue that teaching students to recognize and interrogate their own advocacy practices in social media spaces, whether intentionally or unintentionally, and to analyze texts for the advocacy embedded within them will prepare students to better understand the possibilities for enacting civic engagement, civic responsibility, and advocacy interventions in their future careers. As future technical communicators, these students may be charged with designing documents that will be deeply embedded with intentional or unintentional advocacy, and as such, they must become aware of how their design choices advocate for certain stakeholders over others as well as how these choices provide affordances and limitations for various audiences. I argue that (1) considering the ways *all* texts are embedded with advocacy, (2) encouraging students to recognize their own advocacy practices, and (3) teaching students to carefully construct texts as a result will prepare them to be more social justice minded advocates in the future.

In what follows I first explain the personal impetus for the exigency of this approach before engaging with the scholarly commitments and traditions it arises from. I then provide an overview of the ways that I implemented this approach in an introductory TPC classroom, providing an explanation of course goals and examples of activities and assignments utilized. Finally, I reflect on the results of this effort, highlighting the potential positives of adapting such an approach. By sharing this, I hope to provide a means for other teachers of TPC to consider additional ways to implement approaches to engaging with social media as a route to enacting a pedagogy of social justice in the classroom.

The Exigency for Advocacy

I am interested in developing what I see as a missing connection between considerations of accessibility, ethics, social responsibility, civic engagement, and ultimately, social justice in TPC. I see this missing connection as something that can be addressed through considering the role of advocacy in technical and professional writing professions. I imagine that this role of advocacy lies between a consideration of the ways texts are constructed and/or received and a recognition of the role that technical/professional communicators can play in disrupting power imbalances. Advocacy as a concept and as a teaching tool asks students to consider what language, design, and the very information included in a communication advocate for, as well as who is affected most by this advocacy. In my estimation, advocacy has the potential to become a tie between the notions of accessible design, usability, risk assessment, and social/ethical responsibility. Asking students to consider themselves as always already engaged in advocacy work forces them to consider how their choices as technical and professional communicators affect various audiences and to explore the possibilities for intervention available to them in the process.

In order to properly situate my personal motivation for writing this article, I need to start by telling you a story of my own experience as a technical communicator. Like many technical and professional writing scholars, long before I ever heard the terms "technical communicator," "technical writer," or "professional writer," I performed what would certainly be perceived as this work. Fresh from an undergraduate education in English, I initially worked for a state wide reproductive rights nonprofit organization as its Development Coordinator crafting a wide array of fundraising materials, including grants, mass mailings, invitations to events, materials to solicit major donors to the organization, and, of course, the results of those efforts. Later, I moved into a different position at another organization as the Executive Director of a local housing nonprofit, where was the party ultimately responsible for the entire organization's activities including any lobbying, fundraising, and federal reporting. Finally, I moved into a position working for a local government as a housing program administrator. Throughout my time at these positions, my work became increasingly entrenched in what I would now deem "technical" or "professional" writing. The last job, working for a local municipality prior to the decision to pursue my PhD, was one that really leads me to write this article.

In this position, I worked for my local city government in a dual role as both a sort of technical expert and technical and professional writer on local housing issues. I had been encouraged to apply for this job due to my work at a local housing nonprofit and with the local homeless coalition. In this position as a Housing Programs Manager for a local municipality, I wrote and implemented my first federally funded grant to assist homeowners with needed home repairs. It is important to note that this program, while federally funded, was administered through the state of Michigan. Part of the process of completing the grant application required consenting to a long checklist designed as controls—basically, a very long list designed to ensure that the money was used according to the federal regulations attached to the funding. When I received notification of the funding, I first had to create program guidelines which spelled out all government requirements *and* to submit them to be approved by the local municipality. So, as a new person, I carefully read the regulations and worded things *exactly* the way that they needed to be worded to pass the state's standards for compliance. I was eager to put the money to good use helping people in our community. However, that was when the problem arose: one of the requirements for assistance was that homeowners had to have homeowners' insurance. At the same time, I routinely ran into homeowners who had lost their insurance because they needed home repairs that they could not pay for. So, they applied for repair funding from the agency. I felt frustrated that the people who seemed to need the help the most were unable to access this funding because of this requirement.

Nearly all of these homeowners were distressed about not having homeowners' insurance, and they wanted to have it and would have paid for it if they could. Yet, the insurance companies were cancelling the insurance on these homes because, for example, the roof of the house needed to be replaced.

After struggling with this problem for several months, I finally reached out to my grant contact at the state who told me that the requirement was in place because it was a federal requirement. Frustrated by this answer, I spent time researching the federal regulations, the ones authorizing the funding. I read them carefully and realized that there were no such requirements on the federal money. Later, I crafted an email to my grant contact at the state, carefully citing the passage related to this issue in the federal funding requirements and restating the problem that I was having. After a couple of weeks of being bounced around between different people involved in compliance, I realized that this was one of those "this is the way we have always done things" situations. At some point, someone had thought that adding the homeowners' insurance requirement was a good idea and put it in writing. They even had it passed through various legislative bodies even though the requirement was not connected to the federal regulations at all.

Eventually, I received a very limited authorization to modify my requirements and my previously approved program guidelines and to use a portion of the grant funds to fund the insurance needed during the repair process. The requirement was that the homeowners' insurance had to be reinstated by the families after the repair was completed. Despite this small victory, I realized that I had played a key role in not resolving this problem early on. *I had not done my homework, and I had simply followed established norms and conventions instead of questioning the status quo.* In doing so, I had inadvertently added to the burden of my clients, rather than being part of the solution to a problem. That said, I wish I could tell you that this was the one and only time that I, as a technical and professional communicator, was responsible for creating documents that unintentionally perpetuated unnecessary challenges to the clients I was genuinely invested in trying to serve. There was a series of other situations through which I came to fully realize how critically important even the smallest details in document creation were to ensuring socially and ethically responsible program administration.

All in all, the moral of my story is this: technical and professional communicators need to pay careful attention and recognize the potential implications of their actions and their writing. More important, they need to be aware of their power and their savvy as researchers and communicators—ultimately as advocates—who can make things happen in the world. The pedagogical approach discussed in this chapter is, in some ways, an attempt to reconcile and redeem my own past errors. I believe wholeheartedly that it is necessary to teach future practitioners to recognize the impact and implications of their choices and actions. While considering accessibility is essential, we also need to consider what information is presented, not just how it is presented because the "how" is still complicated by the "what". Students, as future practitioners, should learn how to use their ethical judgement, take initiative when the opportunity to intervene presents itself, and enact social justice. This is where I situate advocacy.

Ultimately, I believe that teaching future technical communicators through the lens of advocacy asks them to consider their roles in advocacy in their future careers. Future practitioners need to understand for who and how they advocate and how they can intervene and reinvent information to disrupt the status quo. Furthermore, using social media as an entry point into considering advocacy in TPC may engage students with the way in which seemingly inconsequential, mundane texts, e.g. their own social media practices, enact advocacy and allow for the discussions of the ways *all* texts advocate on behalf of specific stakeholders. Such an understanding can potentially shift students' views of their role in writing, designing, and disseminating those texts.

A Review of Advocacy in Relation to Technical Communication

The field of TPC has a long-standing commitment to determining the role that technical communicators play in mediating knowledge and values. Carolyn Rude (2009) notes that "Research in technical communication asks questions that are variations of this central question: "How do texts (print, digital, multimedia, visual, verbal) and related communication practices mediate knowledge, values, and action in a variety of social and professional contexts?" (p. 176). Central to this question, in my view, is the phrase "mediate knowledge, values, and action" (Rude, 2009). Since texts are always constructed by *someone*, in this chapter I am interested in considering the following questions in more specific terms:

- How do technical communicators "mediate knowledge, values, and action" based on their research and writing practices (Rude, 2009)?
- As the field has routinely asked, how do teachers of technical communication foster a sense of responsibility for these mediations of knowledge, values, and action in future practitioners?

To engage with these questions is to uncover a multitude of scholarly articles outlining pedagogical and research practices devoted to ethics, accessibility, risk communication, civic responsibility, and most recently, social justice approaches. This work reminds us that there is a danger in not addressing issues of power— the *power* to "mediate knowledge, values and actions"—with students. Courses in TPC should interrogate an inherent risk of abuses of power in workplace settings and community spaces when the "technocratic approach" is used with "a one-way flow of technical information from the 'experts' to the public," an approach which often fails to consider the public's values, beliefs, or goals (Grabill & Simmons, 1998, p. 421).

Scholars have long approached the ability of technical communicators to bring change into their communities by discussing the concept of ethics and by asking students to consider their practices in terms of ethical practice. In fact, most technical communication textbooks dedicate a considerable amount of time to discussing ethics in TPC. For example, Johnson-Sheehan's popular *Technical Communication Today* (2015) describes ethics as "systems of moral, social, or cultural values that govern the conduct of an individual or community" (p. 61–80). As the author acknowledges, ethics can be diversely understood, as layers of ethical considerations that can overlap and complicate discussions. This textbook, like most other introductory TPC textbooks, includes an entire chapter devoted to breaking down the complex and overlapping nature of different meanings of ethics for students. Additionally, the book, along with many other textbooks, includes various scenarios that present ethical dilemmas throughout it for students to consider, weigh, and practice formulating responses to. While the focus on the complexity of ethics (and conflicting ethical perspectives) is certainly one which needs to be attended to, it seems to avoid, or perhaps tiptoe around, large scale social issues, foregrounding the importance of workplace dilemmas that might be encountered by the individual, rather than engaging with issues of social justice more generally.

Indeed, in the introduction to Eble & Haas' *Key Theoretical Frameworks for Technical Communication in the 21st Century* (forthcoming), Savage (2018) notes that "Regarding the perspective of social justice, most teachers, scholars, and practitioners might substitute [it with] 'ethics' as the preferable term—preferable because it does not seem to imply the risky domains of politics, ideology, or social activism associated with social justice" (p. iv). Savage goes on to differentiate between the value associated with thinking about ethics and social justice, noting that there is a "contemporary sense of ethics as a quality of individual character" which he sees "in the realm of the personal" and not "likely to resolve broader issues that fall outside of, if not directly in conflict with, existing laws and policies—that is, issues involving problems of social justice" (p. iv). Savage, in praising the work of the writers in this collection, notes that social justice work can "involve showing how, teaching, campaigning, witnessing, and materially transforming the conditions . . . that perpetuate injustice," which is what he believes contributors have done by sharing their research and pedagogy (p. iv). In what may be read as a call to action, Savage (2018) states the following:

If we are to naturalize the idea of technical communication as a field committed to social justice, I believe we need to adopt a stance that may seem alien to those who have worked in this field for many years. As this book makes clear, there is pedagogical work of social justice to do, which will draw hitherto unseen and unheard people into our classrooms and our professions. It is work that both exposes and undoes the complex and often not readily perceived ways in which technologies perpetuate and reinforce social, economic, and environmental injustices.

(p. v)

In this way, Savage points both to the social justice imperative for the technical communication field, as well as the potential of teachers of technical communication to disrupt systems of inequality by enacting social justice pedagogies. Additionally, Savage points back to including critical interrogation of technologies and the role that they play in mediating knowledge, values, and action. This, for me, connects to the work of scholars who have long urged us to "pay attention" (Selfe, 1999) to the way that technologies are shaping discursive practices (and discourse communities) and to the ways that our students are engaging with them outside of our classrooms (Hawisher et al., 2004). These scholars remind us that "gateways" to technologies are often found outside of traditional school settings. Additionally, I see a connection between the increasing use of technology and the work of technical communication and public rhetorics scholars who urge us not to underestimate the power of the mundane rhetorical practices (Grabill, 2010, 2014; Rivers and Webber, 2011). I would argue that the mundane has much more power than we often give it credit; which is why it is essential to teach future practitioners to recognize this power and to think about how to wield it justly. In order to engage students and to combat the resistance to interrogating both technical documents, digital media interfaces, and technologies more generally (Frost, 2014; Grabill, 2003; Propen & Lay Shuster, 2008), TPC instructors should ask students to examine rhetorical practices which include everyday social media practices. These practices provide a useful point of entry to discussions of advocacy in other documents. Scholars have established the benefits of and need for creating pedagogical approaches that are built on and complicate existing student literacies with social media and "ubiquitous writing technologies" (Dadurka & Pigg, 2011; Pigg, et al, 2014; Verzosa Hurley & Kimme Hea, 2014) by bringing discussions and activities related to the technological affordances and constraints into the classroom.

The next section describes my attempts to use social media analysis in an introductory technical communication classroom in order to engage with existing student interests and literacies with the ultimate goal of fostering a sense of responsibility for their advocacy in a variety of communication practices.

Teaching Technical Communication as Advocacy

Course Context, Goals, and Overview

The course concepts and activities discussed in this section were designed for and implemented in an introductory TPC course at a large public university in the Midwest. It is important to note that these were integrated into the overall course design (rather than used as a replacement for fundamental TPC activities) in order to supplement and further develop the students' skills in recognizing their power and responsibility in writing situations. In addition to being a course requirement for the TPC track, the course also serves as a required communication course for a variety of computer and health science programs on this campus. As such, the students who enroll in the course arrive in the classroom often arrive with widely varying writing and/or communication skills. Several of the strategies utilized were previously implemented in a multimodal composition course predicated on fostering a sense of rhetorical agency by using an advocacy lens to approach texts and were further developed from the experience of teaching that course. The overarching learning objectives specifically related to advocacy for the course were that students would:

- Develop an understanding of the ways that texts advocate through various modes and rhetoric.
- Develop an awareness of the advocacy enacted in social media spaces.
- Recognize how they participate in advocacy in their social media practices.
- Recognize their role in advocacy in the creation and dissemination of texts.

In order to encourage advocacy as a mindset for students, I designed all assignments and activities for the course around a critical interrogation of the ways that *all* texts advocate and the ways that advocacy was enacted through design, language, and genre choices. From the first day of the course, advocacy and the role of technical communicators as advocates (intentionally or not), were discussed as a baseline for the entire course. On the first day of class we discussed the fact that all writing is always already influenced by the historical and cultural contexts in which it is created and that as future TPC practitioners it was essential to develop a sense of the ways that texts advocate and students' potential role in this.

As Elise Verzosa Hurley and I have argued, advocacy, as a concept and approach to teaching and analysis, asks students to consider what is "supported," or perhaps more particularly, what it means to "publicly support" something. Unlike activism, the term "advocacy" implies only public support, rather than any specific and directed action, however, this advocacy can be enacted unintentionally and in ways that reinforce social inequalities that may be unintended, but ultimately have real material consequences (Warren-Riley & Verzosa Hurley, 2017). As such, we argued that it is essential to consider our role in advocacy when we create and interact with texts not just in online and social media spaces, but also in physical ones. Additionally, we must also consider the ways that advocacy is enacted upon us by texts we encounter and how we enact advocacy when we interact with texts and teach students to do the same. Extending this approach into the TPC classroom allows for a recognition that engaging students through social media analysis can be a useful first step to developing this awareness in students.

Arguably, many students arrive to our classrooms as savvy users of a wide variety of technologies. They are constantly communicating, composing and distributing information although they often do not think of these practices in terms of writing. Technologies (computers, the Internet, social media, smart phones, etc.) are integral to their everyday worlds – essential to how they *do* everything. Yet, in many cases, these technologies and the practices that they facilitate have become so naturalized that they become nearly invisible. Thus, many people (students included) have often never taken a moment to step back and think about the effects of that technology on their everyday lives, let alone to consider how the communication practices enabled by them are involved in cultural production and reproduction. Anecdotally speaking, it seems that the one and only pervasive critical perspective on social media use that students have is the ever present one related to its effects on future employment – a lesson which they seem to have taken up well: do not put anything on social media that you do not want future employers to see.

I am interested in following the example of many scholars who have modeled the value of embracing and building from existing student literacies with technologies and acknowledging that these literacies are often developed in non-school settings. I am also interested in working within my students' existing literacies to cultivate a potentially missing critical literacy component for the students in my courses. The activities and assignments shared are geared toward both doing so and also encouraging students to recognize the ways that advocacy is enacted in mundane texts and in everyday spaces.

The following section describes activities and assignments particular to fostering a sense of the power and responsibility for advocating in document creation and dissemination (as future practitioners). As such, one of the overarching goals of the course design was to enable students to recognize their power to "mediate knowledge, values, and action" (Rude, 2009). Another goal was to foster student awareness of the advocacy enacted in everyday, mundane texts.[1]

Sample Activities and Assignments

In order to begin to consider the role of advocacy in texts, students were first tasked with analyzing everyday texts of their choosing, such as advertisements or fliers, for embedded advocacy contained within them. After establishing a sense of the ways that advocacy is embedded in texts, students were then asked to use this approach to analyze various social media texts (such as memes and viral videos) before engaging in an analysis of their own social media practices for the advocacy contained within it. Finally, throughout the course students were tasked with creating texts through a lens of advocacy, an approach which asks them to reflect on the ways that their design choices enact advocacy. The following lists brief descriptions of approaches to these activities and assignments, which have been designed to build upon the knowledge and skills students have acquired through previous assignments:

Textual Analysis for Embedded Advocacy: Tasking students with analyzing texts for the ways that cultural and/or ideological values are embedded within them (however subtly) allows students to begin to engage and grapple with issues of cultural reproduction and advocacy. As such, the learning objectives for these assignments were that students would begin to:

- Develop an awareness of the advocacy enacted in everyday, mundane texts.
- Demonstrate the ability to identify features of texts that reflect particular ideologies or cultural values.
- Articulate how ideologies or values embedded in texts may serve to perpetuate ideologies and cultural values.

Entry level assignments designed to encourage this type of inquiry included analyses of everyday texts (such as advertisements or fliers) to consider how the design choices (including language choice, images, etc.) were used to reinforce gendered stereotypes, heteronormativity, patriotism, materialistic capitalism, ableism, and linguistic discrimination through the features of the texts. In later activities students then applied the skills honed from these activities to analyze forms, brochures, and even government documents and websites, to determine the subtle embedded values and ideologies within them. Students were tasked to reflect on what they had found and offer their suggestions for redesigning documents if they found that the values or ideologies identified were potentially discriminatory or harmful to some groups.

Analysis of Social Media Texts through an Advocacy Lens: In order to encourage students to critically engage with social media texts specifically, students were asked to analyze various social media texts for the advocacy embedded within them. Building from the work previously completed, the learning objectives related to analysis of social media texts were that students would:

- Develop an awareness of the advocacy enacted in social media texts.
- Demonstrate the ability to identify the features of social media texts that reflect particular ideologies and cultural values.
- Articulate the role of social media in perpetuating ideologies and cultural values through the circulation of social media texts.

Particularly useful for demonstrating the everyday advocacy enacted in social media spaces (and the role that these texts play in reproducing social and cultural norms) are memes, viral videos, and popular Twitter feeds. One example that I like to use in my courses are various videos of "fixing" that are pervasive and widely popular on social media. These videos (showing how various surgeries or medical interventions to correct hearing, vision, or other perceived impairments) often go viral, being "liked" and shared across multiple social media platforms, and in many cases, continue to circulate for years across these spaces. These videos provide a unique opportunity to teach students about the power of every-day social media texts, the advocacy embedded within them, and their role in cultural reproduction due to the emphasis they put on correcting perceived limitations in ability. To encourage students to think more critically about unintended advocacy in social media spaces, I used these to discuss problematic narratives that they reinforce about people with non-normative bodies or the way that the videos unintentionally advocate and champion medical intervention and "fixing" of those bodies deemed "less than normal," or "less than perfect." After discussing the potentials of these videos to reinforce narratives that are problematic and socially unjust, I initiated further conversations regarding how often individual people engage in everyday advocacy by liking and sharing content across social media platforms, but do not consider or contemplate the impact of such actions.

Another activity that achieved a similar effect was an analysis of viral memes. First, students were asked to analyze various memes for the embedded values, beliefs, and advocacy in the sample memes. Examples of memes used in this activity ranged from commonly circulated seemingly innocuous memes with identifiable patterns, characters or features (such as the "scumbag" hat, animal memes, or Pepe the Frog memes), to various memes that were overtly politically and/or socially motivated, such as those about protesters, social movements, or political figures. Students analyzed the advocacy contained within these memes by considering the ideologies and values contained within them.

Finally, in order to engage with social media trends, students were asked to share examples of current trends that they had noted in their own interaction with social media. In response, as a class we analyzed the trends identified, dis-cussed whether the trends had crossed platforms and considered the potential reasons that some trends were so popular. Finally, we considered the advocacy embedded in these trends.

Analysis of Advocacy within Students' Personal Social Media: Students were tasked with analyzing their own social media usage, which allowed them to see how they personally advocate or have advocacy enacted upon them through mundane, everyday texts. Assigning students to critically analyze both the tools they compose with (and through) as well as their personal interactions with social media texts provided further insight into how everyday texts advocate. The learning objectives for this assignment were that students would:

- Develop an awareness of the advocacy enacted on them in social media spaces.
- Demonstrate an awareness of their own role in perpetuating ideologies and cultural values in social media spaces.

- Demonstrate an awareness of the role of social media technologies in shaping communications.
- Articulate the connection between social media interactions and offline effects.

Students were asked to answer the following questions focused on a critical interrogation of social media practices and unintended advocacy in social media spaces:

- What digital and social media spaces do you compose in? For what purposes? What are your goals in composing in these spaces and with these tools?
- What are the affordances and limitations of these tools? What can you do/what can't you do with them? What can you control and what can't you control?
- What evidence of cultural values that are embedded in these technologies can you find? What advocacy features are included in the social media tool you use? How do people advocate in these spaces?
- How do you personally advocate (intentionally or not) in your social media practices? How does an investigation into your recent "likes," and "shares" indicate how you advocate in your social media practices?
- After considering how unintentional advocacy can take place in these spaces, discuss your reaction to your analysis. Discuss whether or not you might differently approach the creation, interaction, and/or dissemination of texts in these spaces. How might this analysis affect the way that you approach the creation and dissemination of texts in offline spaces?
- Also, based on our in-class discussions, consider the ways that online/social media texts may influence perspectives in offline settings. Did these discussions affect how you percieve social media texts? Will you approach interactions in these settings differently based on these? If so, how and in what ways?

Creating a Variety of Texts through the Lens of Advocacy: In many ways, the assignments/approaches here are not altogether different from those in other introductory technical communication classes. Students were assigned to draft letters, memos, and emails and to create instructions, technical documentation, and a variety of forms of reports. However, I would argue that by adding advocacy as a lens through which students view themselves and considering how the texts that they are creating advocate in specific ways for particular people contributes to enacting a more social justice focused pedagogical imperative. As such, students were asked to complete a written discussion that addressed how their design choices advocate, for who, and in what ways, which was intended to reinforce this perspective in regards to each of the texts that they create.

Reflections and Implications

Can using social media and everyday advocacy lead to more socially just technical and professional writing practices in future practitioners? While I would like to say definitively that it can, I am unfortunately limited to what I was able to glean from student writing and discussions in the classroom itself. However, based on student engagement with the course concepts, activities, and in-class feedback, I do believe that using this approach did result in fostering a greater awareness of the advocacy embedded in everyday texts and the potential power and responsibility that technical and professional communicators have (the power to "mediate knowledge, values, and action"). At minimum, I can say that students' attention was focused on these aspects of communication that they had not yet considered, which had effects that were repeatedly demonstrated in student work and discussion. And, I did find that bringing social media and the analysis of everyday texts into the TPC classroom allowed for several, perhaps somewhat predictable, yet still unanticipated results, which I think may be useful to other teachers who are considering using such an approach.

First, students seemed to genuinely enjoy talking about and analyzing social media texts, trends, and platforms. As genres that they participate in regularly and are often highly knowledgeable of, students were engaged with conversations and eager to share their experiences and insights about them. This seemed to lead to the development of a lively classroom community where nearly all students regularly participated in both large and small group discussions and appeared comfortable while doing so. Beyond this, what I found particularly compelling was the way that discussions about social media and advocacy often became the impetus for discussions about wider social justice issues, even when they were not intended or expected. These conversations often developed organically as students made connections to concepts across various scenarios. Here I will share just a handful of the resulting conversations to highlight the results.

While completing an in-class activity analyzing viral memes, in response to one particular meme (a "Mexican word of the day" meme which I had included in the set of memes to be analyzed in order to start a conversation about the role of memes in perpetuating language biases or linguistic discrimination), one student rather forcefully reacted. He complained that these memes were a "rip off" of comedian Jeff Foxworthy's "you might be a redneck" jokes and the memes based off his work. This student's criticism of the meme led another student to start discussing cultural appropriation, a topic that while unplanned and unexpected, led to a useful dialogue wherein many members of the class debated the nature of cultural appropriation in general alongside additional discussion of linguistic variations and the way they are represented in both popular media and social media spaces.

In another example, an in-class activity geared toward helping students to identify, analyze, and engage with social media trends again had unexpected results. Discussions of social media trends led to an analysis of the fast-food franchise *Wendy's* Twitter feed, particularly its use of humor to provoke rival fast food chains. One student brought up a teenager's campaign for a year of free chicken nuggets from *Wendy's* and the development of this challenge. (*Wendy's* responded to the teen's initial inquiry Tweet of "how many retweets for a year of free chicken nuggets" with a response of "18 million." The teen's tweet went on to become Twitter's most retweeted tweet. The trend of asking "how many retweets" in exchange for something spread from there.) This conversation led to two distinct and unintended developments. First, it led to a larger discussion of the trends in social media marketing, with some students acknowledging the ways that they were often unwittingly participating in free advertising for various companies when they responded to and/or circulated their messages and the potential implications of this (for themselves and for those in a variety of careers). Secondly, when one student suggested that we attempt to recreate the "how many retweets" trend, our class spent the remainder of class crafting a Twitter message to our university. As we negotiated what our "ask" should be, the student who had initially suggested the activity wanted to ask for something personal (the use of a campus golf cart for a month for himself); however, as a classroom community the students discussed the ethical dimensions of this request, what the "right" thing to do might be, and the ways that asking for something broader could potentially benefit the larger university community – ultimately settling on asking for a pizza party on the quad for the entire student body (which we did achieve through garnering enough retweets).

In an even more intriguing development, when student groups created instructions and posted them to the "Instructables" website, one of the groups' projects (a set of instructions on how to roll t-shirts as compactly as possible) became instantly popular on the site, gathering over 75,000 views and 300 favorites within a few days. Class discussion ensued as to the potential reason this particular set of instructions was so well received. As students debated the issues involved in determining why anything becomes popular on social media more generally, several were inclined to believe that this set of instructions was so liked because it was "practical" and could be used by so many people. "Everyone travels" one student noted, further explaining that packing for travel would be widely useful for a variety of people. Interestingly, one student took issue with this statement quipping back that, in fact, not everyone does travel or can afford to travel. It was fascinating to watch as students grappled with their own assumptions based on personal experiences (for example, that they often travel or know many people who do) and then tease out amongst themselves the problems with this assumption and how it had affected their perceptions. This also led to a discussion about who has access to these instructions (as they are posted to an internet-based site) wherein I was able to further steer the conversation into a discussion of access to the internet and other technologies we tend to take for granted more generally.

All in all, I often found myself impressed with my students' insights and willingness to engage in conversations about issues that developed as a result of in-class and small group discussions on social media, advocacy, and technical communication. And, again, while I cannot say for certain that these were a result of the class focus, I do wonder if simply bringing these together into the classroom played at least some small part in shaping the overall classroom environment and culture.

Conclusion

I realize that in some ways, teaching students to approach technical communication through a lens of advocacy requires relying heavily on the basics of critical thinking, critical reading, and critical evaluation of information. Yet, students also need to learn to analyze the ways that technologies mediate communication and the ways that multiple modes of communication advocate in specific ways. Students' own practices in digital and social media spaces serve as a rich source for discussing intentional and unintentional advocacy and as a means of engaging students in broader discussions.

Once engaged, students can then begin to consider how *all* texts advocate. This, in turn, helps them to recognize how technical communication can be created through a lens of advocacy and in what ways technical/professional writers can affect the presentation of materials that can potentially alleviate concerns related to social justice. The use of this knowledge in future employment situations has the potential to empower writers to present information in more socially just ways. At minimum, this approach seeks to foster awareness of the implications of their writing as future technical communicators. By asking them to consider how their composing practices *can* impact the lives of others, instructors teach students to recognize their power to "mediate knowledge, values, and action," in a responsible way (Rude, 2009). In implementing the course concepts and activities discussed above, I have had success in moving students toward this goal. Such an approach, I contend, is just one of many ways to initiate the enactment of a pedagogy of social justice in the technical communication classroom.

Note

1. For additional general pedagogical suggestions for enacting awareness of the ways that everyday mundane texts advocate, see the appendix.

Discussion Questions

1) The author discusses how engaging students through an analysis of social media texts and their own social media use may be useful for opening conversations related to unintended advocacy and broader social justice concerns. What other activities using social media might prove beneficial for encouraging students to understand the advocacy role of everyday texts in

society? What social media related activities or assignments might also be useful to bring into the TPC classroom to achieve this aim?

2) In thinking about the ways that this article discusses the role of everyday texts and the ways that they advocate for some people over others, how might teachers (or future teachers) of TPC consider their own advocacy enacted through their course design and materials. How might our pedagogy inadvertently advocate for some things not intended? What we teach/how we teach it always already advocates something, what is that? Consider what we advocate in our pedagogy and what the unintended consequences are. In doing so, consider the texts we use to teach, assignments, etc.

3) In the *Sample Activities and Assignments* section, the author shares questions used to stimulate analysis and discussion from students regarding their own social media practices and the advocacy enacted through them. If you were to implement this assignment in your classroom, what additional questions might you add to this list?

4) In response to the social media analysis assignment shared in this article, consider how you might also participate in advocacy in your social media use. Locate examples of both intentional and unintentional advocacy in your own social media spaces. How does your intentional advocacy differ from your unintentional advocacy?

5) In this article, the author argues for embracing and engaging with existing student literacies (particularly literacies with digital and social media) in the TPC classroom. What additional literacies, beyond digital/social media literacies, might we engage with in the classroom? What might activities and assignments geared toward this entail?

6) Beyond the activities and assignments shared in this article, what additional strategies might be useful to fostering a sense of responsibility in future TPC practitioners for the power to "mediate knowledge, values, and action" (Rude, 2009)?

Further Reading

Dadurka, D., Pigg, S. (2011). Mapping complex terrains: Bridging social media and community literacies. *Community Literacy Journal* 6(1): 7–22.

Grabill, J. T., Simmons, W. M. (1998). Toward a critical rhetoric of risk communication: Producing citizens and the role of technical communicators. *Technical Communication Quarterly* 7(4): 415–441.

Pigg, S., Grabill, J. T., Brunk-Chavez, B., Moore, J. L., Rosinkski, P., Curran, P. G. (2014). Ubiquitous writing, technologies, and the social practice of literacies of coordination. *Written Communication* 31(1): 91–117.

Rude, C. D. (2009). Mapping the research questions in technical communications. *Journal of Business and Technical Communication* 23(2): 174–215.

Selfe, C. L. and Selfe, Jr., R. J. (1994). The politics of the interface: Power and its exercise in electronic contact zones. *College Composition and Communication* 45(4): 480–504.

Verzosa Hurley, E., Kimme Hea, A. (2014). The rhetoric of reach: Preparing students for technical communication in the age of social media. *Technical Communication Quarterly 23*(1): 55–68.

Vie, S. (2014). In defense of "slactivism": The human rights campaign Facebook logo as digital activism. *First Monday 19*(4): n.pag.

References

Dadurka, D., Pigg, S. (2011). Mapping complex terrains: Bridging social media and community literacies. *Community Literacy Journal 6*(1): 7–22.

Eble, M., Haas, A., eds. (forthcoming 2018). *Key theoretical frameworks for teaching technical communication in the 21st century*. Manuscript in preparation.

Frost, E. (2014). Apparent feminist pedagogies. *Programmatic Perspectives 6*(1): 110–131.

Grabill, J. T. (2003). On divides and interfaces: Access, class, and computers. *Computers and Composition, 20*(4), 455–472.

Grabill, J. T. (2010). On being useful: Rhetoric and the work of engagement. *The public work of rhetoric: Citizen scholars and civic engagement*. Eds. John M. Ackerman and David J. Coogan. Columbia: University of South Carolina Press. 193–208.

Grabill, J. (2014). The work of rhetoric in the common places: An essay on rhetorical methodology. *JAC: A Journal of Composition Theory, 34*(1–2), 247–267.

Grabill, J. T., Simmons, W. M. (1998). Toward a critical rhetoric of risk communication: Producing citizens and the role of technical communicators. *Technical Communication Quarterly 7*(4): 415–441.

Hawisher, G. E., Selfe, C.L., Moranski, B., Pearson, M. (2004). Becoming literate in the information age: Cultural ecologies and the literacies of technology. *College Composition and Communication 55*(4): 642–92.

Johnson-Sheehan, R. (2015). *Technical communication today*, 5th ed. Boston: Pearson.

Pigg, S., Grabill, J. T., Brunk-Chavez, B., Moore, J. L., Rosinkski, P., Curran, P. G. (2014). Ubiquitous writing, technologies, and the social practice of literacies of coordination. *Written Communication 31*(1): 91–117.

Propen, A. and Lay Shuster, M. (2008). Making academic work advocacy work: Technologies of power in the public arena. *Journal of Business and Technical Communication 22*(3): 299–329.

Rivers, N. A., and Weber, R. P. (2011). Ecological, pedagogical, public rhetoric. *College Composition and Communication 63*(2): 187–218.

Rude, C. D. (2009). Mapping the research questions in technical communications. *Journal of Business and Technical Communication 23*(2): 174–215.

Selfe, C. (1999). *Technology and literacy in the twenty-first century: The importance of paying attention*. Carbondale: Southern Illinois University Press.

Selfe, C. L. and Selfe, Jr., R. J. (1994). The politics of the interface: Power and its exercise in electronic contact zones. *College Composition and Communication 45*(4): 480–504.

Slack, J. D., Wise, J. M. (2015). *Technology and culture: A primer*. 2nd Ed. New York: Peter Lang Publishing.

Scott, J. B. (2003). *Risky rhetoric: AIDS and the cultural practices of HIV testing*. Carbondale: Southern Illinois University Press.

Vie, S. (2014). In defense of "slactivism": The human rights campaign Facebook logo as digital activism. *First Monday 19*(4): n.p.

Verzosa Hurley, E., Kimme Hea, A. (2014). The rhetoric of reach: Preparing students for technical communication in the age of social media. *Technical Communication Quarterly 23*(1): 55–68.

Warren-Riley, S., Verzosa Hurley, E. (2017). Multimodal pedagogical approaches to public writing: Digital media advocacy and mundane texts. *Composition Forum 35*: n.p.

APPENDIX A

In order to foster a recognition of the advocacy work that happens in technical/professional writing settings, I offer the following as potential general key components of a course designed to foster advocacy as a mindset for future technical communicators:

- *Genre Research* – Admittedly, genre research is an essential component to successful writing in any setting. Genre research allows writers to determine established genre conventions to successfully communicate in a given community; however, from my perspective, approaching these conventions needs to be carefully warned against simply repeating the status quo. Interrogating genre conventions from a standpoint of advocacy asks the technical/professional writer to consider the social and cultural forces that shaped those conventions, what those conventions are reinforcing, what they are suppressing information wise from the reader, among other things.
- *Complicating Ethics* – Considering the ethical implications of writing technical documents is important. Ethics alone, however, cannot enact social justice. Discussions of ethics in the technical communication classroom should be complicated with a focus on showing that individual personal ethical or workplace ethical situations are never wholly independent from the larger social and economic inequalities that exist across the globe. Teachers can encourage students to think beyond the workplace scenarios in textbooks to consider how there may be larger implications at stake and discuss potential places where technical communicators can work to disrupt these larger societal inequalities.
- *Communicating to Various Audiences* – Having students create documents to communicate the same information to multiple different audiences (with

different values) asks them to consider how different genres are more, or less, effective for different people. By incorporating activities that task students with doing this, and asking them to reflect on how their design and language choices advocate for specific groups over others, we can further engage students in thinking through not only ethical, but also social justice issues (including issues of accessibility and ethics).

- *Distilling Technical Language into Accessible Language* – Having students practice distilling highly technical or high-level information into genres that various audiences will be able to access helps them to consider the potentials and constraints for advocating as technical/professional writers. Again here, by doing so, and asking students to articulate the choices made in their writing/design (and how those choices involve advocating for specific groups over others), students gain insight into issues critical to social justice imperatives.

- *Understanding Rhetoric (including the way it is employed in multimodal forms)* – Teaching students to understand that all communication is rhetorical, and that the effects of this are achieved through various multimodal forms, is a critical component for establishing the groundwork for an approach such as this. Analyzing the visual, linguistic, gestural, spatial and aural components of texts for the ways that advocacy can (and/or could) be enacted continues to reinforce the ways that social justice work can be engaged with through the creation of texts in a variety of forms.

AFTERWORD

Solving for Pattern in Professional and Technical Communication

Jon A. Leydens

"No education is politically neutral."

bell hooks, *Teaching to Transgress* (1994)

"Language is a means of policy negotiation and of social transformation."

Carolyn D. Rude, *Journal of Business and Technical Communication* (2008)

On November 3, 2017, 13 U.S. government agencies released a *Climate Science Special Report* that reinforced much previous research, stating that climate change is occurring and is primarily caused by human activities (USGCRP, 2017). In itself, that is largely unremarkable. The broad findings in the report had been echoed by many other climate change reports, such as those of the Intergovernmental Panel on Climate Change three years earlier (IPCC, 2014), and other journal articles (see, e.g., Cook, et al., 2013, 2016). But consider a critical layer of the rhetorical context: the document was released by 13 U.S. government agencies at a time in which the U.S. President, several prominent U.S. politicians, members of the President's cabinet, and even the Director of the U.S. Environmental Protection Agency call into question anthropogenic contributions to climate change (Davenport & Lipton, 2016). We live in a time when climate science consensus reports from prominent scientists have been wrapped into one large generalization and dismissed as "a hoax" (Memoli, 2016), an era that has—perhaps hyperbolically (Lloyd, 2016)—been characterized as involving a "war on science" (Kosoff, 2017).

By summarizing the data that have led to a strong scientific consensus among climate scientists, technical communicators of the 2017 U.S. government report were ostensibly delivering facts. Yet technical communication does not happen in a vacuum; instead, it is buoyed, constrained, imbued, and forever involved in the social, political, economic, scientific, and other contexts in which it is produced. To state otherwise is to perpetuate naïve understandings of how texts—via images, statistics, words, and more—shape citizen perspectives and advocate directly or indirectly for certain policy outcomes. An awareness of how texts shape citizens, advocacy processes, and democratic and social justice ideals raises important questions. What role do technical communicators play in citizenship and advocacy? At what point does being a responsible, ethical technical communicator move from reporting data, to serving as an honest broker (Pielke, 2014), to advocacy, to activism? The notion that communicating data is purely neutral work is a relic of the past. In actuality, the lines between communicating information, serving to inform public policy, advocacy—and yes, real or perceived activism—often blur. That blurring becomes more nuanced when we consider the multiple, diverse frames and perspectives on citizenship and advocacy.

Some might consider advocacy to imply pushing an agenda. Unfortunately, those holding such a stance are vulnerable to going along with whatever trends prevail in their times—whether those be toward greater equality and democratic participation by citizens, toward fascism and the relinquishment of individual freedoms, toward gains in social justice and social responsibility, or toward nativism and xenophobia. Such a stance means that rather than steering their destiny, the cultural tide guides them, as their silence becomes a form of assent to any form of status quo.

Edited by Godwin Agboka and Natalia Matveeva, this collection of scholarly essays has contributed to better understandings of the critical junctures between technical and professional communication (TPC) and citizenship/advocacy issues. The chapters have artfully woven together positions on pedagogy, theory, and practice to help TPC professionals—researchers, teachers, and practitioners—better understand how advocacy and civic engagement are always a part of what we do. Moreover, the collection accentuates how such engagement is infused with complexity and opportunities to make a difference. For instance, Emily January Petersen's chapter reminds us that female TPC practitioners are at times most effective *because* they are attuned to issues of audience and social and political contexts, *because* they see how documentation renders visible advocacy and activism, and *because* they understand how social justice requires "a coalition of advocates." In their chapter on community engagement and nonprofit partnerships, Elisabeth Kramer-Simpson and Steve Simpson explore how issues of trust and relationship-building are complex yet crucial in addressing the needs of a local homeless shelter's staff and clients. These and the other chapters in this collection up the ante. Remaining in the TPC field or classroom often means engaging real people with real issues, and diving into the multifaceted sociotechnical terrain that shapes and is shaped by technical communication processes and documents.

In *Pedagogy of the oppressed,* Paolo Freire (1998) notes that critical praxis "involves a dynamic and dialectic movement between 'doing' and 'reflecting on doing'" (p. 43). This reflecting on "doing" citizenship and advocacy should involve briefly looking back on TPC's historical origins as well as looking forward to future frontiers.

Technical and Professional Communication: Historical Origins

TPC professionals have spent much of the late 20th and early 21st century trying to shed and transcend the constraints of the past. This volume represents a continuation—perhaps one of the final stages—of writhing out of that cocoon. One component of that writhing has involved transcending the market model and acknowledging strategies for citizenship and advocacy empowerment.

Collection editors Agboka and Matveeva, in their Preface, "Advocating for the Good of Humanity: Technical Communication as a Tool for Change," mentioned the 20th century "market model" that sought skilled TPC labor for the corporate sector. That model, they note, failed to acknowledge a more complete narrative of what TPC professionals can and should do. Agboka and Matveeva state that critics of the market model "decried the field's attachment to the apron strings of these functionalist, skill-based approaches to the neglect of democratic, humanistic, and social justice approaches that were more responsive to social, economic, cultural, and environmental issues in the community." The latter approach envisions more comprehensive TPC professionals, indeed "more rounded 'public intellectuals' (Cushman, 1999) who would be knowledgeable in their subject matter areas, but also be willing and able to interrogate ways in which their activities would impact their communities of practice." Such an approach accentuated the importance of knowledge mediators capable of, as Agboka and Matveeva state, engaging "practical rhetoric" as "a matter of arguing in a prudent way toward the good of the community rather than of constructing texts" (Miller, 1989, p. 23). As Carolyn Rude (2004) acknowledged over a decade ago, TPC research studies challenging the functionalist paradigm "have helped to disturb the now antiquated notion of communication as the accurate transmission of clear information and have confirmed the close connections between communication, culture, and power" (p. 123). Shedding the cocoon, the TPC butterfly emerges in a world of much greater complexity, where community and other stakeholder engagement processes add multiple layers of communication challenge. Yet it is a world in which we have rendered more visible our sociotechnical responsibilities and opportunities for impact as TPC educators, researchers, and practitioners.

This volume suggests a tendency toward TPC empowerment. Sarah Warren-Riley's chapter on teaching advocacy and social engagement as "a mindset" helps to counter the historical mindsets that limited past TPC practitioners, researchers, and educators. In those mindsets, technical communicators were positioned to communicate facts, but those facts occur in multi-stakeholder contexts, where the facts shape and are shaped by clients, local community members, municipalities, and others. Hence, antidotes to the old mindsets include, for instance, teaching about advocacy via proposal writing—as Diane Martinez has done in this collection—and foregrounding the importance of working with community partners, as Anne Marie Francis' chapter has done. Along these same transcendent lines, Jessica Edwards' chapter showcases effective assignments and strategies for introducing the discussions of diversity and social justice in a technical communication classroom. Although civic engagement and advocacy issues run through TPC scholarship, it is important to remind ourselves that prior to this collection, no coherent body of research existed that focused directly on these issues. Now we have a more intelligible foundation from which to move forward.

Given this important volume of scholarship connecting TPC and citizenship/advocacy, what frontiers lie ahead? What experimentation might occur next in TPC research, practice, and teaching?

Technical and Professional Communication: Future Frontiers

Although this collection has foregrounded several future frontiers for TPC professionals, the focus will be on select issues. These include how we

- Define ourselves as professionals given our past and emerging forms of expertise
- Define culture
- Problematize sociotechnical communication
- Envision local and global citizenship
- Wrestle with issues of power inherent to TPC work
- Engage communities and who defines community.

We end by exploring what critical strategies we can access for citizenship and advocacy.

Sociotechnical Communication Professionals

This volume and other research suggest that among some TPC professionals there is resounding awareness of the inherent interrelations between technical communication and social issues such as citizenship, advocacy, and social justice. That is, we engage in serious forms of sociotechnical communication. The word *sociotechnical* recognizes that technical processes occur in, shape, and are shaped by social contexts. If that is so, why do we still call ourselves *technical communication* professionals? By that term, are we not anchoring ourselves to the past, a past we have worked so hard to transcend? If we redefine ourselves, how might we do so? Ostensibly, *sociotechnical communication* is our emerging area of expertise, yet that term has by no means taken hold in our journals, professional societies and organizations, academic departments, and other important professional TPC contexts. We have a wonderful opportunity for soul-searching and future research. If we are no longer technical communicators, who are we, and what do we do? If technical communicator was the moniker of the 20th century, what will we call ourselves in the 21st? Since nothing should be written about us without us having an active voice in that naming process, TPC professionals should lead that research, even if it means ultimately making no changes in what we call or how we define ourselves. Let this debate carry on.

Where to Now, Culture?

In Laura A. Ewing and Megan M. McIntyre's chapter, they explore how advocacy varies across cultures. This is important work, and can inspire expanded research. Traditional definitions of culture often focus on national culture or ethnic culture. Instead, following the lead of research on intercultural communication, we can expand culture as an umbrella term that encompasses race/ethnicity, social class, gender, ability status, sexual orientation, and more (Sorrells, 2016). Some authors in this collection have engaged many of those topics.

So when we talk about intercultural communication, what definitions of culture guide our way? Is it the anthropological definition of culture, as "a system of shared meanings that are passed from generation to generation through symbols that allow human beings . . . to communicate, maintain, and develop an approach and understanding of life" (Sorrells, 2016, p. 5)? Or is it the cultural studies definition of "culture as a site of contestation where meanings are constantly negotiated" (Sorrells, 2016, p. 7)? Or is it the global studies definition of culture as a resource for "economic and political exploitation, agency, and power to be used or instrumentalized for a wide range of purposes and ends" (Sorrells, 2016. p. 10)? Or is it some hybrid, synthesized version of two, three, or even other definitions? Which hybrid definitions are more viable than any one definition alone? Since citizenship and advocacy are rooted in and need to be tailored to many different aspects of culture, this collection opens up important opportunities to explore what we mean when we say "culture." It also serves as an opportunity to connect with and learn from scholars across multiple disciplines as we refine how culture shapes TPC work in unique, often situated, case-specific ways.

Problematizing Sociotechnical Communication

As the editors of this collection, Agboka and Matveeva have deftly laid the foundations for salient future work in TPC by characterizing some of the issues we face as we move forward as sociotechnical communicators:

> Recent challenges to racial, class, gender, disability, and economic issues raise significant concerns and provide excellent opportunities for our field to engage with, forge, and build new relationships with communities. Scholars very often question the commitment of civic engagement assignments to social justice (Herzberg, 1994), decry the quality of deliverables to community members (Brizee, 2015), raise concerns about the theoretical grounding motivating service learning projects (Matthews & Zimmerman, 1999), wonder about the value of community engagement to students (McEachern, 2001), and worry about the asymmetrical posture of student-community member relationships.

These challenges serve as opportunities to deepen our knowledge and practice. As a field, TPC will be best served if we continue to learn from those who have researched what citizenship means, including global citizenship, as well as what advocacy means, including how advocacy relates to issues of power and community. Several of the guiding ideas below can indirectly or directly help us address these challenges.

What is Global Citizenship?

In an increasingly interconnected world, what does it mean to be a global citizen? How do we integrate yet also go beyond definitions of national citizenship? One problem with being constrained by national citizenship is that the social constraints on human agency and free will are different in different national contexts. It is important to not assume others experience citizenship and advocacy exactly as we do, as our national culture contexts, particularly in developed countries, are not universal. Thinking otherwise can lead to problematic assumptions.

We say we live in a world connected by digital technology. But do we? A 2016 report suggests that fewer than half of the people on the planet use the Internet (Taylor, 2016). To whom are we referring when we say "we?" We may think we live in a time of ever increasing prosperity for all. But do we? A 2016 report on global poverty by the World Bank suggests that despite some gains, "within-country inequality is higher than it was 25 years ago," and "there remains real concern over the share of incomes controlled by top earners" (World Bank, 2016).

Those and other common but misguided assumptions apply not just to technology and socioeconomic inequality, but gender, race/ethnicity, sexual orientation, ability status, religion, and more (Johnson, 2006). Thus, the search for a definition of global citizenship is complicated by cultural, national, and other factors.

Our opportunity for research is to engage multiple definitions of global citizenship in an attempt to understand our own and other cultures in more capacious ways. For instance, Buddhist leader and educator Daisaku Ikeda has identified three qualities of global citizens—wisdom, courage, and compassion (Ikeda, 2005). Those qualities include the wisdom to recognize the interdependence and interconnectedness of all life, the courage to respect differences, and the compassion to empathize with and attempt to co-surmount the suffering of others (Ikeda, 2005). Like Ikeda's ideas, Peggy McIntosh's capacities for global citizenship, including several capacities of mind, heart, and body (2005), and other definitions that inform global citizenship, will each resonate differently in different cultural contexts. Such polysemy provides us with opportunities to better understand multicultural, multifaceted, layered interpretations of local and global citizenship, and hence, local and global advocacy.

Issues of Power

Case studies in community development indicate that project assessment via broad economic measures is useful but inadequate (Nussbaum, 2011; Sen, 2009). If a given community, city, or country increases its gross domestic product, that boost does not tell us about wealth distribution. Community development targeting underserved populations that results in the wealthy becoming wealthier is not attentive to the vagaries of power. In fact, well-intentioned assistance from technical communicators or anyone else cannot only fail to serve those in need, but result in more harm than good (Lucena, et al., 2010; Schneider, et al., 2009). A critical antidote is an awareness of how to conduct contextual listening and identify social structural conditions, as explained below.

It is also important for the next generation of TPC professionals to understand how power shapes citizenship and advocacy processes. As the editors noted in their Preface, service learning has been positioned positively because it:

> offers students opportunities to develop, reflect about, and enact civic responsibility" (Scott, 2004, p. 289); it ". . . prepares students to be responsible community members" and provides ". . . education in engaged citizenship" (Sapp & Crabtree, 2002, p. 412); it produces "critical citizens who produce effective and ethical discourse and work to create more inclusive forms of power" (Scott, 2004, p. 304).

To understand more inclusive forms of power, students will benefit from case studies—including some in this collection—and lived experiences in which individuals and groups in positions of power have framed technical communication in different ways—as community-centric, as biased advocacy, as intrusive activism, and more. It will be vital to recognize the differences between communicating *for* and communicating *with* communities; whereas the former has elements of power relations seen in imperialism and colonialism, the latter aspires to participatory collaboration, democracy, shared power, and social justice as defined by the community. Whereas the former often conceptualizes communities exclusively in terms of what they lack, often called the "deficit model," the latter sees the community more comprehensively, as does Lucía Durá in her chapter, which shows how to integrate the community into technical communication research and practice via "asset-based inquiry."

What is Community and Who Defines It?

This collection and other TPC research have shown that we are increasingly engaging communities. Community engagement will require us to understand complexities surrounding the process by which TPC professionals and others build trust and long-term community relationships. Those complexities emerge from several sources. One of those involves knowing the history of past relations between outsiders and any given local community. That historical knowledge matters whether communities consist of indigenous peoples, members of low-income neighborhoods, individuals who are homeless, or residents subjected to disproportionate amounts of environmental pollution and degradation. Another complexity is not merely seeing any given community through the lens of an outsider, but in terms of how community members see themselves—their own desires, sources of pride, aspirations, and values. Seeing a community through its own eyes means that "voluntourism" (Oppenheim, 2016; Riley, 2011)—coming, doing "good" to note it on a résumé, and then leaving—will be much less effective than spending time listening to community members, situating assistance in terms of community aspirations and structural conditions, and building long-term relationships, as explained below. Multiple methods for understanding a community exist, and we will benefit as a field from learning from anthropologists, sociologists, and others who have spent decades researching sustainable, effective community engagement processes (Baillie, et al., 2010; Bridger & Luloff, 1999; Burkey, 1993; Easterly, 2006; Leydens & Lucena, 2009; Lucena, et al., 2010; Schneider, et al., 2008; Schneider, et al., 2009; Slim & Thomson, 1995; Swan, et al., 2014).

Key concepts matter in effective community engagement. *Self-determination* refers to a community's agency and voice in its own destiny, including its ability to shape its trajectory through its own definition of where the community begins and ends and who is and is not part of that community (Lucena, et al., 2010). Thus, participatory community mapping processes (Bridger & Luloff, 1999; Mazzurco, et al., forthcoming 2018) and contextual listening (Leydens & Lucena, 2009; Leydens & Lucena, 2018; Lucena, et al., 2010) become critical for self-determination. *Cultural dimensions* help us understand some of the ways in which cultures organize themselves based on what they value; these dimensions will (in)directly affect how cultures communicate. Although all such research is prone to generalization, it still holds value. Among cultural dimensions research, Hofstede's cultural dimensions serve as a useful starting point (Hofstede, 1980, 2001). Research on other effective ways to understand community cultures would bolster the ability of our sociotechnical communication to make a more lasting difference in the local and global communities we intend to serve.

Critical Strategies for Citizenship and Advocacy

Strategies for developing TPC students', researchers', and professionals' understanding of citizenship and advocacy are in their opening stages for us as a field, and collections like this one help us see what strategies are (in)effective. Any such strategies we adopt should be seen not as algorithms but as heuristics, guiding rather than determining decision-making processes that affect citizens and advocacy processes. Two particularly relevant, promising strategies are *intercultural praxis* (IP) and *Engineering for Social Justice* (E4SJ).

IP was developed by Katherine Sorrells to "raise our awareness, increase our critical analysis, and develop our socially responsible action in regard to our intercultural interactions" as well as to "address the intersection of cultural differences and hierarchies of power in intercultural interactions" (Sorrells, 2016, p. 16). IP incudes six "ports of entry," which are often enacted recursively, as communicators can shuttle from one to another or enact multiple ports at once. IP can serve as a community engagement strategy that facilitates civic responsibility and advocacy goals. The six IP ports include inquiring, framing, positioning, dialogue, reflection, and action (Sorrells, 2016).

In an increasingly globalized, multicultural world, another critical strategy for developing citizenship and advocacy is social justice. Since that term has multiple and varying definitions, the one used here is situated in and grew out of engineering and sustainable community development research (Bridger & Luloff, 1999; Lucena, et al., 2010) and was refined while designing and teaching courses that incorporate Engineering for Social Justice (E4SJ) (Leydens & Lucena, 2014). The goal was for E4SJ to help evaluate the degree to which community engagement, service learning, humanitarian engineering, and other similar ventures brought about socially just outcomes:

> We define E4SJ as engineering practices that strive to *enhance human capabilities (ends) through an* equitable distribution of *opportunities and resources* while *reducing imposed risks and harms (means)* among agentic citizens of a specific community or communities (Leydens & Lucena, 2018, p. 15). Note: This definition is a unique synthesis of definitions from multiple sources (Barry, 2005; Capeheart & Milovanovic, 2007; Nussbaum, 2003, 2011).

E4SJ consists of six criteria: listening contextually; identifying structural conditions; acknowledging political agency and mobilizing power; increasing opportunities and resources; reducing imposed risks and harms; and enhancing human capabilities. As with the IP ports of entry, the components can be engaged in non-linear ways as intercultural communicators inquire into and engage diverse communities in the quest for enhanced forms of citizenship and advocacy. When the editors wrote about their aims for this collection, they noted that "a good advocate is assumed to ensure that users/audiences have their voices heard or their rights safeguarded." That makes it imperative that we identify effective advocacy strategies, and the E4SJ criteria work toward that end.

Together, IP and E4SJ can help TPC students, practitioners, and instructors inquire into crucial questions: beyond the obvious, practical ends, what is socio-technical communication for? How might such communication artifacts move audiences beyond limiting assumptions? How might those artifacts enhance relevant human capabilities?

As we close this collection, it is worth noting that IP and E4SJ are deeply connected to Wendell Berry's notion of "solving for pattern"—the notion that effective social and community solutions address interconnected parts of a whole. That is not to say analytic thinking is useless, but to acknowledge it is fully complemented by holistic thinking. Effective solutions attempt to solve more than one problem (without creating new ones), and are complex precisely because they "should not enrich one person by the distress or impoverishment of another" (Berry, 2010, p. 446). An ineffective solution, by contrast, does not solve for pattern—it "solves for a single purpose or goal, such as increased production. And it is typical of such solutions that they achieve stupendous increases in production at exorbitant biological and social costs" (Berry, 2010, p. 440). As citizenship and advocacy issues continue to resonate in TPC, it will be important for us to continue learning how to solve for pattern, and to embrace the tremendous complexity that socially just community solutions deserve.

References

All website URLs accessed February 2018.

Baillie, C., Feinblatt, E., Thamae, T., & Berrington, E. (2010). *Needs and feasibility a guide for engineers in community projects: The case of Waste for Life*. San Rafael, CA: Morgan & Claypool.
Barry, B. (2005). *Why social justice matters*. Cambridge, UK, and Malden, MA: Polity.
Berry, W. (2010). *The art of the commonplace: The agrarian essays of Wendell Berry*. (N. Wirzba, Ed.). Richmond: ReadHowYouWant.com, Limited.
Bridger, J. C., & Luloff, A. E. (1999). Toward an interactional approach to sustainable community development. *Journal of Rural Studies, 15*(4), 377–387.
Brizee, A. (2015). Using Isocrates to teach technical communication and civic engagement. *Journal of Technical Writing and Communication, 45*(2), 134–165. https://doi.org/10.1177/0047281615569481

Burkey, S. (1993). *People first: A guide to self-reliant participatory rural development.* London and New York: Zed Books.

Capeheart, L., & Milovanovic, D. (2007). *Social justice: Theories, issues, and movements.* New Brunswick, New Jersey, and London: Rutgers University Press.

Cook, J., Nuccitelli, D., Green, S. A., Richardson, M., Winkler, B., Painting, R., . . . Skuce, A. (2013). Quantifying the consensus on anthropogenic global warming in the scientific literature. *Environmental Research Letters, 8*(2), 024024. https://doi.org/10.1088/1748-9326/8/2/024024

Cook, J., Oreskes, N., Doran, P. T., Anderegg, W. R. L., Verheggen, B., Maibach, E. W., . . . Rice, K. (2016). Consensus on consensus: A synthesis of consensus estimates on human-caused global warming. *Environmental Research Letters, 11*(4), 048002. https://doi.org/10.1088/1748-9326/11/4/048002

Cushman, E. (1999). The public intellectual, service learning, and activist research. *College English, 61*(3), 328–336. https://doi.org/10.2307/379072

Davenport, C., & Lipton, E. (2016, December 7). Trump picks Scott Pruitt, climate change denialist, to lead E.P.A. *The New York Times.* Retrieved from www.nytimes.com/2016/12/07/us/politics/scott-pruitt-epa-trump.html

Easterly, W. (2006). *The white man's burden: Why the west's efforts to aid the rest have done so much ill and so little good.* New York, NY: Penguin.

Freire, P. (1993). *Pedagogy of the oppressed.* New York: Continuum.

Herzberg, B. (1994). Community service and critical teaching. *College Composition and Communication, 45*(3), 307–319. https://doi.org/10.2307/358813

Hofstede, G. H. (1980). *Culture's consequences: International differences in work-related values.* Beverly Hills, CA: Sage.

Hofstede, G. H. (2001). *Culture's consequences: Comparing values, behaviors, institutions and organizations across nations.* Thousand Oaks, CA: Sage.

hooks, bell. (1994). *Teaching to transgress: Education as the practice of freedom.* New York, NY: Routledge.

Ikeda, D. (2005). Forward. In N. Noddings (Ed.), *Educating citizens for global awareness* (pp. ix–xi). New York, NY: Columbia Teachers College.

IPCC. (2014). *Climate Change 2014: Synthesis report. Contribution of Working Groups I, II, and III to the fifth assessment report of the Intergovernmental Panel on Climate Change* (No. 5th) (p. 151). Geneva, Switzerland: intergovernmental Panel on Climate Change. Retrieved from www.ipcc.ch/report/ar5/syr

Johnson, A. G. (2006). *Privilege, power, and difference.* Boston, MA: McGraw-Hill.

Kosoff, M. (2017, October 23). The Trump White House ramps up its war on science. *Vanity Fair.* Retrieved from www.vanityfair.com/news/2017/10/the-trump-white-house-ramps-up-its-war-on-science

Leydens, J. A. (2012). What does professional communication research have to do with social justice? Intersections and sources of resistance. *IEEE International Professional Communication Conference.* Orlando, FL: IEEE.

Leydens, J. A., & Lucena, J. C. (2009). Listening as a missing dimension in engineering education: Implications for sustainable community development efforts. *IEEE Transactions on Professional Communication, 52*(4), 359–376.

Leydens, J. A., & Lucena, J. C. (2014). Social justice: A missing, unelaborated dimension in humanitarian engineering and learning through service. *International Journal for Service Learning in Engineering, Humanitarian Engineering and Social Entrepreneurship, 9*(2), 1–28.

Leydens, J., & Lucena, J. (2018). *Engineering justice: Transforming engineering education and practice*. (T. Nathans-Kelly, Ed.). Hoboken, NJ: Wiley-IEEE Press.

Lloyd, R. (2016, February 16). Is there really a war on science? *Scientific American*. Retrieved from https://www.scientificamerican.com/article/is-there-really-a-war-on-science/

Lucena, J. C., Schneider, J., & Leydens, J. A. (2010). *Engineering and sustainable community development*. (C. Baillie, Ed.). San Rafael, CA: Morgan & Claypool.

Matthews, C., & Zimmerman, B. B. (1999). Integrating service learning and technical communication: Benefits and challenges. *Technical Communication Quarterly*, 8(4), 383–404. https://doi.org/10.1080/10572259909364676

Mazzurco, A., Leydens, J., & Jesiek, B. (forthcoming 2018). Passive, consultative, and co-constructive methods: A framework to facilitate community participation in design for development. *Journal of Mechanical Design*.

McEachern, R. W. (2001). Problems in service learning and technical/professional writing: Incorporating the perspective of nonprofit management. *Technical Communication Quarterly*, 10(2), 211–24.

McIntosh, P. (2005). Gender perspectives on educating for global citizenship. In N. Noddings (Ed.), *Educating citizens for global awareness* (pp. 22–39). New York, NY: Columbia Teachers College.

Memoli, M. A. (2016, September 26). Donald Trump denied during the debate that he has dismissed climate change. His Twitter account proves otherwise. *Los Angeles Times*. Retrieved from www.latimes.com/nation/politics/trailguide/la-na-trump-clinton-debate-updates-yes-donald-trump-said-climate-change-1474940161-htmlstory.html

Miller, C. R. (1989). What's practical about technical writing? In B. E. Fearing & W. K. Sparrow (Eds.), *Technical writing: Theory and practice* (pp. 14–24). New York, NY: Modern Language Association.

Nussbaum, M. (2003). Capabilities as fundamental entitlements: Sen and social justice. *Feminist Economics*, 9, 33–59.

Nussbaum, M. C. (2011). *Creating capabilities: The human development approach*. Cambridge, MA: Belknap Press of Harvard University Press.

Oppenheim, M. (2016, August 23). JK Rowling condemns "voluntourism" and highlights dangers of volunteering in orphanages overseas. *Independent*. Retrieved from www.independent.co.uk/news/people/jk-rowling-twitter-voluntourism-volunteering-in-orphanages-risks-a7204801.html

Pielke, R. A. (2014). *The honest broker: Making sense of science in policy and politics*. Cambridge: Cambridge University Press.

Riley, D. (2008). *Engineering and social justice*. San Rafael, CA: Morgan & Claypool.

Riley, D. (2011). Voluntelling and voluntourism: US approaches to engineering and development. *Engineering, Social Justice and Peace Conference* (pp. 1–5). Bogota, Colombia.

Rude, C. D. (2004). Toward a definition of best practices in policy discourse. In T. Kynell-Hunt & G. J. Savage (Eds.), *Power and legitimacy in technical communication: Strategies for Professional Status* (Vol. 2, pp. 123–142). Amityville, NY: Baywood Publishing.

Rude, C. D. (2008). Introduction to the special issue on business and technical communication in the public sphere: Learning to have impact. *Journal of Business and Technical Communication*, 22(3), 267–271.

Sapp, D. A., & Crabtree, R. D. (2002). A laboratory in citizenship: Service learning in the technical communication classroom. *Technical Communication Quarterly*, 11(4), 411–432. https://doi.org/10.1207/s15427625tcq1104_3

Schneider, J., Leydens, J. A., & Lucena, J. C. (2008). Where is "Community"? Engineering education and sustainable community development. *European Journal of Engineering Education, 33*(3), 307–319.

Schneider, J., Lucena, J. C., & Leydens, J. A. (2009). Engineering to help: The value of critique in engineering service. *IEEE Technology and Society, 28*(4), 42–48.

Scott, J. B. (2004). Rearticulating civic engagement through cultural studies and service-learning. *Technical Communication Quarterly, 13*(3), 289–306.

Sen, A. (2009). *The idea of justice.* Cambridge, MA: Belknap Press of Harvard University Press.

Slim, H., & Thomson, P. (1995). *Listening for a change: Oral testimony and community development.* Philadelphia, PA: New Society Publishers.

Sorrells, K. (2016). *Intercultural communication: Globalization and social justice.* Los Angeles and London: Sage Publications.

Swan, C., Paterson, K., & Bielefeldt, A. R. (2014). Community engagement in engineering education as a way to increase inclusiveness. In A. Johri & B. Olds (Eds.), *Cambridge Handbook of Engineering Education Research* (pp. 357–372). New York, NY: Cambridge University Press.

Taylor, A. (2016, November 22). 47 percent of the world's population now use the Internet, study says. *Washington Post.* Retrieved from www.washingtonpost.com/news/worldviews/wp/2016/11/22/47-percent-of-the-worlds-population-now-use-the-internet-users-study-says

USGCRP. (2017). *Climate science special report: Fourth national climate assessment, Volume I* (p. 470). Washington, DC: U.S. Global Change Research Program. Retrieved from https://science2017.globalchange.gov

World Bank. (2016). *Poverty and shared prosperity 2016: Taking on inequality.* (p. 170). Washington, DC: World Bank.

INDEX